If ONE book can improve your skill as an astrologer—this is it!

One of the world's foremost astrologers takes on astrology's toughest subject. He opens up, as never before in the English language, the masterful prediction tool of Solar Arcs.

Tyl teaches through example. You learn by *doing* astrology, not just thinking about it. Tyl introduces Solar Arc theory in terms of "rapport" measurements, which you begin to do immediately, without paper, pencil, or computer, dials, or wheels. Just with your eyes! *You will never look at a horoscope the same way again!*

You'll be amazed to learn that Tyl wrote the manuscript for this book in November/December 1990, before the war with Iraq. He predicted the state of war, the war itself—exact to the starting date—the involvement of Israel, the change of tactics in mid-February 1991, and the abrupt ending to the war, and much more. *All of which then did occur exactly on the dates as predicted!*

You see astrology make history before the fact! We think this is the first astrology textbook ever to take that chance: to make prediction part of the excitement of learning.

Tyl, in his well-known, very special way, also gets personal. He presents 30 Aphorisms, the keenest of maxims, the most practical of techniques, *to create predictions from any horoscope.* And as if this were not enough, Tyl then presents 20 Aphorisms for *Counseling.*

Look for Tyl's "Quick-Glance" Transit Table, 1940-2040, to which you can refer more quickly than a computer. The busy astrologer will use this Appendix every day for many years to come.

And finally, Tyl has rewritten and updated the entire pioneering body of work involving Solar Arcs and Midpoint Pictures done by Rheinhold Ebertin in Germany in 1940. Tyl gives long-overdue, modern meaning images for every possible direct Solar Arc and midpoint structure in the horoscope.

No matter how much you know about astrology already, no matter how much experience you've had to date, *you'll be fascinated by this book and you'll grow as an astrologer.* Look forward to that! This is a book we present with a passion. This is how we hope you will read it, use it, and remember it. *It's that important.*

About the Author

Noel Tyl is one of the most prominent astrologers in the western world. His 17 textbooks, built around the 12-volume *Principles and Practice of Astrology*, were among the biggest sellers in astrological publishing history, and have led a whole generation of astrologers to sophisticated professionalism. He also founded and edited *Astrology Now* magazine.

He has edited Books 9 through 16 of the Llewellyn New World Astrology Series. In 1994, his master opus, *Synthesis and Counseling in Astrology—The Professional Manual*, was published.

He is one of astrology's most sought-after lecturers in the United States, and internationally in Denmark, Norway, Germany, South Africa, and Switzerland, where for the first three World Congresses of Astrology he was a keynote speaker. Noel is a graduate of Harvard University in psychology and lives in Fountain Hills, Arizona.

To Write to the Author

If you wish to contact the author or would like more information about this book, please write to the author in care of Llewellyn Worldwide, and we will forward your request. Both the author and publisher appreciate hearing from you and learning of your enjoyment of this book and how it has helped you. Llewellyn Worldwide cannot guarantee that every letter written to the author can be answered, but all will be forwarded. Please write to:

Noel Tyl
Llewellyn's New Worlds of Mind and Spirit
P.O. Box 64383-L814, St. Paul, MN 55164-0383, U.S.A.

Please enclose a self-addressed, stamped envelope for reply, or $1.00 to cover costs. If outside U.S.A., enclose international postal reply coupon.

Free Catalog from Llewellyn

For more than ninety years Llewellyn has brought its readers knowledge in the fields of metaphysics and human potential. Learn about the newest books in spiritual guidance, natural healing, astrology, occult philosophy, and more. Enjoy book reviews, New Age articles, a calendar of events, plus current advertised products and services. To get your free copy of *Llewellyn's New Worlds*, send your name and address to:

Llewellyn's New Worlds of Mind and Spirit
P.O. Box 64383-L814, St. Paul, MN 55164-0383, U.S.A.

Llewellyn's New World Astrology Series

Prediction in Astrology

A Master Volume of Technique and Practice

- Great Predictions in History
- Rectification in Action
- Solar Arc Theory and Transits
- Mundane Astrology of World Crisis
- Counseling about the Future
- Exclusive "Quick-Glance" Transit Tables 1940-2040
- Professional Solar Arc Analysis Directory!

Noel Tyl

The Most Complete Presentation of Solar Arc Theory and Practice Written in English

1995
Llewellyn Publications
St. Paul, Minnesota, 55164-0383, U.S.A.

Prediction in Astrology. Copyright © 1991 by Noel Tyl. All rights reserved. Printed in the United States of America. No part of this book may be used or reproduced in any manner whatsoever without written permission from Llewellyn Publications, except in the case of brief quotations embodied in critical articles or reviews.

FIRST EDITION, 1991
Second Printing, 1995

Produced with planetary routines provided by Matrix Software.

Library of Congress Cataloging-in-Publication Data
   Tyl, Noel. 1936–
     Prediction in astrology : a master volume of technique and practice / Noel Tyl.
     p.   cm. — (Llewellyn's new world astrology series)
     "The most complete presentation of solar arc theory and practice written in English."
     Includes bibliographical references and index.
     ISBN 0-87542-814-2
     1. Predictive astrology.   I. Title.   II. Series.
BF1720.5.T85   1991
133.5—dc20   91-32897
                                                                                                     CIP

 Printed on Recycled Paper

Llewellyn Publications
A Division of Llewellyn Worldwide, Ltd.
P.O. Box 64383, St. Paul, Minnesota 55164-0383, U.S.A.

The New World Astrology Series

This series is designed to give all people who are interested and involved in astrology the latest information on a variety of subjects. Llewellyn has given much thought to the prevailing trends and to the topics that will be most important to our readers.

Future books will include such topics as vocational astrology, various relationships and astrology, electional astrology, astrology and past lives, astrological counseling, and many other subjects of interest to a wide range of people. This project has evolved because of the lack of information on these subjects and because we wanted to offer our readers the viewpoints of the best experts in each field in one volume.

We anticipate publishing approximately four books per year on varying topics and updating previous editions when new material becomes available. We know this series will fill a gap in your astrological library. We look only for the best writers and article topics when planning the new books and appreciate any feedback from our readers on subjects you would like to see covered.

Llewellyn's New World Astrology Series will be a welcome addition to the novice, student and professional alike. It will provide introductory as well as advanced information on all the topics listed above—and more.

Enjoy, and feel free to write to Llewellyn with your suggestions and comments.

By the same author:

The Horoscope as Identity

The Principles and Practice of Astrology
       (in twelve volumes, for home study and college curriculum)
    I. Horoscope Construction
   II. The Houses: Their Signs and Planets
  III. The Planets: Their Signs and Aspects
  IV. Aspects and Houses in Analysis
    V. Astrology and Personality
  VI. The Expanded Present
 VII. Integrated Transits
VIII. Analysis and Prediction
  IX. Special Horoscope Dimensions: Success, Sex, and Illness
    X. Astrological Counsel
  XI. Astrology: Mundane, Astral, and Occult
 XII. Times to Come

Teaching Guide to the Principles and Practice of Astrology

The Missing Moon

Holistic Astrology—the Analysis of Inner and Outer Environments

All published and distributed by Llewellyn Publications,
Box 64383, St. Paul, MN 55164

This book I dedicate
to W. P. Canby, Jr.
—my father since I was ten years old—
whose care, inspiration, and support
have made me so much
of who I am.

**Important Note
to All Readers
and to the Public Media**

The central portion of this book deals in great detail with the World Crisis in the Middle East. The predictions were created from astrological data *before the facts*. The bulk of this volume and the Middle East section specifically were completed *before* Christmas, 1990, and not one word has been changed since then. The predictions stand on the verities of the times that have followed.

This is a demanding book about a complex subject. It is an honest professional inspection of state-of-the-art predictive astrology, its strengths and its needs for refinement. There are pride of performance and maturity of practice within the observations presented here. There is no criticism.

Noel Tyl
McLean, Virginia
January, 1991

In Appreciation

The following expert astrologers were particularly helpful to the research supporting this book.

Christian Borup, Director of the I. C. Astrological Institute in Copenhagen, Denmark, for his assistance with the study of King Christian IV and Tycho Brahe.

Dennis Elwell of Stourbridge, England, author of *The Cosmic Loom*, for his assistance with the study of the Great Fire of London and William Lilly.

And very special gratitude to Michael Munkasey of Issaquah, Washington for his patient and gifted help with Fixed Stars and his sharply attentive and warmly encouraging audience to many of the thoughts offered on these pages.

Additionally, thanks are given to Warren Kinsman of Washington D.C. for his calm appreciation for my problems with computers and their programs and for his assistance over and over again with technicalities; and to Michael Erlewine of Matrix for technological and affectionate support.

And finally, the nod of authority and the grace of friendship given to my work by the editor of this book, Tom Bridges, are luxuries indeed.

Table of Contents

Chapter 1 – Great Predictions in History 1
    The Birth of Alexander 2
    Rectified Horoscope 8
    The Birth of Jesus 11
    Rectified Horoscope 13
    The Black Death 14
    Lunar Eclipse Charts for the Plague 16-17
    Long Live the King! Christian IV of Denmark 19
    The Horoscope by Tycho Brahe 21
    The Great Fire of London 26
    The Event Chart 28
    Evangeline's Claim to Flame! 30
    The Great Hotel Fire Prediction
      Rectified Chart for Warren F. Leland 38
    Evangeline Adams's Horoscope 43

Chapter 2 – Great Expectations 49
    St Augustine's Stand 52
    Reliability of Cycles 53

Chapter 3 – Solar Arc Theory and Technique 57
    The Nabod Method 60
    Simmonite's resolution 62
    "Rapport" Measurements 63
    Measuring Arcs precisely 64
    Time Orbs 69
    United States of America Chart 72
    The Fourth Harmonic 73
    Midpoints and Planetary Pictures 74
    Quick Measurement of the Progressed Moon 76
    Exactness? 79

Chapter 4 – Analyzing Arcs **83**
    The Reality Principle 84
    The Arcing Planet 85
    The Sun 91
    Mercury 92
    Venus 93
    Mars 93
    Jupiter 94
    Saturn 94
    Uranus 95
    Neptune 95
    Pluto 96
    The Sensitive Points 96
    Lunar Nodal Axis 99

Chapter 5 – Predictions Down to Earth **101**
    Mundane Astrology 101
    Great Conjunction of Jupiter and Saturn, 1980 . . . 105
    The Kingdom of Iraq 108
    Key Eclipse charts,
      Baghdad and Washington D.C. 111-112
    Triple Conjunction Ingress 116
    Halfway Cycle chart 119
    Grand Mutation into Earth Family 129
    Great Conjunction of Jupiter–Saturn, 2000 130
    The State of Israel 132

Chapter 6 – Getting Personal **135**
    Prediction Aphorisms 138
    Case Studies 144
    George Bush Horoscope 165
    Bush Inauguration chart 167
    Saddam Hussein rectification 169

Chapter 7 – Working with Clients **175**
    The Answer in the Question 176
    How much accuracy? 179
    Major Events? 180
    Counseling Aphorisms 184

Chapter 8 – Working with the Indeterminate **203**
    King Olav of Norway Horoscope 204
    King Harald V of Norway horoscope 206
    Death 210
    Four Key considerations 213

"Quick-Glance" Transit Table 1940–2040 215
Solar Arc Analysis Directory 251
Bibliography 333
Index 337

Chapter One

Great Predictions in History How Did They Do It?

Predictions loom large in the history, pursuit, mystique and criticism of astrology. They thrill everyone in retrospect; they lure all students to continue study; they fascinate and frighten; and success and failure alike in prediction open astrologers to suspicion.

The field of prediction is indeed mesmerizing: the techniques seem eternally elusive; the practice is ever insecure. Yet, as if it were the gold of the alchemists, ever-increasing certainty with prediction is sought as an exercise of faith, skill, and professionalism. For the astrologer, it is the work of a lifetime.

This book will cover three major problems: the complex understanding of times past and future; the techniques that often do indeed fulfill astrology's predictive potential; and how all of this can be of service to ourselves and to our clients. With objectivity and openness in our study, we want to preserve astrology's ever-maturing wholeness, protect astrologers' dignity, and dramatize the excitement of the quest.

But first, let us study some of the most celebrated predictions of all time, necessarily after the facts, of course, but from on-the-scene perspective of just how these predictions may have come about astrologically.

The Birth of Alexander

Medieval myth introduces us to quite a sage, a magician, and an astrologer. His name was Nectanebus. Legends have it that he had been a king of Egypt, with the name Bektanis, capable of conjuring up armies out of thin air to defeat his enemies. Then, there came a time "when the planets were against him," and he moved on, in disguise, to Macedon, in the middle of the fourth century B.C. He reestablished himself as an astrologer.[1]

Nectanebus's great skill brought him into the favor of the Macedonian court of King Philip and Queen Olympias. His "Egyptian" skill was spellbinding, "for the elements of the universe obeyed him."

He is recorded as having proclaimed that there are "many forms" of divination. Nectanebus himself used the stars, wax images, magic wands of ebony, spells, incantations, the interpretation of dreams, and the manipulation of snakes. And, he had an "astrological tablet adorned with gold and ivory, with each planet in the horoscope represented by a different stone or metal."[2]

Nectanebus read the Queen's horoscope and made a prediction: that she would have a son by the god Ammon (Zeus; Jupiter) and that she would become aware of the birth-to-come in a dream.

Nectanebus prepared herbs to induce her dreamstate, created a wax image of her for magical projection, lighted lamps, and "muttered secret incantations."

Supposedly, Nectanebus played the part of the god Ammon himself, transformed into a "dragon which glided into her presence." There are second century reports that tell us it was indeed common knowledge that Olympias had "lain with a serpent before giving birth to Alexander."

At this time, King Philip was off fighting a war. He learned that his wife was pregnant with a child by Ammon, and, needless to emphasize, he finished up his business and returned home in a hurry.

Nectanebus continued to deceive both king and queen, once reportedly appearing in court as a "huge hissing serpent, putting his head in Olympias's lap and then kissing her."

Let us pause here and bring some tighter focus to this tale, which is repeated with unusual congruence of details in many scholarly sources, old and relatively modern. In ancient times, people tried hard to create natural explanations for anything unnatural—anything supernatural or miraculous. We see this still today

---

1. Gleadow, page 59.
2. Thorndike, I; pages 560-563.

when historians search for natural explanations of miracles recounted in the Bible, or of miracle cures at religious shrines, of haunted houses, and, for sure, of the phenomenon of precognition, especially the astrological kind. This seems to be an instinct we have as humans to make the irrational rational whenever possible, to give structure to the amorphous, to "get a handle on things" in order to ward off fear and protect the proud, fragile human condition. We shall see that this is important to understanding the philosophy and practice of prediction even today.

Carl Jung's work with archetypes and the collective unconscious, and his extensive corroborative psychoanalytical work with the symbology alive in the human experience, easily leads us to see ancient symbology archetypically active in this fascinating story.

In all sources, references to snakes and dragons linked with Nectanebus himself and with Olympias's body and bed abound. In the parlance of archetypal interpretation, these references are the means that ancient historians and tale-tellers had, consciously or unconsciously, of skirting censorship—censorship in the mind or in the government, or for their own protection, or just for poetical good taste. In the way of myth, they are telling the story as it was: Nectanebus inveigled himself into Olympias's favor through astrology, introducing his phallus (snake archetype) to Olympias in many ways—once, definitely, while she was in a trance—and conceived with her, her child of Ammon.

It is even reported that Nectanebus, "in having intercourse with Olympias, observed the time when the Sun was entering Leo and Saturn was in Taurus since he wanted his son [the child] to receive the form and power of those planets."[3] The child was to be an extraordinary hero.[4]

Olympias was totally enraptured with the privilege of having the child of Ammon. She told Nectanebus that, should it indeed come to pass, she would no longer "employ" him as a magus but honor him as a god!

Now back to our story of prediction: As Olympias was in labor with her child, Nectanebus, in his office as astrologer, stood by her side—to pick the favorable moment for the birth. All sources agree

---

3. Thorndike, I; page 563; according to Albertus Magnus in the thirteenth century.
4. And here again, we find reference to things libidinal: Jung states that the most widely accepted of all symbols of libido is the human figure as hero, as we see in so many myths, traditions, and tales. The earliest mythical heroes had snake-eyes, were half man and half serpent. The Sun itself is identified with the man-hero. Writers for hundreds of years in ancient times described Alexander as "driven by pothos," a Greek term for desiring, longing—sexual desire.

on this scene and what followed. Nectanebus was studying his astrological tablet and undoubtedly going to the window or terrace to study the sky, waiting for just the right moment to bring into life the world's first hero, its "first famous person."[5]

Nectanebus held back the child within Olympias to avoid astrological portents that the child would be ugly and unsuccessful, a slave and a captive. Imagine that incredible scene: this powerful magus, this ecstatic queen, the incantations and ministrations, the god-like authority of this astrologer as he regulated the moment in time that would identify the person who would change the world! It is no wonder that there are reports that Alexander was born amid an earthquake, thunder, and lightening.

The Astrology

What was Nectanebus waiting for in the heavens? We can only conjecture "how powerful the race of the Egyptians were in mathematics and the magic art," as it is put in the sources. We do not have any knowledge of what was on his bejeweled tablet.

But what would make his prediction work? And what can we learn from this rivetingly dramatic scene of astrological prediction and its development through the ages following this momentous time in 356 B.C.?[6]

The emphasis in ancient astrological history was primarily on conjunctions, both planetary and stellar. There is no doubt about it. They were obvious to the naked eye and were easy to spot-measure through clean, clear skies; they could easily be endowed with dramatic portents because of their inexorable movement coming together—clashing or blending—and because of their apparently purposeful changes of speed and relative positions; and conjunctions were "naturals" for echoing the fundamental interaction of the Sun and Moon and the phenomenon of eclipses. They easily entered into a religiously and politically explained pantheon of god-purpose. They inspired rich archetypal interpretation.

Another emphasis in ancient astrology was on sign significance. Every ancient and very old astrology text reveals rich sign de-

---

5. Braudy's phrase, page 32.
6. As we shall see, this is the correct year of Alexander's birth. All sources agree—except one: in his *A Thousand and One Notable Nativities*, printed early in this century, Alan Leo gave 357 BC, quoting an earlier "Lyndhold" source. Unfortunately, this error has been repeated by many writers in astrology up to the present day.

scriptions, textured to embrace dramatically the dimensions of life in those times. While the descriptions may appear clumsy, severe, or arbitrary to us today, they did indeed reflect the life and language of prediction of those days, especially for the prominently exposed (prone to attack) personages who could afford (or deserved) to have their horoscope done by a mighty magus. It was important to Nectanebus to have Saturn in Taurus for the conception of Alexander. He knew, as well, that Saturn would be in Taurus at the child's birth.

And a third area of emphasis was the fixed stars. The conjunctions and oppositions of prominent stars with planets and with the horizon especially carried extreme significance, which we can easily imagine from the extraordinarily well-developed lore given to these celestial beacons.

During the time of Olympias's labor and delivery, not much would change in terms of planetary motion. Nature would have its way within a span of a few hours on the day of term. What was changing constantly and regularly—and Nectanebus was certainly aware of this elementary and eternal astronomical axiom—was the Ascendant. He had planned a Leo Ascendant for the conception. Was he planning something powerful for the Ascendant axis at birth? A conjunction or opposition with a planet, and even a fixed star, a star associated with renown, visible to the eye, that would crown his predictive election with grandeur?

The British scholar of classics and oriental languages Rupert Gleadow tips us off—unfortunately through an oversight. In his *Origin of the Zodiac*, page 58, Gleadow quotes a book dubiously attributed to Aristotle covering the things Aristotle was supposed to have taught Alexander. In one quote about making a "talisman for lordship and dominion," there is the instruction "let the Ascendant be in Leo," and Gleadow injects parenthetically, "This is quite correct since Alexander the Great was born with the Sun in Leo conjoined to Regulus."

And so today we see the few conjectural horoscopes for Alexander drawn with the very late degrees of Leo rising—the position of Regulus in modern times![7] At Alexander's birth, 356 B.C., Regulus was positioned at 26 *Cancer* 30' 39" on the ecliptic.[8]

How did this ecliptic position of Cancer affect the constella-

---

7. Epoch 1900: right ascension longitude for Regulus was 28 Leo 36, with ecliptic longitude of 28 Leo 27, advancing by R.A. 8.4 minutes of arc every ten years; see Johndro, page 88.
8. Computed by the United States Naval Observatory and by James Neely, through Michael Erlewine of Matrix Software.

6 / *Prediction in Astrology*

tional archetype for Regulus at *Cor Leonis*, the "heart of the lion"? Perhaps it was not until Ptolemy's work some five centuries later that Regulus was recognized as completely "leonine."[9] Or perhaps the ecliptic position had nothing to do with fixed star archetypes, the constellations themselves being the sole source of interpretive significance.

The fact remains, however, that if indeed Nectanebus was waiting for Regulus, with its fabulous symbolism of heroism, grandeur, and nobility (Ptolemy associates it with Mars and Jupiter), he would have been keyed to the ecliptic longitude area of 27 Cancer.

Finding the date of Alexander's birth has been extraordinarily difficult. As it turns out, many spurious dates have been put into astrology books and even a few history books.[10] The most reliable reference is offered by Plutarch.[11] He states that Alexander was born "on the sixth of Hecatombaeon" (pronounced hecka-tom'-biahn), which was called Lous by the Macedonians. He also records the well-known fact that, on the same day (that is, historically linked with Alexander's birth), the Temple of Diana burned at Ephesus. This was thought to be an omen, a precursor to calamities that would devastate all of Asia. People ran through the streets in fear. [12]

The sixth of Hecatombaeon—according to several scholars[13]— was "about July 20th in their calendar." Each state in Greece had its own calendar references, using different names for the months and having a different number of months, and having the months in different sequences.[14]

Now that we have a date to work with, sign symbolism, a conjunction, and a fixed star can come together to reveal the prediction conjured by Nectanebus.

The Moon's position on July 20, 356 B.C., was Virgo. On the 21st and 22nd of July, the Moon was in Libra. Isabelle M. Pagan, author of the brilliantly insightful book on astrological symbolism, *From Pioneer to Poet* (first published in 1911), writes like an ancient. One of her descriptions for Moon in Virgo reads "practical and businesslike

---

9. Ptolemy refers to Regulus as "bright at the heart" (*cardias lampros*).
10. Again, Alan Leo's notation of July 1 was off. The month is right, but the date is far off. Evangeline Adams later took Leo's data for Alexander's birth for her book *Astrology: Your Place among the Stars*.
11. *The Lives of the Noble Grecians and Romans*, page 802.
12. Several sources say that the priestess of the Temple was with Nectanebus attending the birth of Alexander—neglecting her duties at the Temple—and that this may have led to the conflagration.
13. Conferring on behalf of my request, led by Dr. Robert A Hadley, Associate Professor of History at George Washington University in Washington, D.C.
14. See Bickerman, *Chronologies of the Ancient World*.

methods, attacking work, habits of industry, irritability, and a critical rather than an appreciative turn of mind and style of expression." She goes on to say further, "having no thought of recognition or reward."

This is simply not Alexander the Great, who was consummately self-absorbed, who expected adulation from the world continuously, was totally oriented to public appeal, and was so glamorous and popular.

But for the Moon in Libra, Pagan suggests "a tendency to pass easily and naturally from one kind of work to another, to adapt oneself to changing conditions and environment and to make the best of them. This position gives a well-balanced, lovable and loving nature, and ensures a certain amount of popularity." She goes on about statesmanship, and then, writing of Libra at the Midheaven, about the "ambition for personal popularity and public recognition."[15] Pagan develops so much more insight—themes of persuasion, opportunism, and the attainment of social honor.

By anyone's knowledge of astrological symbolism and the character of Alexander's life (his extraordinary charisma; his gigantic achievements within only 33 years of life), Alexander the Great was born with Moon in Libra, not Virgo.[16]

For the ancients, the Moon was Artemis, Selene, Diana. Diana! Was this why the priestess of the Temple of Diana had been summoned by Nectanebus, since he knew the child would have a Libra Midheaven (and a Libra Moon near the Midheaven)? Was the burning of the Temple indeed an omen, a sign, a corroboration of the birth of Alexander, the son of Ammon—Zeus and Jupiter—through Nectanebus?

On July 22, 356 B.C., the Moon was in late Libra. The Sun and Venus were conjunct in late Cancer, the latter just 30 minutes of arc away from precise conjunction with Regulus.

What was Nectanebus waiting for? Why did he delay the birth? Imagine him consulting his tablet, searching the sky, probably having assistants perched on nearby rooftops signalling to him. Imag-

---

15. Pagan possessed truly astounding sensitivity of insight, and her words weave a spell of discovery. For twenty years, this book and Pagan's rich grasp of astrological symbolism have always impressed me and have never appeared off the mark.
16. It is interesting to note the following passage from *Rhetoric to Alexander*, mentioned previously, attributed to Aristotle: "And there was good reason for my having this intention; for just as it was your desire to wear the most *splendid attire of all mankind* [my emphasis], so it is proper that you should attempt to attain the most distinguished ability in rational discourse." Could we ask for a better description of Libra at the Midheaven?

8 / Prediction in Astrology

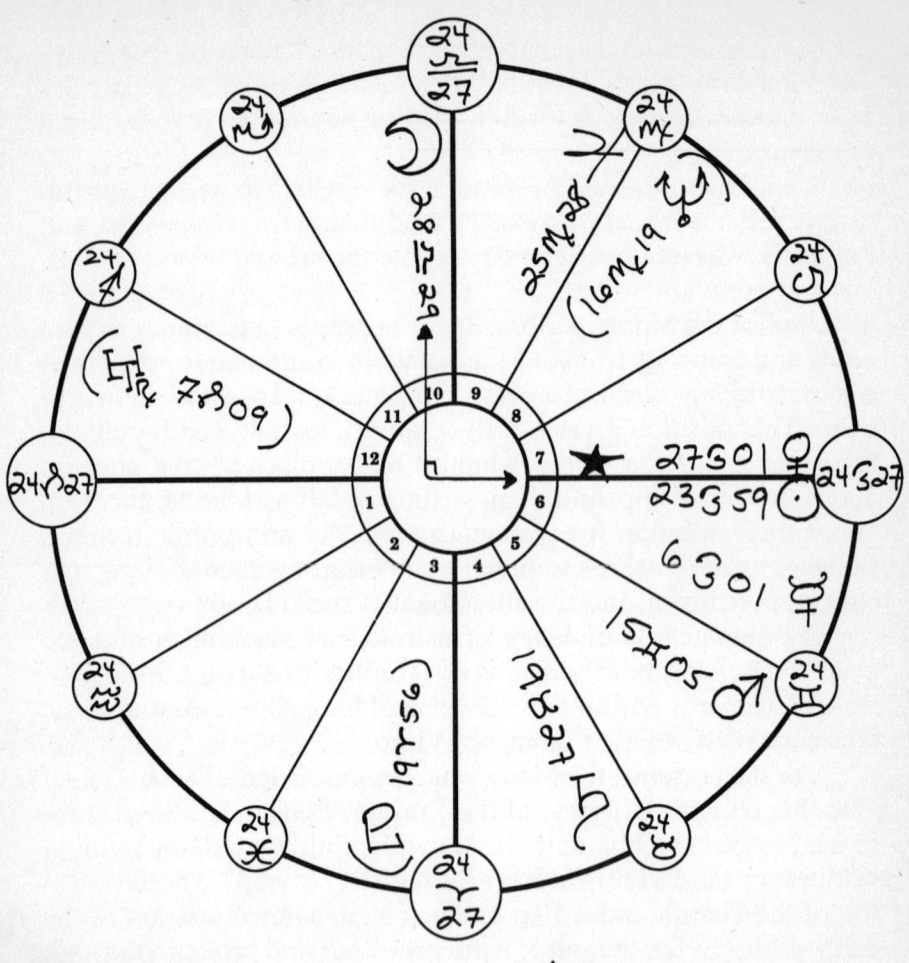

Alexander the Great
Rectification
July 22, 356 B.C.
7:27 p.m. LMT
Pella Macedonia
21 E 45   42 N 00
Equal Houses

★ Regulus: 26° Cancer 30′ 39″

ine him scanning the horizon from the terrace of the Queen's palace chamber. Nectanebus was waiting for the sunset—for the western horizon to meet the Sun, Venus, and Regulus together. The scene actually becomes beautiful!

Imagine that the Sun was just setting. This would put Venus and Regulus right at the horizon only some 15 time minutes later.

Venus in Cancer—an extraordinary emotional "swoon," the *pothos* which historians have recorded time and time again in connection with Alexander (see footnote four). And we may know from Alexander's horoscope, printed on the preceding page, that the Moon was in Libra, in the sign of Diana, indeed conjunct the Midheaven, and, at that moment, square to Venus, the Sun, and Regulus—a tremendous developmental aspect.

This moment gives a powerful Capricorn Ascendant to the hero. According to Pagan, "Capricorn as Ascendant suggests attainment through social or political ambition, personal or vicarious, leading either to strong concentration and unceasing hard work, or to the development of diplomatic ability and of the tendency *to be all things to all men*" (my emphasis). She continues by pointing out a longing "to scale the heights, to arrogance and magnificence."

We see that the ruler of the horoscope, what the ancients called the planet ruling the sign on the Ascendant, was Saturn, and, according to Nectanebus's plan at conception, Saturn was still in Taurus, sextile to the Sun and Venus. Evangeline Adams writes (also in a rich symbolic style): "Saturn in Taurus sextile the Sun ... an ideal disposition for a great conqueror. Only the most concentrated patience and steadiness of push could have carried him through into India; an expedition, by the way, which would appear hopeless for a modern army of any size. He is an example of Saturn in Taurus at his best." In addition, Adams cites Ulysses S. Grant and credits Saturn in Taurus with "giving military genius."

As Alexander came into the world, his Mercury was in Cancer and his Mars was in Gemini. Both of these positions may seem uncharacteristic of the laser-like intelligence and lethally concentrated application of energy and force that typified Alexander's manner of thinking and behavior. But we may note that neither of these planets makes any major aspect except to planets which weren't known in Alexander's day. Mercury and Mars are not clearly integrated within the whole of the personality and are prone to running away with or dominating it, spilling out unleashed upon the world. Here was the extraordinary acquisitiveness, the hoarding nature of Cancer full-blown through Mercury and the extraordinary resourcefulness, diversification, and inventiveness of Gemini full-blown through Mars.

When we add Uranus, Neptune, and Pluto to the picture, we see the intensification of all that Nectanebus had anticipated (we feel him acknowledging that the gods Mercury and Mars would, in this hero, be freed from all the other gods, free to be unmodified and pure, to reign unfettered in the heavens and upon the earth). Mercury is opposed to Uranus, corresponding to the laser-like quality of Alexander's mind; Neptune is square to Mars—magnetism, military leadership.[17] We see, with the outer planets added, that Mercury and Mars are no longer unintegrated, but intensified by dynamic aspects with mighty planet symbols.

Pluto is at the bottom of the chart, opposed to the Moon, square the Sun. This astounding T-Square—Moon opposed Pluto, the axis squared by the Sun—discharges directly onto the Ascendant of this god-hero become man.[18]

There was thunder and there was lightning ... and the Temple of the Moon was aflame.

After his success with the conception and birthing of Alexander, Nectanebus ended life similarly in close touch with the stars. One evening, Nectanebus and his pupil were out walking for an astronomy lesson. Alexander was twelve years old.[19]

In one version of the story, Alexander, in his incredible, constantly reiterated and verified arrogance,[20] pushed Nectanebus into a steep pit. Nectanebus lay there to die from a broken neck. Alexander explained that he had done this to register with Nectanebus the "futility of his art" (astrology), since Nectanebus had been staring at the stars and was unaware of what could threaten him from the ground.

Nectanebus—this extraordinary astrological personage linking ancient Egypt with the rise of European thought through his student, the conqueror Alexander (who would next be tutored by Aristotle)—had one more astrological prediction to fulfill: he had told Alexander that the stars had shown him a warning, that he (Nectanebus) would be killed by his own son. In this way, Alexander learned the secret of his birth.

---

17. Grant Lewi, in his classic *Heaven Knows What*, writes that Mars square Neptune is found "among great military leaders who have an unusually magnetic personal hold over their men" (page 206).
18. Pluto was also opposed to the Midheaven. As presented in *The Principles of Practice of Astrology* (Tyl), Pluto: the masses, the collective, perspective of values; opposition: a measure of fate, of circumstances that place the identity within the flow of life development beyond the working of will; Midheaven: public standing.
19. Thorndike, I, page 563.
20. Through his mother, Alexander was supposedly a direct descendant of Achilles. Later, Alexander was to visit Achilles's grave and weep that he, Alexander, did not have "his" Homer to record "his" greatness.

In another version, Nectanebus tells Alexander about the extraordinary prediction the stars had presented him about his own death, and *then* Alexander pushed his master into the pit *to foil the prediction*; Nectanebus's own son would not kill him! Alexander would!—Indeed, this fulfills the prediction as well.

In this very early story about prediction, we see the power that astrology and its symbology have upon human sensibilities, so long ago and still today—a power influencing life and death, religion and the very reasons for existence—all dramatically played out in the richest of symbologies and most tyrannical of pronouncements.

We are seeing the human condition dictating the use of symbols to say the unthinkable, the threatening, the uncomfortable, the holy. We are seeing the eeriness of self-fulfillment within prophecy, and we are recording the undeniably tenable suggestion that, generally speaking, magic, astrology, and the ability to make predictions are all wrapped up together—in astrology and in every astrologer.

The Birth of Jesus

As Nectanebus engineered the birth of Alexander to fulfill the prophecy for this great man-hero, we may ask who made the prediction—who "chose the time"—for the birth of Jesus in Bethlehem? Who predicted the date and time when someone would be born who touched almost all the world forever? What was the astrology of this moment, this special moment that attracted awed astrologers from the East to Bethlehem in Judea, this moment that entered world consciousness as no birth time has since?

For centuries, there has been conjecture about the birth date of Jesus, and of late, about the birth time, too. The issue appears settled finally, and the astrologer who "picked the time" through brilliant rectification technique and scholarly study almost 2,000 years after the fact was the late Don "Moby Dick" Jacobs, who maintained a popular astrological practice in Hawaii until his death in 1981.

In 1603, Johannes Kepler computed what he thought was the "Christmas Star." He surmised it must have been the Great Conjunction of Jupiter and Saturn that occurred in 7 B.C.[21] Due to retrogradation, that conjunction took place three times during that year.

---

21. The Great Conjunctions of Jupiter and Saturn will be discussed in much more detail later in the book, especially in Chapter 5.

With historical cross-references, assiduous study of the political scene in Judea, creative and sound deductive logic, and an identification with the trek taken on by the Magi (magoi, Greek, from Persian, meaning diviner or astrologer), this surely is the greatest detective work ever done in astrology. Jacobs was able to focus on March 1, 7 B.C. What argument can stand up against this determination?[22]

Working only with the sure notation from historical and biblical references that Jesus was born in the middle of the night, Jacobs looked for this Jupiter-Saturn Great Conjunction to coincide with a New Moon in Pisces. Pisces sign-symbolism permeates the early Christian era. In ancient times, world geography was sectioned according to the zodiac, and Judea was Pisces.[23] The Great Conjunction was building to last for seven months in Pisces. The astrologers in the East recognized this astronomical configuration as very auspicious. They journeyed to Judea in search of a "king."

The secret sign of the early Christians was a fish.[24] Jesus was called "the Fisher of men." There was the miracle of the loaves and fishes (the Virgo/Pisces polarity). And all of this was taking place at the dawn of the Age of Pisces.

We astrologers learn most of what we know about the premise and technique of prediction through the technique of rectification. We place ourselves before a mountain of life evidence and examine the upheaval of time and space that gave it all birth. Sometimes we are lucky to have only a few snippets of evidence. In any event, we are dealing with birth potential and event possibilities *already corroborated within past time*. Although it is philosophically elusive, in astrology, *effects often come before causes*.

As our experience and sophistication grow, we refine our skills to higher levels of surety. We begin to see the extraordinary power of conjunctions.[25] We revive within our vocabulary the richness of sign symbolism. We develop new enthusiasm for researching still-unweighed analytical anchors such as the fixed stars and eclipses.

---

22. There have been many attempts. The substantive ones are covered in Jacobs' superb account of the whole rectification process for Jesus' birth: *Astrology's Pew in Church*.
23. In the second-century A.D., Ptolemy reorganized the growing world and allocated Aries to Judea, based on the temperament of the people living there. This notwithstanding, Judea was Piscean in earlier traditions.
24. The Greek for Pisces is "Ichtheon." Today we call the branch of biology that deals with fishes ichthyology.
25. Ptolemy considered conjunctions so fundamental in astrology that he took them for granted, not even mentioning other aspects with them.

Great Predictions in History / 13

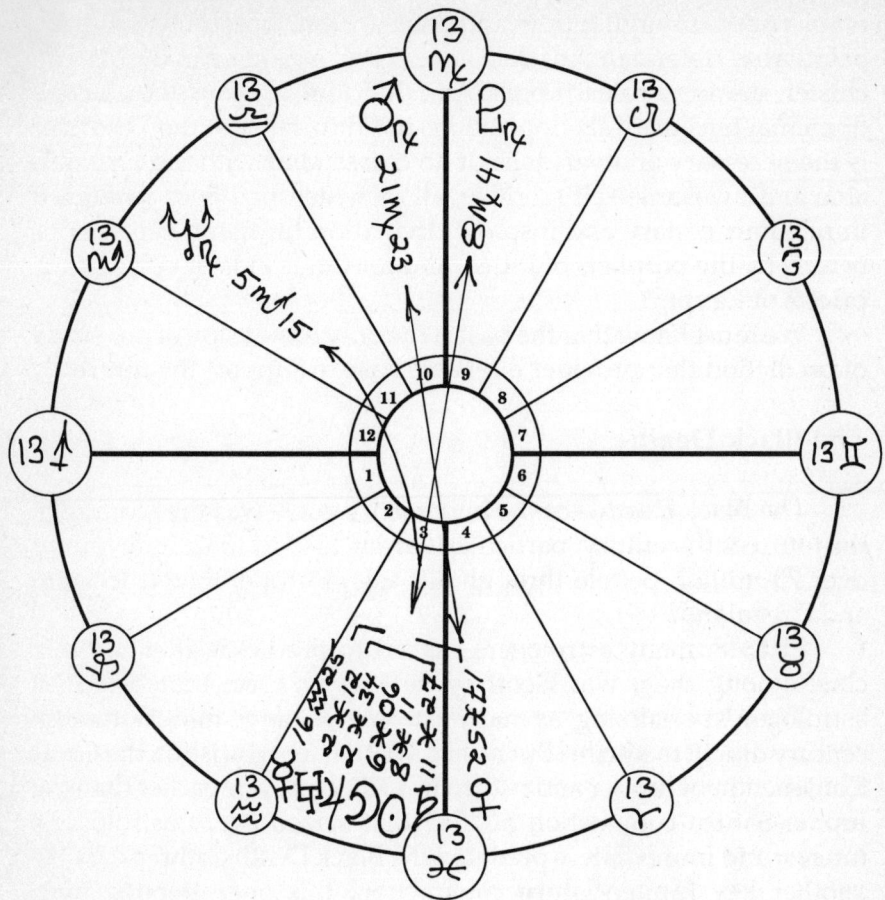

Jesus of Nazareth
Rectification by Don "Moby Dick" Jacobs
Copyright 1977
Reprinted with permission from
The Joshua Foundation
San Francisco, CA.

March 1, 7 B.C.
1:21 am, LMT
Bethlehem, Judea
35 E 13   31 N 42
Equal Houses

Study the horoscope of Jesus shown above, and then on your own study Jacobs' research. The chart of Jesus contains ten conjunctions, six oppositions, and five trines: some twenty close planetary contacts, extremely rare in any horoscope.

Notice the retrogradation above the horizon, reinforcing the power in the opposite hemisphere below the horizon, withdrawn to the Imum Coeli. Notice also the overwhelming focus upon the IIIrd House of communication, the dimensions of learning and teaching

14 / *Prediction in Astrology*

emphasized through Jupiter and Saturn. Note that Jupiter rules the Sagittarius Ascendant, in itself a mighty complement of the Piscean cluster, sharing a ruler, Jupiter. And then look at the extreme developmental tension of six oppositions to Pluto, ruler of the XIIth: this is the necessary and vast tension to correspond with the unavoidable and awesome self-sacrifice, all of which had been predicted in religious ecstasy and inspired divination for many generations before, by the prophets of Judea, and for thousands of years by the priests of Egypt.[26]

We must know that the past is the only dimension of our study of prediction that provides a reliable base to support the future.

The Black Death

The Black Death—or the bubonic plague—was the scourge of the fourteenth-century, particularly from 1348 to 1352. It devoured over 75 million people throughout Asia, Europe, Egypt, Iceland, and Greenland.

In 1348, many astrologers rushed to predict it after the fact; chief among them was Geoffrey de Meaux, a celebrated French astrologer, specializing, as many astrologers of the mid-fourteenth century did, in medicine. But he had written his treatise on the Great Conjunction of Jupiter and Saturn in 1325, one cycle earlier than the Jupiter-Saturn conjunction of 1345 that seized every astrologer's interest and immediately predated the Black Death outbreak. Yes—another key Jupiter-Saturn conjunction, this one attended by a lunar eclipse.

Jean de Murs, another Parisian, a prominent astronomer and musician, did make the prediction ahead of time. Through frequent astrological correspondence with Pope Clement VI (on calendar reform and, eventually, on startling astrological predictions about the Holy Roman Church), we can keep track of "John," as the literature refers to him. He annotated everything, and we can surely place his prediction of the Black Death between late September 1344 and the end of that year, preceding the Black Death by three years and preceding the planets as mapped in the prediction chart by several months.

---

26. Well-annotated in Glass, pages 15-16. There is a tremendous amount of lore and legend about Jesus or Jesus-like figures in ancient Egypt, alarmingly congruent in detail with the life of Jesus of Nazareth—enough for the study of a lifetime.

When astrologers realized that the Black Death should be linked to the Jupiter-Saturn conjunction that had "corrupted the air" three years earlier, they all ran to judgment. But John had beaten them all to it, before the fact, and had based his analysis on three additional measurements that were to be conclusive: the lunar eclipse of March 18, 1345 just 17 days after the Mars-Jupiter conjunction, 14 days after Mars would conjoin Saturn, and two days before the all-important Great Conjunction of Jupiter and Saturn; second, the fact that this massively symbolic configuration occurred just six days after the vernal equinox in 1345; and third, a mass of fixed stars in Aquarius.[27]

The theory then—and now—is that an eclipse aggravates a point, zone, or span of time in a horoscope and that fixed stars endow a point with lasting significance.[28] Both circumstances, along with the Great Conjunction, Mars, and the vernal solar ingress, were at work here for John, and he made his brilliant best of them:

> Three chieftains [planets] of the celestial militia, born of noblest lineage, are hastening from remote parts o'er many a desert and by tortuous route to a general council [conjunction] in the year of Christ 1345 [cryptic language follows, indicating a time one week after the vernal equinox], that in which the creation occurred.
>
> One of them is an old man, dark, and of sombre visage [Saturn]. The second is just, pious, handsome, chaste, devout, merciful [Jupiter]. The third is ruddy, bellicose, impetuous, no other than Mars.
>
> [John goes on that the second chieftain will meet the third on the first day of the month after midnight and will bring to the world] "wars, slaughter, floods, corruption of the air, epidemics, discords, and unexpected catastrophes from above.... On the fourth day before daybreak, the first and third will meet and that event will bring discords, deceits, and frauds, wars, violent winds, and disease. Later in the month, the first and second will meet and there will ensue changes of kingdom, appearance of prophets, sedition of peoples, new rites, and finally a horrible blowing of winds. After accomplishing these their appointed tasks, our three heroes return to their own countries by another route.[29]

---

27. Think of these day-spans as "time orbs," a concept to be discussed in detail later.
28. See Jansky, Chapter 5 of his book on eclipses. Jansky uses the words "emphasis" and "crisis."
29. Graubard, pages 109-110; Thorndike, III, pages 306-307.

16 / *Prediction in Astrology*

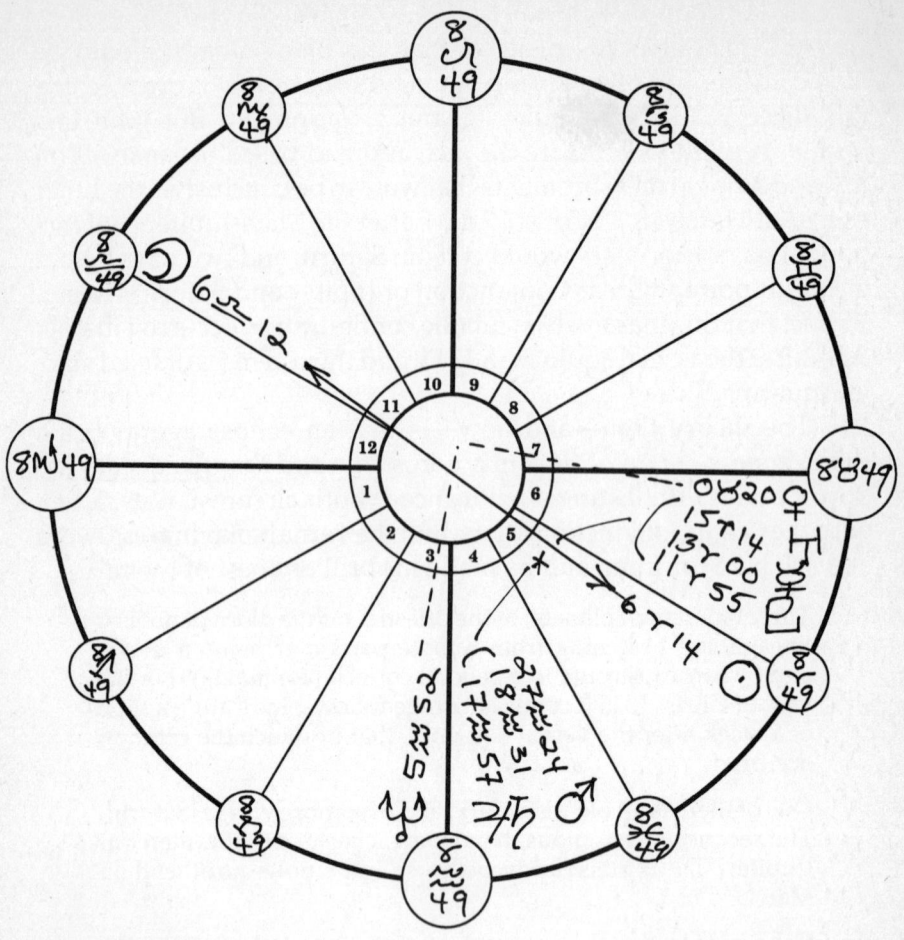

Lunar Eclipse
March 18, 1345
9:25 pm, GMT
London
000 W 10   51 N 30
Equal Houses

Well, John covered the waterfront! He wrote of this prediction again several times, with less flowery verbiage. He then included the eclipse, dramatically, as an intensification of the dire portents for the world.[30]

Look carefully at the horoscopes which follow. John probably

---

30. Subsequent reiterations of the prediction were made in collaboration with an astrologer named Firminus de Bellavalle.

Great Predictions in History / 17

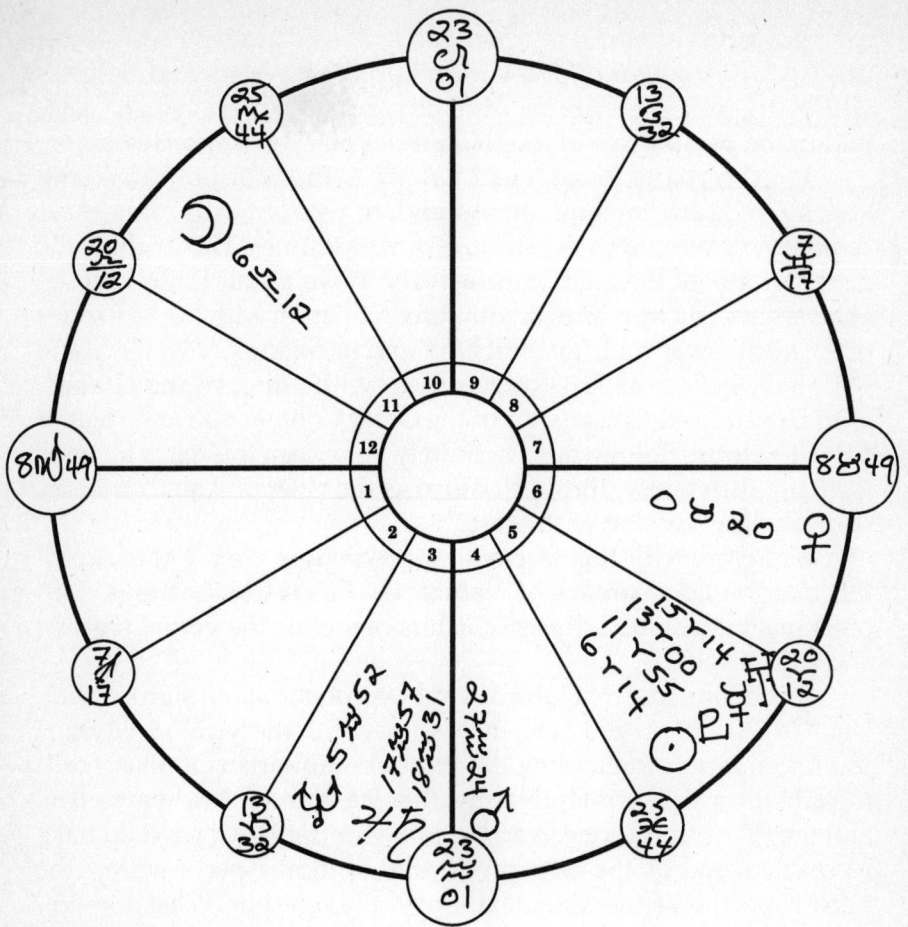

Lunar Eclipse
March 18, 1345
9:25 pm, GMT
London
000 W 10 51 N 30
Placidus Houses

would have cast the eclipse/Great Conjunction horoscope using equal Houses and yet he would have been aware of the Angles.

Look at the horoscope, also set for London, the intellectual center and certainly the astrological center of the Middle Ages, using the Placidus House system, in which the IVth House cusp is also the lower Angle of the chart, the Imum Coeli, opposite the Midheaven. The Great Conjunction, along with Mars and all the fixed stars that attracted John's attention, are strongly positioned at this point. We get a powerful, stressful midpoint picture: Midheaven = Mars/Saturn (the Midheaven opposes the midpoint of Mars and Saturn), which suggests the extreme difficulty, sorrow, bereavement, and, within the perspective of tough lifetimes 600 years ago, death.

In both charts, of course, Mars rules the Scorpio Ascendant, and, as we know for sure, the Ascendant was critically, almost excessively, important to all astrologers in past times. This anchors the dire portents of the chart conclusively. If we admit Pluto into the analysis, we can be alarmed with its conjunction with the Sun, ruler of the Midheaven and "giver of life," and its opposition to the Moon within the eclipse axis; its conjunctions with Mercury and Uranus, with Uranus as the dispositor of the Great Conjunction and ruler of the IVth House. John would definitely have seen this extra focus as well, but differently, through Saturn as the ruler of Aquarius, in its own sign, in "combat with Mars."

So again, with this fascinating prediction, we see the importance of the large strokes of Nature: the Great Conjunctions, conjunctions in general, eclipses, clusters or stellia, the vernal ingress, and the horizon.

It is interesting that John did not wax poetic about sign symbolism. He certainly could have in this case, with the Mars-ruled Scorpio Ascendant commanding the chart, the Aquarian emphasis calling attention to general humanity, the rich Aries/Libra symbolism, and the IVth House zone. And I would wonder how he would have reconciled one of the two supportive, minor aspects within the horoscope, the Venus-Mars sextile over the sign-line. What does Venus "do" with Mars on this battlefield? Perhaps a grace from the Creator, eventual surcease of scourge?

Of course, John would not have seen the outer planets and the VIth House Venus square Neptune, Neptune also squaring the Ascendant. But these great astrologers rarely spoke of aspects as we know them. It seems they had an eye for only the strongest astrological indicators. This gave them a predictive courage—and perhaps recklessness—about that in which they were confident, based upon the techniques of the ancients handed down through wars, national upheavals, and pestilence.

We have more astrological ammunition in our modern interpretive lexicon. We have computers to do so much work with almost no error. But have exacting measurements and technical expertise become a plague for us, dominating our astrological posture in the name of science? Can we face up to the increased demand to do "everyman's" horoscope with sensitivity that approaches art?

It is one thing to predict for a nation or, indeed, for the world, with highly vaunted, impersonal symbolism and dramatic language, and quite another to help an individual who is not a grand hero, who is *not* a king, who is not off to win a battle . . . to see his or her way into the future. What about the *people* born March 18, 1345 in the evening in London, or the other Judean babes born March 1, 7 B.C. during the night?

The difference in our practice of astrology from the mundane to the personal is the adjustment of our language and the temperance of our bravura. For the individual, we must adjust the language of our symbology and we must feel the individual's own life perspective. These points will be explored several times through the development of this book by way of introducing the concept of an individual's Reality Principle.

Then, working with the large and small strokes of nature, we can learn a more personal kind of courage, built on grace, sensitivity and insight, rather than on the general, sweeping, and sensational. In this way, we become effective and helpful on the humanistic level.

As perhaps one benefit of studying the historical cases in this chapter, we should reapproach our astrology with some revival of the anthropomorphic splendor and passionate feel of the planet-gods; and then we should update the drama to modern behaviorist language sensitive to individual perspectives. Many astrologers do this, of course. Even so, it is good to be reminded that we should always recall the poetry of astrology in order to relate astrology to the art of living. We shall explore this in Chapters 6, 7, and 8.

Long Live the King!

Tycho Brahe (1546-1601) was a formidable observer of the heavens. His enormous contributions to the field of astronomy have overshadowed his skill and importance as an astrologer, even in his native Denmark. Historians acknowledge his powers of seeing into the sky and his brilliant inventiveness with astronomical instruments—but they barely mention his honored position as an astrologer to two kings of his land.

Brahe [Brah'-heh] was a powerful man: Sun in Capricorn conjunct Saturn and Mercury, with the Moon conjunct Uranus in Virgo, Mars in Aries, and a wide conjunction of Venus and Jupiter rising in Aquarius. This was an exacting, privileged scientist.

In Brahe's time, astronomy and astrology were hardly separated at all. The telescope, which would give astronomy its autonomous future, would not be created until 1608. All scientists were still debating the concept of the Copernican system, which, in a manner of speaking, had just moved the earth. Still, working without planetary tables of any real reliability (that is, unable to use transits except in the most general terms), astrologers were hard-pressed to accomplish meaningful delineation of horoscopes, especially for individuals and kings.

At this time, astrologers relied on only five planetary aspects: conjunction, sextile, square, trine, and opposition. It was not until Kepler devised his laws of planetary motion (working with Brahe's acute observations as a base) that improved accuracy with prediction was possible. Fixed stars were still very important for filling the measurement gaps. Brahe's private study of 777 (!) stars (*by line of sight*), was published by Kepler, three years after Brahe's death.[31]

King Frederick II summoned his "court astronomer" to Frederiksborg Castle to attend the birth of his son, Christian. Brahe's duty was to cast the complete horoscope, including predictions, for the new prince, born April 12, 1577, at 4:30 p.m. King Frederik asked him to prepare the horoscope "as soon as possible," and we must note that it took Brahe *until July* to prepare it. Perhaps it took a lot of time to imprint the chart figure in gold upon green velvet and to write the life overview in Latin, but we can be sure that what took so much time was the measuring. Without reliable data for the future position of the planets, the measurements of planetary significance for prediction were focused practically solely on complex Primary Directions, which in our time have been mostly supplanted by more manageable Solar Arc and Secondary Progression techniques.

Brahe's predictions for the life of the newborn who would become King Christian IV are examples of the purest, most grounded astrology one can find in the Middle Ages and early Renaissance. Before the facts, Brahe was able to construct a life

---

31. And it was not until 1618 that Kepler established other aspects meaningfully for astrology, the quintile, biquintile, and sesquiquadrate, and then later suggested still more, including the semisquare. See Thorndike, VII, page 20.

Great Predictions in History / 21

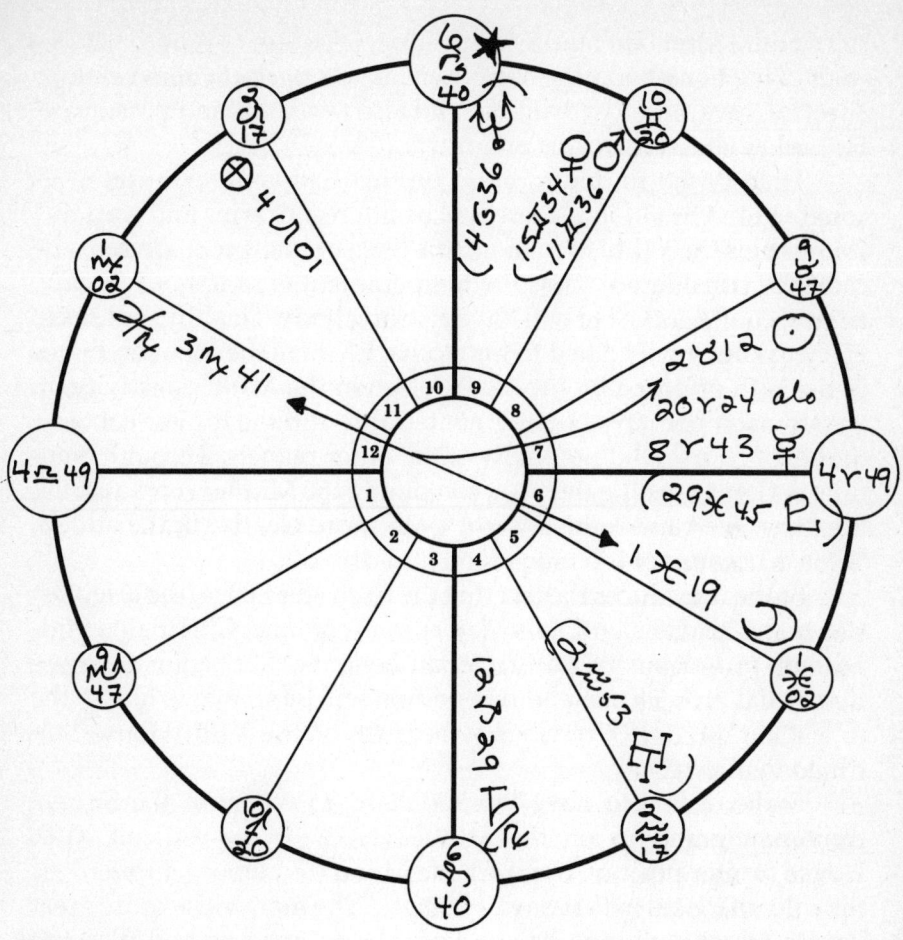

King Christian IV of Denmark
April 12, 1577
4:30 p.m. LMT
Frederiksborg Castle, Denmark
12 E 18   55 N 56
Campanus Houses, by Brahe

★ Sirius: 5 Cancer 55 in 1577

projection that eventuated in almost every instance exactly as he had predicted.

Brahe divided his treatise into certain age-spans of life, citing favorable and unfavorable times in childhood, in matters of health, matters of state, etc., and into character description with specific, years-of-life prediction.

So matter-of-factly, Brahe began with a description of Venus ruling the Ascendant (and as dispositor of the Sun): "When Venus is ruler of the horoscope, the native will have a pleasant demeanor, be cheerful, lovable and dreaming, and also sensuous and passionate. He will have a sense of art and music."

Then Brahe started to build on this Venus observation in its conjunction with Mars: "there will be interest in arms and warfare" (Mars rules the VIIth; for a king, this level of interpretation must be carefully considered) "and the temperament is sanguine" (ruddy, hearty, confident). "He will have a strong body. Healthy, but stout. His weakness will be tied to his stomach" (note the Moon in Pisces in the VIth opposed by Jupiter in Virgo in the XIIth: sensitivity, in the stomach perhaps, but augmented through the Jupiter contact). Brahe, of course, did not know of the outer planets. Through Neptune in Cancer, ruling the VIth, conjoining the Midheaven, squaring Mercury, we can see his insight even more clearly. Brahe added, "This is because of too much food and drink."

Brahe introduces the fact that the fixed star Sirius (the brightest star in the heavens, in Canis Major), was conjunct Christian's Midheaven, promising grand Jupiterian benefits: "He will have more than usual luck. Honor and recognition will be shown to him to the fullest extent" (also, obviously, because of the VIIth House Sun trined by Jupiter).

Brahe seems to have worked hard to reconcile the Sirius/Jupiterian grandeur on the Midheaven with the difficult XIIth House Jupiter position opposite the Moon (remember, Jupiter was the ruler of Pisces in that day). He says, "The man will acquire great wealth which will give rise to discord. He will not gain pleasure from the Church. And he will travel widely to foreign lands" (again, very important considerations for a future king).

This last observation concerning Jupiter also brings Brahe back to the Venus-Mars conjunction in the IXth: "He will be more interested in love affairs than in marriage, and there will be many affairs" (King Christian married twice, had numerous affairs, and sired 21 children).

About children, Brahe was off the mark. He said Christian would have stormy relationships with women and difficulty having children. Clearly, Brahe based his insight on the Venus-Mars conjunction, with Mars ruling the VIIth, and on Saturn—very strong in its own sign—also ruling the sign on the cusp of the Vth, Aquarius. Had Brahe known about Uranus and seen its position in the Vth exactly square the Sun, he would surely have intensified his prediction of affairs and allowed for a flock of children!

Brahe goes on: "He will have many friends among kings and princes" (Brahe had noted the part of fortune in the XIth, disposited by the Sun; and perhaps he felt something was conspicuous about the western orientation of the planets, echoing the social-contact profile set up by the Ascendant). "But he will have many enemies among the clergy and among lawyers" (here is the Jupiter focus again, in the XIIth) "and with warlike people" (Mars ruling the VIIth, conjunct the Ascendant ruler, Venus, in the IXth).

Then the keen astronomer adds a warning, still working his deduction out of the Jupiter considerations, which were so important because of Jupiter's isolation in the eastern half of the chart, in the XIIth, opposing the Moon, the ruler of the Midheaven, trining the Sun. (It seems that Brahe got himself into a back-and-forth set of considerations between IXth House concerns and Jupiter in the Jupiter-Moon axis).

The warning, so clearly dictated by the symbolism, was, "Do not send your enemies to jail or exile them" (surely, for fear of secret retaliation—the prominent XIIth House).

There was much more of this kind of simple and yet oh-so-telling character delineation in Brahe's horoscope for Christian. The king fulfilled so much of it, including grand building plans and museum construction for his people (the Venus promise) and even Brahe's famed observatory tower.

Brahe then closed Christian's life this way: "There is no sign of a violent death. It will be perfectly natural as in sleep, but it will be due to the indulgent way of life, eating and drinking." (The naturalness of death is not clear: Venus conjoining Mars but ruling the VIIIth. For a king, one might consider in this case a battle wound or the like. The reference to dying "as in sleep" probably was added to placate King Frederik and balance the harshness of the often-repeated description of Christian's indulgent way of life.)

King Christian was an inveterate letter writer. He wrote his last letter on February 9, 1648, two months before his 71st birthday. He had returned to Frederiksborg Castle the preceding Christmas, feeling tired and ill—with stomach problems and no appetite. We see Brahe's prediction coming to pass through the Moon-Jupiter axis, the symbols that suggest an indulgent life; the placement of Jupiter in Virgo symbolizes the diet; the Cancer reference through the

Moon suggests the stomach; and there is Mercury, dispositor of the powerful Jupiter, sextile Venus-Mars.

Christian wrote, in the royal third person singular, "The king *knows what is going to happen* [my emphasis; the king had lived with Brahe's analysis for 70 years] but he wants to die in his beloved castle."

On February 21, 1648, King Christian was carried down from his castle rooms to a sleigh and was rushed to his castle in Copenhagen. The speed and excitement of the portage were reported to have been so extreme that, as soon as the sleigh stopped in Copenhagen, one of the horses dropped dead.

On February 28th, the king died. The attendant physician records, "The gentleman died very softly, without any pain or struggle with death, as if falling asleep."

Beyond the extensive descriptions of character, Brahe submitted many specific time periods for key developments in King Christian's life. For example, he specified the young age of three to be a most auspicious time. In April, 1580, on his third birthday, the young Christian was designated successor to his father's throne.

Brahe had worked this prediction through the fulfillment of the Jupiter-Moon opposition through Primary Directions. We can see an approximation of this by simply noting the orb necessary for the Moon to close with Jupiter—2°22'—and suggest two and a half years.

Brahe predicted that the age span of 17-20 would be extremely important to Christian's career. The Prince was crowned King on August 29, 1596, at age 19 years, four months. Measure the orb between natal Saturn and its square position to the Sun—from 2 Aquarius—and call the degrees "years." This degree-for-a-year system grew into our modern system called Solar Arcs. (From here on, the prefix SA refers to a Solar Arc directed planet.)

This SA projection of Saturn to square position with the natal Sun in the VIIth House also corresponds to the occurrence of Christian's first marriage on November 27, 1597, at 20 years, seven months. SA Venus is at the Midheaven.

Brahe made many such predictions; one very important one must yet be included here. He stopped his horoscope overview for Christian at the ages 56-57. He goes no further, saying, "Great dangers are threatening the King at this time. If he survives, he will live to be very old." The Solar Arc projection for this final observation could well have been the Midheaven opposite the Moon and then conjunct Jupiter on the axis with which Brahe had been so occupied throughout the reading. Brahe did not include the fixed star and eclipse phenomena that helped with his delineation. Our objectives here, though, have been fulfilled: to show the poise and insight of a brilliant astronomer/astrologer; to dramatize pure, grounded astrology on the level of an individual life; and to introduce Solar Arcs.

One final note about this case concerns introducing the outer planets and examining their absence over millennia of astrological practice.

It is extraordinarily clear how powerfully helpful these positions would have been in Christian's chart: Uranus, square the Sun, in its own sign, ruling and posited in the Vth, quincunx Jupiter, sextile Pluto; Neptune, conjunct the Midheaven, trine the Moon, sextile both Jupiter and the Sun (Neptune = Sun/Jupiter), square Mercury and Pluto (Neptune = Mercury/Pluto) and quincunx Uranus; and Pluto closing in powerfully by Solar Arc projection (through an age—degree—span from 5 to 34) to square Neptune, oppose the Ascendant, square the Midheaven, conjoin Mercury, square Saturn, conjoin the Sun, and square Uranus.

Without these three outer planets, Brahe and all the other astrologers of times past did not have the six major aspects possible to eleven other planets and points; they lacked the potential for 36 different House placements and 36 autonomous rulerships. Well over 270 meaningful, symbol-rich measurements simply were not there as a resource for these astrologers!

As a result, astrologers were forced to read a great deal into the symbols they had. On the one hand, this is perhaps why Saturn, as the end of the planetary line, took on such onerous demeanor, which indeed fits into the context of harsher times but now often taints our interpretations in more resourceful times. On the other hand, this is why classic horoscope interpretations from the past are so fascinating: fewer measurements focused the symbolisms much more strongly, requiring the pithiest language to place them into life.

With the technological bonanza presently existing in astrology, *more measurements must have more meaning,* and not just exist for their own sake. With these measurements as colors on our palette, the responsibility is greater to develop an artful portrait through pure, grounded astrology. This is the key to successful astrology, to analysis, and to prediction: relating busier symbology to busier lives, always within definitely individualistic frames of reference.

The Great Fire of London

Probably the most famous prediction by astrologers of the past concerned the great fire of London, England, which took place on September 2, 1666, lasted four days and burned two-thirds of the city to ash, leaving 100,000 people homeless. This fire had been preceded by yet another monstrous outbreak of the bubonic plague (this one called the Great Plague) in 1665. The English astrologer William Lilly[32] predicted *both*. His prediction was first published in 1648 and then, with a harrowing woodcut known as "The Geminian Twins," in 1651 in his treatise *Monarchy or No Monarchy*—18 and 15 years before the facts.

Unfortunately, there is little astrology to go along with the dire predictions. But, according to Zadkiel's early nineteenth-century book on Lilly's life (*The Life of William Lilly*), we learn that these predictions were made by means of the fixed stars. He quotes Lilly as saying, "the asterisms and signs and constellations give greatest light thereunto" (read: the stars are all-important).

The entire basis for the prediction (according to Zadkiel) was, incredibly, the position of "the Bull's North Horn," which is the fixed star Elmath (or El Nath), Beta Tauri (that is, the second brightest star in the constellation), having, according to Ptolemy, the nature of Mars. Elmath, in 1666, would take the position of 17 Gemini 54, "the exact Ascendant of London."

Zadkiel is careful to check this. He shows the computations used to take Elmath back from 20 Gemini 15 at the time of his research in 1834 to the London Ascendant of 17 Gemini 54. This difference of position of 2°21' equals 8460 seconds of arc, which divided by 50 and a third seconds of arc (the annual progress of a fixed star) gives 168 years, exactly the number of years intervening between the 1666 fire and 1834.

---

32. Born April 30, or "in May," 1602, seven miles south of Derby, England, presumably with a 5 Pisces Ascendant; this is according to Alan Leo, who quotes John Gadbury, a contemporary and arch-rival of Lilly, in the latter's *Collectio Geniturarum*, published in 1662. Lilly himself says, in the preface to his own masterwork *Christian Astrology*, "I was born at Diseworth in Leicestershire May 1602 in an obscure village."

But then Zadkiel coyly points out that Lilly "was not very nice in his calculation"; Lilly had published that the Ascendant of London was the *nineteenth* degree of Gemini. Surely, Lilly knew it was very late in the eighteenth degree. But in his *Almanac* he spoke in a general fashion to a general public, and it could also have easily been a typo, what with coarse typesets and early printing presses. (Later, we will detect a gross error in Lilly's Table of Houses.)

That is the story. Zadkiel is adamant in reinforcing that 17 Gemini 54 is the true Ascendant of London: "It was that which ascended at the moment of driving the first pile of the new London Bridge."[33]

Here is what Lilly said in his prediction:

> In the year 1665, the Aphelium[34] of Mars, who is the general signification of England,[35] will be in Virgo, which is assuredly the Ascendant of the English monarchy, but Aries of the Kingdom. When the absis[36] of Mars shall appear in Virgo, who shall expect less than a strange catastrophe of human affairs in the commonwealth, monarchy and Kingdom of England. There will be then, either in or about these times, or near that year, or within ten years, more or less of that time [talk about protecting one's prediction!], appear in this Kingdom so strange a revolution of fate, so grand a catastrophe and great mutation unto this monarchy and government as never yet appeared of which as the times now stand, I have no liberty or encouragement to deliver my opinion—only, it will be ominous to London, unto her merchants at seas, to her traffique on land, to her poor, to all sorts of people, inhabiting in her or to her liberties, *by reason of fire and consuming plague*"[37] [my emphasis].

Lilly clearly makes no reference to Elmath, which Zadkiel was so sure commanded Lilly's prediction.

Sources suggest that the great fire of London broke out at 1:00 a.m. on Sunday, September 2, 1666. The event chart is . . . uneventful. If it were significant, someone in that competitive astrological market would surely have taken credit for it.[38]

---

33. Zadkiel, page 5. Interestingly, historical sources suggest specifically that the fire began in the King's bakery on Pudding Lane very near the London Bridge. This London Bridge is not the London Bridge presently standing (which underwent reconstruction in 1824 and reopened in 1831), but an older and also celebrated span over the Thames.
34. Aphelion: the point on a planet's orbit most distant from the Sun.
35. Which refers presumably to the Aries Ascendant of the Coronation chart of William I on Christmas Day, true noon, 1066 in Westminster.
36. Apsis, line of Apsides: the major axis of an elliptical orbit; the aphelion/perihelion axis.
37. Glass, pages 111-112.
38. In 1962, Van Norstrand (see bibliography) averred that the conjunction of Uranus and Neptune at 18 Sagittarius in 1650 (opposite the London Ascendant), fifteen years before the plague and the fire, "caused" these calamities. Of course, Lilly did not know about these outer planets, discovered in 1781 and 1846 respectively.

28 / Prediction in Astrology

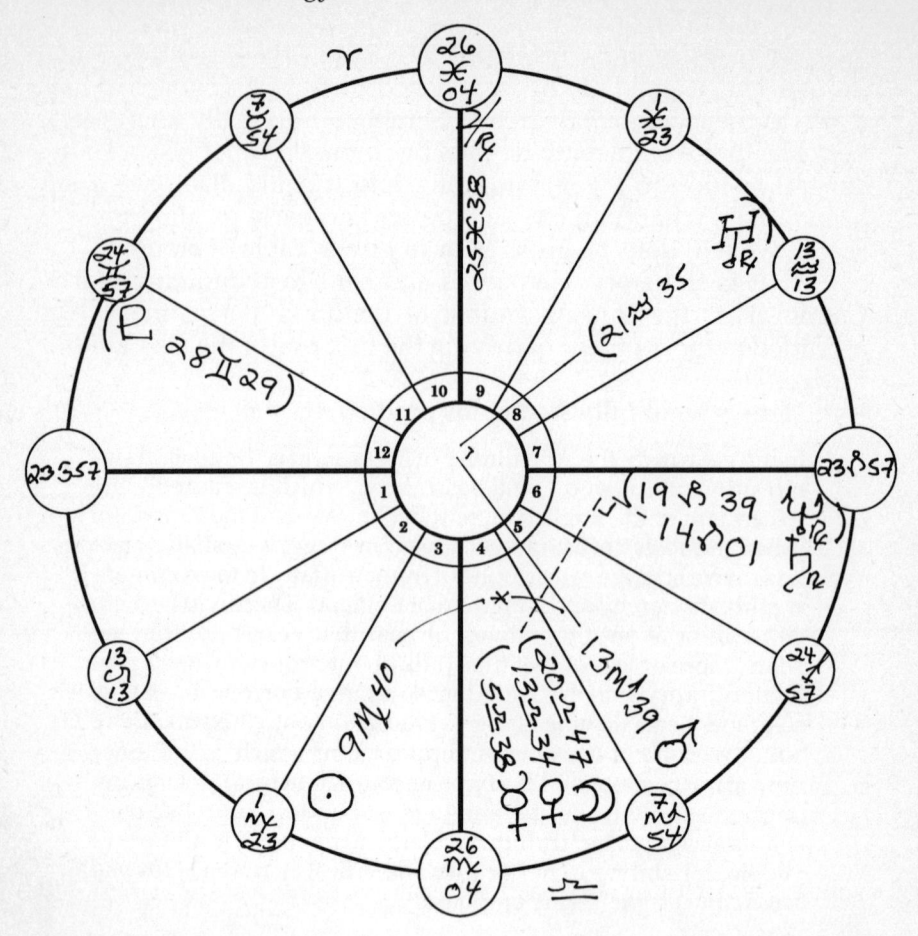

The Great Fire of London
September 2, 1666
1:00 am, LMT
London
000 W 14 51 N 31
Regiomontanus Houses

This chart was computed with reference to Lilly's own published Table of Houses. These are Regiomontanus Houses devised early in the 14th century. Lilly's Tables contained a huge misprint/error for the eleventh/fifth cusp axis, here corrected.

    This astrology—what there is of it—is certainly not enough for such an extraordinary prediction. But Lilly was no lightweight. His mathematics throughout his major, three volume work, *Christian Astrology* (1647), is indeed sharp and painstaking (except for a major lapse in his Table of Houses); his timing of the example horary charts is always to-the-minute; his knowledge of Ptolemy's work with Primary Directions and the refinements of the system throughout the centuries is thorough; and his language always has that subtle edge to it, a quiet cleverness, which usually indicates keen perception.

Certainly there is more than we can ferret out today, or more that Lilly never revealed. The astrologers of his day were at each other's throats with jealousy and competitive barbs—constantly. Thorndike cites these astrologers' "vilification of one another." There was name-calling in public ("Gadbury the Arch-Conjurer"). There were accusations that Lilly "wrote to please his friends and to keep in with the times [in other words, for popularity] and not according to the rules of the art." The suggestion is that Lilly was protecting his techniques from his competitors while titillating his public.[39]

Let us realize that these astrologers were promoters; they were earning a living not from kings and queens, as in older times, but from the public, under the harshest scrutiny and expectations. One big-time prediction to attract attention demanded another one even bigger in order to sell more books and pamphlets. Lilly was a *full-time* predictor. We have no record of how many predictions failed.

For sure, Lilly did cause quite a stir. On October 25, 1666, some six weeks after the great four-day fire, just as the plague was subsiding, he was summoned before the House of Commons (not for the first time!) to answer for any "cause of or design" behind the fire. There actually was suspicion that perhaps Lilly caused the fire to fit the prediction.

Lilly acquitted himself eloquently, persuading his questioners that only "the finger of God" had been at work.

In closing the case of the great London fire, it is interesting to note that Lilly began a study of magic twelve years after he began his study of astrology in 1632.[40] This phase did not last long, but it does show us more about this man, emphasizing his Pisces Ascendant, his Sun exactly conjunct Venus eleven degrees from Uranus, and his Moon conjunct Neptune (the latter two unknown to Lilly, of course).

---

39. It is interesting to note this passage from Lilly's preface to *Christian Astrology*: "Annual and Monthly judgements I have not yet digested into a Method, I hope to live to performe it; I am the first of men that ever adventured upon Monthly Observations in such plaine language, yet is it my hearty desire to communicate hereafter what ever I know unto Posterity. Having been of late traduced by some halfe-witted fooles, I deliver my selfe to Posterity who I am, and of what profession...."

40. Glass, page 112.

The fame of Lilly's prediction is possibly due in large part to the fact that he echoed the prognostication made by Nostradamus 111 years earlier:

> Le sang du juste à Londres fera faute,
> Bruslez par fue, de vingt et trois, les six.
>
> (The blood of the just requires London
> to be burned with fire in sixty-six.)[41]

Lilly surely knew of this prediction.[42] Was the Magic of Nostradamus involved here as well?

Clearly, behind the historical tale, there is much we do not know. Lilly was an extraordinary astrologer, and, in his 68th year, becoming a medical doctor, he used astrological knowledge in new directions very effectively. He became blind in 1681 and died that same year on June 9, five weeks after his 79th birthday.

This example has again revealed a great emphasis on the fixed stars, on one in particular. If we pay attention to those stars, most definitely an extension of the prevailing order of our solar system, they begin to close in upon us from so far away. In our astrology today—mundane and personal—are we losing sight of something? Or are we starting to see it again?

Evangeline's Claim to Flame!

New York City, March 16, 1899. Evangeline Adams comes to New York City, and history bears witness still.

The soon to be celebrated astrologer, traveling the difficult trip down from Boston, was 31 years old at the time. At the Fifth Avenue Hotel in New York, she announced that she was an astrologer and had come to the city to practice her "science." She was welcomed as a guest but was refused admission as an astrologer, and she found herself "homeless on the sidewalk of Madison Square."[43]

Adams continues:

> I staggered along under the weight of my carefully overpacked portmanteau.... I was in a mood to defy assistance—and the world. So I put off up the Avenue with my dignity in one hand and my luggage in the other.

---

41. Many sources, including Roberts, page 60; Century II, quatrain 51.
42. And also, the Nostradamus quatrain supposedly prognosticating the Great Plague in 1665 as revenge for the execution of Charles I; see Roberts, page 60; Century II, quatrain 53.
43. All references to Adams' experience are recorded in her book, *The Bowl of Heaven*, pages 36-39.

By the time I reached the Windsor Hotel, in that day the New York home of many visiting notables, my feelings had calmed... I entered respectfully the portals of the great building which was destined to bring me sudden fame.[44]

Upon her arrival at the Windsor Hotel, Adams met with Warren Leland, the proprietor, who is the vitally important focus of this case study and rectification. She was taken to her room on the first floor ("twelve dollars a day, a large sum") after eschewing, without explanation (later, crediting "favorable auspices"), a suite first shown her at a much lower rate on the fifth floor. She checked in "about eight o'clock in the evening, Thursday, March 16, 1899."

Adams writes that Mr. Leland said, "in his jovial way [note "jovial"], 'Tomorrow will be Friday, a bad-luck day. You better give me a reading now!'"

She did indeed. And so will we.

So I took out one of my charts, entered the day and hour [note] and place of his birth, and began to calculate the position of his stars [planets]. Suddenly, I saw something which made me hesitate. The man was under one of the worst possible combinations of planets—conditions terrifying in their unfriendliness.

I remember telling him that the danger was so imminent that it might overtake him on the morrow. And his reply: [hear the joviality], "Oh, tomorrow's a holiday [St. Patrick's Day?]. Stocks can't go down!'"

Adams describes Leland as "a great speculator [note, she uses a Vth House word; she could have said "investor"] and even when he learned that the unfavorable conditions affected not only him but his entire family, his mind still reverted to the stock market."

Adams says he was very impressed with the "general accuracy of the reading" (note "general"; curious in the light of what follows). "He sent guests to me that evening until long after midnight" (Adams was a workaholic: Leo Moon in the VIth House; more about this Moon and her horoscope later).

The next morning [important], Leland visited Adams again and asked for a projection for the next week (undoubtedly for use with the stock market; Leland was definitely a millionaire—before the time of taxes!). She comments:

---

44. The Windsor Hotel is not to be confused with the Hotel Windsor presently on West 58th Street in New York City. There is no historical connection between the two. Adams' Hotel Windsor burned to the ground, as we shall see. One feels that the Windsor was the first hotel Adams came across on her trek to find lodging that early evening. There is an eerie feeling indeed that circumstances seemed to be bringing her, Warren Leland, and catastrophe together.

My mind was still so filled with the horror which was hanging over this kindly, hospitable man that I forced myself to consult his chart again. There could be no doubt of the accuracy of my first reading. The danger which confronted him was so clearly indicated and so imminent that it seemed as if the man in front of me was being pushed at that very moment into the very depths of disaster. I tried to be calm and professional in my warning, but I could not control the chills which ran through my body.

The jovial stock-market speculator, this kindly, hospitable Mr. Leland, got up to leave Evangeline Adams, opened her door "and walked into the greatest hotel disaster of all times, the famous Windsor fire!"

Adams writes of rushing to gather up her most important papers and fleeing the hotel (fortunately from the first floor), and then watching with horror as people dropped to their death from upper windows, as people blackened with fire and soot ran screaming out of the hotel, as its grand Fifth Avenue facade collapsed. An enormous fire. Adams writes:

> A grim success, you may call it, my first astrological reading in New York. And such it was! I would have given anything I possessed at the time if my prediction had not come so terribly true. But the stars had decreed otherwise.
>
> And they had decreed that so far as I was concerned, good should come out of evil. For the next in importance to the news of the fire, was Mr. Leland's statement, printed in big type on the front page (of the next day's New York Times, March 18, 1899) that the disaster had been predicted by Evangeline Adams of Boston!

Leland lost his wife and daughter in the blaze. They both died that day, March 17, 1899, and—as we shall see—Mr. Leland would join them, dead from appendicitis 18 days later.

What did Adams see? What possibly could be the combinations of planets she saw in Mr. Leland's horoscope? To know the answer to those questions, to share the prediction on-the-scene with Adams, we have to know about Mr. Leland.

The search for Mr. Leland's identity and his birth data would fill a large chapter in itself. It has been a laborious and yet intriguing task, finding out who this man was. The New York Times obituary for his death April 4, 1899, was substantial. Leland was from a celebrated family of hoteliers which dated back to a grandfather in the Inn business in Vermont in 1814; he hobnobbed with the famous;

governors called in condolence for the loss of his family.

The obituary was one year off on Leland's birth (1844 instead of 1845, as was discovered) and wrong in the name of the Chicago cemetery where Leland was finally buried.

Warren Leland was born in Londonderry, Vermont, in 1845, definitely. Yet, the archives office in Londonderry has no record of his birth, which, I was advised, is not unusual for that era. Montpelier, the capital, has no record. No birth or school records of any kind seem to exist in Vermont. We shall learn that Leland left Vermont as a boy. He was surely born at home and no one thought of registering his birth.

Leland married Isabella Cobb of Cleveland (according to his obituary). The Cleveland City Archives do contain their marriage certificate for December 16, 1868, but again, no birthdate is listed for Leland. This marriage date proves to be very helpful in the rectification of Leland's horoscope.

Another clue came through research in Newport, Rhode Island, since Leland had taken over a hotel there in 1894, before he came to New York (again, according to the obituary). He was so popular that, upon his leaving, he was feted by Newport's finest at a testimonial dinner. There was tremendous press coverage of the event in the Newport Journal, September 2, 1895. But there was still no birthdate.[45]

There were many dead ends like these, but every research probe added important details to help build a portrait of Leland. One final clue takes us as far as we can go: Leland's obituary said that he was to be buried in "Lakewood Cemetery in Chicago." This turned out to be the wrong name for what actually was the Oak Woods Cemetery.

Leland died on April 4, 1899. His body was delivered in Chicago under the care of the C.H. Jordan Funeral Home (now the Blake-Lamb Funeral Home). They took it to Oak Woods, where it was kept in a 100-casket storage facility until the ground would thaw enough to allow the digging of his grave.

Warren F. Leland was buried on June 6, 1899 at Oak Woods in Section I-1-877. There is a large monument marking the Leland

---

45. Newport's 91-year old (in 1990) Curator of Manuscripts, Gladys Balhouse, immediately recognized Newport's "Ocean House," later "Leland's Ocean House." She said, "The original was built in the 1840s; *burned down, the next year*, I think; and then rebuilt, and THAT one *burned down in 1899*, about the same time as the Windsor. It was over there on Beltvue Avenue where the shopping center is now."

family plot. Warren Leland's individual gravestone simply states his name and the dates 1845-1899. Still no birth data!

But the old burial archives bring us very close to what we need: "Warren F. Leland died at age 53 years, ten months, and four days" (how did *they* know?).

Whew! Finally, we can focus on May 31, 1845.

What are we going to find? Just what did Evangeline Adams see during that evening of March 16, 1899 that related so drastically to Leland's portion of time brought to life in 1845?

As we have already seen, rectification is a rigorous challenge for astrologers. But it is well worth the effort, since it forces us to predict *before a birth time is determined*. We exercise deduction strenuously. We exercise creative and logical use of what we know about astrology and how its symbology translates into life, especially under conditions of stress, change, or catastrophe. This type of prediction within the past trains us to predict into the future. Much of the rest of this book will deal with this vital premise.

Here are some observations about Leland, gleaned from careful reading of Adams' brief account of her meeting with him and picked up here and there during the search for his birth data.

1. According to Adams, Leland was "a most charming host, sympathetic with my work and aims." Leland had to have been charming; he was in the hotel business within a long family tradition. Adams was 31 years old, very tired that evening after a long trip and an inhospitable confrontation at a competing hotel. She was glad to be settled down in the big city. She loved the welcome she received to the ritzy surroundings of the Windsor. She felt flattered and supported. She needed that attention, unabashedly, through her Leo Moon and her Venus in Pisces, rising just above her Pisces Ascendant.

2. Adams described Leland as speaking in a "jovial way." This is a very important observation. Here is a keen astrologer using an astrological word. Astrology was always on her mind and, at that time a hundred years ago, there was no more "Jupiterian" word in the vocabulary. We can start to feel an insistence on Jupiter, perhaps on Sagittarius.

3. Adams wrote that she "entered the day and hour and place of his birth." This tells us that Leland did indeed know the time of his birth.

The problem of knowing birth times was a lot more pronounced then than it is now, a century and a half after Leland's birth, especially when we can be almost positive that Leland was delivered at home.

The birth time, we can deduce further, through Leland's remembrance of it, must have been pegged down around some established time of day, such as "a little while after dinner that night, which we all missed, of course"; or "just before the sun came up."

Of course, Adams was accustomed to this. In her book, *Astrology: Your Place in the Sun*, she provides time-tables of Ascendants, based upon hourly intervals of the day, every four days of the year. These tables are not unsophisticated or clumsy. They appear to be accurate within two degrees most of the time. In other words, *astrologers then were well-organized around the unsure*. Additionally, as is essential in working with suspect birth times, Adams surely asked Leland many questions to test the grounds of his recollection.

4. Adams wrote, "I began to calculate the position of his stars." She obviously had established his Ascendant (probably through tables not as reliable as the ones in her later book), working with his recollected time of, say, late evening. Indeed, Leland may have added something like, "My father always liked to recall that he never did get his supper that night, until almost midnight!" Or maybe he startled Adams by saying something like, "Well, I happen to know it for sure. My father—Simeon, he loved the Bible—wrote the time down in the Good Book! He was very proud of that."[46]

5. Then Adams wrote: "Suddenly I saw something which made me hesitate"—when she saw the "worst possible combination of planets." She was looking at transits in relation to a major, pop-off-the-paper situation in Leland's developing horoscope.

The horoscope for that reading time which follows shows a very strong opposition between Saturn and Neptune (Pluto was not yet known; Neptune was the end of the line), 29 days or 1°25' of arc past partile.

---

46. In the rectification process, conversations like this—apparently idle banter—are extremely important in crystallizing deductions. Every seasoned astrologer has learned how to listen creatively.

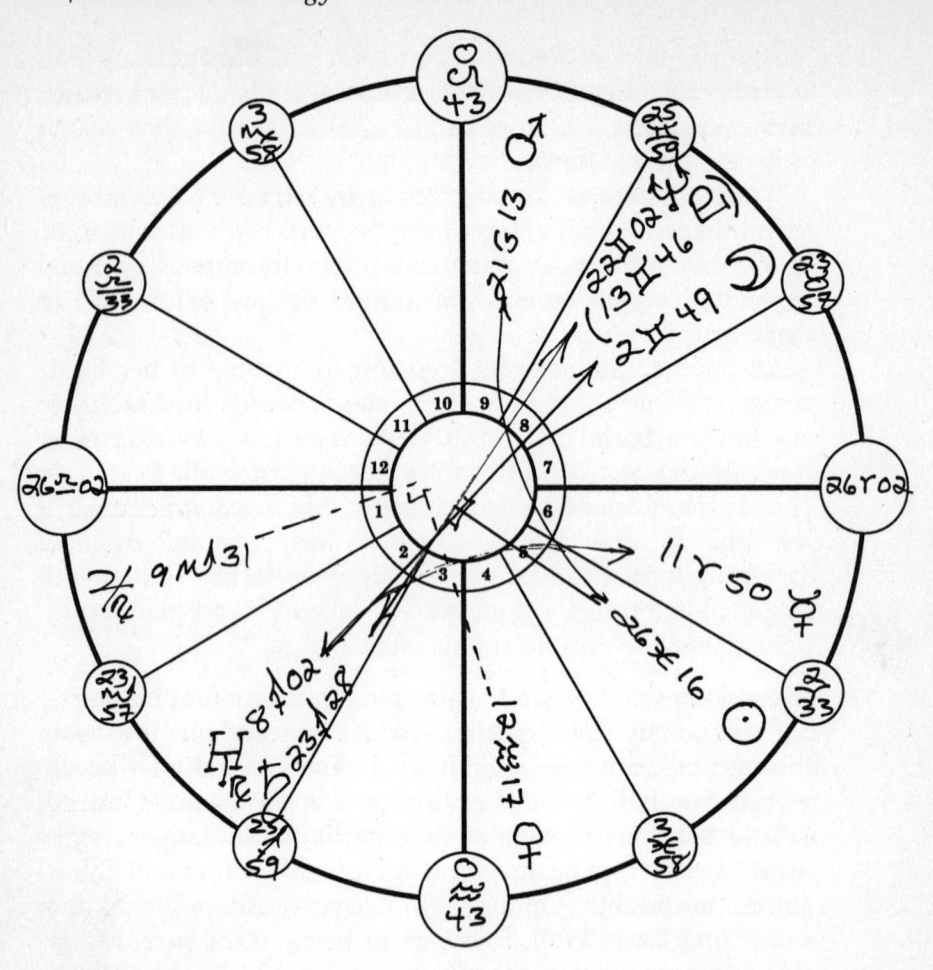

Adams Reading
March 16, 1899
08:30 pm, LMT
Manhattan, NYC
073 W 59   40 N 46
Placidian Houses (used by Adams)

This had to be the dominant configuration Adams saw. (The opposition between Uranus, also in Sagittarius, and Pluto is extremely telling here as well, but as noted, Adams would not have known of Pluto.) She would also have seen that the Sun was involved with that opposition axis, forming a transiting T-Square.

Immediately, she would have seen the Moon opposed to Uranus, to be exact in only about twelve hours of time (early the next morning). She would have viewed this as a potential "trigger." Any skilled astrologer would have.

Instantly, her eyes would have searched out the position of Mars. She would have seen that it was trine the Sun, and really not threatening anything in transit. Now, Adams was not looking at this "reading chart," which just records the transits of that general time. She would have *known* and been refreshed at that moment by her ephemeris; on the long train ride from Boston she would have ruminated about the transits of that day in relation to her first trip to New York; she would have been ready for action with her first clientele in the big city.

The Saturn-Neptune and Moon-Uranus oppositions were immediately measurable, recallable, with only a minimal calculation required for the Moon's position.

6. The Saturn-Neptune and Moon-Uranus oppositions in transit that evening were in the Sagittarius-Gemini axis. For Adams to relate those measurements instantly to Leland's horoscope under construction before her, something must already have been there on the paper—from her steps of calculation—which related dramatically to the transiting oppositions. It had to have been the Ascendant, the first step in calculating an astrological chart.

Remembering his "jovial" way (observations one and two above help us with an initial hypothesis), and appreciating points four, five, and six that lead us to the Sagittarius-Gemini axis, we can assign Leland a Sagittarius Ascendant, upon which horizon axis the Saturn-Neptune transiting opposition fell dramatically. This would give Leland a birth time of, say, 8:25 p.m. LMT in Londonderry, Vermont. This time easily fits with observation four above.[47]

7. Adams makes several references to Leland being a "speculator." Here is another astrological word, relating to the Vth House, IInd House, to the VIIIth House of "other people's

---

47. Hard work with this case has repeatedly corroborated a birth time of 8:25 pm. Evidence now follows in the text to show how the rectification process works.

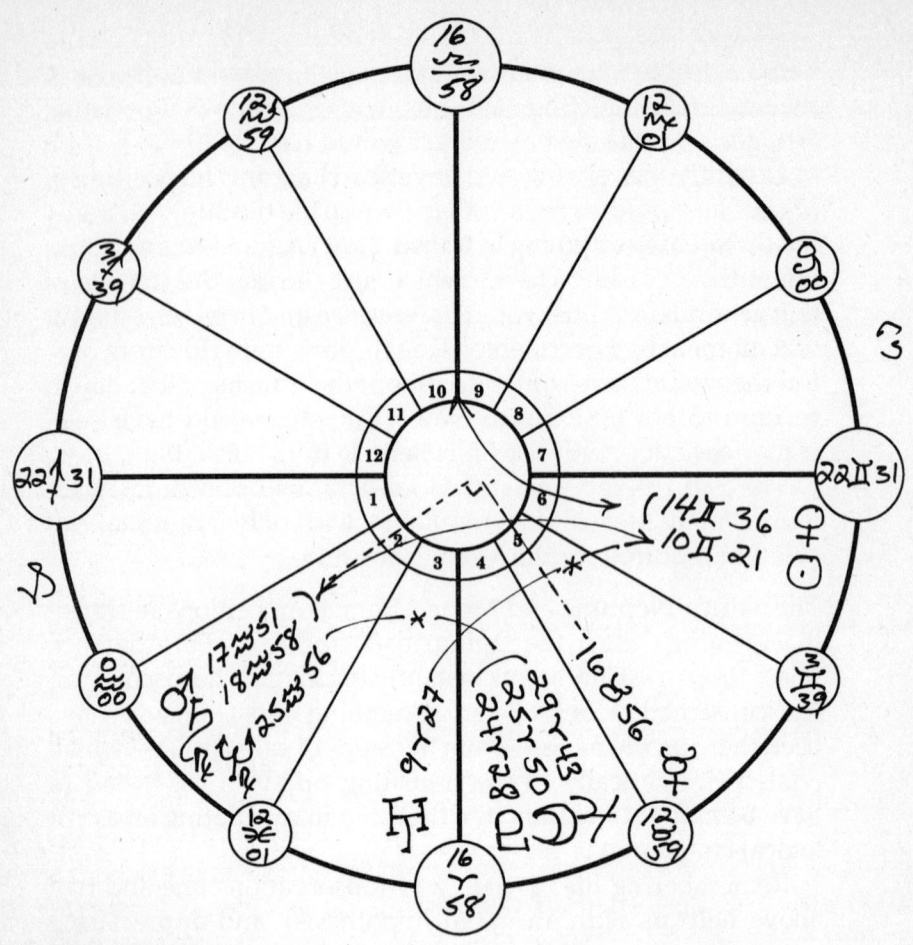

Rectification
Warren F. Leland
May 31, 1845
08:25 p.m. LMT
Londonderry, Vermont
072 W 49   43 N 12
Placidian Houses

money," and to Venus and Jupiter.[48] We must remember, Adams "talked astrology," very, very well, sometimes quite

---

48. Adams hardly ever mentions Houses in her published works. I might say "never," except once, in her construction instructions and fleetingly in her barest of presentations about horary astrology, when she does mention the word. But Adams knew her astrology—the symbology and the rules—all with a classicist's flair. She knew Houses, of course, but for some reason she didn't use them conspicuously in her work.

poetically, always dramatically.

In Leland's rectified horoscope, the ruler of the Vth House of speculation is Venus, which is conjunct the Sun, in mutual reception with Mercury, ruler of the "public" VIIth; it is trine Mars and Saturn in the "money" IInd, ruled by Uranus, which is sextile to the Sun and Venus. The Sun rules the VIIIth and trines the planets in the IInd. Venus rules and trines the Libra Midheaven; Jupiter (big money, big wins) rules the Ascendant, is powerfully strident in Aries, conjoins the Moon (and Pluto), and sextiles Neptune in the IInd.

A lot of corroborative evidence—through planet symbolism, House placement, aspect, and rulership—anchors the dimensions of the speculation and money-dealing in this man, who worked very hard all the time to fulfill strong ego needs for recognition.[49] Money is all-important here. Leland was extremely wealthy.

This is how the rectification process goes. The first step is *to relate all details at hand*, all conversational tidbits, anything at all, including *all the classical astrological lore* that so pithily encapsulates the symbolism of signs and planets.

Here are some more "brush strokes" to add to the portrait: the Moon in the IVth House usually suggests, in vocational considerations, that the individual works at home or makes his or her workplace look like home. This seems so very simplistic, yet it can be extremely helpful in vocational guidance counseling, and it can be an important touch or corroboration in rectification. In this horoscope, it is perfectly appropriate: a hotel owner who always lives in the hotels he owns.[50]

We note that Uranus at 9 Aries 27 would come to the Imum Coeli (opposite the Midheaven) in about seven and a half degrees, or about seven and a half years. A 1°/1year generalization is the basis for understanding Solar Arc theory. The probability is extremely high under this measurement that the person would experience a major change of residence, take a new start in life, change vocational direction, etc. We read in Leland's obituary, "When a boy, he was

---

[49]. Moon in Aries, overcompensating for some very early homelife struggles, not germane here, but suggested in part by the organization of all planets under the horizon; while embraced by the superb trine between Mars and Sun-Venus, one parental ruler, Mars, is clearly stressed by the conjunction with Saturn, which is retrograde.

[50]. See Tyl, *The Principles and Practice of Astrology*, Vol. IX: "Success, Sex, and Illness," pages 5-10.

40 / *Prediction in Astrology*

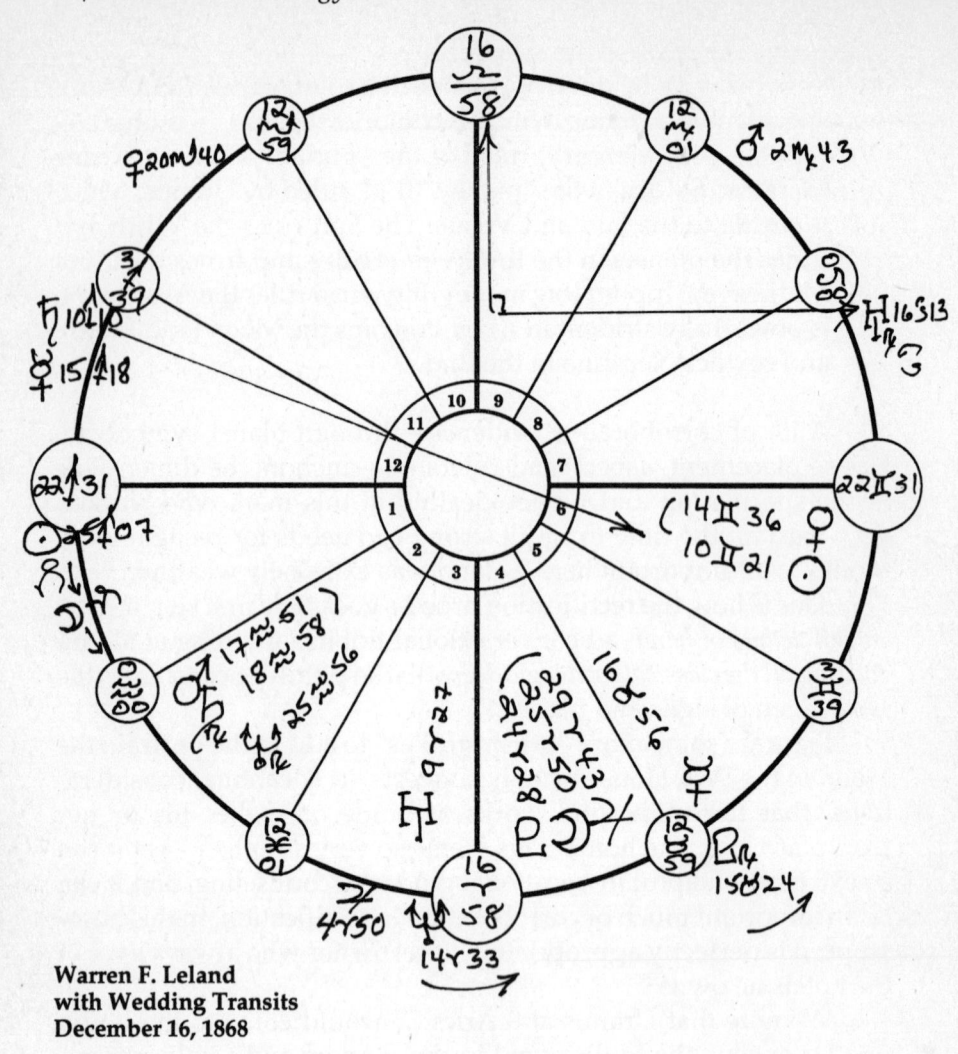

**Warren F. Leland
with Wedding Transits
December 16, 1868**

taken to Cleveland, Ohio, by his father, Simeon Leland, Jr." This could well have been the time.

When Leland married Isabella Cobb on December 16, 1868, transiting Uranus was at 16 Cancer 13 tightly square to Leland's Libra Midheaven from his VIIth House. Any arc or transit to an Angle is a vitally important test of rectification. In addition, transiting Saturn at 10 Sagittarius 10 is almost exactly opposite Leland's Sun; Neptune is at 14 Aries 33, nearing Leland's Imum Coeli; and, although not yet discovered, Pluto at 15 Taurus 24 is one and a half degrees from conjunction with Leland's Mercury, ruler of the VIIth.

All of this is extremely strong corroboration of the birth time as presented.

Leland's obituary reports that, in March 1892, Leland sold a hotel he had refurbished in Chicago. The sale was for $1,000,000—a colossal sum one hundred years ago! Leland was 47 years old and just beginning to register the momentous 45 degree Solar Arc accumulation (see Chapter 3; a slow arc here). He was also perhaps at the culmination of his career in financial speculation. The very important semi-square (45 degree) arc accumulation moment was exact for Leland in July 1892 and certainly applies to the bonanza four months previous.

This would be an easy prediction and a sound rectification confirmation for the importance of Jupiter and Venus in Leland's horoscope. The distance between natal Jupiter and conjunction with natal Venus in general Solar Arc projection is just seven minutes of arc short of 45 degrees! The measurement of SA Jupiter conjunct Venus is indeed exact in 1892, right on schedule.

Interestingly, Leland's professional history, as much as we have of it from his obituary, highlights two times of his life when he took over hotels and renamed them with his own name. The million dollar sale in 1892 was for the "Leland Hotel" in Chicago, formerly the Gardener House on Michigan Avenue. In Newport, Rhode Island, Leland took over the Ocean House and named it "Leland's Ocean House." This is clear fulfillment of the reigning needs of the Moon in Aries, especially as it conjoins Jupiter (and Pluto), swooshing to prominence in his life, indirectly through hotel names, over the potentially suppressive horizon line.

When Leland's SA Pluto conjoined his natal Sun in July 1893 (age 48; slow arc of 46 degrees; see Chapter 3), Leland had built the Chicago Beach Hotel in connection with the World's Fair of 1892-93. In four months, he netted $244,000, "eclipsing all hotel records for rapid and enormous profits" (obituary).

Leland took over the Windsor Hotel in New York City on May 1, 1896. The negotiation period just before this extraordinary moment in his life—coming to New York City, taking over a Fifth Avenue palace, etc.—is power-packed astrologically: all through March and April 1896, the preceding two months, transiting Jupiter was stationary, barely in motion relative to the earth for the longest time, in the last degree of Cancer, exactly square to Leland's own Jupiter in the IVth House of properties, hotels, new starts . . . and

42 / *Prediction in Astrology*

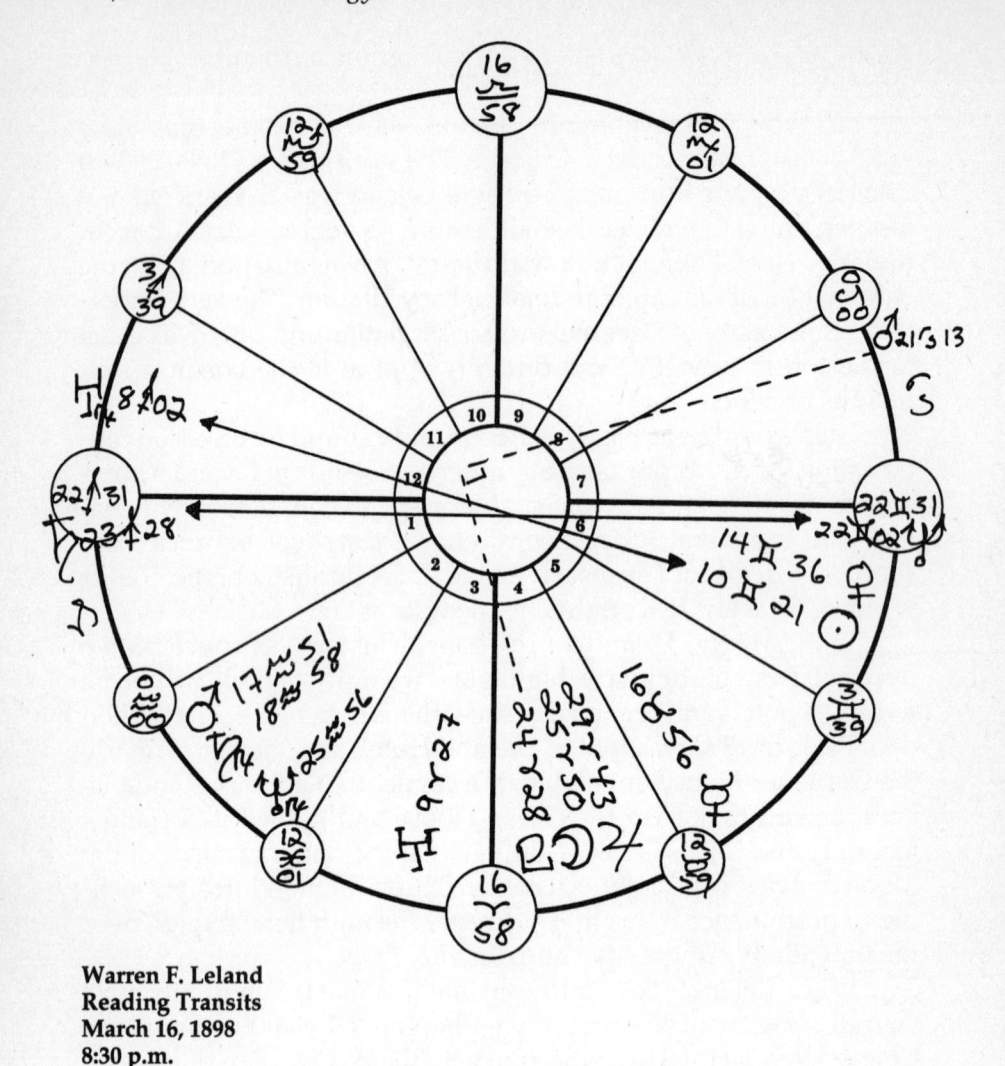

Warren F. Leland
Reading Transits
March 16, 1898
8:30 p.m.

ends of matters. Of course, Jupiter had just squared his Moon-Pluto conjunction earlier, when all the plans and excitement of change were being cast.

NOTE: It is extremely important in dynamic astrological analysis to see the drama of planetary movements quickly in terms of life activity, the common sense and actuality of growth, problems, concerns, struggles, plans, strategies, and, most important, the orderly procession of events within real time. Otherwise, the

Great Predictions in History / 43

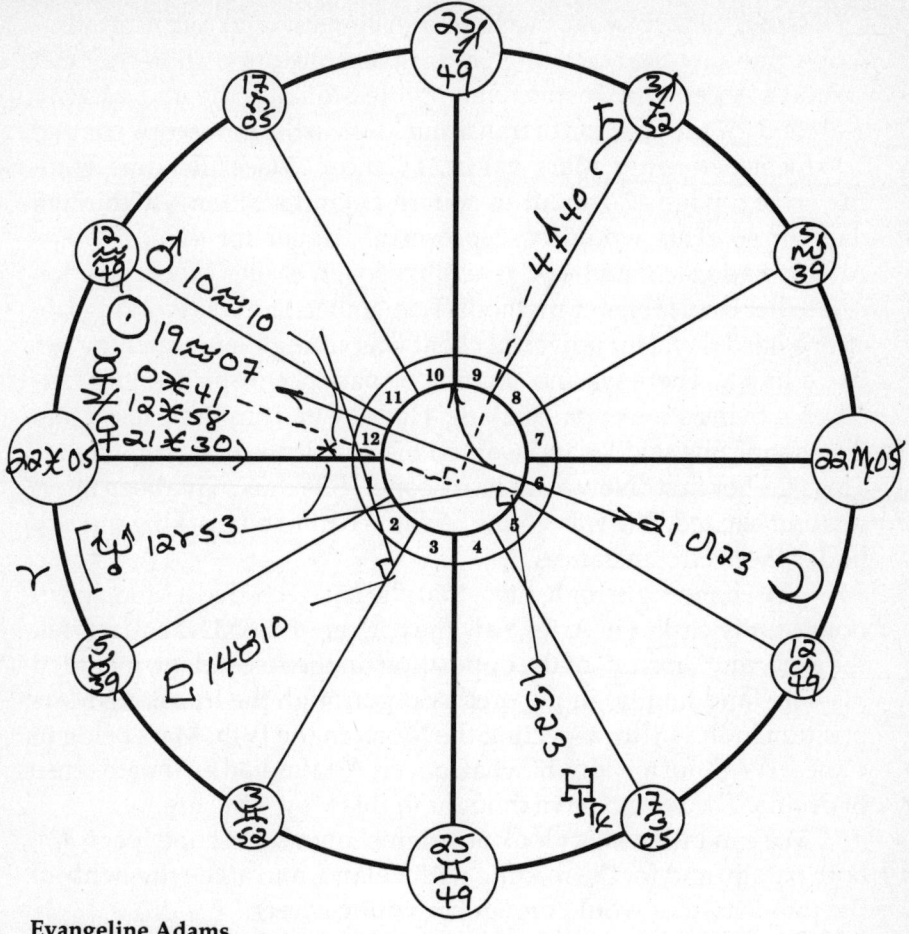

Evangeline Adams
Sources: McCaffery, Jones
February 8, 1868
8:30 a.m. LMT
Jersey City, New Jersey
074 W 04   40 N 44
Placidian Houses

astrologer can easily get lost in a maze of measurements and never make it back to reality.

The real proofs of rectification are in Solar Arc projections and major transit movement to the Angles of the horoscope. This will be discussed further in Chapter 3, but for our work on fascinating predictions and the "stuff" behind them, the insights shared here suffice to anchor Leland's horoscope as we have it, at 8:25 p.m., LMT.

Now, back to what Evangeline Adams saw in Leland's horoscope. She saw the transiting Saturn-Neptune opposition conjunct Leland's Ascendant. Instinctively, professionally, she immediately searched for the position of transiting Mars in the horoscope coming into focus before her. Mars was in 21 Cancer 13 (see "Reading Transits" chart, page 42), about to square Leland's Moon—within ten days or so. This would be a powerful trigger for sure. Perhaps Adams had calculated—or generalized—an earlier Moon position due to her own tables or methods. Remember, she was working late after a hard day. Her powerful client was sitting there watching her like a hawk. There was no stamina or patience or professional excuse for being slow or painstaking. Had she had anything to eat that afternoon? She said Leland wanted his horoscope done right away. This was her first "New York horoscope." She must have been nervous and excited. She was young. Adams had to be working quickly under these circumstances.

The chances are high, then, that she had recorded a Moon position slightly earlier in Aries, saw the trigger of the Mars square, felt the dormant "horror" of the opposition on the Ascendant, included his wife (and family) in the prediction through the transiting Mars position in the VIIth, aspecting the Moon in the IVth, Mars being in Cancer. Without any doubt whatsoever, Adams had an innate sense of drama. She would have thought in this way, I'm sure.

We can take a short look at Adams' own horoscope (page 43), both natally and for the reading with Leland, and at the fire, with all the publicity that would crown her young career.

We have already felt the powerful Leo Moon: her dramatic turn of phrase, flair, her need for the center of the stage, and indeed her sense of self-importance, in full awareness (opposition) with her Aquarian Sun. This is a formidable Queen complex for sure, but benevolent, magnanimous, sincerely eager to be helpful. It is her way to fame; the Moon is trine to the Midheaven. She assumed it all naturally.

But all of this was counterbalanced and indeed enriched by a tremendous sensitivity: Pisces rising, Neptune in the Ist House squared by Uranus in the IVth. Note the concentration of planets in Pisces in the XIIth, not in conjunction but in cluster, her faculties of mind, learning, and social relations all sensitive as litmus paper. And all of this is grounded by the powerful square-of-wisdom (as the ancients might say) between Mercury and Saturn, the only close aspect that either planet makes.[51]

Mars is close enough to conjoining her Sun in theory, and most certainly formatively by progression in her ninth and tenth years of age.

Pluto, not known to Adams of course, is square her Mars (rebellion, force, temperament). This lady, with her sensitivity and insight, was a powerhouse. We see Aries intercepted in her Ascendant; but it is like a hot poker plunged into cool water; the steam is intense.

Fascinatingly, the Saturn-Neptune opposition she saw in Leland's chart, conjunct his Ascendant, was nearing her own Midheaven. Saturn crossing the Midheaven was the beginning of her success.

When we acknowledge Pluto, we can project Adams' SA Neptune to conjunction with Pluto, ruler of her VIIIth. The arc measures 31°17'—roughly three months after her 31st birthday. Measuring the arc exactly (see Chapter 3), we see it was indeed exact on March 22, 1899![52]

Neptune's contact with Pluto by Solar Arc symbolism seems to correspond to things of supernatural dimensions, states of being that are morbid and unusual, or inexplicable, or transcendental. Events may transpire which make one think fatalistically, with horror or dread, or indeed with inspiration and mysticism. All of these colors were in the aura of this meeting with Leland. That her career blossomed in the midst of all the smoke, flames, and drama is clearly suggested by the Solar Arc measurement of Uranus sesquiquadrate (135°) her Midheaven, connoting a sudden turn of fortune, even to the extent of being touched somehow by destiny. In her own words, "I entered respectfully the portals of the great building which was destined to bring me sudden fame."

Now we must return once more to Leland and our exercise of deduction. Evangeline Adams stated one observation in her account of the reading that is bothersome to our entire discussion: "I noticed that he [Leland] had been under similar conditions twice before in his life—though not nearly so malefic—and I asked him if

---

51. Adams herself writes in *Astrology: Your Place Among the Stars*, page 225: "Mercury without Saturn is like an egg without salt."

52. Although such exactitude with Solar Arcs is not that important, as we shall see, a computer needs to give an exact date, which, in this case, happens to be just five days after the catastrophic fire.

misfortune had not pursued him at those times. The most that he could remember were two fires, small ones, which had broken out in the hotel—and he was inclined to dismiss all thought of his present danger until the market opened on Saturday morning."

What was so drastic in this transit-natal configuration that had possibly occurred twice before in his life? Adams' statement "in his life" may be throwing us off in light of Leland's answer about two fires in the hotel. For Leland had only been proprietor of the hotel for 34 months. Maybe Adams said, or meant to say, "in the recent past" or "since you've been here at the Windsor."

If Adams had been talking about Mars (fires; the planet faster in motion than Saturn and Neptune; the free-roaming trigger of any classic configuration like the major transiting conjunction), she knew, of course, that the Mars orbit around the Sun takes approximately 22 months. What else could have been so quickly observed in terms of two drastic "hits" in 34 months?

Maybe she was thinking back one Mars orbit almost two years before, when Mars would have been squaring the Moon from the same position it occupied during the reading [actually May, 1897, exactly 22 months]; and then once earlier, during his tenure at the hotel. She surely would have asked about his tenure at the hotel in their social time together (or his Aries Moon would have "told" her). At this time, transiting Mars would have been passing over the Moon in the IVth.

But this is too much to expect of Adams under the pressured conditions she faced that evening.

Another point: She went on with readings after Leland's ("He sent guests to me that evening until long after midnight"). This is either improbable or she was working "psychic fair" style, doing quick general readings. I think what we have here are the remembrances of youth talking with a definite aura of retrospective self-drama. Evangeline Adams was 58 years old when she wrote this account in the *Bowl of Heaven*. Her story reached back 27 years (Saturn's return to the event), and enchantingly, she sprinkled it with all sorts of self-aggrandizing phrases and sentence structures.

But this statement is disconcerting: "He was so amazed by the general accuracy of the reading." How in the world does the word "general" slip in here, when the entire thrust of her story is the extraordinary specificity of her observations and prediction?

And finally, Adams writes: "and the next morning, he again showed his interest by coming in to see if everything was comfortable." Then, after she repeated to him the horrid observations she had made the night before, "he opened the door—and walked into the greatest hotel disaster of all times. The famous Windsor fire!"

Now, Leland arrived the next morning and left, say, some 20 minutes later. He was very wealthy, very busy, and very active. She was there to see clients. Time was important. And he could well have been privately unnerved by her reading.

Contrary to her account, the fire did not start until about 3:00 p.m. that afternoon, according to the front page story in the New York Times of March 18, 1899. A guest on the second floor above the hotel office was beginning to smoke in the front parlor. The guest lit a match, used it to light the cigar or cigarette, and attempted to throw the wooden match out the window to extinguish it. The lace curtains covering the window caught fire quickly, spread voraciously, and the hotel and Leland's family were gone.

Quite a tale! Quite an extraordinary experience. And quite an enriching exercise in astrological deduction and rectification. What did Adams actually see in the horoscope, which had been around twice before, connoting fires? We do not know.

And why did she never annotate the case publicly for further fame, especially some 30 years later? Indeed, even with her listing of 100 horoscopes in *Astrology: Your Place Among the Stars*, there is not one single delineation demonstrated.

How much of a role did her great sensitivity, her "other dimension," play in the feeling and the prediction of that moment of fate she shared with Warren F. Leland? It is all admissible, as we see in these great cases.

The moment has a magic. To measure it is science. To interpret it is art. To understand it is growth.

Chapter Two

Great Expectations

This is a book not about rules, but about judgment. It gives a nod to science and a bow to art. In my opinion, we cannot study prediction any other way since, if prediction *were* methodologically reliable, it would be standardized in its practice, it would be ubiquitous in its application, results would always be the same, and every astrologer would be a hero.

In short, in our work in astrology, especially in our efforts to predict, we should ask ourselves just how much accuracy can we expect? How much accuracy do we need? Astrologers and clients have great expectations from astrology. Too great. The answers to these concerns are not within the measurement methods of astrology but, rather, they are within the adjustment of professional expectations and practice.

Great expectations are the lure within our quest, to be sure. But great expectations are also our problem: expectations set up failure, failure sparks greater effort and renewed expectations, as well as elaborate explanation and rationalization, and further disappointment finally brings on embarrassment and criticism. Who is the astrologer who has not felt this bewildering sense of impotence?

Kepler felt it, poignantly. He condemned the general run of "vulgar" astrological predictions. He wrote that only one was correct against a hundred that were wrong.[1] In 1601, he drew up a special treatise of Directions (Primary Directions, the complicated, highly mathematical forerunner of Solar Arc theory) which he

---

1. Thorndike, VII, p .19.

called the noblest part of astrology, strongly confirmed by experience, despite the fact that both his own first son and the son of Michael Maestlin (a prominent astronomer, mathematician, and colleague), for whom at their birth he had predicted a favorable future, died in their first year of life.[2]

As astrologers, we tend to sell our craft and ourselves with big stories about astrology's successes—how often is the Evangeline Adams fire prediction cited, even today!—and big promises about what astrology can do in the future. This is only human. Other business people try to be proud and persuasive about their jobs, products, and services. They advertise and make promises all the time. They even make predictions about your future with what they have to offer, and artists sell themselves with their works and plans for works to come in order to get commissions.

The public loves astrological stories. Just look at the tabloids! The neat stories about past predictions are always found to be amazing and intensely interesting. But as soon as the perception becomes personalized and projected into the future, a fear emerges. Astrology is often warded off through ridicule or as harmless entertainment. Yet, the "sale" is often accepted, and the astrologer begins work against a spectre of client expectations that is formidable. Can the astrologer's performance match up with the implicit guarantee of accuracy, indeed, of revelation or even a miracle that the client feels? Will we have two heroes in consultation together?

In offering predictions, *we imply infallibility*, of astrology and often of astrologers. We get a rush of hope and power when we begin to prepare a horoscope. We long to see the "right" measurements come up to vindicate our anticipations. And when those measurements appear, we feel such security!—And then, so often, we confront another anxiety from our client, *the fear for astrology to be right, to be accurate*. What happens to individual self-awareness under such existential anxiety? How circumspect our counseling techniques must be (Chapter 7).

A case in point: Margaret Thatcher recently resigned (November 22, 1990) as Prime Minister of England after a tenure of eleven years and an overall government career of 32 years, all prominently in the public eye. Her horoscope is well-known [October 13, 1925;

---

2. Thorndike, VII, p. 21; and on page 27 cites Kepler's occult explanation of the relations of cause and effect between heavens and earth. It is bizarre if not pure rot. It was too much for the great French astrologer Morin (1583-1656), who concluded simply that "Kepler was quite ignorant of astrology."

9:00 a.m., GMT; Grantham, England]: it shows Saturn rising in Scorpio ["the iron lady"] at 13 degrees and an Ascendant of 15 Scorpio 16. Instantly, an astrologer knows that transiting Pluto was in 18 Scorpio in November, 1990 and had been crossing her Saturn/Ascendant conjunction in September. In fact, during the entire Summer of 1990, Pluto was seemingly stationary in the 16th degree of Scorpio. Here is tremendous corroboration of her complete change of life perspective.

And the question arises, could we have predicted this 32 years ago, or even two years ago, before her resignation? In this case, involving one of the most powerful transits in our symbology, the answer is "Yes." (We could have predicted the "pressure point"; see Chapter 7). But there are pressing questions that arise in relation, not to the astrology, but to the astrologer's management of the prediction, his or her poise and performance.

How would we have presented the prediction? Such a prediction—if it were accepted by her personally and not put out of mind—would lurk in her consciousness for her entire career or at least for a very uncomfortable Summer. What is the responsibility for the astrologer in moments of prediction? Later in this book, in Chapter 7, we will address counseling techniques with prediction, but here and now we should simply be keenly aware that prediction is made up of measurement in a very small way—and, in very big ways, of insight and humanity.

Wouldn't Mrs. Thatcher ask, "What does that mean? Why should it be? How will it come to pass? Will I have done something wrong?" These are powerful questions that become the *life* of the prediction, that take the simple measurement or set of measurements and give them the colors of human experience, the pleasure, pain, and shock of living yet another day.

We must consider what makes things happen. Astrologer Zipporah Dobyns echoes an eternal astrological axiom that *character is destiny*; that "pain is the warning signal of life, indicating the need to change one's direction or actions...One person's actions cannot produce an effect on another person's life unless the latter individual's character is in harmony with the situation."

Dobyns suggests that "Our character draws us to the people and to the events and circumstances which give us the consequences related to our character." She concludes, "The problem for many people is that they are not consciously aware of the character which is producing the life experiences."[3]

What does the prediction mean? Why should it be? How will it come to pass? Am *I* going to do something that will make this happen? What can I do about it?

These are very, very complex questions. A prediction accosts a person's entire being, his or her character. It touches dreams, it prods memories, and it challenges values.

In the 5th century, St. Augustine wrote eloquently and copiously to repudiate astrology (and magic) almost entirely on religious grounds. His argument basically was that God was being *excluded* by the premise that the stars managed our actions and our passions: "And what part has God left Him in thus disposing of human affairs if they be swayed by a necessity from the stars, whereas he is Lord of stars and man?"[4]

Yet, to the people of almost all periods of time, but especially the Middle Ages and the Renaissance, astrology was simply common sense, a universal folklore common to all cultures. It was then as heinous and outrageous to deny astrology as it was to assert other cultural truths such as all men are created equal or that we descended from primates. Augustine felt the pressure; he gave in a little, writing that astrology *would* be understandable or tolerable if astrologers only claimed that the stars were "signs, not causes of such effect."

Here we have some answers. To feel that our character attracts destiny to us may be valid indeed, but it is frightening at the same time. It is embedded in the human condition to expect, to deserve, to assume times and places where bad things do not happen to good people. Dreams, memories, and values are quickly alerted in defense of identity, trying always to make meaningful the phenomenon of living. We fear effects. Therefore we fear causes.

There is a resistance to change. For example, within the symbology of Taurus (especially the Moon in Taurus), the tendency is to resist change in order *to protect the status quo*. People will consider staying even with a negative situation because, as they say, "it is predictable (!)"; it is secure. With a new order, something new threatens. In short, what is predictable here then is nothing at all; we are simply preserving what is. There are no causes to deal with that have not already been assimilated and reacted to routinely.

---

3. Dobyns, p. 5.
4. Augustine, *City of God*, Fifth Book; see also Graubard, p. 75.

Something that we do understand without fear is the sense of cycle. We see cyclic repetition in the seasons, in history, in birth and death and family growth, in the weather, in the stock market, etc. In fact, we humans are passionately appreciative of cycles: they give us security and a kind of predictability that's reliable. There is a proven 18.3-year cycle in real estate activity; a 4.33-year cycle in the city of Baltimore's precipitation between 1820 and 1960; an 11.2-year cycle in international battles, from 1760-1947.[5]

If we are part of a cycle, somehow we are not being acted on by causes. Effects emerge according to some "respectable" and less-fearsome condition. The present expands somehow to link past and future more gracefully. The spotlight is less individual and more collective in its illumination. We watch for "signs" rather than causes.

The greatest security we have in prediction is in *the reliability of cycles*. Eclipses occur in sequences, and so does character development. In cycles, the past *supports* the future. All of us collected in the same human condition in similar environments become individual through our reactions to the emerging cycles.

A woman has natal Pluto at 16 Cancer opposed by Jupiter at 24 Capricorn. This is a powerful opposition suggesting an indomitable need to control the environment and protect herself at all costs. It is a lot of energy for a woman in our society to assimilate, especially when she is retired and living alone. With no ready outlet, the energy seems to back up and, in her life history, emerge in illness practically every time the axis is triggered by transit and/or Solar Arc contact. Pluto rules her VIth.

At the same time, this woman must assimilate a very strong natal opposition from Uranus to her Moon, ruler of her Ascendant. This powerful axis is also muted in her life expression at many levels and also erupts in the form of illness, or suspicion of illness, of physical problems, whenever it is triggered by transit and/or Solar Arc contact. The Moon ruling her Ascendant is in Scorpio, disposited by her Pluto, ruler of the VIth.

What we see here in her life is an individual cycle made up of a complexity of interplanetary contacts that set up conditions *that themselves become predictable*. There is a time ahead now when both axes in her horoscope will be activated at the same time. Sharing the understanding of the cycles with her establishes fair warning and

---

5. Dewey.

dictates strategically protective procedures and regimens for optimal security.

A young law student made a major life decision when he left law school, wanting to be "his own man," and not emulate his father. He took up banking instead, indeed in his father's bank, but on his own individual terms. Transiting Jupiter was exactly conjunct his Taurus Sun.

Twelve years later, still at the bank, as president, the man took a wonderful international vacation trip, which was very meaningful to him, then and still today. A most positive Jupiterian time, as transiting Jupiter, in its 12-year cycle, once again conjoined the Sun.

Eleven years after that, the banker was pressed by complex collection problems at his bank. Times were tough. One year thereafter, transiting Jupiter was due to cross his Sun once again. The cycle had been established. The levels of manifestation had been clearly Jupiterian and individualized. The prediction was made by projecting the banker's position within his personal Jupiterian cycle, promising resolution to his problems and reward. The transit conjunction took place, and his telephone report began, "We've just had a miraculous resolution of collection problems at the bank!" Properties were "falling into my lap," and he had even received a buy-out offer. The transit and the events coincided to the week.

Can we say then that everything that happens somehow relates to our astrological pantheon *in terms of some cycle*? Complex, multi-dimensioned, subtle, whatever, but within some set of cycles that, in accumulation, prescribe the beat of life, the way of growth, and the reason for being?

If an event is not indicated as part of any corresponding set of astrological measurements—i.e., a cycle sweep known or not yet known to us in our studies—do we call it an accident? All the dead and injured in a plane crash may accidentally accompany the cycle of one pilot's error, or all may be victim to a weather cycle we do not understand and could not anticipate. Think of the life cycles arbitrarily extinguished by a bomb blast. *Accidents interrupt cycles.*

With the comfort we do have within established cycles, can we say that the inexorable—that press of fate we identify so fearfully with the harshness of causality—becomes opportunity? Can what develops within our life from out of cycles—as with all life and matter in our microcosm and macrocosm—be seen as halls we must walk, as doors we must open and close, to appreciate our Mansion? *It is only within opportunity that we exercise choice.*

In the late 1930s, there was a paraphysical school of thought that conjectured that the future is within the present, that it has already happened. A busy debate ensued among philosophers.

There was some real data too: according to Brad Steiger, researcher of the paranormal, a man was photographed at the edge of the Grand Canyon seven years before he actually visited the site. The camera he would buy in 1955 is clearly visible in the photo of him exposed in 1948.

What is productive for us out of such arguments is the link that can be made between foreknowledge and memory. Both are cognitive functions on an axis of time, focused in the present. Memories can be as real upon recall as "hunches" or specific predictions can be. The weatherman, predicting a rough winter ahead based on his awareness of climatological cycles, can recall similar rough winters from the past. They merge in the present.

Light comes to us from a star. Its light is from the past, due to the vast distances the light has traveled to reach us. The star has gone on, so to speak. The light may be what "happened" 10,000 light years in the past, but through our sophisticated measurements of that light now in the present, we can know where the star will be 1,000 years from now in the future.

This thought—"memory about the future"—is less a tease and more an instruction. We find the future out of the past. Through cycles. Through individualized reactions to opportunity. Through the acknowledgement of signs. As with memory, we can be inaccurate; and likewise with our projections into the future. But the process can work. We can predict. We do predict. And when we adjust our expectations and manage our practice with insight and humanity, we get closer to reality all the time.

There are ways to predict and to present prediction that grow in reliability as we ourselves grow within the time we measure.

Chapter Three

Solar Arc Theory and Technique

"But now we come to handle the measure of time in Directions, wherein there are at this day [1647] three severall opinions, yet not such as doe make any great difference in the matter ."[1]

This is William Lilly writing. He cites Ptolemy first, of course: "The opinion of Ptolemy hath continued since his time until this last age without any contradiction." He quotes from a Latin translation of Ptolemy's works the rigorous technique of Primary Directions involving measurements of right ascension, oblique ascension, interpolations of latitude, concerns of declination, and many more technicalities. These issues are summed up innocuously by Ptolemy in his *Tetrabiblos* in Aphorism XXV: "The progression of a significator, posited in the Midheaven, is to be made by Right Ascension; of another posited in the Ascendant, by the Oblique Ascension of the particular Latitude."[2]

These terms are "Greek" to most astrologers in our day, except to the especially mathematically comfortable and research-gifted. For the record, right ascension is the measurement taken on the Celestial Equator—a great circle determined from an extension of the Earth's own equator—starting from 0 Aries and continuing in the direction of the apparent annual motion of the Sun.

Oblique ascension (and descension) is determined by that point on the Celestial Equator that rises at the horizon when the planet or star does.

---

1. Lilly, III, p 708.
2. Ptolemy, p 155.

There are many other technical considerations in Primary Directions: ascensional difference, diurnal arc, nocturnal arc, semi-arc, and polar arcs. Reference tables and logarithms are constantly employed in the mathematical work-ups.[3]

Probably from the earliest history of astrology, astrologers were intrigued with the numerical closeness between the measure of 365 [365.25] days in one year and 360 degrees in the circle. Granted, horoscopes were not drawn in circles until late in Tycho Brahe's time, around 1590, but the concept of the circle, of course, has always been of paramount importance to all astrological reckoning.

Add to this, in the Middle Ages and Renaissance, the biblical reference in Ecclesiastes (3: 1-15): "For every thing its season, for every activity under heaven its time..." and the clear confirmation of many, many astrological references elsewhere in the Bible, and those contained in the "clean" and accurate translation from the original Greek of the Lord's Prayer—"Our Father who lives in the heavens, Let your name be honored, Let your Kingdom come. Let your will be done down here on the earth, as perfectly as it is in the sky."[4]— and you have great expectations on the part of astrologers for some symbological progression system like a day-for-a-year to work.

The concept of equatorial arcs, which Ptolemy concretized in the second century A.D., was based on the Sun's movement in one day in right ascension, originating from that place on the equator touched by a circle drawn through the particular planet's position and the pole (which was then coordinated with the measurement of the planet's declination, the position of the planet from the equator to the nearest pole), equated to one year of life.

This was the reasoning: the time it takes for *one degree* to pass the Midheaven is four minutes of sidereal time or 3.9890 minutes of mean solar time; the first four minutes after birth then could symbolize the first year of life; the next four minutes, the second year of life, etc.

The problem then became that only six hours of time were needed to form arcs throughout the horoscope to cover developments for 90 years of life! The planets and points in the horoscope

---

3. For relatively modern presentation of Primary Directions in Ptolemy's methodology, see Robert De Luce, *Complete Method of Prediction*; also Alan Leo, *The Progressed Horoscope*, pp. 273-350.
4. Jacobs, p. 22.

simply did not move enough symbolically to give astrologers enough to work with developmentally and interpretively. Just six hours of time, or much less! This system was philosophically exacting in concept, computationally tedious in operation, and narrow in results. And I must add, as one can say with regard to any system in any discipline, if the system had worked with high reliability, it would have prevailed. We do not use Primary Directions in astrology, even with the resources we have with computer technology to help with the mathematics, because results have been scarce over centuries of testing.

So, different hypotheses sought to expand the symbolism of one day equaling one degree equaling one year, linked to the Sun, into other directions: relating one 24-hour period to the whole of the heavens carried around the circle in that time period. Somewhere along the way (as we shall see, in the middle of the 19th century, some 1,600 years after Ptolemy) the arc of the Sun in one day was indeed going to be applied throughout the heavens, throughout an individual's personal portion of time, his or her whole sky, to the entire horoscope.

Lilly next cites "The Second Measure of Time," propounded by Antonius Maginus, published in 1604, "induced hereunto (as he saith) by an Aphorisme of Doctor Dee of London, and something else gathered from the writings and opinions of the famous Tycho Brahe the Dane."[5] Lilly referred to Maginus as "an Italian of singular learning, and one of the greatest mathematicians of Europe, the first that questioned this measure of time delivered unto posterity by Ptolemy."

Maginus propounded that the *Sun's true motion one day to the next after birth* should be the arc of singular importance. This was probably the birth of the system which today we call Secondary Progressions—each day after birth representing a successive year of life—although it was not then thoroughly systemetized as we know it today, since Maginus still clung to Ptolemy's arc orientation *to the equator*. The ties to the past were very strong, but Maginus was extremely close to the method of Solar Arc measurement we use now.

---

5. John Dee was an original Fellow of Sir Isaac Newton's own Trinity College at Cambridge. He was arrested in 1553 shortly after Mary I's accession to the throne, accused of trying to murder the Queen by means of magic! He was acquitted and returned to court 5 years later to use astrology to select the best day for the coronation of Queen Elizabeth. Newton and Dee are regularly cited together in references to mysticism and alchemy, the pursuits of which were very significant and absorbing for Newton. —Christianson, p. 220.

The third and last measure of time which Lilly presented was perfected by Valentine Nabod (or Naibod) who was a mathematics professor at the University of Cologne in Germany in the 1560s. (He was a vocal proponent of the Copernican theory about which academe was still arguing 48 years after its formulation).[6]

Nabod worked hard to create easier prediction methods using arcs of time related to the primally important arc of the Sun's daily movement after birth.

Maginus himself published Nabod's work in 1619 and joined Lilly as seeing it "In my owne judgement, the most exactest measure that hitherto hath been found out."[7]

Nabod established the use of the *mean daily motion* of the Sun as the increment of progression: 59'08" of arc symbolically equaled one year of life. The mean motion is the rate of motion that divides the interval (between 57' and 61' minutes of arc, the span of possible Sun motion) at a point with the same number of incidences of divergency above and below this measure, with a constant, graduated development between the two extremes.[8]

Lilly was quite open in applauding the ease of this system, working with just one quick-reference table.

Three hundred and forty-some years later, the British astrologer Sepharial joined a list of astrologers who had tried to refine Nabod's refinements, all of them searching for an even more facile way and, indeed, more accurate one—to capture the symbolic significance of the Sun's movement from day to day (from year to year in terms of degrees) and apply that to the entire horoscope in terms of lifetime. Sepharial did not add much of anything. The work, put forth in his *Science of Foreknowledge*, was pure Nabod.[9]

---

6. Nabod died tragically according to his own prediction: he had retired to Padua to write still another commentary on Ptolemy's work. He took an old house, filled it with food, and closed himself within it; he feared "death from steel," obviously a serious Mars direction in his horoscope, about which he had commented to many colleagues. Robbers thought the house abandoned, broke in and killed Nabod with swords. Another story, in the Sloane manuscripts in the British Museum, says that the landlord came to collect rent from Nabod, was barred admission, broke the door down, and found Nabod "transfixed by a sword whether by his own hand or another." (Hopefully the rigor of Ptolemy's calculations were not to blame!)
7. Lilly, III, pp. 708-715.
8. Each degree of Right Ascension equalled one year, five days, and eight hours of life; each minute of arc, six days and four hours. In short, the mean daily motion of the Sun equalled one year of life.
9. Sepharial's real name was W. G. Old. 19th-century astrologers took occult names or names of angels of the Zodiac to create a transcendental atmosphere about predictive astrology and/or to protect their identities against harsh criticism and law suits when their predictions were wrong. There were many Raphaels; a Mercurius Herschel; R. J. Morrison became Zadkiel, and W. F. Allen became Alan Leo. —See Howe.

Throughout these centuries, working without accurate ephemerides—or any ephemerides at all in the earlier times—until Kepler established his rules for planetary motion early in the 17th century, there were enormous drives, motivations, pressures, urges, and mandates to predict in the name of all that was holy what would affect the affairs of man. Life had to have meaning, strategy, and control.

At this time, we must take pause to realize how *inaccurate* so much of the astrology was, with so little recorded data, without the three outer planets, and under the greatest of expectations.

Constantly, in studying old astrologers' work, we find error after error after error; not large necessarily in astronomical reckoning, especially in the late 16th century and thereafter thanks to Brahe's instruments, inventions, and observational skill and the discoveries by Kepler and Galileo; but grossly large in the dating and timing of births and fundamental interpretive assessments. Citations of birthdates constantly turn up different in different sources, and reckless commentaries abound.

For example, with Nabod's own horoscope, not too long after his death, an anonymous commentator surely armed with Nabod's published birth data (there were two different versions), says: "Yet it is credible that he killed himself, since Saturn is the lord of the horoscope and of the eighth House, and Venus the other lord of the eighth House declining in Aries."[10] That's an impossibility: "lord of the horoscope" meant "ruler of the Ascendant." Saturn rules Capricorn and Aquarius, two *adjacent* Signs. Additionally, Venus does *not* share Sign rulership in any way whatsoever with Saturn.[11]

Returning to time projection systems: let us recall Lilly's words cited at the beginning of this chapter, "three severall opinions, yet not such as doe make any great difference in the matter." All the theorizing about the equation of one degree to one day to one year notwithstanding, *error was still haunting every system*. The Nabod application of the mean motion of the Sun was easy to use; it had the "large-stroke" feel about it that signaled something "right." But after about 30 years of age, the correspondence between events and planetary significators in an individual's horoscope, i.e., that which

---

10. Thorndike, VI, p. 123.
11. I suggest that astrologers used to alter birth times to make their calculations work *after* the fact, from the wrong facts. To this day, rectification carries with it that same potential bias: the reality of the birthtime is adjusted to support the expectations of the meaurements. Yes, that's the purpose and the proof of rectification, but are we ever sure?

was predicted, *seemed to be about a year off*, especially for people born during the Summer. As those people—and everyone else eventually—got older, discrepancies between events and predicted ages got bigger. This system did not work reliably either.

What was happening was that the Nabod measurement did not take into account the very prominent *changes in daily Sun motion throughout the seasons of the year*. In the name of simplification—simply using the mean daily motion of the Sun—Nabod did away with the *individual measures* linked to the different rate of movement of every person's Sun.

The Sun appears to move much more quickly during our Winter months than during the Summer months. In the Winter, the Sun is lower in our sky and "races away" in the ephemeris. In the Summer, the Sun "takes its time" and arcs high in our sky.

A person born with a slow diurnal Sun motion (less than the Nabod mean measurement) would gradually accumulate a discrepancy away from the one day/one year equation. By about age 30, the discrepancy accumulates to about one degree, or one day or one whole year! It would take 31 years to live out the more slowly accumulated arc of 30 degrees.

It appears that this problem did not get smoothed out in astrological practice until the middle of the 19th century, through the work of W. J. Simmonite, a major figure in astrology in Victorian England. He was a popular practitioner, writer, and publicist for astrology, as well as a medical herbalist and meteorologist.[12] He was predominantly a horary astrologer, as many astrologers were in those times and for some two hundred years before, to Lilly's time, probably because the time of a question was there and then, eminently reliable, as opposed to a birth time recollected in strange ways and requiring risky, time-consuming rectification.

Simmonite noted that using the standardized mean motion of the Sun could amount to an error of 2 degrees and 49 minutes over a span of 45 years, at the extreme. As we have seen, this would introduce a symbolic prediction error of almost three years. That is what had been infecting the practice of predictive astrology for so very long.

Simmonite advocated using the *actual* motion of the Sun in progression after the birth date (the Secondary Progression Sun meas-

---

12. Howe, pages 48-49.

urement) as the individual's projected symbolic time factor. There would be no problem with slow or fast Suns. The measure would capture exactly the individual's measure of time and development.

The distance the Sun traveled in the ephemeris one day to the next would capture the flow of life one year to the next year. This distance that the Sun traveled became the Solar Arc.

Simmonite's work was basically a revival of the work of Maginus, which Simmonite surely knew, having studied Lilly's books (both men were the most celebrated horary astrologers of their eras). But Simmonite's presentation had no mathematical ties to Ptolemy; it did without worries about the equator, ascensions, interpolations, and the other mathematical impedimenta that were packed into astrology from times past. Simmonite simply measured the Solar Arc on the ecliptic (in the Zodiac) rather than on the equator.

It then seemed so natural to take the Solar Arc increment for any given year of life and apply it *to every planet in the individual's birth horoscope*. This was so streamlined and so simple. Most important, *it worked*, very, very often. The Solar Arc positions created new aspects to the natal planetary positions. Life unfolded through grand symbolisms enriched with time. Here was another large stroke with the ring of truth. Here was Solar Arc theory born to our time, distilled from centuries of investigation into symbolic systems supporting reliable prediction.

Today's Practical Method

First, to train the eye and alert a sense of interpretive anticipation, we need to consider what I like to call "rapport" measurements within the horoscope.[13]

Rapport between two planets or between a planet and an Angle is measured by the distance between them. It suggests that there is a potential that will be realized when one planet arcs through the space between them and symbolically conjoins the other (or aspects the other). In Chapter 1, this kind of abbreviation, this generalization of Solar Arc technique, was introduced into the text to show

---

[13]. "Rapport" is the French word meaning the state of understanding awareness in relationship. In astrology, its use originated with Dane Rudhyar (French born) and appears in *The Astrology of Personality*, page 429, in his presentation of Progressions. Rapport measurements are sometimes called Radix measurements or the Radix System, simply referring to the exclusive orientation to planetary positions in the Radix, the "root," the birth horoscope.

how Tycho Brahe, in part, prepared his predictions for Christian IV, and how we tested the horoscope for Warren F. Leland. (Brahe indeed used Primary Directions; but the two systems are very close, just separated by complex mathematics and centuries of habit.)

Clearly we are doing what the ancients did: we are equating one degree with one year. But first off, in abbreviation, we are doing it knowing that it is not going to be as accurate as the measurement can be (except, of course, if the individual's day-to-day progressed Sun motion is exactly 60' of arc each day). We use these rapport measurements knowing that they *are* generalizations and that they will help enormously to orientate our time analysis of a particular horoscope and alert us to where we must measure more carefully.

With our awareness of the problematic time/motion dynamics behind Solar Arc theory, we can add an extra year or so in our use of rapport measurements when generalizing about measurements in a horoscope with a Summer birthtime (slow day-to-day Sun movement)—after some 30 years of life.

For example, take a horoscope that has Saturn at 8 Gemini and the Sun at 12 Cancer, a distance (a rapport) of 34 degrees. But with the early July birth (Cancer), we know the Sun's progressed movement will be slow (about 57' of arc) and, over 34 years, 1° 42' of arc would not be covered, i.e., would still remain to even out at 34 degrees (3' discrepancy from 1° daily—yearly; multiplied by 34 years gives 102' or 1° 42').

In other words, Solar Arc Saturn would come to the Sun in 34 degrees, yes, but, in this case, that would equal about $35^{1}/_{2}$ years! Note: the age projection with a slow Sun will need more life time, it will be longer than the number of degrees.

This is extremely simple. In practicing now with the generalization of rapport measurements, we must make a quick mental accommodation to a slow-moving Sun when it occurs, usually from late April to early September. The Sun—the individual human being in development—will take a little longer in years than the arc number in degrees to fulfill the generalized Solar Arc measurement.

A female's horoscope shows the Moon at 21 Virgo, ruling her IVth. Pluto was just behind the Moon at 8 Virgo at birth, a rapport measurement of 13 degrees. Her Mars is at 17 Gemini 53 in the IIIrd House in rapport with the fourth cusp (opposition to the Midheaven) at 00 Cancer 38, a distance of 12° 45', almost 13 degrees.

Here are two Solar Arcs that can be seen so quickly, timing out almost the same: SA Pluto will conjoin the Moon, ruler of the IVth at almost the same time as SA Mars will be at the fourth cusp in opposition to the Midheaven.

With a little practice and faith, any astrology student can make this kind of observation quite quickly. These two measurements just mentioned immediately prompt a question about a major change in the home—probably a disruption in the child's whole life perspective, since Pluto and Mars are involved together. Indeed, the child's father left the family when she was 13 years, 6 months old. She was an August birth; it took her developmentally about six months longer at that age to fulfill the rapport measurement of 13 degrees.

Rapport measurements are extraordinarily helpful in preparing the initial framework for rectification. After evaluation of planet/Sign identification, rectification demands the testing of time development, especially through Solar Arc projections of planets to conjunctions or squares with the Angles of the horoscope. There is no other way to accomplish the task. Rapport measurements are the swift approximations that open the door to more accurate formal measurements.

As you read these pages, simply project any planet that may be in your IXth or XIIth or IIIrd or VIth House to conjunction with the Angle ahead of it (or any planet in aspect to any other planet, of course; but start simply). Translate the distance into years. Make the mental correction for a slow Sun (say, 6 months per 15 degrees, that is, 15 years) if it applies, and recall what transpired in your life at that time. Think about it carefully. If it is not immediately clear, give yourself, say, a six-month Time Orb. Search. Discover events and development. Enrich the symbolisms in your own horoscope with the dimension of time.*

Another introductory observation concerns the accumulation of an Arc of 45 degrees in anyone's horoscope. This is always a time of adjustment and change and challenge. The Solar Arc applied to all the symbols in the horoscope, to all faculties of behavior and dimensions of need, is a *semi-square time of developmental tension*.

It is uncanny how major times of life are so very often signaled by *several* Solar Arc background measurements becoming exact at

---

* If your planet is too close to the Angle, you may have been too young for something to register. The heavier the planet, the more emphatic. Minutes on the Angles are very important.

nearly the same time, as we saw with two aspects in our example above. Rapport measurements exercise our interpretive skill as soon as we can spot the measurement and introduce us to both past *and* future.

For precision, nothing could be simpler: calculate the Secondary Progressed Sun position (or have your computer go right into a Solar Arc program which is doing just what we are describing now), that is, the Sun's position at the birth time a specific number of days after birth to correspond to the same number of years in life. A birth on June 3 will reveal its 18th year, for example, through a Sun position calculated at the birth time on June 21, 18 days after the actual birth date; the 42nd year would be a Sun position calculated at the birth time on July 15, 42 consecutive days later into the next month following the actual birth date.

The next step is a simple subtraction: from the Secondary Progressed Sun position—again, calculated using the natal birth time, *not* the noon or midnight position—subtract the Natal Sun position. The answer is the Solar Arc increment to the birthday month in the selected year of life.

The final step is to advance every planet, the nodal axis, the Midheaven and Ascendant axes the distance of the Solar Arc. Simply add (or the computer does it) the Solar Arc to every planet and sensitive point in the horoscope. *The primal symbol of life development, the Sun, is being shared with every symbol in the horoscope.* Life development is bringing the birth horoscope forward in time while maintaining the individualistic relativity of the natal positions. Dynamic new aspect relationships are then created to reflect the developmental tensions in the process of becoming. Dane Rudhyar said it quite succinctly: "Destiny is essentially the individual *schedule* of growth." [14]

---

14. Rudhyar, p 421; my italics.

Shown here is a portion of my horoscope.[15] Three rapport measurements—potentially significant Solar Arc times—literally jump off the paper:

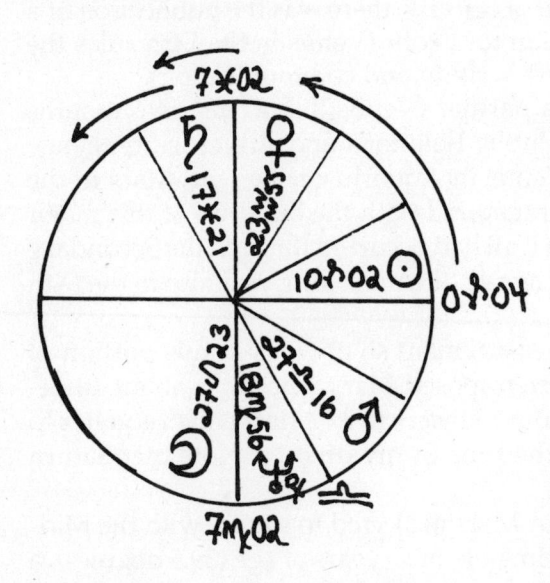

- SA MC conjunct Saturn; the Midheaven projected into the very strong opposition in the parental axis;
- SA Sun conjunct Venus;
- SA Saturn opposed Mars.

The birth date is at the end of December, suggesting that the Sun's movement in progression will be very close to one degree. Our rapport measurements of arc will equate very closely with years of life.

SA MC conjunct Saturn has an arc of a little over 10 degrees (7 Pisces 02 to 17 Pisces 21 is an arc of 10° 19′). For months before and after my tenth birthday, my home was in upheaval, and my father left the household permanently.

SA Sun conjunct Venus normally corresponds to romance, an affair, a time of marriage or having a child, when it occurs within time spans that would reasonably support such events. The arc for my Sun-Venus conjunction scans to some months after my 43rd birthday on December 31, 1979 (20 degrees to finish Capricorn plus 23 degrees, almost 24, to reach Venus in Aquarius). At that time, I had just finished writing my book *Holistic Astrology* and was publishing it myself as a first-time effort (IXth House significance). The book went onto the market February 1, 1980. The Solar Arc was

---

15. Noel Tyl, born December 31, 1936; 3:57 PM, EST (Birth Certificate) in West Chester, PA, 75W36; 39N58.

precise in measurement in February 1980.[16] (I planned it that way; or did I?)

Here we have an example of another level of symbolism emerging for the classic Sun-Venus aspect. Personal realities at that time in my life excluded any of the major archetypal possibilities; however, in my real realm of activity, there was the publication of a major book and speculation for profit (Venus in the IXth rules the Vth; the Sun rules the IIIrd, writing and communication).

Additionally, with a partner (Venus; Libra) just five months earlier, I had opened a Public Relations and Advertising agency (again the IXth House; Venus in Aquarius; trine with Mars in the Vth). All of this activity transpired with the build-up of this major Solar Arc; the inception of it all had occurred through the Secondary Progressed New Moon at age 42, the preceding year also in the IXth House.

The third rapport measurement so obvious in this portion of the horoscope is SA Saturn opposed Mars. The arc is about 40 degrees (Saturn projected from 17 Pisces to 27 Aries) which equates to the end of 1976, age 40, the time of my divorce. Note that Saturn rules the VIIth.

We can go further: SA Mars projected to square with the Midheaven equates to approximately $39^{1}/_{2}$ years of age (39.5 degrees), a second Solar Arc indication of the dissolution of my marriage and my divorce. Here then, two powerful Solar Arcs—Saturn opposed Mars and Mars square Midheaven—suggest the importance of that time around my 40th birthday. This would lead the astrologer into more thorough measurements of that time-span and certainly into a meaningful discussion with the client.

And still further: SA Venus came to conjunction with Saturn at approximately age $23^{1}/_{2}$, precisely when I decided to become an opera singer, to go to New York City, find a teacher and build toward an international career. Here creativity, the arts, international aspirations (Venus in the IXth) *illuminated*, if you will, Saturn, the dispositor of the Sun, our two symbols for ambition.[17]

---

16. With computer exactness, the reference date for the completed Solar Arc is "February 18, 1980 at 6:13 PM."—This precision is essential to the computer only but really does not affect our application of Solar Arcs. We will see soon in our discussion the management of a Time-Orb concept for Solar Arcs. This is no caveat to assimilate inaccuracy; rather, it's a way to assimilate the nature of human affairs in their inception, development, and fulfillment.
17. As we shall see later, there is a difference in interpretive anticipation and value manifestation between SA Saturn conjoining Venus, for example, and SA Venus conjoining Saturn. This has not been studied in the literature to date. Here is a perfect case in point. I suggest that the operable word in this instance is "illuminated."

And even more: SA Saturn to square with the Sun, projecting Saturn to 10 Aries, equates, just before age 23, to a series of life-changing events that led to the time of SA Venus conjunct Saturn at $23^{1}/_2$ as noted above. This was a change of life, from one career to another; decisions that altered every dream and opportunity and resource in my life for over twenty years. The astrologer who understands Solar Arc theory and practice would see these rapport measurements quickly, anticipate one after the other, zero in on the main ones with more exact measurements—not always necessary as we shall see—and be extraordinarily well-armed to begin a meaningful conversation with the client. Additionally, the individualistic core meanings of the horoscope begin to surface from just these few measurements drawn from just a portion of the horoscope. The framework of time begins to speak eloquently about the past. This makes it possible to speak insightfully about the future.

Still a tighter focus. We have proceeded from the general year-of-age orientation established through rapport measurements to the measurement of the exact Solar Arc distance for any given year of life. That Solar Arc determination (the natal Sun position subtracted from the Secondary Progressed Sun position) is equivalent to the birthday month position in the projected year. We have to be able as well to apply the Solar Arc to months before and after the birthday month.

As an example: we saw the rapport measurement between Sun and Venus in the horoscope portion on page 67 to measure 43°+. The exact Solar Arc measurement for the 43rd birthday month (December 31, 1979) was 43° 46', with the Secondary Progressed Sun coming to 23 Aquarius 48. Only 7' of arc remained for the Solar Arc projection to be precisely conjunct natal Venus at 23 Aquarius 55.

Maneuvering Solar Arc minutes and life months is very easy. We can generalize again, as with rapport measurements, the measure of 60' of arc for one year of life. There are 12 months in one year; one degree (60') divided by 12 gives a monthly increment of 5' of arc. In our example case, with 7' of arc remaining to partile, we project that the Solar Arc conjunction between the Sun and natal Venus would be perfect $1^{1}/_2$ months after the 43rd birthday month. It was.

Time Orbs. At the same time as we acknowledge minutes of arc as a measurement orb of application to aspect partile or to separation from partile, we must also acknowledge a corresponding Time Orb in the possible manifestation of the Solar Arc measurement within life activity. Two very important considerations must be noted.

First, the symbolisms of Solar Arc aspects with natal positions seem to function as a *backdrop* to life development. More often than not—unless there are several Solar Arc aspects forming simultaneously—the Solar Arc "picture" waits for a *transit-trigger* to bring it into focus.

The second consideration: transits are real-time movements of the planets, as we know. More often than not, they key Solar Arc potentials into manifestation. The astrologer must be aware of "the grouping of forces" within a Time Orb before or after exactness of the Solar Arc picture.

For example, again using the SA Sun conjunct Venus measurement from my horoscope: five months preceding the SA conjunction (that is about 25' of arc; 5' x 5), transiting Jupiter was conjoining my natal Moon in Leo in the IIIrd House, and transiting Saturn, ruler of the public and partnership VIIth, was trining my Sun in the VIIth. This is when my partner and I opened our Public Relations and Advertising agency. The Time Orb of this extremely important Solar Arc conjunction stretched 25' of arc, i.e., 5 months, into the application time period, the time before exactness.

During the five-month approach period, I also prepared the new book and saw to all the production plans with my partner. Transiting Jupiter was trining my Sun from my IIIrd House (writing). In the month of exact Solar Arc conjunction, transiting Jupiter was still trining my VIIth House Jupiter and Sun and transiting Saturn was exactly sesquiquadrate that Sun.

It is very clear indeed that the powerful SA Sun-Venus conjunction dominated a portion of my life for approximately 5 months in aspect application and—what with marketing success immediately after publication and planning for foreign editions (IXth House)—three months in separation.

The concept of Time Orb is not inexactness. *It is gradualism.*

Note: with the exclusive "Quick Glance" Transit Tables in the Appendix of this book, the astrologer can rapidly check the times suggested by rapport measurements and find important transits that, in relation to the natal horoscope, would trigger development.

We must be very careful not to fall under the spell of the great expectations that haunt and hurt astrology in its practice and presentation. Predictions about major opportunities or change, supported by specifics out of the individual's practical realities of the time period, must establish an expanded present of potential, *not a bull's-eye focus of criticality*. In looking ahead to a major measurement, we must understand what is reasonable in build-up, in prelude, in preparation, in strategy and, as well, what is reasonable in the aftermath—should the Solar Arc potential manifest in the life. In my life leading up to the Sun-Venus conjunction, the potentials were predicted, and the events were planned to happen in congruence.

The United States of America is under enormous tension in late 1990, most of 1991, and, as we shall see in a later chapter, much beyond. Its horoscope (page 72) shows an expanded present of great difficulty: SA Neptune came to a square with Mercury, the ruler of the U.S. Ascendant, in July, 1990, suggesting disillusionment, false speculation (Mercury also rules the Vth holding natal Neptune in Virgo), indecision, and incorrect behavior. At the same time, SA Pluto came to a semi-square with natal Saturn, a powerful measure usually suggesting loss, hardship, and the potential for self-destruction.[18]

Then in November, 1990, SA Saturn came to a semi-square with the U.S. Venus, ruler of Taurus in the XIIth, conjunct Jupiter in Cancer in the U.S. IInd. Here is financial drain and hardship, stringent efforts to ameliorate tensions, possibly a brittle semblance of a peaceful approach or a strategic delay.

Then, from February, 1991, through April, we see SA Moon squaring Mars (temper, mobilization, fight) and SA Mars sesquiquadrate Uranus, which is rising at the U.S. Ascendant and rules its Midheaven (a test of nerves, a struggle for survival; unusual achievement; power and effort).[19] SA Mars will oppose Mercury 35' later, i.e., 7 months, or November, 1991. This is another direct attack upon U.S. interests.

The point here is that these major Solar Arc measurements *command a longer time period* than just the month of their occurrence. There are overlapping Time Orbs that seem to respond to the punctuation by real-time transits. For example, *transiting* Uranus, for the entire period outlined above, was opposing the U.S. Jupiter, ruler of the VIIth, and, in February, 1991 (and again in July and December), transiting Uranus will oppose the U.S. Sun in Cancer, ruler of the

---

18. Ebertin, p 188.
19. Ebertin, p 158.

72 / Prediction in Astrology

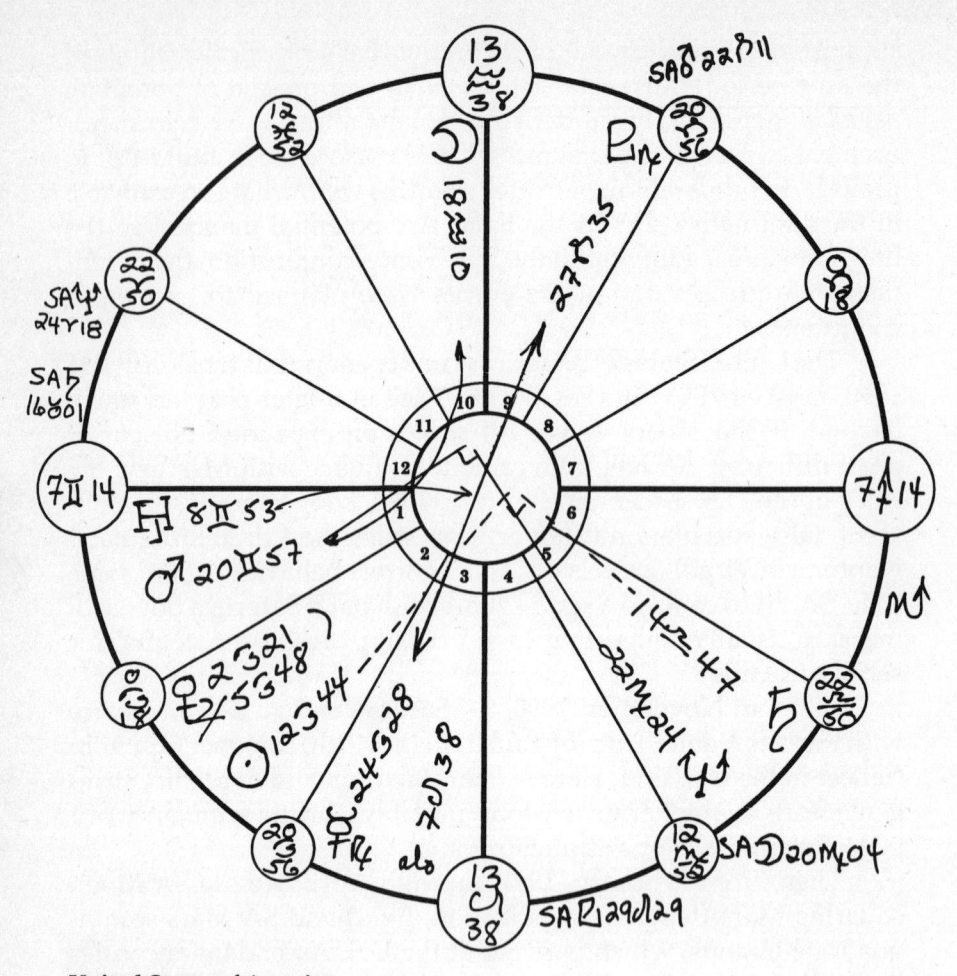

United States of America
July 4, 1776
2:13 a.m. LMT
Philadelphia, Pennsylvania
075 W 10   39 N 57
Placidian Houses

IVth (home security for sure). Transiting Uranus joins transiting Neptune (oil concerns, subterfuge) already opposing the U.S. Sun. Transiting Mars conjoins the Sun in late April, 1991. In November, transiting Neptune will square the U.S. Saturn.

The United Nations has established January 15, 1991 as the deadline for Iraqi evacuation of Kuwait before international force would be applied. Fascinatingly, on that very day, there will be a total eclipse of the Sun at 25 Capricorn 20, almost exactly opposite the U.S. Mercury, ruler of the Ascendant. The eclipse falls into the U.S. IXth House, clearly within orb of the U.S. Pluto.[20]

This is how predictions are *assembled*—the proper word. Measurement parts of a significant time period are put together into a framework that supports the past and tries to build the future. This reflects reality. Indeed, there are sudden "happenings"; there are accidents; there is the inexplicable. And I am one astrologer who admits that we do not yet have the tools to understand all this. We must not let expectations that are too great cause us disappointment with the revelatory reliability of what we *do* have in astrology.

The Fourth Harmonic. The fourth harmonic in astrology labels the family of aspects gained by division and subdivision of the circle by four and two: conjunction, the square (360/4); the semi-square (360/(2x4)); the sesquiquadrate (a square plus a semi-square, 135°); and the opposition (360/2). In Solar Arc theory, these so-called "hard" aspects are the ones that are used almost exclusively. The family of square-related aspects "makes things happen"; trines and sextiles "keep things as they are." This has been a prevailing, operational aphorism in astrology for a long, long time.

Indeed, a Solar Arc trine between the Sun and Uranus often signals a period in the life that abounds with things positive and rewarding, but for truly practical assessment of life development, it is the management of strong developmental tension that is telling, and it is this tension that is the predominantly important measurement in our work with Solar Arcs.

Basically, there is a general hierarchy of importance among the fourth harmonic aspects: the conjunction seems to be the most clearly focused and predictable; then the square seems to be obviously vigorous; the opposition, discernably challenging or confrontational; and the semi-square and sesquiquadrate have echoes of developmental tension akin to the square turning up the heat. But Solar Arc theory does not make a major issue out of this. What is important is *contact, contact within the fourth harmonic*. The fact that the contact is a conjunction, an opposition, or a square becomes instantly obvious to the eye, with a bit of practice and confidence; and then, the sense of the semi-square and sesquiquadrate follows.

---

20. Additionally, the preceding Solar Eclipse was on July 22, 1990 at 29 Cancer 04, conjoining the powerfully important U.S. Mercury-Pluto axis; the great Saturn-Neptune conjunction of November 13, 1989 was at 10 Capricorn 22, opposed the U.S. Sun; and there are many more aspects of accumulating tension.

Therefore, astrological notation uses the concept of the equals sign to denote contact; Saturn=Sun; Solar Arc Saturn is in fourth harmonic contact with the natal Sun. The eye quickly tells us this point of contact's position within the aspect hierarchy. It is not something to worry about or from which to anticipate complication.

Midpoints and Planetary Pictures.[21] Another aphorism in astrology is that *all* planets are indeed in aspect with each other regardless of the degree-distances between them. This reflects the idea that our rich symbologies are thoroughly interrelated within the Order. The discipline of astrology has simply defined a handful of specific aspect-relationships to bring a measurement manageability to the philosophical whole. We could put it another way and say that all planets are related to each other to one degree or another, some very strongly and some in ways we do not yet know.

For the most part, the minor aspects in astrology are hard to measure and, although now computer-generated, still are not empirically illuminated satisfactorily enough in their symbolisms to be used in our everyday work. Along with England's John Addey and his thorough and pioneering work with harmonics, we are always making the effort to fill the vault of the heavens, the circle of the horoscope, with meaning, with symbolic statements that work together to create a human portrait.

The theory of midpoints is another means of establishing more synthesis among the planets and points in the horoscope: the point exactly half-way between any two planets or between a planet and a sensitive point is a point that apparently *synthesizes their interrelationship.*

The concept of the midpoint is everywhere, throughout Nature, throughout man's ordering of awareness of two or more variables. Dawn is the midpoint between night and day; twilight, the midpoint between day and night. A compromise in a discussion is the midpoint between two polarized views. A child synthesizes its two parents. One planet is located at the midpoint between two other planets.

We have Mother-Child-Father; we have planets A-C-B. These are *direct midpoints*; something is precisely in between or issues out

---

21. As we have seen, consciousness and exploration of Solar Arcs are not new to modern times. And neither is the study of midpoints. But in this century, an extraordinary amount of theorization and practical formulation have been given to Solar Arcs, midpoints, and the structures of planetary pictures by Alfred Witte (1878-1941) founder of the Uranian School of Astrology, and Rheinhold Ebertin (1901-1988) founder of the Cosmobiological School.

of the central point between two other points.

Indirect Midpoints. Indirect midpoints introduce a developmental tension factor, an astrological aspect, which colors interpretation of the synthesis. Back to our Mother-Child-Father example, perhaps the child is born severely ill and must be removed from the family unit. This introduction of stress affects the relationship among all family members, but, quite especially, between mother and father. Astrologically, the "middle" planet *may not actually be* at the midpoint between two others; it may oppose the midpoint, square the midpoint, semi-square it, or make a sesquiquadrate to it. Indirect midpoints measured in the fourth harmonic create telling "planetary pictures" that are very important to Solar Arc practice. (Needless to say, these midpoint pictures can be calculationally demanding; but now with astrology's computer programs, they are computed quickly and presented securely measured and dated.)

For example, several Solar Arc midpoint pictures formed in July, August, and September 1990 in the United States horoscope as the dramatic build-up of the international commitment for operation Desert Shield in Saudi Arabia began.

- SA Ascendant opposed the midpoint of Sun/Jupiter (SA AS = ☉/♃)[22]: this brings the national identity focus of the Ascendant into full awareness of good objectives and good fortune. In the reality of what was transpiring internationally, we could add the thought of hopes for shared successes among the assembling world coalition.

- SA Ascendant square to Mars/Pluto (SA AS = ♂/♇): at the same time, however, the national identity was under high developmental tension with the use of force, with aggression, and enormous magnification of an energy build-up. This is the stirring up of danger (the square).

- Also at the same time, there was SA Neptune conjunct the Jupiter/Midheaven midpoint (SA ♆ = ♃/MC): here we see befuddlement or delusion placed in the midst of hopes for luck, success, and glory. The aspirations can somehow be unrealistic or self-deceiving.

---

22. In midpoint pictures, the equals sign is used to show synthesis, that is, contact. Again, the actual nature of the indirect aspect is not crucial since we preserve measurement by fourth harmonic and all such aspects connote degrees of developmental tension.

- Then, as the United States entered Saudi Arabia, SA Moon made a sesquiquadrate aspect to the midpoint of Pluto/Midheaven (SA ☽ = ♇/MC). This indirect midpoint brings the symbol of the United States' need to take charge (Moon in the Xth at the Midheaven) and to play the humanitarian role (natally in Aquarius, dispositor of the Cancerian Sun) into developmental tension with magnified public attention and a hope for glory. For this picture, Ebertin adds: "The ability to exercise a great influence upon others on account of one's own inner qualities."[23]

This is an astoundingly accurate portrayal of the hot Summer of U.S. involvement in the Kuwaiti crisis. Along with the major Solar Arc aspects, as we have seen—SA Neptune square Mercury; SA Pluto in contact with Saturn; SA Saturn = Venus; SA Moon = Mars, and SA Mars = Uranus—there are these four midpoint pictures that add more details conclusively.

Solar Arcs are measurements of a master cycle built upon the movement of the individual Sun in symbolic progression. While the Solar Arc increment is derived from computation of what we call Secondary Progression (a day for a year), the similarity between the two systems goes no further. Secondary Progressions are indeed helpful symbolically, since they are consistent within the regimen established through the day-for-a-year equation, but the Sun's all important increment is applied *only* to the Sun's position and not to the other planets and sensitive points, as we have seen in Chapter 3. The other bodies and points are progressed *at their own rate* within the daily progress forward through the ephemeris. As a result, for the planets Jupiter, Saturn, Uranus, Neptune, and Pluto, there is hardly any progression at all within a lifetime.

In Secondary Progression, there are many limitations on interpretive opportunities. Yet, since the Secondary Progressed Moon (reflecting the Moon's swift diurnal motion in the ephemeris) moves a considerable distance, offering many, many more new aspects with natal positions than any symbol in any system (in just one year, the Moon may cover 10 to 15+ times the distance of Solar Arc progress!), it is very helpful and significant to predictive astrology.

To keep things simple within the streamlined system of Solar Arcs, astrologers can add and utilize the Secondary Progressed po-

---

23. Ebertin, p 219.

sition of the Moon *without computing it* by emulating the rapport measurement generalization we see working effectively in Solar Arc measurements. We can take the Moon's average daily (yearly) motion as 12 degrees and count ahead from its natal position the number of degrees to any conjunction or aspect with any natal planet or to the crossing of an Angle. When we divide that degree distance by 12, we get the number of years, that is, the age when the Secondary Progressed Moon aspect will occur (remembering that the application or separation orb would be 1 degree per month).

The Secondary Progressed Moon's aspects with natal Saturn are very telling—an architecture of advance. We can count ahead to the first quadrature aspect made by the SP Moon and natal Saturn, translate that distance into years by dividing by 12, and then know that, starting from that age, *we can establish a lifetime cycle*, involving a quadrature aspect with natal Saturn every six-and-one-half to seven years thereafter. (The Lunar Cycle, of course; approximately 28 days/years.)

In my horoscope, Saturn is at the Midheaven at 17 Pisces 21. My Moon is at 27 Leo 23 in the IIIrd House. In Secondary Progression measurement, the Moon would reach the opposition to Saturn (i.e., opposing from 17 Virgo) in 20 degrees (3 to finish Leo, 17 further into Virgo); divided by 12 gives almost two years of age. This begins my Secondary Progressed Moon-Saturn cycle, in increments of seven years from age two: age nine (square), severe home problems with father preparing to leave; age 16 (conjunction with the Midheaven Saturn), excellence in school, athletics, college plans; 23 (square), major job success out of college and major new career focus; 30 (opposition), operatic debut in New York City; 37 (square), international move back to the United States, earliest book being published; 44 (Midheaven Saturn conjunction again), self-published my 16th book, opened Public Relations and Advertising agency; 51 (square), career changing again.

This generalization technique for those astrologers who work well with the Secondary Progressed Moon comes easily with a little practice. Imagine how easy it is when the natal horoscope shows the Moon and Saturn (or the Moon in relation to any planet or Angle) *already in aspect*. All we need to do to begin a lifetime cycle is bring the Moon to the starting position, divide the distance traveled by 12, determine the age in years and go forward in lifetime in increments of $6^1/_2$-7 years.

Try one more projection: my Descendant is 0 Capricorn. That's 270 horoscope degrees (9 completed signs x 30°). My Moon at 27 Leo translates to 147° (4 completed Signs = 120° + 27 into the next Sign = 147°). Projecting the Secondary Progressed Moon to conjunction with the Descendant is simply 123° (270-147; or, from 27 Leo, project a trine to 27 Sagittarius and then add 3 degrees to 0 Capricorn). That 123° is a little over ten years of age. Again, a strong corroboration—which we have seen over and over again in the Solar Arc measurements as well of the extraordinarily important time of family break-up between ages nine and ten. The Secondary Moon had just earlier been squaring Saturn in the Xth, as we have seen, when I was nine, and then crossed my Descendant (my mother's fourth cusp; fourth House from my IVth) when I was ten.

The remainder of Secondary Progression measurements simply can not match the vast spectrum of arcs and midpoint pictures possible in the Solar Arc system. It is interesting to note that the system of Secondary Progressions was introduced to the United States by British astrologers at the turn of the century. Meanwhile, Europe was building the system of Solar Arcs to eventually bloom with the Cosmobiological work formulated by Rheinhold Ebertin. Astrology on two continents developed in different directions to harness the cycles of time.

It is *our* time now—for astrologers in the United States to work with Solar Arcs in tandem with transits, together the most powerful prediction system we have in astrology. These measurements are easy to make for Direct and Indirect Solar Arcs, and, with computer program assistance, the Solar Arc midpoint pictures exact no effort from the astrologer in terms of computation.

Solar Arc measurements are not at all limited by the system that supports them or by celestial mechanics, and they are dramatic and basically unlimited in symbology. Most important, so very often, they do indeed crystallize the past and illuminate the future.

On the average, throughout a year, a horoscope will exhibit about 25 Solar Arc contacts, perhaps three Direct Arcs—planet to planet or Angle—and some 20 or so Indirect Midpoint pictures. This is not a cumbersome amount to interpret by any means. The Direct ones are very easy to see through rapport orientation with just the simplest extra calculation, if necessary. Using a Solar Arc computer program, the astrologer can prepare a spread-sheet over a span of, say, three years in just a few minutes. This small effort literally can enrich a lifetime.

During an astrological consultation, reference to rapport measurements (generally prepared in advance) and the "Quick-Glance Transit Guide" in the Appendix can guide conversation into the past, dramatically and with minimum effort. Then, the spread-sheet prepared ahead of time along with transits is already before the astrologer, taking on meaning from discussion about the past, crystallizing potentials for the future.

It is important here to reiterate the danger of great expectations. Our objective is not to find some magic measurement, some consummately precise measurement to give us control over our existence. It simply is not astrology's nor any other discipline's calling to say, "When you walk through that door, you will find this building aflame!" Instead, we should look for appreciation of our life within the infinitely callibrated cycles of time, *to translate the sense of the inexorable into the sense of opportunity*, and to help others not be alone in understanding that life process we all share.

In fact, it is tenable that the more exacting any measurement—or, indeed, the more bizarre any measurement or system is—*the narrower our perception becomes*. Just last week, as I prepare these pages in December, 1990, the time had come for large populations along an earthquake fault in the Midwest to await their ruin, as predicted with the most exacting measurements and confidence by a well-credentialed scientist! The populace had believed. The media had supported the sensationalism. Businesses had closed in fear. Fatalists were revelling. Nothing happened. Life goes on. The scientist promptly made *another* meticulously backed-up prediction about another time in the near future when a force majeur *would* strike!

Measurements can begin to exist *for their own sake*. How many astrologers pursue measurement to avoid the challenge of interpretation? Why should we confine a client's life by relating him or her to the horoscope, to what we know about astrology? What if we turn the process around and relate the horoscope to the person? We will literally be bringing the horoscope *to* life!

Every skilled astrologer learns that several extremely well-posed questions, based upon careful, reasonable, and interpretively translated measurements, can begin to reveal the substance, quality, and individualistic timing of life development much more than one magic, perhaps arcane measurement can.

Exactness is something of the imagination in the art of astrology; there are simply too, too many vagaries in our work, in our presentation of it, and in our life that we seek to understand. There are the problems with exact birth timing, with pre-natal considerations, exact longitude measurements, exacting latitude considerations, different House systems, the interaction among horoscopes all around us, moments of happenings, events we have forgotten, events we dream about, events elsewhere that will catch up with us somehow, sometime, somewhere; with the other-dimensioned dilemma of the future already having taken place; the subjective bias of value judgments and choice we instinctively use to protect our identity, our systems of thought, our understanding of life; the intangibles of extrasensory cognition; out-and-out accidents; the touches of the miraculous, from the naturalness of prayer to the contrivance of altered states of consciousness; all the books we have read; all that our teachers have told us; the corroboration we have or have not received in our experience and its relation to our level of confidence... and so much more.

This is the human condition. How much measurement *do we need* in order to begin a meaningful conversation with our client?

The coefficient pi (π) is not exact, can never be exact, from 3.1416... to infinity, but its power to capture the interrelationships of circle measurements is sufficient to put someone on the Moon.

Rudhyar asked over 50 years ago (*Astrology and Personality*, page 460), "why *should* events be foretold accurately? The coefficient of inaccuracy is the coefficient of freedom!"

In all of my experiences, I remember only several instances of prediction that approached the magically precise.

> One will suffice: an out-of-work teacher was meeting with me at mid-day on a Sunday. She had lost her job two months before. She was hurting for work, income, and self-esteem. After much discussion, I suddenly said, "But there is such a positive opportunity for you now; there is, there is and it's today! But how can that be, it's Sunday?"
>
> I had simply noticed that transiting Jupiter was precisely on the woman's Sun on that day. She had responded well to the Jupiterian cycle in the past. And I just blurted out that gush of enthusiasm. It almost sounds like an on-the-run observation at a Psychic Fair!
>
> But it was not. Something had happened in the room; within me, between me and the client.
>
> She telephoned four hours later: she was employed again as a teacher! She had impulsively gone by her School District headquarters; it was open; she met a senior official working over the

weekend; a new job opening had come up; he offered it to her then and there, that Sunday.

What had happened? Astrology simply does *not* work that way, contrary to all the fictions about astrology that we ourselves would love to believe.

I went back to the horoscope to check: the Jupiter transit was simple, of course, but it applied to a grander time period. The partile exactness that day could have nothing to do with what had happened to her that afternoon, or such exactness of measurement would have this kind of miraculous corroboration much, much, much more often. Astrologers really *would* be heroes!

How many astrologers return to the horoscope some months after a consultation, after having said something significantly predictive and received full corroboration by the client after the future time had joined the present, *and found nothing or little to reinforce what had been deduced and predicted in the first place?* What was it?

What is that other dimension that operates within us, that touch of magic in our art, that touch of the magician in us all? What allies us to the conundrums of time ever so much more the more we study and practice?

Is it sensitivity as much as it is knowledge? Is it inspiration as much as it is regimen? Is it confidence more than it is insecurity?

Yes. But it is *all* these things.

Chapter Four

Analyzing Arcs

Please share with me this lengthy quote from Lilly, written in 1647; enjoy the language and absorb the message:

The Effects of Directions. "Before I handle this point, I must give this generall instruction to the younger sonnes of art, that in judging of the effects depending upon any Direction, they maturely consider the age of the native, for events are to be accommodated unto the difference of times, and therefore one should extreamly deceive himselfe, that upon any strong Direction of the Ascendant or Midheaven... [aspects enumerated involving Venus and Moon]... should predict marriage unto a native that is then three, four, or five yeers of age; how much, I say, should the artist misse the mark if he should attribute that action to an infant, of which he cannot then be capable; or what madnesse were it to predict to an aged man the begetting of a child, when in reason itselfe, and by reason of his extreame feebleness, no such thing can or may be expected; we must therefor prognosticate *things possible and naturall*, befitting and agreeing unto every one, according to the difference of his yeers, etc. We must also in all our predictions have the world to understand, that the common or generall fate of any nation or place, is of more efficacy then any ones particular. We must also consider the region where any one is borne, if we will exquisitely judge of the shape and form of the native, and of the manners of his mind, etc. ever considering the most powerfull cause, etc."[1]

We can use astrology as artists by reaching to understand what *can be* only in terms of things possible and natural, suiting the cli-

---
1. Lilly, p. 708.

ent's Reality Principle, including origin, acculturation, mannerisms, and stated potentials. These humanistic awarenesses give life to measurements. Our vision should be *expanded* by our measurements, not narrowed.

An obvious example is in analysis of a horoscope of someone born in Germany or any other war-torn country during the war years or earlier and then experiencing maturity conditioned by very taxing memories. In our own society, what considerations must be made for minorities who have suffered social deprivation during development? What about education related to achievement in different areas of the country, etc.? No astrological measurement in a personal consultation can outweigh the Reality Principle of the client's world.

And to complete our introduction to this chapter, please share with me this statement by Dane Rudhyar, written the year I was born:

> "...system after system of progressions or directions are propounded—each apparently most satisfactory in many cases, most unsatisfactory in just as many others. Hardly ever is an attempt made to give a philosophical, coherent interpretation of what 'progressions' really mean and of why they operate at all—when they do.
>
> "... A birth-chart is the symbolical macrocosmic representation of the potential fullness of the perfected microcosm. It is the 'blue-print' of the complete man. It is therefore *nothing but* a set of potentialities, it is entirely abstract. Because it is a representation formed by macrocosmic factors (planets, horizon, etc.), it is purely symbolical. It indicates nothing factual; nothing concrete; nothing precisely 'fated.' ... There is not one single precise event of a man's life to be found as such in his birth-chart. What can be traced are more or less definite types of potential eventualities, with varying degrees of 'actualizability' at certain more or less accurately determinable times of his life."[2]

Both Lilly's and Rudhyar's statements are courageous, even by today's expectations. We must constantly remind ourselves that *human beings* make things happen, not planets. We have to admit we do not know *why* there appears to be such a correspondence between what is above and what is below—and, in Mundane Astrology, as will be seen most dramatically in the next chapter, this can be mind-boggling.

---

2. Rudhyar, pages 418-419.

We have to recognize potential and how it can be tuned to the real circumstances and dreams in a person's life.

Specifically, we must note that sometimes the most powerful of Solar Arcs, the most powerful of transits can occur in a horoscope and there appears to be no corresponding manifestation in the person's life—even within a Time Orb consideration for possible or likely birth time error, for example, of three or four years in either direction, equivalent to $\pm$ 15 minutes of time on the Midheaven.

In 1987, I had powerful Solar Arc measurements focused in the months of February and March: SA Pluto was conjunct natal Neptune in my IVth House (my mother), ruling my Midheaven. And, at the same time, SA Midheaven was square natal Pluto. There was a simultaneous string of strong Jupiter transits to natal Jupiter and the Sun, and a repetition three times throughout the year of transiting Saturn square its own natal position from my VIth House.

The entire symbolism suggested two things: major professional readjustments and employment and/or matters of illness or death concerning my mother. *The latter potential was admissable* because in my Reality Principle my mother had become quite frail and sickly, though mentally robust and reasonably mobile; she was losing her eyesight rapidly.

My mother did die, suddenly, six months later in September, at which time there was *no* Solar Arc measurement anywhere within sixty days in my horoscope. There was *no* transit of note. The Secondary Progressed Moon was crossing my Ascendant.

Now, after the fact, we could glibly see the Secondary Progressed Moon as the mother symbol; we could see it corresponding to major adjustments in my life due to her. The fact of the matter, of my life, was that her death did not affect anything objective in my life whatsoever, and there was no emotional upheaval. Rather, the Moon measurement corresponded to very focused professional aspirations in a new direction, which I was pursuing strongly—conceivably a new identity. I was strategically aware of these measurements to come and I conducted my life and development accordingly late in 1986 and early 1987. Recognizing my mother's sense of humor, I observe only that she died six months late!

In the interpretation of Solar Arcs, it is very easy to feel daunted by how many there are, how interchanging the symbols are: we have 144 Direct Arcs and 858 Indirect Midpoint pictures! We must become familiar with the symbols in terms of Arcs just as we learned them in terms of basic horoscope analysis—the planets in signs, in aspects, etc. We can not spend all our time looking them up in the Appendix of this volume, for example. Looking things up constantly takes away our concentration and feel for the horoscope; we get separated from the time-sharing experience.

When we learn the *principles* of interpretive judgment of Solar Arcs—instead of reaching for mastery of all the specifics, we soon become comfortable with the "feel" of an Arc and we do not necessarily need a specific label of meaning. Confidence comes with time and practice. And, when we do need a boost, we can check the book. It is very much like a medical doctor's situation with the flood of prescriptions on the market or, indeed, all diverse symptomatology relating to his or her practice: most of them are known, the chemicals and their combinations, the syndromes of disease, but there are directories that help out when help is needed.

Another benefit from gaining an understanding of the principles behind synthesis for Solar Arc interpretation is that we become better astrologers the more we use our head, hone our perceptions, and learn to express our art. We artists must know our colors.

Direct Arcs. The key to analysis of Direct Arcs is found in the arcing planet, the planet symbolically on-the-move. In its symbolism, it is bringing a value, a color, an energy *to* the natal planet. The arcing planet's symbolism is brought to the natal planet's symbolism and significance in the particular horoscope: if the Arc is a conjunction, there is a blend, a get-together, a meeting, a focus or, as it would have been noted in the 14th century, "the lord of attack is meeting with the lord of caution far away from our King's land" (SA Mars conjoining Saturn in the IXth). Actually, these old-time picturesque ways of distilling our symbolisms are very helpful as a base for our modern images! They keep us objective in our analyses.

When the Direct Arc is a square, semi-square, or a sesquiquadrate (strong developmental tension in the square, then less, and still less, respectively), we need *to add a verb* to the image that shows a stirring up, a readjustment, a push for development originating with the arcing planet and being received by the natal planet: "the lord of attack *argues* with and *enflames* the lord of caution" (SA Mars square Saturn).

When the Direct Arc is an opposition, there is the feel of full awareness, confrontation, challenge brought into the horoscope picture, sometimes possibly complementary, depending upon the natures of the planets and the Reality Principle that may be valid in the individual's life. The arcing planet *alerts* the natal planet; "the lord of attack has been sent to *assess* the lord of caution; the warlord meets the holy man for battle or for learning." The arc axis must then be fitted to the real-life situation in (or potentially in) the client's life.

These SA Mars to Saturn contacts set up the drama for better or worse through energy interacting with discipline, with plan, with strategy, seasoned by experience gathered over time. The oxymoron "aggressive constraint" captures the opposite natures of Mars and Saturn. The analytical goal then becomes the meaningful management of this "meeting" between the two within the horoscope.

The arcs gain individualized significance through reference to the Houses. More often than not, along with its own symbolic energy values, the arcing planet brings with it strongly *a reference to the House it rules in the natal horoscope*. We know how important House rulership networking is in the dynamic analysis of natal horoscopes, facilitating the expansion of synthesis out from a planet's House position through an aspect to another planet and its House position, to the significances of the Houses both rule.[3] In Solar Arc analysis, so very often the arcing planet brings with it House references from the natal horoscope in terms of its own House rulership *first*, its own natal House position, second, and the target-planet's House references third.

One more very important point must be presented before we continue with some examples: as suggested in footnote 17 on page 68, there is a difference in potential manifestation between SA Mars=Saturn and SA Saturn=Mars. To date, Solar Arc theory has not dealt with this sufficiently.

I have maintained this difference to be so for some 20 years, and more often than not, observation and experience have borne out the hypothesis. It seems that the *arcing planet gains the upper hand*; being on-the-move highlights the arcing planet's "mission." SA Sun arcing to conjunction with Saturn certainly is not "the King rushing to gather up trouble"; that would go against the integrity of the life force and defeat the hierarchy of values established for all the planets, all of them being essential to the "allness" of the human experience.

---

3. Tyl, *Holistic Astrology*.

Rather, the King could be bringing illumination to a great, austere Minister of the Budget or Minister of Education or Minister of Marriage, all depending on rulerships, etc. Illumination meets crystallization; if all is well in reality, we expect to acknowledge fulfillment; if all is not well, the King might indeed have to learn a new strategy.

Then, if we see SA Saturn arcing to contact with the Sun, we must change the image: "the lord of caution is advising the King, is strategically restraining the King (square), or is confronting or reminding the King of difficult responsibilities (opposition)."—"Do this in remembrance of me, Sire!"

As we have discussed in Chapter 1, *the language of symbolism* is crucial to our understanding and application of astrology. These simple medieval images here and there in these modern paragraphs should help anchor us to primal symbolisms and allow us to build modern significances more easily.

For example, in the fragment of my horoscope introduced on page 67, we saw that SA Saturn opposed natal Mars in about 40 degrees or 40 years of life, my birthday on December 31, 1976. The lord of caution, the state, the exactor, arced to oppose the lord of energy, procreation (Mars in the Vth in powerful aspect configuration). In short, cold faced off with hot. SA Saturn rules my VIIth, the marriage partner, and was making the opposition from the XIth, love received (i.e., the fifth, love-given, of the VIIth).

My divorce came through in June of 1976. The rapport measurement alerts us to the general time period; actual measurement of the SA Saturn=Mars was April 1976. the Time Orb of such a strong measurement, evaluated beforehand, certainly indicated the significance of mid-1976, that it was to be vital to my marital status.

We have seen that SA Mars signified the divorce as well, at the same general time, squaring the Midheaven, stirring up real anxiety about my profession and its finances (Mars rules the XIth, the second of the Xth) for child support (Mars in the Vth natally). This Solar Arc Mars=MC (Medium Coeli) was exact in February, 1976, two months before SA Saturn=Mars, and just four months before the divorce decree, the period of time when all the financial debate was taking place about the terms of the divorce and the singular focus upon child support. The astrology fit the reality.

As it happens so frequently, a major transit-trigger seemed to gather the background symbolisms of the Solar Arcs and focus them transiting within real time. In this instance, transiting Jupiter and transiting Uranus were in opposition in the 6th degree axis of Taurus-Scorpio, exactly conjunct my natal Uranus at 5 Taurus 42 in the XIth House, ruling my IXth, the House of legal affairs!

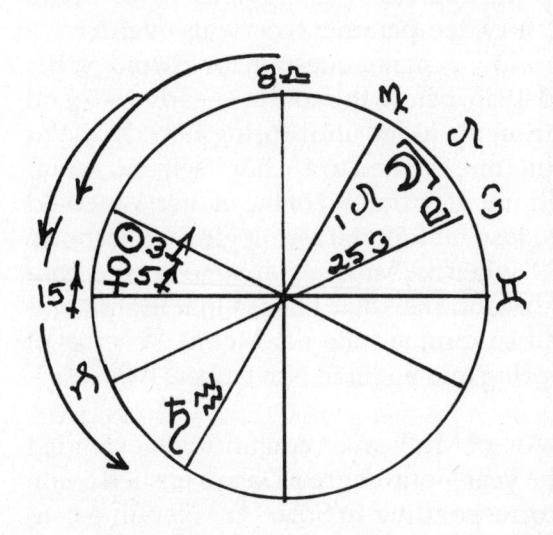

Here is another example. This second horoscope portion shows another set of measurements that corresponded perfectly with real events, and was used predictively. The predictions often seemed off-base in their protracted time projections because they went so against the time norms of the activities at issue. Neither client nor I could believe the court issue would last so incredibly long.

This woman's SA Sun came to opposition with natal Pluto in 52° (general rapport measurement). Exactly measured, the opposition took place in July 1986, $3^{1}/_{2}$ months before her 52nd birthday. At that time exactly, with transiting Saturn in conjunction with her Sun, she sought out a prominent lawyer and began a divorce action and preparations for a major court case. The objective of the case would be solely her husband's very large and enormously complicated estate. This is symbolized perfectly here this way: SA Sun is opposing Pluto—the Queen (her Sun, poetically; but note her Moon in Leo in the VIIIth) is facing (opposition) a new perspective (Pluto), a major change in the direction of her life (always with Pluto, as we shall see). The VIIIth is her husband's estate, the second House of her VIIth.

She had been feeling extreme financial deprivation for some time (transiting Saturn conjoining her Sun in the XIIth, Saturn ruling her IInd and placed there natally). She took action.

The case came to court nine months later. Transiting Jupiter opposed her Midheaven and corresponded to a favorable position.

throughout the exacting trial. The complexities of the legal presentations necessitated several trials about different segments of the case; there were delays after delays for any number of reasons.

Tensions built to a high point by the end of 1987. (SA Uranus formed a square to Mars—not shown here—the individuation force, Uranus, stirring up the aggressive energy, Mars, for her to stand up and be counted; fury, temperament, nervous overdrive.)

"When will this case end?" A major question for astrology. Begun in preparation in mid-1986, before the courts in early 1987 and later, and still no verdict from the judge until Spring 1989! No Solar Arc or transit in the interim time seemed to anchor itself and set up the sense of fruition or fulfillment or the end of the matter. We could not believe it; we began to lose faith in the astrological projections, *until* precisely March, 1989, when SA Midheaven came to exact conjunction with her natal Sun (and the Solar Eclipse that month was square her Ascendant and sesquiquadrate her Moon). A series of pronouncements in the Spring and again in November, 1989, clarified she had won.

The dominant Solar Arc of Midheaven conjunct Sun extended a Time Orb throughout the year—one degree. Delays ensued again before final settlement, corresponding to Solar Arc Neptune conjunct her Jupiter, dispositor of her Sun and ruler of her Ascendant. This befuddling Arc began shortly after the Midheaven=Sun Arc began.

Then came the appeals and the reconvening court schedules for specific estate settlements, which finally focused on January 1991 (another enormous delay), *when the Solar Arc Midheaven would continue on to conjoin her Venus* in the XIIth with the Sun (exact Arc measurement: January 5; final court date: January 4). This would be it. Venus rules the Midheaven; transiting Saturn will be semisquare her Pluto at the same time: the break-up of her husband's estate, or at least some loss from his point of view.

(Now, at the time of writing these pages, two months before that key date for my client, her affairs are already improving steadily in all phases of her life: her work, her relationships, and her great expectations for the finale of her four and one-half year wait for the "arc of settlement.")

Interpreting the Planets

We have seen that the arcing planet *carries the lead in the Solar Arc drama*: that planet blends its symbolism with the other in conjunction, registers developmental tension in the fourth harmonic aspects. The synthesis begins best, normally, with the arcing planet's symbology, then the symbology of the "receiving" planet, and then reference to the House the arcing planet rules in the natal horoscope. In preparing an analysis image, it is helpful to revert back to the ancient, primary, basic symbologies as an objective start for modern interpretations; this helps keep the arc picture simple. And finally, *every analysis must fit into a past, existing, or projected reality in the life of the client, or the arc should be set aside.*

☉ In all relationships involving the arcing Sun, we are bringing the illumination of our life ("the King") to some other symbol of psychodynamic awareness, behavioral potential, and focus of needs. When the Sun relates to the Moon, for example, we see the drama of male and female, the King and Queen, illuminated achievements and inner needs, outer successes and inner feelings. SA Sun to Moon suggests highlighted relationships of all kinds (note: the word "highlighted" is not a value judgment; if the reality situation is poor, a Solar Arc of the Sun to the Moon may just make the situation devastatingly clear).

Reversing this: the arc of the Moon to the Sun seems to suggest a bringing to focus of one's personal sensitivity about the major needs one has for a sense of fulfillment. When my SA Moon came to square with my VIIth House Sun (43 degrees), I was about 42. This was a time of deep self-questioning (Moon rules the Ascendant) and relationship considerations at a pivotal time in my professional life, with transiting Saturn approaching my fourth cusp.[4]

When SA Sun *opposed my Moon* in the IIIrd, ruled by the Sun, my whole life had switched to a different form of communication, from opera to promotion, and my private personal relationship was under developmental concern.

---

4. Transits are not included in this part of our discussion in order not to complicate images. Power transits are covered in Chapters 6 and 7.

☿   When we are analyzing arcs by Mercury, we should think of bringing the image of "thought" to the symbology of the other planet, first in terms of the House Mercury rules in the natal horoscope. If Mercury comes to the Sun, we should expect common sense in terms of House references; to Venus, idealism; to Mars, thoughts about strong reactions, planning, even impulsiveness (the square, for example); to Jupiter, perhaps magnanimity or enthusiasm or vacation travel or study; to Saturn, self-control, thinking how to be wise; with Uranus, perhaps inspiration or using one's resources cleverly; with Neptune, imagination may be alerted or some spiritual awareness awakened; and with Pluto, the sense of being persuasive or, indeed, even obsessive about some particular line of thought or objective.

These images are not hard to *feel*. When we get so many of them out in our study, there are too many to memorize. *Getting the feel* is what is very important and is the path to real skill in applying Solar Arcs to past and future time, throughout general rapport measurements—then and there, on-the-spot—and/or through specific measurements of especially important times.

Now, if Mercury is the "receiving" planet of arcs from other planets, I suggest that the manifestation will be different in terms of our analytical images and the dimensions that fit our client's reality.[5] The Sun will illuminate the mind; Venus will idealize or romanticize it (for fulfillment, for rationalization); Mars will stimulate (anxiety, restlessness, speaking out, traveling to get things done); Jupiter will fill out the thinking process, expand it (higher level of reasoning; extended education; longer, more enriching trip); Saturn will offer the awareness of controls necessary for wisdom, even if it must emerge through temporary fall-back or depression; Uranus will excite the mind, the nervous system, the impulses; Neptune may suggest suppression of perceptions of what is real (things may be other than they seem) and Pluto, arced to contact with Mercury, often correlates with a major alteration of personal perspective, a complete change of orientation (SA Pluto in Cancer ruling the Scorpio IXth conjoins Mercury in Virgo in the VIIth: the woman leaves the country for an extended length of time and marries a foreigner).

---

5. With the Sun, Mercury, and Venus, the adjustments of symbolisms is not very marked since these bodies are always so close to each other in space as well as in interactive analysis.

♀   Arcs by Venus can add grace, awareness of things harmonious, loveliness, lovingness, and suggest the brighter side of things. Venus *receiving* arcs will take on illumination from the Sun (SA Sun-Venus contact is classic, as we have seen, for romantic affairs, marriage or childbirth, if age and circumstances support the potential); intensification from Mars, often sexiness, surely vitalization of relationship; from Jupiter, the aura or actualization of good luck; from Saturn, a maturation, a call for reevaluation, or a relationship with someone of great age difference; from Uranus, great sexual interest and or excitation; from Neptune, possibly a socio-romantic magnetism, idealistic dreaming, romantic charade, or clandestine love concerns; from Pluto, a driving focus to the extent that emotions and affections may be wasted and bring difficulty because of excess, or, again, the change of family or relationship perspective through marriage, childbirth, or disruptive affair.

♂   Arcs by Mars add energy, stir things up, in terms of the planetary pairing, often through reference to the natal House ruled by Mars; and then, of course, to the House dynamics of the planet receiving the arc. "The lord of attack" relates exceedingly clearly in Solar Arc projections. Think in terms of the old-time prediction images and get the feel for modern application.

It is interesting that, when SA Mars relates to Neptune, there is the suggestion of magnetism, of great appeal. It is as if one's aura is stirred up and people react to it favorably. If this kind of energy finds an outlet in the client's reality, it can be considerably inspiring; if there is no outlet, the absence of life organization or project plans may appear as weakness or disillusionment.

SA Mars to Pluto suggests extreme force, possibly rebellion, even assault (with the client as perpetrator or victim), but, as well, the kind of energies that, when channeled productively, are concomitants of great success: "the lord of attack confers with the lord of his Domain to speak of overthrow or vindication with the causes at hand."

Arcs projected toward Mars suggest *adjustments* to the client's application of energy, rather than that energy being brought by Mars to different behavioral faculties and dimensions of identity. Again, Mercury will suggest a sense of planning and task tension; Venus, a sense of grace and a touch of libido; Jupiter, a broader application; Saturn, a temperance for strategy or out-and-out frustration if there is no outlet; Uranus, extreme intensity, temper, even rashness and anger, as the individualism factors stir the ego into action impetuously; Neptune, an obfuscation of energies, a dissipation; and Pluto, again a tremendous awareness of potentials (Pluto is always "the sense of perspective," the lord of the Domain) and the drive necessary to fulfill them and, as in all these powerful arc images, if there is no outlet, the shot cannot leave the gun; the kickback, the implosion, can cause concern and problems, frustration, rebound reactions, including ill-health.

♃ Jupiter arcs introduce education, gain through experience, and enthusiasm, and, with Saturn, a sense of patience, possibly a pleasure in aloneness, an awareness of a new order issuing from an old order. In all these contacts, there is always the touch of luck possible. The Jupiter arc to Uranus seems to heighten the glory of individualism and, if things are going well, can correspond with a very fortunate change in the client's world. With Neptune, there can be signs of spiritual enrichment, heightened idealism or, if the reality profile already shows difficulties with dishonesty or subterfuge, more of the same leading to instability. Jupiter's arc contacts with Pluto are definitively descriptive of the urge to power (as are the natal aspect configuration of Jupiter and Pluto, especially the opposition). And again, the urge to power must have a place to go to express itself in leadership of some kind, of controlling the environment. If there is no outlet, the urge to power can take on forms of exploitive control and even collusion, leading to entanglements, upsets, separations, and loss.

Arcs toward Jupiter alert the mind, the social graces, the enthusiasms, and, from Saturn, prudence and a sense of knowing, which can be related to religion, the law, or higher learning; from Uranus, intense hope, speculation, and innovation; From Neptune, a spiritual sensitivity; from Pluto, again an urge to power, but here it appears less dramatically.

♄ Saturn arcs symbolically establish caution, prudence, patience, the sense of necessary controls or, indeed, the sense of depression, inhibition, frustration, self-doubt (to Uranus); laborious realization of plans, or suffering and emotional torment (to Neptune). The arc of Saturn to Pluto is extremely difficult: it almost always seems to correspond to loss, to struggle, and the fight to get out from under oppression. "The Grand Inquisitor shall meet, deal with, confront the lord of the Domain. Who shall survive this meeting upon the mountain?"

In my opinion, the reciprocal arc of Pluto to contacts with Saturn is identical to Saturn arcing to Pluto. There seems to be no nuance of difference between these two Direct Solar Arc images. At best, the client's life is securely routinized to such a degree and the client feels comfortable and rewarded enough in relation to needs and dreams that the Saturn-Pluto or Pluto-Saturn period goes unnoticed.[6]

In my life, SA Pluto came to opposition with my natal Saturn exactly in July 1985, an arc of 49 degrees by rapport measurement; late 1985 in terms of exact age measurement. In the time period March to August 1985, my business partnership dissolved, my private relationship dissolved, my residence changed, and my business was spiraling to failure. Pluto, making the arc, ruling my employment VIth, was coming from my natal IInd (self-worth, money), opposed Saturn from my IVth (home, ends and new starts); Saturn in my Midheaven (profession) ruled my VIIth, the House of partnership and relationship.

♅ Arcs made by Uranus add extraordinary individualistic intensity to the natal symbolisms, behavioral faculties, and needs suggested by the natal planets. Just as with Mars receiving arcs from the other planets (page 91), Uranus receives arcs that manifest potentially in nervous awareness, charisma, energetic drive, opportunism, strategic refinement, magical sureness with Neptune, and extreme self-awareness and drive from Pluto.

♆ Neptunian arcs suggest a softening of the edges in the classic symbolisms we have repeated many times in this discussion (and which are covered in the Solar Arc Directory in the Appendix), with the addition sometimes, especially when the client's reality is at an apparent standstill, of not going forward in an organized fashion, so

---

6. Astrologers are certainly aware of the tone poem called "The Planets" by Gustav Holst. It depicts the planets' images in symphonic colors out to and including Neptune. For Pluto as musical image, there can be no greater moment than in Bartok's *Bluebeard's Castle*: when Bluebeard proclaims his Domain as endless, the grand, C-Major section.

that idealism becomes an overt defense mechanism, with dreams taking the place of action; subterfuge is experienced or is applied. Sometimes, in relations to Jupiter or Pluto, Neptune contacts can register a dimension of the supernatural; affairs of death, deep thoughts about one's existence, leading possibly to esoteric studies or self-help pursuits.

℞ Plutonian arcs intensify differently than Uranian arcs. Where the Uranian are "electrifying," the Plutonian are "totalitarian," that is, having no limitations or qualifications. The Uranian image is highly focused, like a welder's torch; the Plutonian image encompasses a *domain* of concern, a megaproportioned surfeit. Uranus zaps and drills; Pluto explodes and annexes. Pluto is the adverb among our planetary symbologies, the only symbol that lives on the concept of "how much." Plutonian arcs will add that kind of perspective to the perception with Mercury; the sensual with Venus, the application of energy with Mars, the hope for opportunity and reward with Jupiter, through strong exploitation; the potential for shattering the existing order, experiencing loss, and building anew with Saturn; rampant individualism and the avant garde with Uranus; the potential for scandal through calumny, or self-deception through aggrandized perspectives with Neptune.

Sensitive Points. Direct Solar Arc aspects to the Midheaven and Ascendant are extremely important in preparing and testing rectification and in analysis of developments in the past and projections into the future. In the process of rectification, rapport generalizations will start to suggest a strategically valid birth time, but exact measurements are then mandatory, incorporating heavy transit-triggers as well. It seems that Solar Arc projections over or in square to the Angles of the natal horoscope manifest with even more time precision than Solar Arcs between planets do. Through a great deal of experience with Solar Arcs—and this should not then sound naive or simplistic to say—the Midheaven and Ascendant seem to be truly alive, very sensitive, and strategic in the measurement of life development as if these axes are *within us* somehow.[7]

The most telling aspects, of course, are from Mars, Saturn, Ura-

---

7. I am reminded of Marc Edmund Jones's suggestion that the MC-IC axis is the "spine" of the horoscope; that all religions identify the horizon with physical awareness; of Paracelsus, the great Swiss seer, doctor, astrologer saying "The planets are within."

nus, Neptune, and Pluto. In those cases, we see the potentials for dynamic change: contact with the Midheaven, change in the early home through the parents' life development activities, later in age through one's profession, through one's social status and, still later in life, through cooperation with one's children (the Midheaven is the sixth of the Vth through derivative House rulerships)[8]; to the Ascendant, change in one's personal projection, how one begins self-awareness in the early years, what events affect that tender time; major adjustments of self-awareness during the years of trial and error, during maturation.

Solar Arc activity with the Descendant obviously refers to relationship factors and, in early life, changes in one's young society or growing personality image through whatever was happening in the parents' lives (since the seventh cusp is the Midheaven of the parental Xth or the fourth of the parental IVth). Similarly, Solar Arc activity with the Imum Coeli (the fourth cusp in most House systems), signals new beginnings, especially concerning residence, moves, relocations that really matter, and new starts in general.

Solar Arcs from the Sun and Mercury will carry, again, the sense of illumination, self-emphasis and the thinking process and, often, travel. Solar Arcs from Venus, especially to the Midheaven or Descendant during marrying years, can suggest romance, marriage, or childbirth very reliably.[9] Remember, none of these observations is a hard and fast rule; these observations are guides to judgment.

What emerges here with the very important Sun-Venus relationship, and the Moon and Mars, and the combinations of these male and female symbols is that relating them by Solar Arcs to the Angles of the horoscope very, very often corresponds to the time of romance and children if the reality will support it, or, as we saw in my personal case something as clearly symbolized in the horoscope but at an entirely different level.

For a long time, I have looked forward to my time of life from mid-1990 forward, almost upon me, my time now of writing this book. I would have gone through an enormously powerful and protracted period of strong transit conjunctions with my VIIth House Sun at 10 Capricorn (Neptune, Saturn, and now Uranus!). Every

---

8. See Tyl, Holistic Astrology.
9. Both Lilly and De Luce make much of this Solar Arc activity from Venus: the former mentions either Venus or the Moon directed to the horizon line or Midheaven; the latter promised marriage through the arc of Moon or Venus to an Angle for a man, Sun or Mars to an Angle for a woman. Lilly even allowed sextile and trine; De Luce allowed only conjunction.

relationship in my life experience would probably change (they all did), and I would be intensely alert to and bewildered by a new direction in my professional development.

At the same time, along with very supportive Solar Arc midpoint pictures, especially Mars=Jupiter/MC (high energy development of professional opportunity for reward), SA Uranus was conjoining my Ascendant in July 1990; one of most powerful measurements in the Solar Arc lexicon, which would certainly dominate the entire year (especially with transiting Uranus simultaneously upon my Sun).

In transit theory and Solar Arc theory, Uranian contacts with the Ascendant carry with them a very high percentage of probability of geographic displacement. The probability is extremely high due to the intensification of individuality, the drive for independence, separation, new start, adjusted identity, etc. The same applies even more dramatically to the Solar Arc measure which can extend its Time Orb over an entire year.

I planned a year of strategy around these predictions, filled out with many other measurements and deductions. I worked as hard as I could to make things happen, to engineer major changes in my professional life, any one of which would take me away from where I lived and place me in a new environment for a new life. I literally rearranged my reality in terms that were hopeful but not speculative; in terms that had high security and little whimsy; in terms that could happen; that should happen. But all these thrusts failed.

This meant that the prime level of anticipated manifestation drawn from the astrology of the situation did not manifest. When this happens, there is nothing "wrong" or lacking in astrology, especially in a horoscope so carefully refined over many years of testing—*there are simply other considerations the astrologer must deal with*. (This book is one of those considerations; and it is fascinating how much of this book, as you will see, quite by accident deals with the 10th degree of the Cardinal Signs all in relation to my Sun position so under developmental tension at present.)

We cannot force one level of interpretation or prediction into being. Another one may simply be waiting to emerge in a kind of Law of Naturalness. When we force, we bring the bias of what we think we know about astrology into what we presumably know about a person's life. With major Solar Arcs and transits, when the front line—the prima fascia level—of symbolism does not seem to manifest in the life development of the client, there will almost always be a *parallel symbolism*, another level of symbolism to search out, adjust to the client's reality, and use as strategy.

There will always be a *variety* of appropriate manifestations, for the most powerful predictive measurements especially. Just as we may say that there will almost always be a list of appropriate measurements for a specifically developed and manifested event.

For contacts of Uranus with the other Angles of the horoscope, we have to be aware of the potential for something to rupture the status quo.

On the other hand, Solar Arcs by Neptune tend to blur ego awareness (Ascendant), blur selfhood as seen through the job or through whatever is emerging through the home and family situation (Midheaven); in relationships (Descendant); and, again, through the early home life (if that is the time of application), or in the home of the client as an adult (the IC). As well, SA Neptune conjunct the fourth cusp is also opposed the Midheaven and suggests a possible wipe-out of identity, often for the strangest of reasons or from the strangest of causes. Alcohol and drugs are often represented. Neptune's House rulership may clarify the elusive measurement meaning.

Solar Arcs of Pluto to the Angles are usually extremely powerful. Quite simply, especially in relation to the Ascendant or Midheaven, we can anticipate major turns of destiny. I experienced SA Pluto conjunct my fourth cusp (opposed my Midheaven), Pluto ruling my VIth, the twelfth House of my VIIth) with a rapport measurement of 39 degrees, or 39 years of age. It was exactly seven months before my 39th birthday, in May 1975. This Solar Arc dominated my entire year then, and, in ways, still to this day. Transiting Mars and Saturn were in opposition, Mars upon my Sun; transiting Pluto was square my Sun in the VIIth House ... all at the same time in February, 1975. These transits triggered the major Solar Arc measurement, and I experienced a major turn of destiny: I left my marriage and proceeded with plans for a divorce, late in February, 1975.

The Lunar Nodal axis, in natal astrology, without any doubt whatsoever, according to my years of research and practice with the hypothesis, represents the maternal influence in one's development: when the nodal axis is tightly configurated in conjunction-opposition with a planet in the horoscope—and as well in square—the influence of the mother through the need symbolism represented by the planet is undeniable.

Yet, in Solar Arc interpretation, that insight does not seem to apply. Rather, Ebertin suggests that for SA Node there is the connotation of groups, associations, contacts. This hypothesis was probably founded on the fecundation symbolism involving the Node's occurrence in tandem with the Sun-Moon relationship, i.e., where the Moon's orbit around the Earth cuts the apparent path of the Sun, the ecliptic.

Working with the nodes in Solar Arc theory requires much more study. My opinion is that somehow the Lunar Nodal Axis is "once removed" from the pulse of our grand Solar Arc sense of cycle. Its measurement is made from a different cut of time and space than are our measurements of the planets and Angles, which are based solely upon the symbolism of the Sun's progress from one day to the next.

I respect the efficacy of nodal interpretation within the natal horoscope, where the Sun-Moon relationship is of real importance. But within Solar Arc projection, I do not yet see enough comparable, reliable manifestation. (Curiously however, the Ebertin idea of "contacts" often fits aspects made by the *transiting* nodal axis—forecasting dates important for business meetings, interviews, etc.)

Finally, in our overview of Arc analysis, we can easily understand Solar Arc projections of the Midheaven axis or Ascendant axis to contacts with natal planets. A key example was already introduced on page 67 showing the Midheaven conjoining natal Saturn.

Solar Arc projections of these two major axes simply pick up the symbolic content of the planets with which arcs are made. The sense of "picking up" echoes the function of an aerial to pick up radio waves, for example. Authors in the past have portrayed the two great axes of our horoscope as antennae, and in Solar Arc interpretation the image is indeed appropriate.

The Directory of Solar Arcs and Midpoint pictures at the end of this book has been devised through the reasoning shared in this chapter and supported by years of practice. The principles of analysis are simple because they are based upon the primal symbolisms of our craft. The colors are rich and variegated. Along with transits, Solar Arcs become the major source of depiction that we have in astrology to bring past and future times to life.

Chapter Five

Predictions Down to Earth

Mundane Astrology—the astrology of nations and celestial phenomena related to the Earth—is a rich testing ground for astrological measurements, analysis, and predictions because very little that is subjective can get in the way. We are less afraid than we are with human beings to "tell it like it is," to see our symbols more clearly, more objectively, the way the old astrologers did. While Mundane Astrology is technical—many measurements are involved with so many factors present throughout large spans of time—there is nothing fancy or subtle about it. It is an extremely rewarding practice for astrologers with which to improve analytical skill and increase confidence.

Why do horoscopes of nations and, especially, celestial phenomena speak so eloquently? Why do interpretations of the symbolisms in these areas appear so fated? Perhaps it is that myriad millions of people, living, working, planning, evolving in any country all reinforce national positions within time's grand cycles. In a real sense, these millions of energies make the history and define the times.

Additionally, when analyzing a Great Conjunction, for example, neither planet "says" anything to corroborate or dispute an observation. Neither does a nation. (Perhaps the planets are better than most nations in predicting their futures... at least they know where they will be in times to come.) But history does record relentlessly the realities that ensue, the facts of the past, and the eventuations in the future.

102 / *Prediction in Astrology*

In Chapter 1, "Great Predictions in History," we saw that conjunctions, eclipses, and Fixed Stars were the major auguries for astrologers of the past. These phenomena were translated into pithy symbolic language and related dramatically to happenings of extreme significance, often before the fact. Over and over and over again in the history of astrology, we see the importance of these three special areas of astrological study.

It would be easy to establish the case for the Great Conjunction of Jupiter and Saturn as the most astonishingly significant measurement in Mundane Astrology, or of all astrological time. We have already seen the conjunction as the Christmas Star in Jesus's horoscope (page 13) and accompanying the Lunar Eclipse chart tied to the outbreak of the Black Plague in 1348 (page 16). And now, dominating much of the rest of this book, Jupiter-Saturn conjunctions will take us on the thrust of history out of the past, through our times, and into the future.

The Great Conjunction of Jupiter and Saturn occurs approximately every 20 years. From 1842 to 1981, the conjunctions have occurred exclusively within Signs of the Earth Family, and, curiously, every United States president who assumed office under this conjunction in the Earth Family has died in office (William Henry Harrison, Abraham Lincoln, James Garfield, William McKinley, Warren Harding, Franklin Roosevelt, and John F. Kennedy).

When the cycle of conjunctions between Jupiter and Saturn changes into a new family of Signs, it is called a Grand Mutation. This occurred from December 31, 1980 to July 24, 1981 in early Libra, with the inauguration of Ronald Reagan as president. A symbolist would point out that the change to the Air Family would shift the concentration upon administration, organization, and doctrine in the Earth Family symbology to society's greater well-being, living together in peace, sharing inventions, resources, information, escaping from the grip of stratification—or, indeed, fighting over whose peace was the correct one to share.

A quick mind-sweep over the last decade certainly reveals efforts in the Air Family direction—the Arab-Israeli accords engineered by Carter, Sadat, and Begin; the achievements in space and the cooperation among several countries on that frontier; and the historically awesome reorganization of Germany, Eastern Europe, and Russia emerging out of the Soviet Union, all in the name of Air Family values.

But the transition to a new world order is gradual. There is still so much agony and terror on Earth. The Grand Mutation will take *five more cycles* (until the year 2080) to become completely settled within the Air Family. We can literally see this thrust of historical change when we study the *last* Great Conjunction that occurred on December 31, 1980 in 9 Libra 30. This Great Mutation Grand Conjunction signalled the onset of religious war throughout the Arab world, throughout the Middle East, and much of the rest of the world for many years to come. *At the moment it occurred, Jupiter and Saturn were rising precisely on the Ascendant at Mecca.*[1]

Astrologers 300 years ago would have waxed eloquent over the symbolism that literally blazes off this horoscope (page 105): "The great lord of the gods and of all learning, he that rules the heavens in the name of Allah, meets with the lord of time who teaches wisdom, that lord also who enforces the law of the land and the laws of life. Together they oversee our world from a place that has long been holy." This image portrays the symbol of religion, philosophy, and learning (Jupiter) in the leaden grip of conjunction with the symbol of time itself, the rigor of tradition, and the administration of dogma (Saturn).

That this conjunction was exactly rising at the most important shrine of the Islamic world places extreme focus, demand, and responsibility upon Islam and the Arab world, *divided from the world of the Jews by a schism tied to an ancient debate:* which people truly issued from the seed of Abraham as the "promised" people?

When the Bible was assembled from many chronicles, some of known authorship, some of ascribed authorship, some written by students in their famous teacher's name throughout approximately 600 years (the Old Testament compiled about 250 B.C. and further in the 6th century A.D.; the New Testament from the 3rd and 4th centuries), the world was inferentially divided into two spheres, the Jews (Hebrews) and the rest of the world. The presumption was that the Jews were the chosen, the promised people because they issued from Jacob, renamed Israel ("contender with God") after he had

---

1. Mecca is the birthplace of Mohammed, the founder and prophet of Islam, dating from 622 A.D. Mecca draws some two million pilgrims to its shrine during April every year, more than 15 million annually. The Kaaba is for the religion its greatest focal point, in the great mosque El Haram. The 50-foot square Kaaba holds a black stone supposedly given to Abraham by the angel Gabriel to symbolize the founding of the shrine to Allah. Outside the cubic structure is a holy well, to have been used by Hagar, Abraham's wife's servant and the mother of Ishmael, founder of the Arab "tribe." Mecca is the spiritual home for over one-half billion Muslims. In prayer throughout the world, the faithful face in the direction of Mecca.

wrestled with the angel of the Lord (see Genesis 32:28). Jacob was the son of Isaac, the (second) son of Abraham, through his wife Sarah—*after Abraham had had a son, Ishmael, through Hagar, Sarah's servant.*

Abraham was the founder and first patriarch of the Hebrew people. He was chosen by God (Jehova) to establish a new nation. Leaving Ur (now in Iraq), Abraham and his wife and nephew (Lot) traveled to Canaan. Sarah was old and infertile. With Sarah's permission, Abraham begat a son with Hagar, Sarah's Egyptian servant. This first son in the new land was Ishmael.

After the birth of Ishmael, Sarah became fertile, supposedly at age 90. She gave birth to Abraham's son Isaac.

At this point, Hagar and Ishmael were sent off into the desert. An angel of the Lord protected them. Ishmael married and begat twelve sons, *from whom the Arab people trace their lineage.*

There is an interesting prediction in Genesis 16:12 that Ishmael "will be a wild man; his hand will be against every man, and every man's hand against him."

Meanwhile, back in Canaan, Abraham's faith was tested when Jehovah ordered him to sacrifice Isaac. An angel intervened at the last moment when Isaac was upon the stone. Canaan became the "promised land" because God then promised that the land indeed would belong to the descendants of Abraham, Isaac, and Isaac's son, Jacob (Genesis 12:7; 26:3; 28:13). Jacob, who was renamed Israel, as we have seen, also begat twelve sons, *who were the founders of the twelve tribes of Israel.*

This fascinating story from ancient times lives still in the present spirit of the Middle East, throughout the extraordinary tensions between Jews and Arabs, between Judaism and Islam. It is complicated and profound, and, in that scope, it is not too much of a leap of astrological inference to suggest that the Great Conjunction rising at Mecca indeed resurrects and reflects this grand issue about the identity of "the chosen." It could be seen that God's will would aggressively develop Arab dominance of the Middle East and, quite possibly, through strategies tied to oil, exert a major influence upon the rest of the world. There would be aggression from other nations—Moon, clearly, through the Mars square to the Moon, ruling the Midheaven, Mars ruling the VIIth House—and also "trouble at home," which we see through the very strong IVth House emphasis through very close Sun-Mercury squares to the conjunction, with

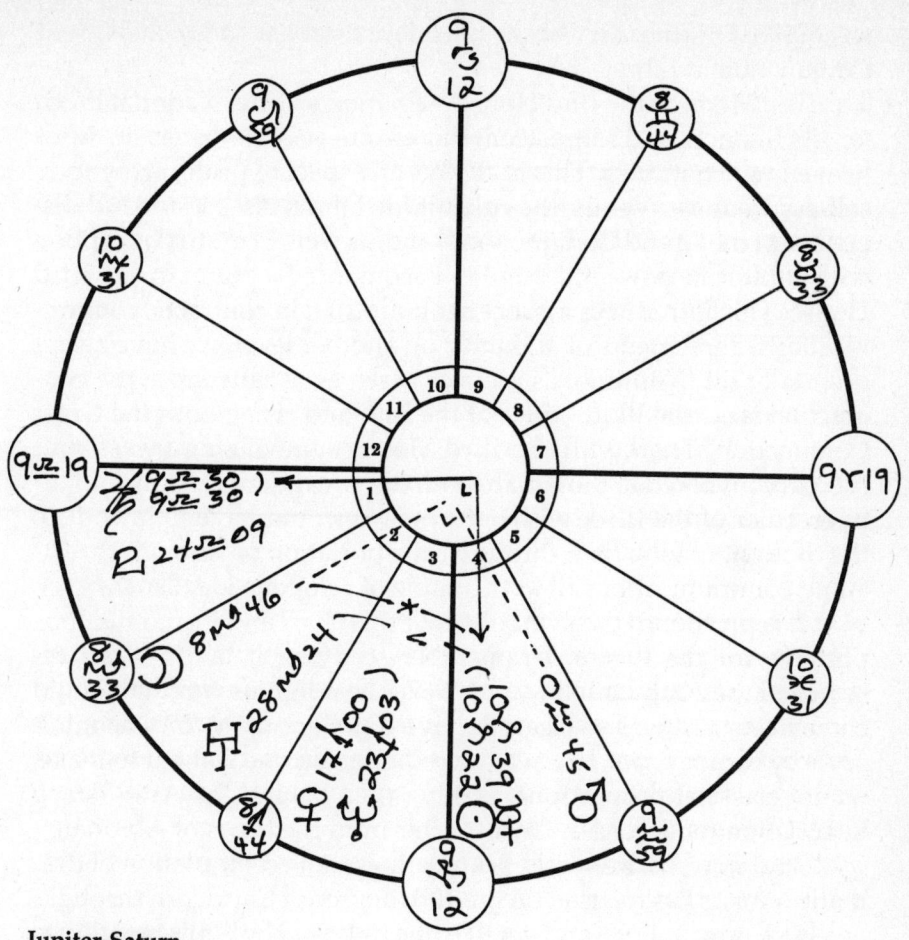

**Jupiter-Saturn
Great Conjunction
December 3, 1980
11:19 p.m. EET
Mecca, Saudi Arabia
39 E 49   21 N 26
Placidian Houses**

Saturn ruling the IVth. It is definitely an indication of an internecine struggle, Arabs warring with Arabs.

The Moon in the Grand Conjunction chart is in Scorpio (religious dogma; the Sign of prophecy) and is, as we have seen, squared by Mars. The VIIth, ruled by Mars, is the house of a nation's or people's relationships with other nations, of war and trade, of public reactions to the nation, and of public enemies. Mars in Aquarius re-emphasizes the Air Family purview established by the Grand Conjunction in Libra.

The Moon in the IInd House—a nation's Gross National Product, its finances and self-esteem therefrom—closely trines the Midheaven which it rules. This is always an aspect of pride, arrogance, self-assuredness. Venus, the ruler of the Libran Ascendant and dispositor of the Grand Conjunction—and, as well, in mutual reception with Jupiter (a powerful bond)—is conjunct Neptune in the IIIrd House. This introduces a concern about trust in contracts, communications, agreements of all kinds; on another level, we have a suggestion of oil (Neptune) as a major asset, especially since the conjunction is sextile Pluto, ruler of the IInd and rising with the Great Conjunction. Then with the IIIrd House symbolizing travel, and Mercury involved in the square with the Great Conjunction, and Jupiter, ruler of the IIIrd, with Saturn—we would have to introduce the thought of terrorism through transportation or through threatening communication, all in the name of religious idealism.

It is profound: the symbolism of this chart and its momentous portents for the future. I remember studying it in 1974 as I researched the Arab-Israeli war of 1967. The religious war that would come in earnest was so clear; the five-day flare-up in '67 was miniscule by comparison. This was a prediction no one wanted to make, one of classical proportions, lurking then behind the Arab-Israeli negotiation for accord—like a specter from the times of Abraham.

And now, as the world bears witness, an accumulation of dramatic transits has focused on the 10th degree of Capricorn throughout 1989, now in 1990, and yet to come in 1991. The Sun's position at 10 Capricorn in this Great Conjunction chart is square the Ascendant—and the Great Conjunction itself. This Sun tightly opposes the 12 Cancer Sun of the United States, and is in square to the U.S. Saturn at 14 Libra, ruling the U.S. IXth House. In January, 1991 (and thereafter in October/November), transiting Uranus conjoins the Great Conjunction Sun, opposes the United States Sun, and squares the all-powerful Great Conjunction itself. Again, war among Arabs is clearly indicated to begin with United States involvement.

The extraordinary transits through the first decanate of Capricorn have unleashed the most dramatic symbology of the Grand Conjunction chart and its incredible ties to the United States chart. Upon the passage of these conjunctions, the portents of peril have reached the apex of danger.

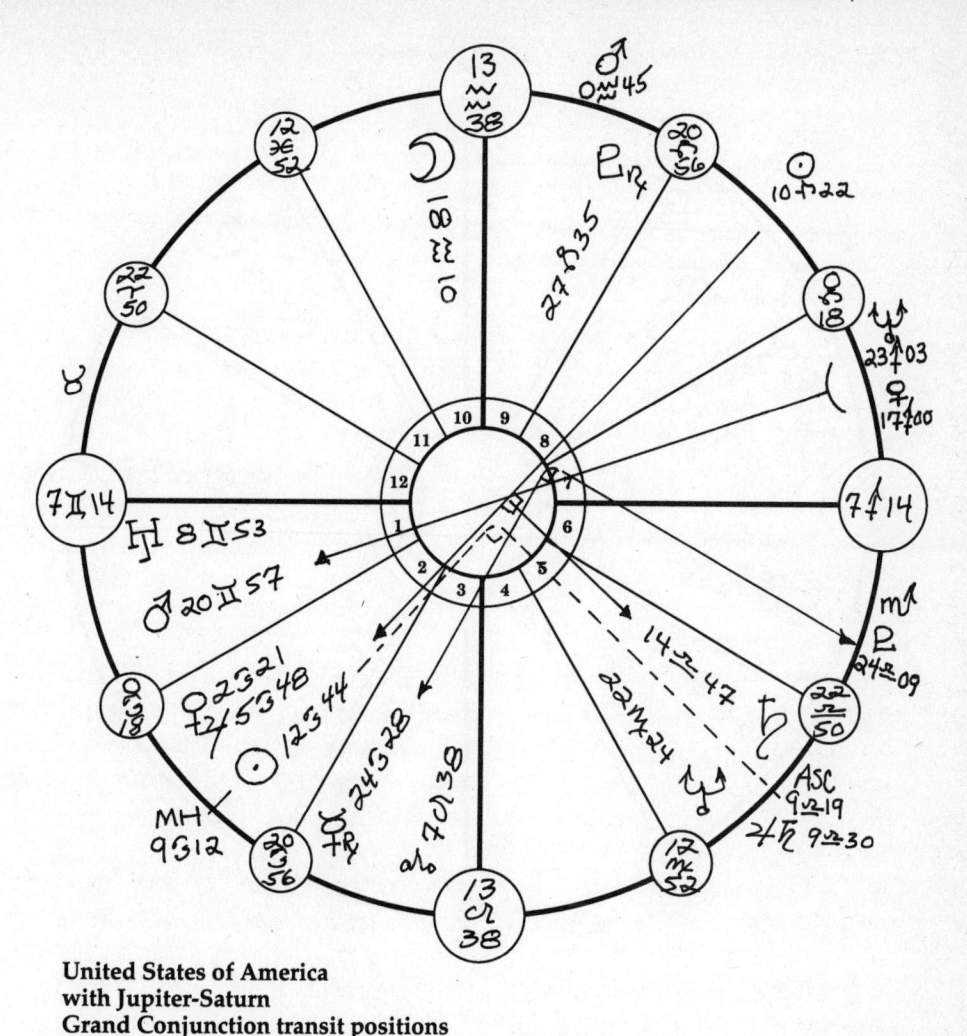

Predictions Down to Earth / 107

**United States of America
with Jupiter-Saturn
Grand Conjunction transit positions**

On August 23, 1921, Amir Faisal Ebin Husain ascended to the throne of Iraq, to become King of the territories put together mainly by the British and the French after World War I (and then given the stamp of approval by admission to the League of Nations on October 13, 1932.) The horoscope for the founding of the Kingdom of Iraq—the supposed site of the Garden of Eden, the historically rich desert given life by the Tigris and Euphrates, that land of Nebuchadnezzar and Hammurabi—in its modern identity has the Sun conjunct the Fixed Star Regulus (Epoch 1990: 29 Leo 41′ 24″) and, as well, a Great Conjunction of Jupiter and Saturn!

108 / *Prediction in Astrology*

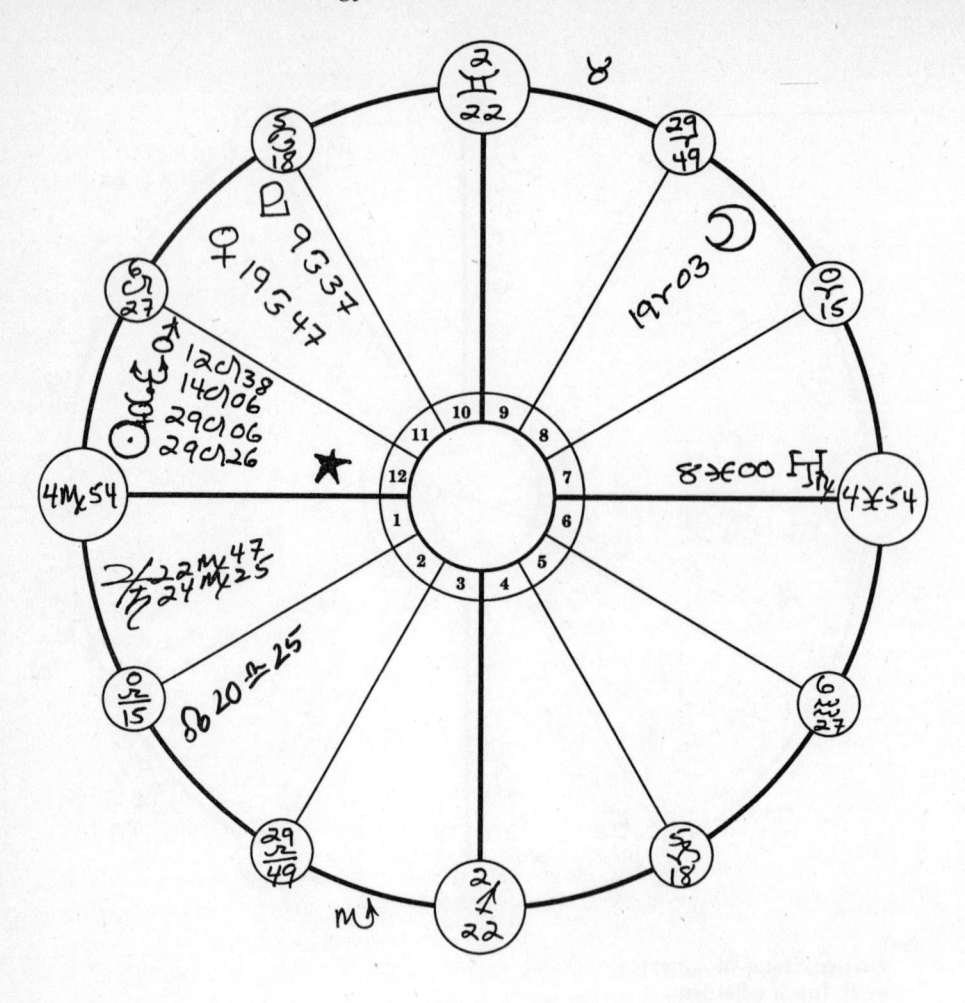

Kingdom of Iraq
August 23, 1921
6:00 a.m.
Baghdad, Iraq
44 E 25   33 N 20

Sunrise is very important to Islam, the symbolic renewal of life every day. Sunrise that day was 5:34 a.m. British civility prevailed for 6:00

An Associated Press news dispatch from Baghdad, reported in the August 24, 1921 edition of the New York Times, describes the formal recognition of the kingdom of Iraq the assumption of the throne by Faisal on August 23, 1921, 6 a.m. A great gathering was witness to the event, and Sir Percy Cox read the proclamation of the kingdom and brought personal best wishes from England's King George.

Predictions Down to Earth / 109

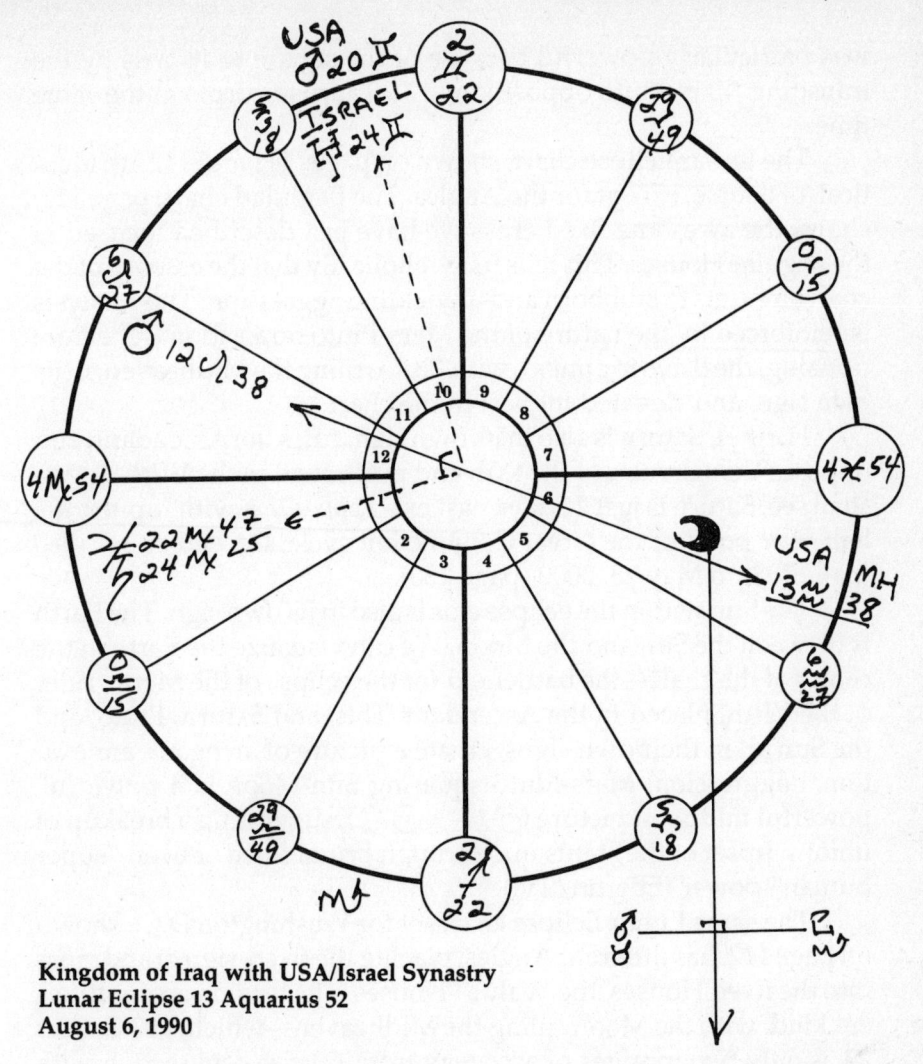

Kingdom of Iraq with USA/Israel Synastry
Lunar Eclipse 13 Aquarius 52
August 6, 1990

    The awesome outreach of this set of phenomena continues: the Iraqi Jupiter-Saturn conjunction closely squares the United States Mars in 20 Gemini and the Israeli Uranus in 24 Gemini! The Iraqi Mars is opposed by the United States Midheaven within one degree!
    On August 6, 1990, four days after Iraq invaded Kuwait to seize its oil fields, and one day before U.S. President George Bush ordered American military forces to Saudi Arabia to defend their oil fields, a powerful Lunar Eclipse took place at 13 Aquarius 52 on the opposition axis with the Mars of the Kingdom of Iraq and exactly conjoining the Midheaven axis of the United States. This Full Moon eclipse

was particularly powerful because of the square to its axis by the transiting Mars-Pluto opposition in 16 Taurus-Scorpio at the same time.

The Lunar Eclipse chart, shown on pages 111 and 112 are identical, of course, except for the Angles. The Baghdad chart, page 111, shows the awesome fixed cross we have just described focused in the angular Houses. This tells us symbolically that the essence of the chart amounts to stubborn and unyielding aggression. This analysis is reinforced by the nature of the Mars-Pluto opposition (rebellion; uprising; the drive to annex), with Pluto ruling the Midheaven, in its own sign, and elevated highest in the chart.

Further, Saturn is also in its own sign, rules the Ascendant, and opposes Venus, ruler of the IXth and positioned in the VIIth. As we shall see, Saturn is just 24 days past exact *opposition* with Jupiter, the half-way point of the Great Conjunction cycle, December 31, 1980 (page 105) to May 28, 2000 (page 130).

The Sun within the eclipse axis is also in its own sign. The Earth is between the Sun and the Moon. We can visualize the Earth in the center of the chart—the battlefield for the eclipse of the Moon, ruler of the VIIth, placed in the Ascendant. This, and Saturn, Pluto, and the Sun all in their own signs, create a picture of arrogant, annexational aggression. Mars-Pluto squaring Sun-Moon is a powerful, powerful midpoint picture ($\male / ♇ = \odot / ☽$), suggesting a breakup of unions, upset of the status quo through brutal force or even "super human" power (Ebertin/Tyl).

The same Lunar Eclipse chart set for Washington D.C., shown on page 112, has different Angles, placing the fixed-sign grand cross into the fixed Houses, the "value" Houses. The tension is of a different kind: with the Moon ruling the Midheaven—which, at 2 Cancer 22, is only two minutes of arc away from precise conjunction with the U.S. Venus at 2 Cancer 20—the eclipse takes on a threat to United States world position, to efforts for peace and values of security and status. The Aquarian Moon registers the humanitarian sense of the Air Family gradually trying to emerge in the Grand Mutation cycle. And, as we have seen, this eclipsed Aquarian Moon is precisely conjunct the U.S. Midheaven!

The analysis quickly starts to show the United States threatened by strife in foreign lands (Saturn opposed Venus, ruler of the Ascendant in D.C., placed in the Midheaven with Jupiter, and also ruling the IXth). Mars in its opposition with Pluto calls immediate

Predictions Down to Earth / 111

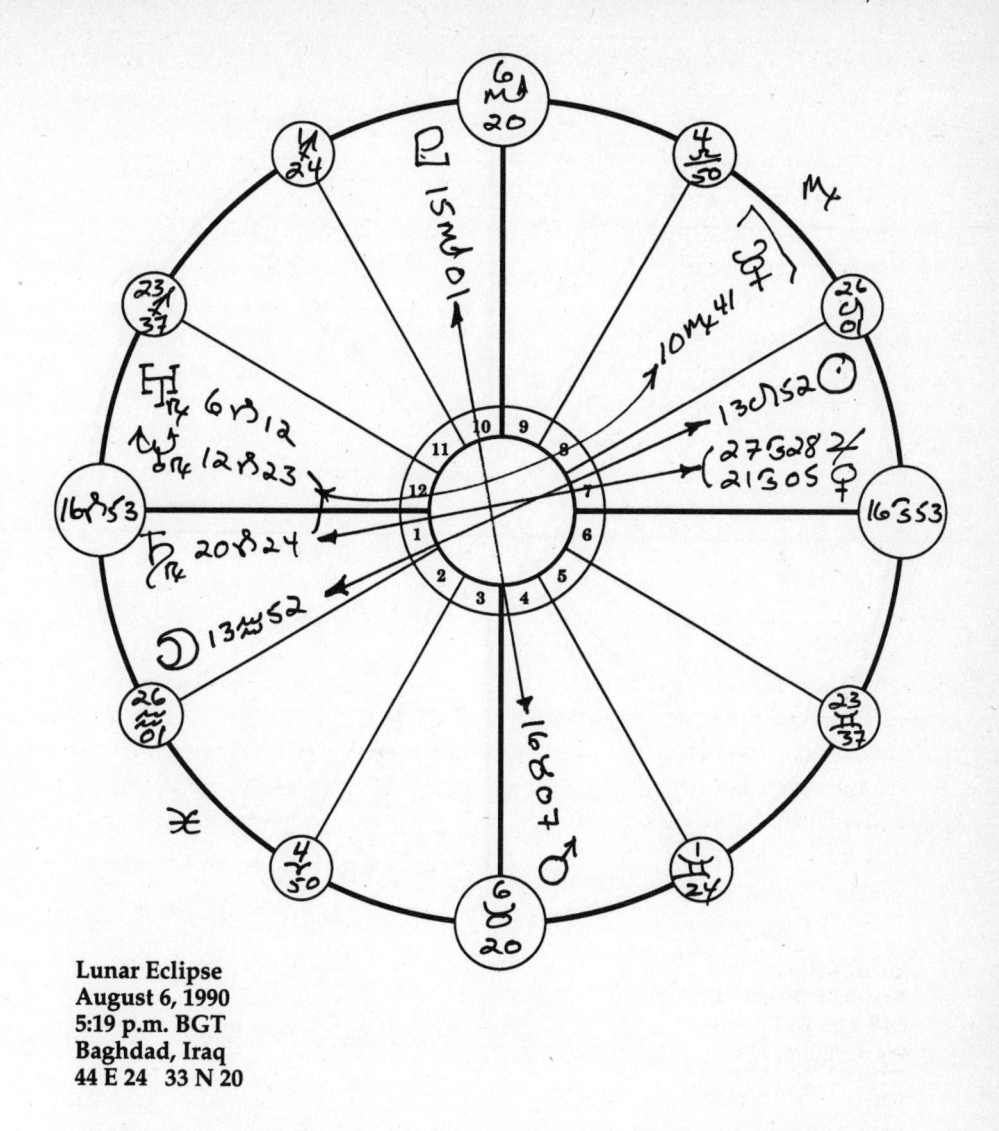

Lunar Eclipse
August 6, 1990
5:19 p.m. BGT
Baghdad, Iraq
44 E 24   33 N 20

attention to the VIIth House of "other nations" (as opposed to the IXth of "international trade and law" in Mundane symbolism) and to the VIIIth House where Mars is placed, where it also rules. The VIIIth represents other nations' resources, riches, and public loans.

All of this—which takes so many words to describe but can be seen and felt quickly with a command of symbolism and confidence of articulation that come from study and practice—shows extreme threat to the resources we rely on from other nations, to our

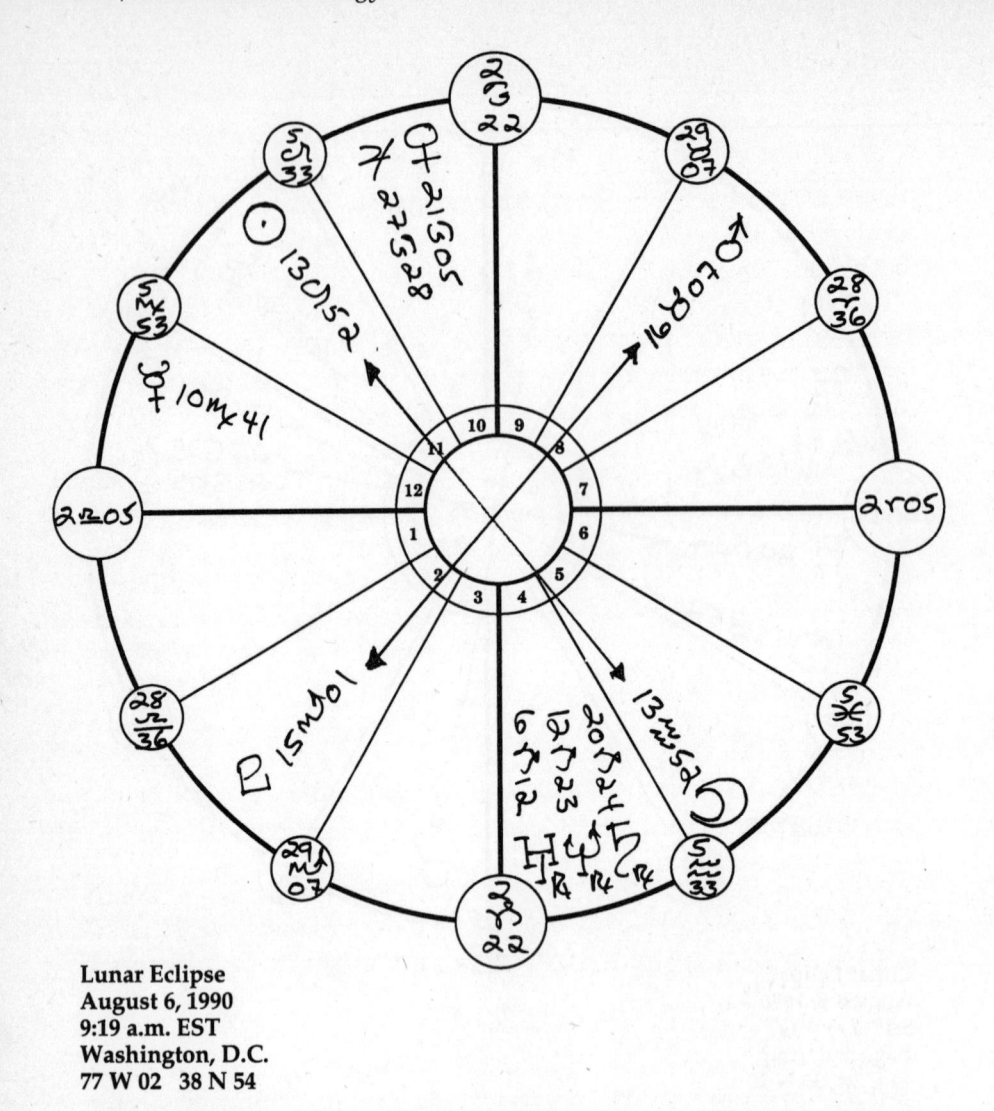

Lunar Eclipse
August 6, 1990
9:19 a.m. EST
Washington, D.C.
77 W 02   38 N 54

spectrum of values, material and philosophical. The Venus symbol in the Eclipse Chart is more prominently significant for the United States than it is for Iraq because of the conjunction between the eclipse chart Midheaven and the U.S. Venus, the elevation of the Venus-Jupiter conjunction in the Eclipse Chart Xth for the U.S., and the Venus rulership of the IXth, the Ascendant, and the IInd.

Finally, it is crucially important to see, at this moment in time when so many dimensions of astrology and reality are coming to-

Predictions Down to Earth / 113

gether phenomenologically, that one more detail spells the insidious terror of the situation: Neptune in the Eclipse Chart is exactly opposed the United States Sun—and in the D.C. IVth House, is conjunct Saturn and Uranus, all retrograde. We see clear suggestion of the trouble, anxiety, and indecisiveness on the home front about the declaration of war, especially from the political party not in power (opposed the party that is in power in the Xth) and the people.[2] There is a strong dimension of mistrust and secrecy about the entire operation to help Saudi Arabia protect its own values. There is also possible here corroboration of the fear of Iraq's use of chemical weapons (Neptune again), that is, the threat (Neptune-Saturn) to the people's "health," with Neptune ruling the VIth.

This Neptune at 12 Capricorn, seen from the Iraq Eclipse Chart (page 111) is rising. Neptune joins Saturn as the Iraqi identity within this entire upheaval: inscrutable, collusive, camouflaged, iron-principled infliction of tyrannical dogma. This Neptune also relates to the thrust for values (rather than the defense of them; or perhaps the rationalization of aggression in terms of identity values—restoring its lands and oil fields out of Kuwait) through its trine with Mercury in the VIIIth, ruled by the Sun, and by its own rulership of Pisces intercepted in the IInd.

We see final corroboration of the overall symbolism of this powerfully important Lunar Eclipse in the defensive reaction strategy that immediately followed the annexation of Kuwait and the rush to defend Saudi Arabia: international sanctions were gathered from the nations of much of the world to support a veritable blockade to deprive Iraq of life-sustaining supplies. What is an eclipse if not a blockade of light?

The extraordinary Grand Mutation Great Conjunction at the end of 1980 (page 105) clearly signalled an era of history that is now being played out, at times productively and at other times savagely. The social upheavals throughout the Soviet Union, Eastern Europe, and in Berlin are all extensions of this Grand Mutation symbolism. They have not all been peaceful. There is astrology to tie those events into the scheme of change as well, but, for our study here, I focus on the celestial phenomenon related to Mecca, which threatens to touch almost all the world.

---

2. The IV-X axis in the Iraq Eclipse Chart, page 111, holds Mars opposed Pluto, so clearly recording the rabid, fight-to-the-death demeanor of the Iraqi people and military during the seige of Kuwait and preparations for war.

The process of Mundane Astrology begins with ascertaining the birth data of nations, which is not an easy task. There are some source books that can help, but research of newspaper reports to back up history-book notations is the most reliable way to start. Checking with astrologers or their professional organizations in the nations at issue is also important. Gradual refinements can be made within a given day of political organization, based upon common sense, observation of history in great detail, and the testing of predictions—backward and forward in time—against current event records.

At the same time, celestial phenomena such as the Great Conjunction and, indeed, the very important conjunctions between Mars and Saturn which occur every two years or so, must be related to national capital cities on earth. *Where the conjunctions are found rising or overhead at the Midheaven tells us to expect with highest reliability events in keeping with the particular conjunction chart's symbolism, related to the chart data of the nation, including transits and Solar Arcs.*

When more than one nation or phenomenon is brought into consideration by the chart significators—as we have already seen to an almost incredible extent among Iraq, the United States, the Great Conjunction, and the Lunar Eclipse—we have to organize analysis carefully and orderly around dominating measurements. This is perhaps where the science part of astrology ends and the art part begins. And the key to interpretation, as we are seeing time and time again in this book, is the *classical* interpretations of the symbols, the planets and the signs, brought down to earth.

In Mundane Astrology, we are not dealing with the psychodynamic nuances of an individual's personality, for which our astrology also has great symbolic facility; rather, we are addressing a massing of millions of individuals within a structured state organization known to the world as it was known to Ptolemy: by the temperaments and actions of the people and the development of national history, the "stuff" that creates the nation's horoscope.

We must assimilate the brutal facts of life as well as the graceful ones, the bad and the good from one perspective or another, knowing *that all are somehow necessary*. It is neither nihilistic nor defeatist nor negative to recognize that time is inexorable and that life is difficult. These are wisdoms that help us to learn and to define more clearly what we do know and what we don't.

Three more considerations within our mundane overview of the Middle East Crisis will illustrate analytical procedures further to support understanding of the past and anticipation of the future, not just to next month or next year, but to a decade and beyond into the next century, the next millennium.

First, it is clear throughout the astrological record presented in this chapter that we are dealing with the phenomenological concentration of astrological symbolism in Capricorn, around the degree areas 0-1, 8-12, and 23-28. These areas relate with very strong dynamic tension to the same areas in the other cardinal signs by squares with Libra and Aries and by opposition with Cancer. *The Cardinality promises strong action*, a catalytic leadership of historical development.

When did this "entrance of the mighty lords into Capricorn" take place? In Mundane astrology, such an entrance is called an ingress. And the one shown on page 116 for the triple conjunction of Mars, Saturn, and Uranus in 00 Capricorn, with Neptune at 9 Capricorn, can take one's breath away. It occurred exactly on the Midheaven over Washington D.C.[3]

I studied this triple conjunction in the Spring of 1976 when I was preparing my *Teaching and Study Guide to the Principles and Practice of Astrology*. My notes were concise: "Pres., sudden war plans; pressure; defensive; but we initiate?"

I put the chart away and did not see it again for 13 years. But now, I see those remarks emerging within the harrowing reality of the Middle East crisis.

The analysis, the prediction, is clear as can be:

- Our nation, the president, the party in power (Xth House) would soon be faced with (the triple Conjunction squaring the Ascendant) sudden pressures of conflict (Uranus, Saturn, and Mars). There will have been and perhaps continue to be collusion, deception, something secret, some other dimension involved (Neptune). This latter insight is now clarified when we see that the triple conjunction chart's Neptune is exactly square the Ascendant, Jupiter, and Saturn of the

---

3. In researching conjunctions and relating them to earth geography, it is practical to create a chart for London at the time of aspect partile (see astrological calendars and aspectarians). Then, *count the number of degrees East or West* to adjust the key planets to conjoin the Midheaven or Ascendant in London. This gets the astrologer into the right world zone. For this triple conjunction at London, the key planets were in the VIth House, 77° from the Midheaven, i.e., West of the London Midheaven; at the Midheaven at 77W02, Washington D.C.

116 / Prediction in Astrology

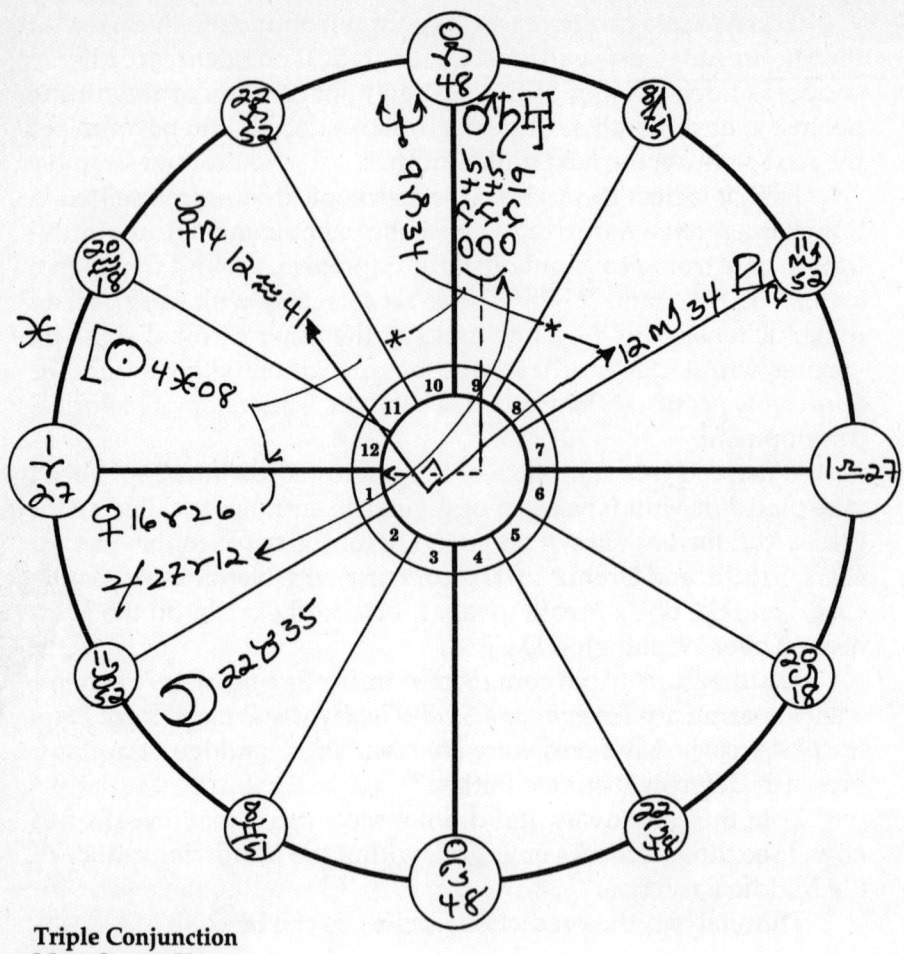

**Triple Conjunction
Mars-Saturn-Uranus
February 23, 1988
8:01 a.m. EST
Washington, D.C.
77 W 02   38 N 54**

Great Conjunction chart at Mecca (page 105). We have the symbolization of oil concerns and the rationale of religious zeal throughout the Arab world. How many times do we hear reference to *jihad*, to Holy War?

- I felt the conflict would be defensive: Aries rising, and its ruler, Mars, the "lord of attack," while squaring the Ascendant, *refers back to "his own domain"*—as opposed to coming from relationships with the VIIth, for example. At the same time, the organization of the horoscope is *protecting* the Ascendant, especially the sweeping trine of Jupiter in Aries (over-the-sign-line into Taurus to make the trine) from the Ascendant to the triple Conjunction, with Jupiter ruling the IXth (the support of other nations); and the supportive sextile between the Sun and the triple Conjunction.

- The exact Mercury-Pluto square is a classic symbolization of more than one concern because of the retrogradation of both planets: something "other than what appears" will be going on. This is especially valid because Pluto receives a supportive sextile from Neptune (Neptune's only aspect), because this Mercury is almost exactly conjunct the Midheaven of the United States chart (page 72).

- A confounding detail is that the Moon in the Triple Conjunction chart is void-of-course (classically void-of-course, although interestingly it does form a sesquiquadrate aspect with Neptune). Ordinarily, we can expect a void-of-course Moon to be ineffectual. In Mundane Astrology, void-of-course may symbolize a period of waiting, waiting for a means of expression for the implied symbology.

Here in Taurus, there is definitely the need for structure, *for resisting change*, for keeping things the way they were/are. In this awesome horoscope, it is clear that these tendencies are linked to national resources (the IInd House) on the home front (Moon ruling the IVth). For the United States, our point of perception for this triple Conjunction chart, the focus through this Moon is *protecting what we have*.

The Moon is waiting for a structured cause. Could that be the clue to our *defensive* reactions up to the brink of war and beyond? It is a sensitive position here: on August 16, 1990, ten days after the crucial Lunar Eclipse (chart, page 112), transiting Mars conjoined this Moon Triple Conjunction Chart position at 22 Taurus 35. This was the day of "attack," when Iraq announced its hostage-human shield plan and enraged the United States and much of the world. Transiting Pluto will oppose this very sensitive 23rd degree axis of Taurus-Scorpio in December, 1992, from Scorpio. Does this portend an extension of present conflict or the resurrection of it?

Or is it aggression about our internationalism here at home, with the Moon ruling the IVth?

The second consideration to round out our study here involves the half-way point of the momentous Jupiter-Saturn cycle between 1980 and 2000: the time when these symbols will be in opposition, just as Full Moon (opposition) supplements the symbology of the lunation cycle seeded at New Moon (conjunction).

Again, the chart (page 119) is crucially corroborative; we gather even more detail and confidence for the sense of the future. The exact opposition occurred on July 13, 1990, just 20 days before the Iraqi invasion of Kuwait, on the axis of 22 Cancer-Capricorn 07. The mundane astrologer, with all the charts organized by key positions, quickly sees these startling corroborative measurements:

- Jupiter and the Sun are conjunct the key 21 Cancer Venus position in the vitally important lunar eclipse chart (page 112); Saturn opposes it. Settlement is crushed. Peace is trampled. Acquisition is commanded.

- Uranus and Neptune are opposing the United States Sun. Indecision. Shock and doubt. Holding back to explode suddenly.

- The Jupiter-Saturn axis conjoins the very sensitive United States Mercury-Pluto axis, with Mercury ruling the United States Ascendant and the axis anchored by Pluto in the international IXth. The United States has entered the grand imbroglio for *generations to come*. The Mideast struggle has become a part of United States identity for a long, long time into the future.

- The Sun/Jupiter-Saturn axis is conjunct the Venus in Cancer in the Iraq chart (page 109): this is the extraordinary justification and rationale offered by Iraq for its own actions.

- And, of course, just as we would anticipate (and anticipation becomes a key to all prediction), there are tie-ins between this half-way (opposition) chart and the formative initial Great Conjunction chart (page 105). It is literally as if the opposition chart (actually a chart of transits) triggered the conjunction chart to explosion:

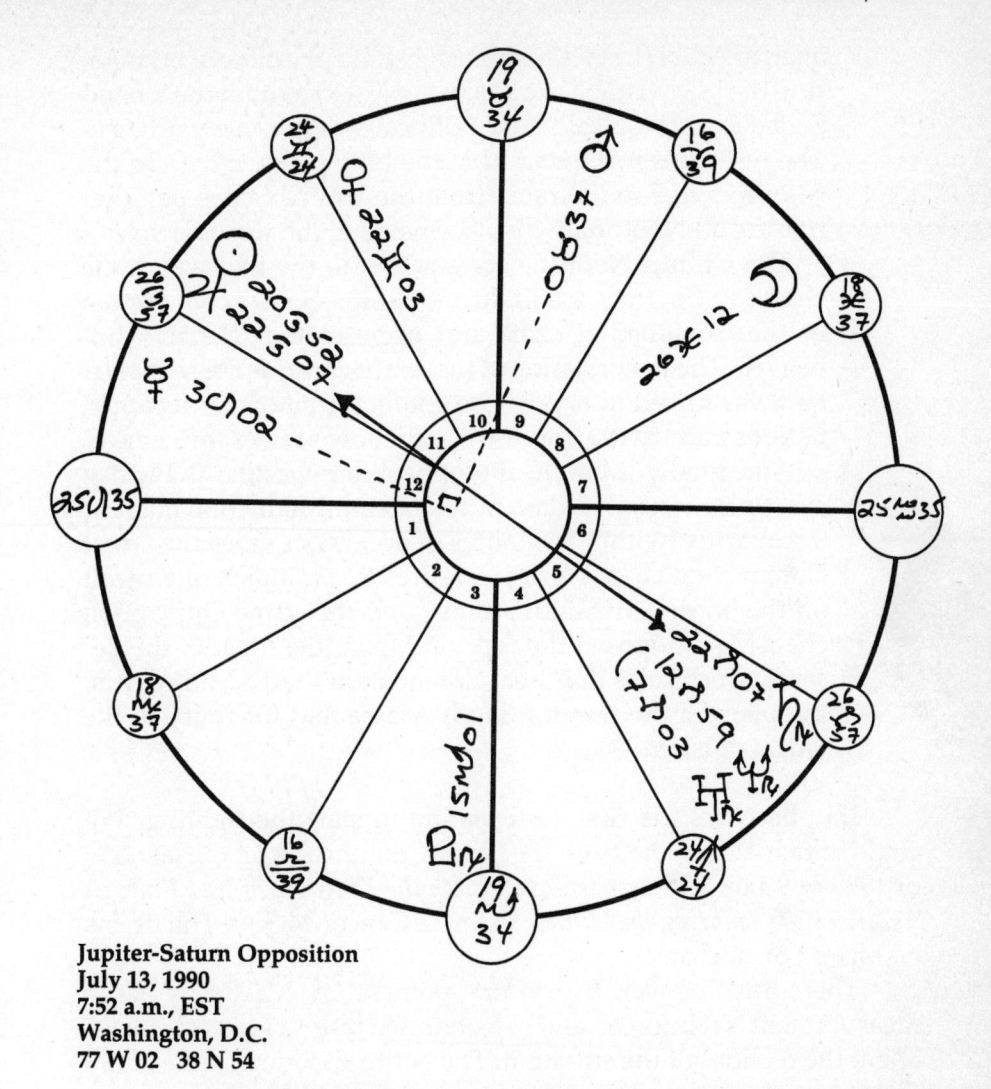

Jupiter-Saturn Opposition
July 13, 1990
7:52 a.m., EST
Washington, D.C.
77 W 02   38 N 54

The Opposition axis squares the Great Conjunction chart's Pluto, ruler of that chart's IInd House, *the resources in Saudi Arabia*, really in the Arab world as presided over by Islam; in Mecca, in the oil fields. (Remember, we continuously see the oxymoron "holy war" as land and oil fields annexed for resources to isolate, squeeze out, and defeat non-Arabs—specifically the Jews, the people of Israel—*all in the name of religious vindication as "the promised people."*

The IVth House tensions in the Great Conjunction chart (page 105) should never leave our attention: Arabs fighting against Arabs, but with the background objective of eliminating the Jews (Israeli expansionism), with whom the United States is astrologically and politically very closely aligned. The resources in Kuwait from the Iraqi perspective and the resources in Saudi Arabia from the United States perspective are all Neptunian displacements of the *real* objectives.

The Uranus-Neptune conjunction in the half-way cycle chart squares the Ascendant and Jupiter-Saturn conjunction in the Conjunction chart and opposes that chart's Midheaven. The major nation of the Arab world, as the seat of Islam, was forced to expose the conflict from one of its allied nations and try to suppress it somehow at the same time.

And finally, Mars in the opposition chart, at 0 Taurus, exactly squares the Mars in the Great Conjunction chart at 0 Aquarius (within 8 minutes of arc). Mars rules the Great Conjunction chart's VIIth; it represent *the* attack of Kuwait on the borders of Saudi Arabia; and this same Opposition chart Mars opposed the Scorpio Moon (the viper of the desert), which rules the Great Conjunction chart's Midheaven, the place in the Sun for Saudi Arabia and for unity in the world of Islam.

Iraq becomes the first Arab nation to start the fighting. We could anticipate that because the Great Conjunction on the last day of 1980 in 9 Libra 30 was *in square with the Kingdom of Iraq Pluto* at 9 Cancer 37, *squaring the United States* 12 Cancer 44 Sun. The tie-ins go on and on and on.

There must be war. Everything points to it; practically every measurement is reinforced and corroborated by every news bulletin about the realities of the situation. The entire situation is celestially phenomenological and mundanely phenomenological; the above and below enmesh. The punctuation by the Lunar Eclipse is more than dramatic; it is fateful. The rationales are difficult to understand and the objectives are confused within the symbolisms of Neptune and the politics of internecine carping and fighting for Arab world leadership. At the end of the chains of analyses, Mars emerges dominant.

There *must* be war. And this war will be on-going in different ways; nor will it be the last one in the Middle East within this decade.

Our third measurement, in conclusion, involves review of the Solar Arc backdrop of the nations involved. While Solar Arcs are often very telling in accurately timed personal horoscopes, there is always a difficulty in Mundane Astrology since the timing of a national chart is usually general or unsure, and a discrepancy of four minutes of time (one degree on the Midheaven) equates to *one year* of error in Solar Arc timing with regard to the Angles.[4] The problem does not manifest so boldly with the planets because their motion in a short passage of real time—four minutes or one hour, say—is not appreciably significant to upset Solar Arc measurement.

For the United States, the dominant Solar Arc measurement late in 1990 at the onset of Iraqi aggression is SA Pluto semi-square Saturn, exact late in July 1990. As we have seen in the last chapter, Solar Arc contacts between Saturn and Pluto appear to register severely as situational demand and incipient loss.

SA Pluto=Saturn suggests enormous struggle, the application of megaforce, the threat of great upset. In the United States chart (see page 122), Pluto rules Scorpio in the VIth which, in Mundane Astrology, rules the armed forces of a nation. The symbolism of that House includes the Civil Service, the police, laborers, unions and labor organizations, etc. The armed forces are the primary reference.

The arcing planet in the Solar Arc picture, then, introduces the military. Pluto has come from the IXth House in the national horoscope—internationalism.

Additionally, the U.S. Saturn is ruler of the IXth and, in 14 Libra, opposes the Aries Moon of the Kingdom of Iraq. Saturn is in the Vth House which represents diplomatic ministers, ambassadors, the Senate; all the people and groups that project the national identity. (The Vth House is naturally always trine to the Ascendant; and trine to the IXth; with the IXth, the symbolism becomes international diplomacy.)

This powerful measurement is corroborated by the enormous activation of the Armed Forces, sending them to a foreign land, exploiting all diplomatic channels possible at home and throughout the world to try to achieve peace (Saturn in Libra), to right a wrong,

---

4. The Kingdom of Iraq horoscope (page 108) is dated and checked from historical records and news reports; but, since the 6 a.m. time appears generalized, the Angles can not be relied upon in analysis without caution. The United States horoscope (page 72; see note) has proved itself once again in this presentation. No organization information is available for Kuwait—the actual issue made by Iraq!—whose borders were defined also in 1921 by the British and French after World War I, but leadership has continued unchanged from "about 1756" when the Sabah family began its direction of the Emirate.

122 / *Prediction in Astrology*

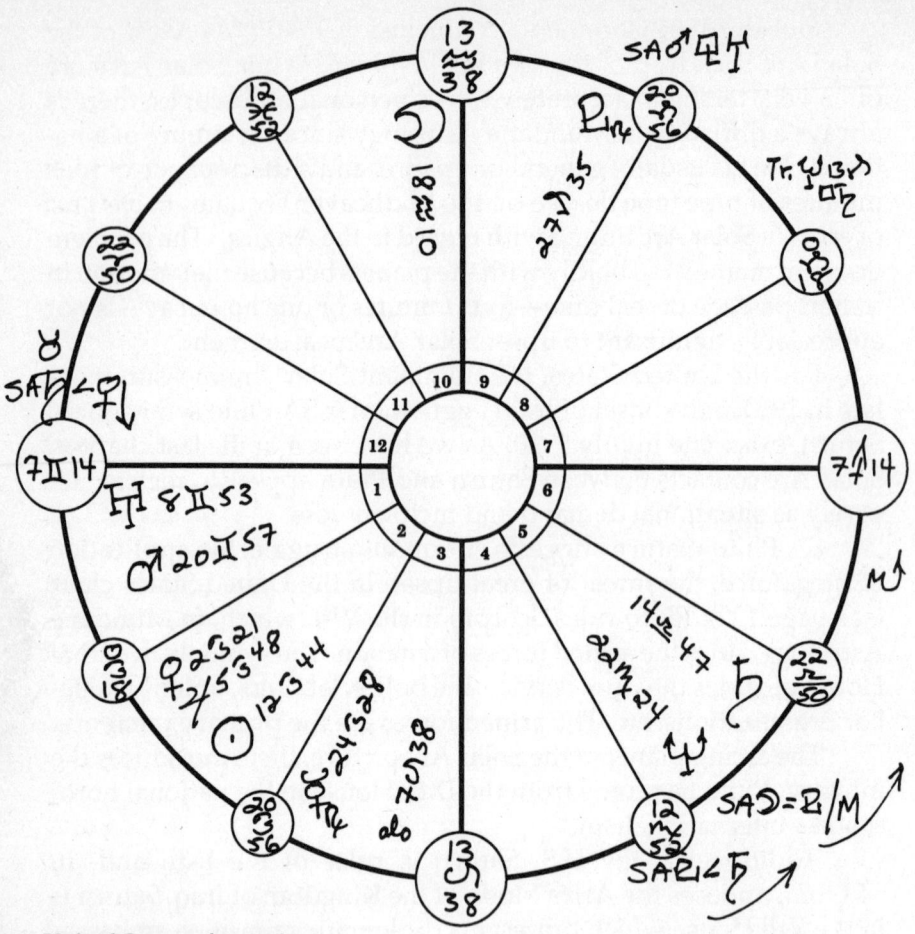

**United States of America
with Key Solar Arc Positions
in late 1990**

and to preserve the status quo. With the United States Saturn natally square to the Sun, the pressure of the times now (the Great Conjunction; the Triple Conjunction; the Lunar Eclipse; the Opposition) forces the United States to save face, to prove rightness, to transcend difficult at all costs, to ward off the threat of extreme loss, and emerge the winner in war or diplomacy, all in the name of humanitarianism (U.S. Moon in Aquarius) and honoring international treaties (again the symbolism of Saturn in Libra disposited by Venus in conjunction with Jupiter). This is not the first time the United States has put on the save-the-world-from-others mantel.

United States of America		
Date	Aspect	
JUN 03, 1990	♃ ☌	☽/♇
JUN 05, 1990	☋ ∠	♃/MC
JUN 15, 1990	♂ ⚼	♅/AS
JUL 21, 1990	♇ ∠	♄
AUG 25, 1990	♆ ☌	♃/MC
SEP 17, 1990	♅ □	♅/MC
SEP 21, 1990	♇ ⚼	♀/♇
OCT 04, 1990	MC ∠	☿/☋
OCT 12, 1990	☽ ⚼	♇/MC
	♇ ☌	♆/☋
OCT 14, 1990	♀ ⚼	♀/AS
OCT 16, 1990	☽ □	♀/♅
NOV 20, 1990	☋ ⚼	☉/☋
NOV 22, 1990	♄ ∠	♀
NOV 23, 1990	♇ ∠	☿/♃
DEC 15, 1990	♄ ∠	♇/AS
DEC 17, 1990	☋ ∠	☽/♀
FEB 04, 1991	AS ∠	♆/♇
FEB 10, 1991	♆ □	☉/☋
FEB 11, 1991	♄ □	☉/♆
FEB 14, 1991	☽ □	♂
MAR 06, 1991	MC □	☽/♄
MAR 08, 1991	♆ ☌	☽/♀
APR 10, 1991	♂ ⚼	♅
MAY 23, 1991	AS ⚼	♃/♄
MAY 31, 1991	♄ □	♂/♄
JUN 15, 1991	☉ ⚼	☿/AS
JUN 26, 1991	☽ ⚼	☽/☿
JUL 02, 1991	☉ ☌	☽/MC
JUL 13, 1991	AS □	MC/AS
JUL 23, 1991	☿ ∠	☽/AS
AUG 03, 1991	☿ ⚼	☉
AUG 04, 1991	♀ ☌	♇/MC
AUG 09, 1991	♀ ⚼	♀/♅
SEP 04, 1991	☽ □	♇/AS
SEP 15, 1991	♄ □	☽/♇
SEP 21, 1991	☋ ∠	☿/♇
OCT 10, 1991	♄ ∠	♅/♇
NOV 03, 1991	☽ ∠	♂/♆
NOV 06, 1991	♂ ☍	☿
NOV 26, 1991	☋ ☍	♄/☋
DEC 07, 1991	♀ ⚼	♂
DEC 11, 1991	♆ ☌	☿/♇

This SA Pluto=Saturn arc dominates the times in the middle of 1990 and for some months beyond.

In October 1990, the Solar Arc midpoint picture formed in the United States chart putting the Moon sesquiquadrate the midpoint of Pluto/Midheaven (SA ☽=♇/MC): SA Moon, coming from its natal Midheaven position, makes a tension aspect to the synthesis of Pluto and the Midheaven, falling in the IXth House. This midpoint picture suggests tremendous potential change of international positioning and a threat of using power.

In November, 1990, SA Saturn semi-squared the natal Venus (SA♄=♀). Saturn, the arcing planet, rules the U.S. IXth and is in tension with Venus in the IInd House (international drain on national funds) ruler of the VIth (the Armed Forces again) and of the XIIth (Taurus intercepted), along with Mars. This is a suggestion of foreign enemies domestically and internationally; also of the armies of other nations (the sixth of the VIIth). It also shows the diplomatic pursuit of peace and its suppression, recalling the Saturn of the Opposition chart opposing the Venus in the Lunar Eclipse chart (see page 112).

As we have seen, time and time again, the transits do corroborate the Solar Arc suggestions: in November, transiting Neptune is closing on exact square to the U.S. natal Saturn. The square will be precise on January 18, 1991—three days after the United Nations deadline for Iraq's departure from Kuwait, after the total Solar Eclipse in the 26th degree of Capricorn conjunct the U.S. Pluto in the IXth House.

Transiting Uranus opposes the United States Sun from February through June, 1991, and transiting Mars conjoins the United States Ascendant at 7 Gemini 14 during February 12-16, 1991. This time in February will see an escalation of the war that itself will have taken place January 16, 17, or 18; in February we can expect a change of tactics in response to an Iraqi initiative.

Early in 1991, in April (but casting a Time Orb throughout the preceding months), the United States will have Solar Arc Mars= Uranus (see table, page 123), a measurement of further extreme, rash, explosive actions. With Mars ruling the XIIth in the U.S. chart, there is a suggestion of a heavy attack; natal Uranus is at the U.S. Ascendant. For the world of Islam, this time in April is extremely critical; it is the holiest of times, Ramadan, with some 2,000,000 pilgrims to arrive in Mecca. Will they come regardless of the war, willing to risk being martyred to Allah? Will they become human, practically "untouchable"shields, and bring religion back into the war? Will the Arab countries within the coalition begin to feel sympathy for Hussein, with what they perceive as the over-killing of all of Iraq in an ageless Arab land? Will there be a stand-off to the utter frustration of the United States? (SA ♂=♅ with transiting Mars conjunct its own natal position in the U.S. chart.)

A strategic ploy early in the conflict, especially with this most holy time of Ramadan approaching, could very well be for Iraq to direct retaliatory force, not onto Arab soil to the combined forces from many nations that will be assembled there, but *to Israel as a dramatic political diversion*. (The astrology of Israel's involvement follows soon in this chapter.)

There are many more Solar Arc measurements in effect, but the ones listed here make the point for our discussion of the construction of prediction and the techniques of measurement and analysis.[5]

For Iraq, while the date and time are correct, the time has not been finely tuned. Six o'clock is general, and within general clock times we have to be wary of our measurements involving the Angles, as we already discussed. We have to be watchful for suggested adjustments of those Angles—adjustments of the time in the process of analysis to help with eventual rectification of the horoscope for greater measurement security in the future.

But, uncannily, several major Solar Arc measurements involving an Angle present themselves to dominate the closing of 1990. Our testing of the horoscope comes at a most critical time.

SA Saturn may have opposed the Midheaven in November, 1990, but it certainly casts its Time Orb over several months (say, 15' minutes of arc, which is three months of calendar time and one minute of clock time in the founding of the nation) back into the past, certainly to August, 1990. This measurement represents enormous struggle, fighting against enormous odds, tremendous exertion, and the adamant assertion of iron-clad dogma to establish one's public position. (See table printout, page 127.)

As the arcing planet, Saturn comes out of the powerful Jupiter-Saturn conjunction in the Ascendant, ruling the Vth, which brings to the foreground ambassadors, diplomacy and government speculation. This was the time of Iraq's world propaganda mission to rationalize its seizure of Kuwait.

At the same time, we see SA Sun=Pluto/ASC: a ruthless maneuver for national projection.

And still two more: SA Jupiter=Sun/Midheaven is exact around the turn of the year, suggesting an attainment of objectives, a smugness, a confidence; then SA Mercury=Pluto/ASC—the Sun and Mercury are in conjunction in the Kingdom of Iraq horoscope, and the Pluto/ASC midpoint is strongly emphasized: here is the urge for the national point of view (Mercury) to dominate and be projected to the world. The symbolism of Pluto tied with the Ascendant or Midheaven always registers the potential for prominent or exposed self-assertion, a kind of exhibitionism. The role of Mercury is crucial because it rules the Ascendant and the Midheaven, no

---

5. In transits, especially with the slower moving planets, one should not "wait for" exactness. Traditionally, a 1° orb usually is telling. See Van Norstrand, who suggests, "The greatest force of any aspect or position is exerted when it is one degree or less of being perfect, the reason for this is that its resistance is reduced." (page 71). This observation suggests through all the measurements we have made that the United States attack will come sooner than later after the deadline.

126 / Prediction in Astrology

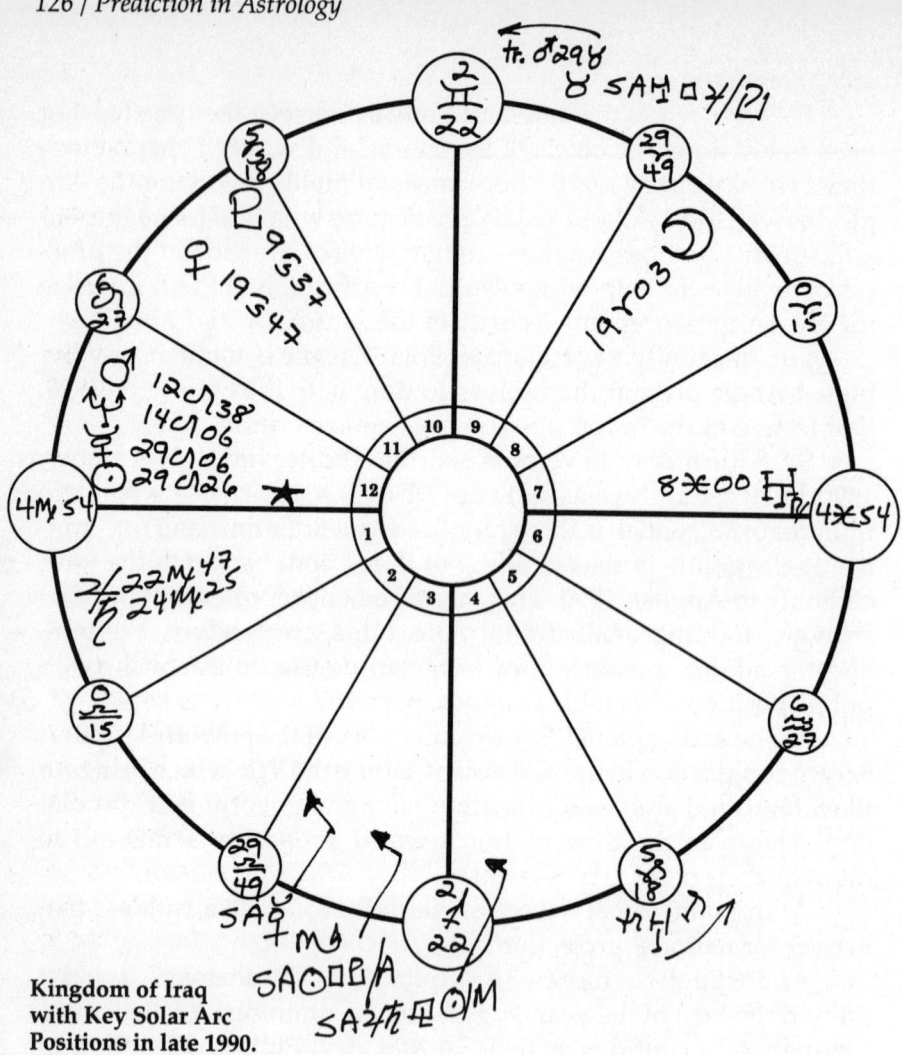

Kingdom of Iraq with Key Solar Arc Positions in late 1990.

matter what specific time the kingdom was "born" that morning in August, 1921.

There is only one power Solar Arc picture created for January and February, 1991 that does not involve an Angle: SA Uranus=Jupiter/Pluto. This suggests a sudden uprising, a fanaticism, an explosion. It is rockets, even the concern about nuclear energy. The picture is exact in February for the 6 a.m. birth time, but surely casts its Time Orb back into January.

Kingdom of Iraq Date		Aspect	
JUN 13, 1990	♂	☍	♅/MC
JUN 20, 1990	♂	∠	♀/☊
JUN 21, 1990	♀	∠	♀/AS
JUL 01, 1990	♄	☐	☿/AS
JUL 26, 1990	MC	∠	☉/☊
AUG 23, 1990	♇	☌	♆/☊
AUG 25, 1990	AS	☐	♂
AUG 29, 1990	♄	☐	☉/AS
SEP 05, 1990	☊	⚼	♂/♆
SEP 30, 1990	☉	☐	♇/AS
OCT 05, 1990	AS	∠	☊/AS
OCT 07, 1990	♀	∠	♂
NOV 01, 1990	☽	☌	☽/AS
NOV 02, 1990	☊	☐	☽/♅
NOV 08, 1990	♄	☍	MC
NOV 11, 1990	♃	⚼	☿/MC
NOV 15, 1990	♂	☌	☊
NOV 17, 1990	♀	☌	☊/AS
JAN 09, 1991	♃	⚼	☉/MC
JAN 27, 1991	☿	☐	♇/AS
FEB 12, 1991	♅	☐	♃/♇
MAR 14, 1991	☽	∠	♀/AS
MAR 15, 1991	☊	⚼	♀/♅
MAR 16, 1991	♄	☐	♂/♃
APR 06, 1991	MC	☐	☽/MC
APR 08, 1991	☉	∠	♃
MAY 18, 1991	AS	☐	♂/♆
MAY 28, 1991	☊	⚼	♆
JUN 29, 1991	♀	∠	♂/♆
JUN 30, 1991	☽	∠	♂
JUL 14, 1991	AS	⚼	☽/♅
AUG 05, 1991	☿	∠	♃
AUG 10, 1991	☽	☐	☊/AS
	☊	☌	♅/☊
AUG 17, 1991	MC	∠	♀/MC
AUG 26, 1991	♀	☍	☽/♅
SEP 20, 1991	♂	⚼	♅/AS
OCT 24, 1991	♆	⚼	♅
NOV 24, 1991	AS	☍	♀/♅
DEC 06, 1991	♄	☐	♃/♆
DEC 08, 1991	♅	☐	♄/♇

Corroborating transits are extraordinary: transiting Uranus opposes the Iraq Pluto—tremendous, wrenching upheaval at the turn of the year to come, 1990-1991; transiting Mars will be at 29 Taurus, exactly square the Iraq Sun-Mercury conjunction (and Regulus) at 29 Leo for five days in January, 1991: *January 13 through 18*. There can be no more arrogant stance possible.

The power eclipse we have discussed occurring on the ultimatum day, January 15, 1991, *trines* the kingdom of Iraq chart's Jupiter-Saturn conjunction—again a suggestion of enormous confidence and spiritual conviction: almost as if the whole world political machinery were playing into the hands of the Iraqi vision of ascendancy! The eclipse will be in close orb with a semi-square to the Iraq Uranus in the VIIth, the House that represents the enemy, the United States (really, the supposed expansionist policies of Israel), and ruling the VIth, Iraq's own army.

The United States will make the attack shortly after the United Nations deadline. One day or two days; three at most.

In March/April, the powerfully important month for Islam, for Saudi Arabia, the land of Mecca, and for the United

States with its Solar Arc Mars in contact with Uranus (see page 124), Iraq will have *SA Sun=Jupiter* (semisquare). This Iraq arc is a very benefic measurement. It is success; curiously, it is the fulfillment of objectives; it is perhaps peace in some terms that help the country save its pride among all other Arab countries and re-enter the Arab world. That will be the effort. This will be a tremendous frustration to the United States (SA Mars=Uranus). And always present: Israel, whose 23 Taurus Sun is squared by its 28 Leo Mars (conjunct the Iraq Sun!).

These predictions have been easy to see but difficult to make. This is usually the case with projections into the future, which, no matter how small, always make us feel awkward, as if we have transgressed somehow into a place beyond our normal limits. I have presented here the means of measurement, the measurements themselves, and the deductions possible from them. You have made the predictions with me.[6]

Going further into the future, we must complete our study within the history-changing cycle of Jupiter-Saturn conjunctions beginning in the Earth Family of Signs at 5:21 a.m., GMT on January 26, 1842. The past supports our future projection to 2000, the next Jupiter-Saturn Great Conjunction. In the process, we will be able to predict further, perhaps as a keynote for the next millennium, the eternal clash of Israel and the Arab world—as the Bible established it: the Hebrews and all other peoples.

The chart on page 129 is cast for the Grand Mutation of the Jupiter-Saturn Great Conjunction into the Earth Family of Signs, January 26, 1842. It is easy to see the beginning not only of the pressure focus in the early degrees of Capricorn (in opposition to the United States Sun) but a focus upon the Ascendants of the national capitals that were to make much of the history of the 20th Century.

---

6. It is not reliable to cast a national chart for Saudi Arabia. Affairs of government and religious issues are deeply intertwined. After World I, a conservative religious movement called Wahhabism had brought about a good bit of unification among the desert tribes. The people of the growing territory fought the British for years to bring lands back into the fold. Most of Saudi Arabia was in place around 1926, except for the small coastal areas of Oman and Yeman. The ruling family (al-Shaykh) emerged through the wars and skirmishes.

Some historians link the Saudi national identity to Mohammed's flight from Mecca to Medina in 0622. The date is variously given as July 15 or July 16 at Sunset. One of those dates is usually also given as the first date of the Muslim calendar. While Mohammed left Mecca then to establish his Faith, the first date of the calendar was July 19, 0622. That date at Sunset (the established time of reference) was 01/01/01 of the Calendar, the first of Muharam. That day captures the crescent Moon (semisquare Sun) that was part of Mohammed's great vision, which appears on Arab flags to this day, and originates the Islamic lunar calendar.

There is good argument to be made that this Calendar inspired by religion *is* the event chart to portray the Arabian nation, but that is study for another book.

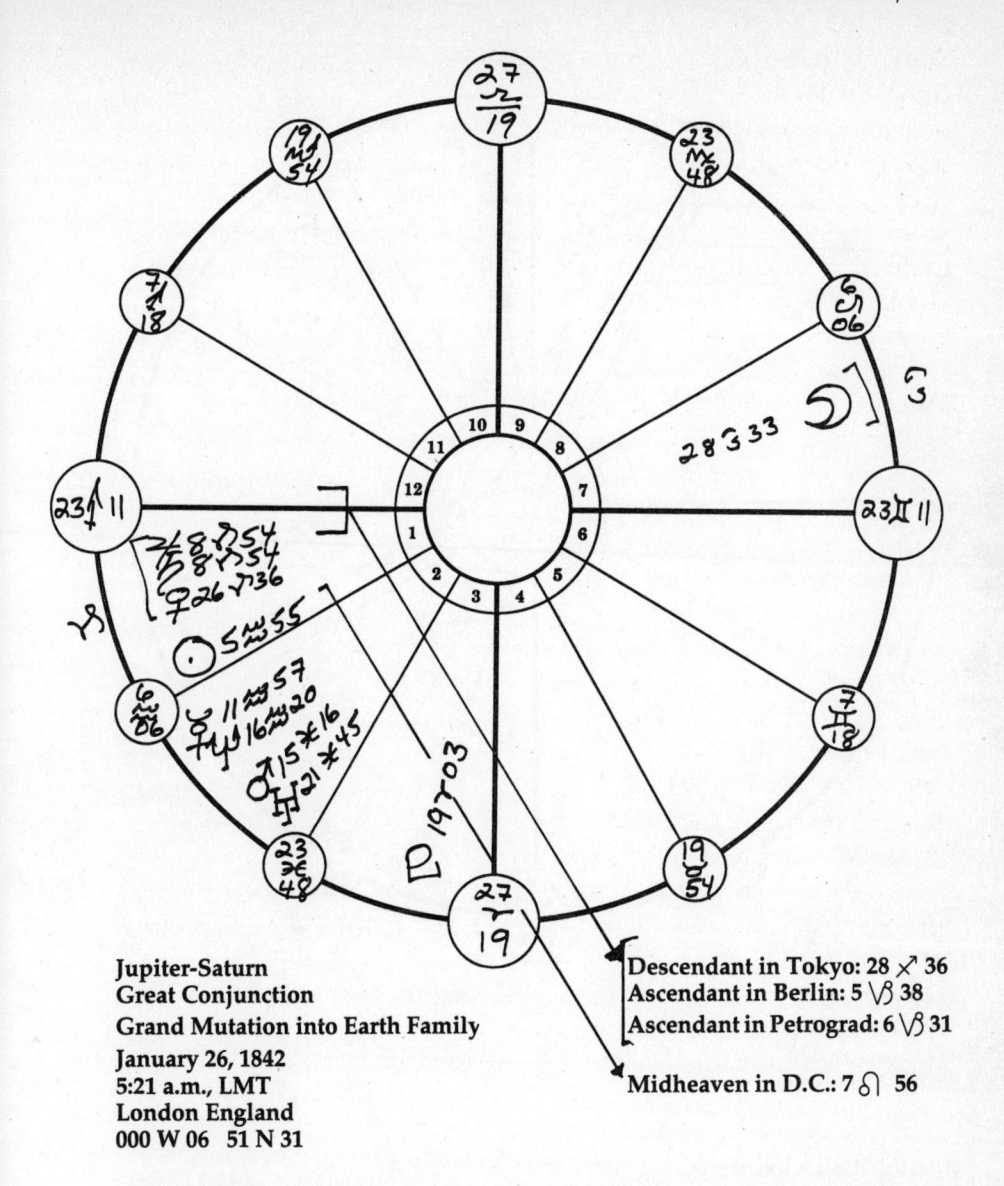

Jupiter-Saturn
Great Conjunction
Grand Mutation into Earth Family
January 26, 1842
5:21 a.m., LMT
London England
000 W 06   51 N 31

Descendant in Tokyo: 28 ♐ 36
Ascendant in Berlin: 5 ♑ 38
Ascendant in Petrograd: 6 ♑ 31
Midheaven in D.C.: 7 ♌ 56

Immediately following this Great Conjunction—the beginning of this enormous cycle—outbreaks of war occurred throughout the world, continuously, including the United States Civil War in 1861; populist uprisings toppled national leaders everywhere; nations were reorganized; there were countless border disputes; presidents began to die in office (not just in the United States) within the 20-year cycle of these conjunctions. The events are simply too

130 / *Prediction in Astrology*

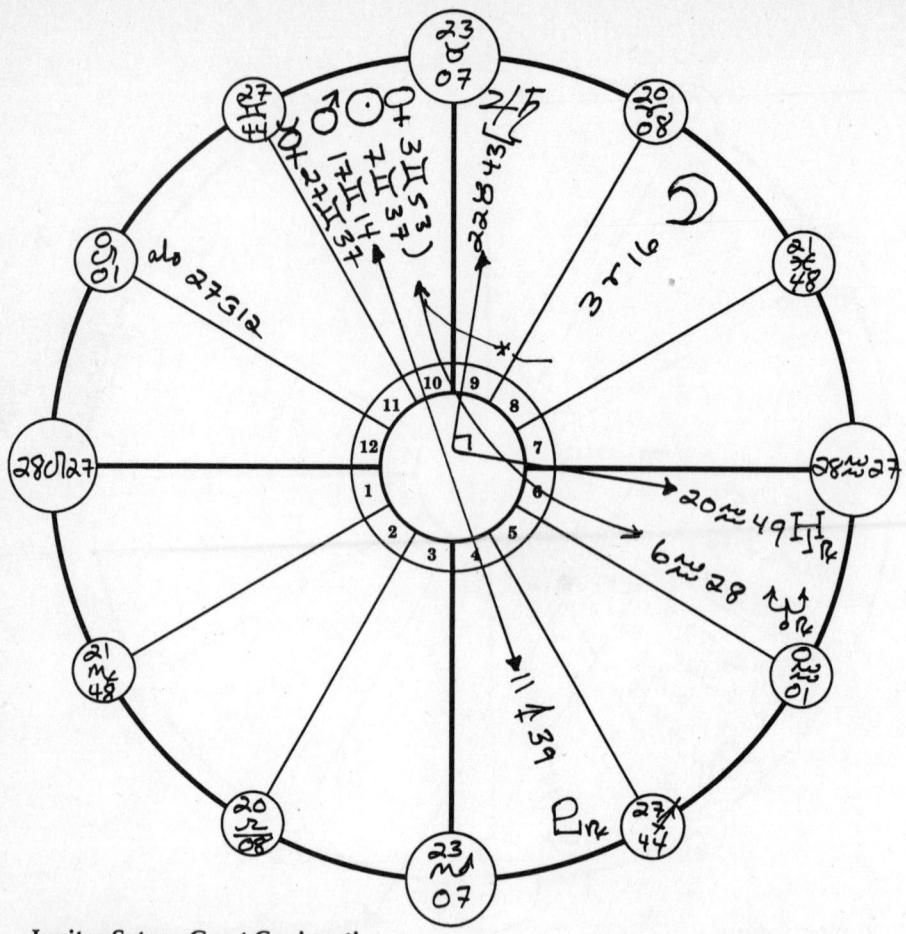

Jupiter-Saturn Great Conjunction
May 28, 2000
11:05 a.m., EST
Washington, D.C.
77 W 02   38 N 54

numerous to list here.

The next Jupiter-Saturn Great Conjunction chart in 2000 back into the Earth Family is alarming (see above): the Great Conjunction in 22 Taurus 43 is only 24' of arc from precise conjunction with the Midheaven of the Washington D.C. Great Conjunction chart at time of partile. The Great Conjunction is powerfully squared by Uranus in its own Sign, ruling the VIIth: other nations, warring or otherwise.

The Sun of the 2000 chart is exactly conjunct the United States Ascendant! The prominence of the United States' role into the next years is undeniable. It will be belligerent: in the Quick-Glance Transit Guide in the Appendix, we can see that transiting Uranus will be conjunct the United States Moon in the Spring and Fall of 2000, and Mars will square the Great Conjunction in August. The last time (one cycle ago for Uranus) that Uranus conjoined the U.S. Midheaven and Moon was during 1915-1917, signaling our complicity in World War I (transiting Saturn was then conjunct the U.S. Sun): defending our allies in true Aquarian spirit.

It is important to note that transiting Pluto will be in the 12th degree of Sagittarius and will have just crossed the United States Descendant (other nations), opposing the national Ascendant, in January-May, 1998, again in November, and a third time from July through September, 1999, with transiting Saturn heading for the Grand Conjunction and squaring the U.S. Midheaven and Moon June, 1999 through April, 2000. These are measurements *for great alarm*, especially with the pressure on the U.S. Midheaven having a history symbolically linked with war involvement and with the Pluto symbolism linked to Atomic Energy.[7]

The Solar Arc background measurements for the United States throughout that time are SA Uranus=Sun/Pluto (tremendous sudden change and upheaval; the arcing planet ruling the U.S. Midheaven); SA Pluto=Uranus, another powerful picture of transformation, explosion, radicalism, and the application of force, with Pluto, the arcing planet, ruling the United States VIth, the Armed Forces, and, again, with Uranus ruling the Midheaven.

Another Solar Arc occurring in that millennium period is confounding because it is so peaceful. It occurs at the same time, July, 1999: SA Venus conjunct the United States Midheaven. This is love and peace—and also alliance with some other country, as in a marriage. Translated into mundane terms, within the Cancer/Aquarian thrusts of the national identity ("Give me your tired, your poor..."), perhaps it suggests the belligerence that will be roiling up at the close of the century will indeed be on behalf of another nation whom we must defend in our eternal vigil as custodian to the countries of the world.

---

7. The chart for the first Atomic Chain Reaction (see McCaffery) was timed for December 2, 1942 at 3:35 p.m., CWT, in Chicago; 087W39, 41N52. The chart is dominated by a Saturn-Uranus conjunction opposing Sun-Mercury-Venus in the VIIIth. Saturn is at 8 Gemini 57, conjunct the U.S. Ascendant. It was a "new horizon" indeed for the United States and the rest of the world. There is only one square aspect in the chart: *Pluto, ruler of the VIIth, squares the Ascendant.*

132 / *Prediction in Astrology*

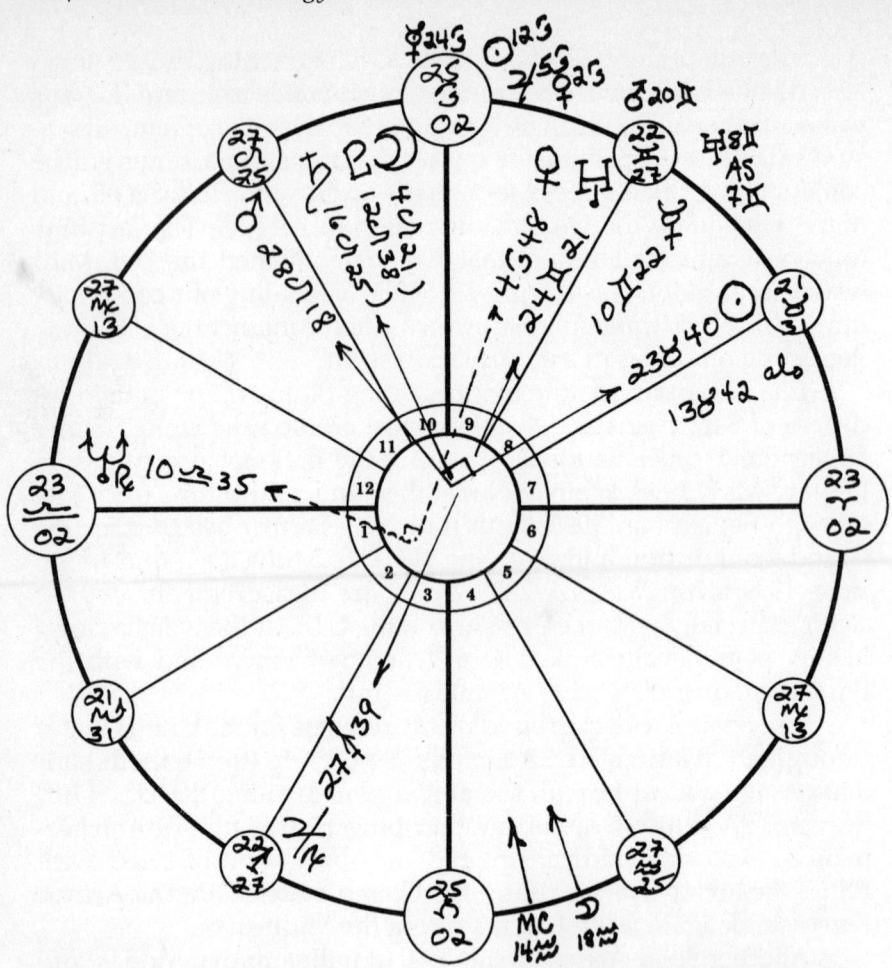

Israel
May 14, 1948
4:00 p.m., Eastern Europe Time
Tel Aviv
34 E 49   32 N 02
Outer Ring: United States Contacts

Note: There was definitely *no* Daylight Saving Time in effect in Israel at this time, contrary to other published charts for Israel. The meeting to proclaim independence from British rule began precisely at 4:00 p.m. The reading of the proclamation ended at 4:37 p.m. Ben Gurian regarded 4:00 p.m. as the critical time and recorded it as so in his diary.

That nation will be Israel, and it will continue to be Israel. The chart for Israel shows the extraordinary ties Israel has with the United States.

In the chart for the next Great Conjunction, May 28, 2000 (page 130), the Great Conjunction itself at 22 Taurus 43 conjoins the Israel Sun at 23 Taurus 37. The Conjunction chart Uranus opposes the Israel Mars which itself is exactly conjunct the Ascendant of the Conjunction chart, as viewed from Washington D.C.

The final note for this Mundane astrology overview—so clear, so anticipatable—is that the Sun of the 2000 Great Conjunction chart is precisely upon the United States Ascendant, identifying the United States with the entire symbolic force of the next Grand Conjunction. As the Grand Conjunction spoke so dramatically at Mecca in 1980, so we can anticipate a similar marriage between the portents of the next millennium and at least the first 20 years of United States involvement.

These measurements are epic.

We have been studying cycles at work, specifically the great cycle of the Jupiter-Saturn conjunction. Throughout history, this Great Conjunction has seemed *to create* history. From understanding the past in relation to this celestial phenomenon, we can afford to have keen, reliable, and seasoned expectations for the future. Our present era is dominated by warring Earth Sign values giving way to Air Sign values in time-tandem with the Jupiter-Saturn cycle. In an earlier time—in the Grand Mutation to the Water Family—it was the Christmas star, followed by wise astrologers who were in the East. It was the Age of Pisces.

Are we now, truly, at the rupture of light that is witness to the dawning of the Age of Aquarius?

The signal for Mecca, for Islam, in 1980 brought religion and politics together, a perfect synthesis of Jupiter and Saturn symbolisms. And supposedly wise men continue to wage war, beginning in Iran and escalating still?

The Great Conjunction, the Grand Mutation, speaks a message from times past to times to come, bringing nation after nation deeply into its augury. For the Arab nations, behind the stores of oil is the exacting fuel of faith, a "Victory by God's Will." This thrust will not stop with the end of the Iraq war.

For the fate of Israel, of one thing we can be sure, because we see it now as we have looked ahead into time: the seeds of Abraham—the concerns of Ishmael and Isaac—are already sown for still a third millennium of strife. And the United States, with its extraordinary ties with Israel, is still bound to the stone.

Chapter Six

Getting Personal—Looking at the Past Ahead of Time

Marcel Proust, the celebrated French novelist (1871-1922), bridged the passage into the present millennium, the birth of the 20th century, with compellingly revealing creative output. While literarily inspired, Proust was also the focus of so many things personally problematical, intrinsically and of the times: he was the son of an eminent Catholic doctor and a Jewish mother; he was an early and chronic asthmatic, became manifestly neurotic, hypersensitive, homosexual, and hypochondriacal. He retreated from the world and, shortly after his parents died early in the new century, he repaired to his cork-lined bedroom rarely to emerge.[1]

In 1912, he completed the first draft of *Remembrance of Things Past*. World War I delayed full publication and distribution of the book; Proust revised it to twice its length, and it became his masterpiece: memories with grand symbology, destined to live on into the next millennium. The work was nihilistic and dismal, but it was real.

Proust's title, remembrance of things past, is compelling indeed. How much time *do* we give to the past? What does it do for us? How do we evaluate it? *Do we see why it was necessary?*

It is clear that Proust's work was a psychological catharsis for the intense anxieties he had absorbed in his early homelife; he projected his fears, pains, and idiosyncracies upon others in the

---

1. Proust was born on July 10, 1871, according to M. Gauguelin, at 11:30 p.m. LMT, in Paris, with a stellium in Cancer (Jupiter, Mercury, Sun, and Uranus) in the IVth, square Neptune rising; Saturn is retrograde at the Midheaven (coincidentally a Jupiter-Saturn opposition), with that axis squared by Mars in Libra.

rambling stream of consciousness, bedroom-discourse novel. I ask again, though, do we ever search within ourselves for the *necessity* of our past? When we do, we learn about the present, and we are fortified for the future.

Dane Rudhyar's *The Astrology of Personality*, which was published in 1936, totally changed the perspective of astrology in modern times. He wrote, "Only as every factor of his life-history stands out with clear meaning in terms of the whole life-destiny—only then is man really prepared to face his future with intelligence and understanding; in other words, in function of his true individual selfhood."[2]

"Nihilism" is often used in connection with Proust's work. Nihilism (from the Latin *nihil* meaning "nothing") was a socio-philosophical label developed in the late 19th century when, to the philosophers and writers of the day, life did not seem worth living. There had been terrible wars, and a constant disregard for human life and dignity; the American Civil War, the Franco-Prussian War, a major revolt in Paris to proclaim the third Republic and the onslaught of the Prussians; Civil War in Spain, financial panics in Vienna and New York; wars in Turkey and between the Egyptians and Ethiopians. There were wars everywhere, from France annexing Tahiti to Chile fighting Bolivia and Peru; the Germans in South Africa; changes among the leaderships of many, many governments; the Chinese defeated by the Japanese at Wei-hai-Wei; Armenians massacred in Turkey; Italians defeated by Abyssinians; among others, a Shah of Iran was assassinated; Germany declared war on Spain over Cuba. Then later, there were some 90 wars in the world between 1945 and 1988, and then still more.*

The code of the early nihilist movement (a Russian concept that spread quickly to France) was elimination of God in order for there to be *personal* freedom; elimination of the individualistic sense of "rightness," which only meant power; and the eradication of civilization, property, marriage, morality, and justice—all the values that had not brought happiness and stabilization to the world. The existentialist doctrine of letting one's own happiness be one's only law should prevail.

This was a code of self-indulgence for sure: there was nothing

---

2. Rudhyar, p. 464.
* And we should recall the Jupiter-Saturn Grand Conjunction chart, in the Earth Family, January 26, 1842. page 129. Its astrology touches all these conflicts.

else to rely on. Does some of that radical, lonely spirit live on today in the passage into the *next* millennium? With our astrology getting personal, are we able *to justify* the future for our clients? Is that part of our "job"?

Remembrance of things past brings extraordinary perspectives into life in the present and life into the future: do we want to lose the past? Do our clients gain by learning to understand their past? Do we enrich our passage as we take the past with us into the future? Then, is it a matter of accuracy or is it a matter of degree? Is it a matter of measurement or a matter of communication?

These are powerful questions for astrologers. We will return to them from different perspectives in Chapter 7, dealing with counseling about the future. But now, as we do get personal, as we begin to look at the past ahead of time, in individual horoscopes, we have to know that remembrance of things past must always be linked to the particular significance of having been born, of living now, of having emerged through a mesh of parental influences, formative experiences and self-projection, of hoping to live into a dream, into times to come. An event is an event, but the value one gives that event is a personal choice. *You give the event value*. The astrologer helps the client give value to the remembrance of those things past.

The following list of Prediction Aphorisms is not a list of rules. The list holds 30 observations about how the astrologer can get into position to see life through astrology in a way that makes the past meaningful and the future anticipatable. They are concise statements of principles that suggest ways to get into the horoscope quickly, not particularly through the analysis of substance, but, *assuming* that, through the discovery of time structures of development, of cycles upon cycles that transport the process of becoming into the future. As the astrologer detects the framework, the client adds the substance, the value judgments, the choices and then the projections, the hopes and dreams. These Aphorisms reveal developmental truths in American society and their astrological counterparts; they track important cycles as they emerge in life. They come from my personal experience and the satisfactions of having shared lifetimes with well over one thousand others. With understanding and practice and confidence, these steps can be accomplished quite quickly, resorting then to more careful measurements when the general structure clearly dictates.

Prediction Aphorisms

1. *Acknowledging Self-worth*—the process of becoming is the process of ascertaining self-worth, measured in many different ways throughout lifetime development.

2. *Measuring Self-worth*—To appreciate an individual horoscope in depth, we must first search out the self-worth dimension by checking planets within the IInd House or those ruling the IInd: whichever one stands out under high aspect-tenion in the horoscope, that planet initially leads on to further analysis, especially to the significators of the parental axis.

3. *Saturn Retrograde*—The phenomenon of Saturn retrograde is a crucial key. Its occurrence immediately introduces IInd House concerns and the significators of the parental axis (IV-X) and their aspect condition.[3]

4. *Nodal Axis*—Any planet in close conjunction (or square) with the Moon's nodal axis will suggest a powerful maternal influence in terms of the natal planet making the contact.

5. *Relationship Concerns*—Self-worth anxiety naturally extends to relationship concerns, and we look to the aspect condition of the significator(s) of the VIIth House (the planet(s) in or ruling that House) for suggestion of the amount of tension. Discussion will reveal how constructively it was managed in the past.

6. *Needs*—Self-worth concerns relate to the *needs* of individuals, shown through the Moon and its sign in the particular horoscope, energized by the Sun in its sign; together, the Moon and Sun define the energies propelling development through challenge within time, the needs working for fulfillment in the past and for the future.[4]

7. *Retrogradation*—Retrogradation suggests secondary levels of concern; need fulfillment pressing at more subtle levels or indirectness, especially with Mercury or Venus. Multiple planets in retrograde motion tend to collect in one hemisphere or the other, sort of as an exclusive group, calling attention to the concerns of the *other* hemisphere as counterpoint within meaning. Retrogradation

---

3. The Saturn retrograde phenomenon is fully discussed in Tyl, *Holistic Astrology*, as well as rulership and significator dynamics throughout the Houses and needs among the symbology of the planets and Signs. In short: Saturn retrograde suggests a legacy of inferiority feelings usually linked with the father figure in the early home, his absence, passivity, or tyranny.

4. Simply insert the word "need" into descriptions of the Moon's signs: Moon in Aries *needs* to be number one; Moon in Leo *needs* to be dramatic; behavior follows to fulfill the need, coloring the entire horoscope development.

emphasis in the West calls attention to the East, the protection of the Ego, especially in relationship dynamics; emphasis West (retrogradation in the East), insecurity about giving one's self "away" to others, charade; emphasis South (above the horizon), unfinished business at home; emphasis North, protected and incomplete, potentially victimizable by experience.

8. *Education*—The significator of the IXth House and its aspect tension will suggest whether or not the education was interrupted, a very important consideration in American culture and in individual self-worth development, a past occurrence that often haunts future development.

9. *Early Development*—In the course of gaining orientation within the horoscope, particularly strong planetary positions should be noted. The planets in the Cadent Houses can be quickly projected by Solar Arc rapport measurements to the Angles ahead, suggesting key development times in the earlier, most formative period of life time.

10. *Rapport Measurements*—By noting the rapport distances of natal planets to conjunctions with Angles, we build the basis of time projection throughout development into the future. Timings to younger years will be absorbed through the parents; in independent years, these arcs will generally be more important, what with greater exposure to life.

11. *Repetitive Measurements*—Certain rapport generalizations will clearly appear repetitive or in a series. When this is the case, these time measurements become important keys for discussion and analysis, related to the individual's needs, self-worth assessment, relationships, social mobility, professional status, etc.

12. *Transit Superstructure*—Analyses of the major transit superstructure of time, based upon Saturn's transit to its natal position (ages 7, 14, 21, 28-30, 35, 42, etc. [5]), should concentrate on the formative years first; awareness of this transit activity, especially when crossing Angles in those years will begin to work in synchronization with the Solar Arc contacts that are forming in the earlier years.

13. *Planetary Relationships in Development*—Building awareness of the horoscope will then reveal greater rapport measurements between planet and planet. It is helpful to organize these contacts to reflect time frames of the realities of development: Venus and Mars in the teenage years and early twenties; Jupiter and the Sun in the

---

5. Lewi.

early thirties; Jupiter and Saturn and the Sun and Saturn in the forties; Uranus and Venus, Mars, Neptune, and Pluto may manifest most significantly from 20 or 42 onward. This organization idea is only a guide; exceptions abound and call attention to individuation, of course. The point is to keep what is natural in mind as one measures for corroboration or divergence.

14. *Neptune*—Whenever transiting or Solar Arc Neptune comes to an Angle, special note must be made of that age for the possible manifestation of serious self-suppression; somehow ego definition may get lost or may be overtaken by someone else or, indeed, may be taken up with nefarious activities.

15. *Pluto*—Whenever transiting or Solar Arc Pluto comes to an Angle, there can be a tremendous change of perspective in the life, especially if upon the Ascendant, then usually accompanied by breaks in relationships (opposite the VIIth); on the fourth cusp, a whole new start affecting home, occupation, whether of one's own making or through the spouse (the fourth is the tenth of the VIIth). Realization is similar with Pluto in contact with the Midheaven, but here major change is usually accompanied by the show of success, excess, and bravura; over the seventh cusp, we can expect a major change in perspective with regard to formal relationship or a major change within the spouse (the other person's Ascendant in the relationship).

16. *Clusters*—Especially telling about time development of natal potentials are transits to natal *planetary clusters*, since several behavioral faculties and needs are symbolized together to relate to the transit and/or Solar Arc projection. Most subtle of these perhaps is the natal conjunction of Mercury and Venus (often with the Sun and/or Jupiter), suggesting a very strong strain of idealism in character development (usually a defense mechanism).

A strong transit or Arc to this position or in aspect to it out of the natal configuration will suggest marked effects for the entire mental outlook. Saturn can register disappointment and/or depression. (Ask why. What else is going on? How old is the person? What are the values normally at that age? What is coming up next in the general time scheme?) Uranus can suggest an urgent zeal; Neptune, a self-absorbed or self-righteous state; Pluto, perhaps a complete wrenching change of a lifetime point of view. These transiting or arcing planets will engage much of the human being's life process over an extended period of time.

17. *The "Feel" of Development*—The pressured times of development begin to emerge, involving parental relationships, self-worth development, the support or lack of education, the focus of giving love and managing sexuality (Vth House significator), and the ease and quality of relationship dynamics, all reinforced by major transit and Solar Arc movements. (The major transit activity throughout many years of past development is now simplified to just a few moments by the Quick-Glance Transit Tables in the Appendix).

What emerges is very much a "feel" of the person rather than a descriptive list of measurements, and that "feel" has general timing frames throughout. With experience, the astrologer will be able to anticipate these patterns; not just their timings, but, as well, the substance of the corresponding realities that will be corroborated by the client. In any culture, society, or sub-group, there are ways of behavior and reliable expectations that become predictable patterns of development.

18. *Age Reality*—All transits of Jupiter, Saturn, Uranus, Neptune, and Pluto and all Solar Arc projections of these planets (and the Angles) to fourth harmonic aspects with natal planets (and Angles) will register usually through the parents while the son or daughter is still under their protection and leadership. Rebellion and separation may develop, but initially the registration of significance is not directly through the young person. *Reality must accommodate age.*

Parents are important for both nurturance and contrast. This is how growing individuals define who they are. Tension builds identity. (How much tension was there in the early home? How well was it managed? The aspect condition of the significators of the parental axis tell the story.)

19. *The Fourth Cusp*—Transits of Saturn or Uranus over the fourth cusp will always suggest a new start, usually a change of home or vocational direction, through the parents when young, through one's own efforts or the press of the environment when independent of the parents.

20. *Saturn, Uranus Transits*—Transits of Saturn or Uranus over the Ascendant or the Descendant usually suggest a new start through the father's job (the Ascendant is the fourth of the Xth and the tenth of the IVth); it is similar over the Descendant, through derivative House relationships from the parental axis. During the greater part of life after leaving the home, these transits are

extremely telling: a peak of activity when at the Midheaven or Ascendant; a new start at the IVth; and very often a "whole new look" at the Descendant, often to rupture the old to birth the new.

21. *Consideration of Marriage*—First marriage is often regarded consciously or unconsciously as an escape from a homelife unsupportive of ego needs or plans or dreams, or acquiescence to pressure from the home extending its influence. *Precipitousness of marriage can be a function of time development as much as it may be a function of emotional values.*

22. *Arcs of Marriage*—Romance/marriage is suggested by rapport measurements between the Sun and Venus, between the Moon or Venus and the Angles (especially the Midheaven or Descendant); between the Sun or Mars and the Angles, or major Solar Arc reference to the ruler of the VIIth, usually accompanied by significant transit activity, usually to the Midheaven or the fourth cusp.

23. *Framing Questions*—The objective of time analysis in the horoscope is to frame general questions of significance to gain specific elaboration from the client and establish the client's value assignments with events in the past. These then will color value projections into the future.

24. *Larger Measurements*—Very soon, projections begin to leave the formative years and enter the testing years and then approach the future. Larger arcs approach fulfillment, and transits begin to repeat cycles. The significance of key times past within arc movements and within transit cycles is always the key to the times of cycles to come in the future; what they meant, they *will* mean for the client.

25. *Jupiter*—Jupiter's 12-year cycle is one of opportunity and reward. By noting when the next transit of Jupiter will conjoin the Sun (project one sign per month, generally, from a benchmark position in the present), we can make reference to a period first back into the past to the previous conjunction, usually twelve years back to the month. What happened then in the person's life should occur again in similar terms at a different level. If the past situation was not rewarding, serious Solar Arc and other transit activity surely complicated the growth picture somehow; the time then requires finer study and discussion, which will help make the next Jupiter-Sun contact maximally fruitful and rewarding.

26. *"The Future Was"*—To escape the inhibition of measuring into the future, the astrologer might speak about the measurements

in the past tense, in private, just to keep the analytical process moving: "Then, next September, transiting Pluto *came* to the Midheaven and that hope for career change *was* realized." This is surprisingly helpful to the astrologer to build confidence and to lead symbol interpretation quickly out into the open without natural reservation and instinctive caution.

27. *The Big Semi-Square*—When someone is 43-46 years of age, major change takes place determined by the accumulation within that time period of a Solar Arc semi-square—every planet and point in the horoscope is semi-square to its natal position. There are also transit oppositions by Jupiter, Saturn, and Uranus to their natal positions, and a transit square by Neptune to its natal position.

28. *Houses as Backgrounds*—The House zones in which the planets Saturn, Uranus, Neptune, and Pluto are transiting at the time of consultation can often suggest the background concerns in the client's life at that time and help with future strategies: Saturn will suggest hard work, a slowing down, perhaps, a sense of responsibility, or the sense of controls or limitation; Uranus, excitation or change under foot; Neptune, a lack of clarity or a fearful state; Pluto, a large time period of special concerns that figure to be prominent in the next decade of life.

29. *The Progressed Moon*—The Secondary Progressed New Moon and the Secondary Progressed Full Moon, suggesting a whole new thought or activity-focus or a phase of awareness fulfillment, respectively, in terms of the House in which they fall, can be very helpful. The day/year can be so quickly noted just by looking at the ephemeris; no computation is required: just count ahead from the birth date a day-for-a-year to the part of the lunation cycle that is nearest the present age of the client or just past or, most importantly, just ahead. Astrologers have become so reliant upon computers and their programs that they have gotten away from use of the ephemeris. In many measurements, the ephemeris is still faster than the computer!

30. *The Client's Projections*—The client is the vital measure of times past and times ahead. The client's poise, involvement, confidence or lack of it, opinionation, energy deployment, creativity with insights, and, most important of all, what he or she projects into the future (see Chapter 7) are vital measurements for the astrologer to make. Through this assessment, astrologer and client come together.

144 / Prediction in Astrology

"Bob"

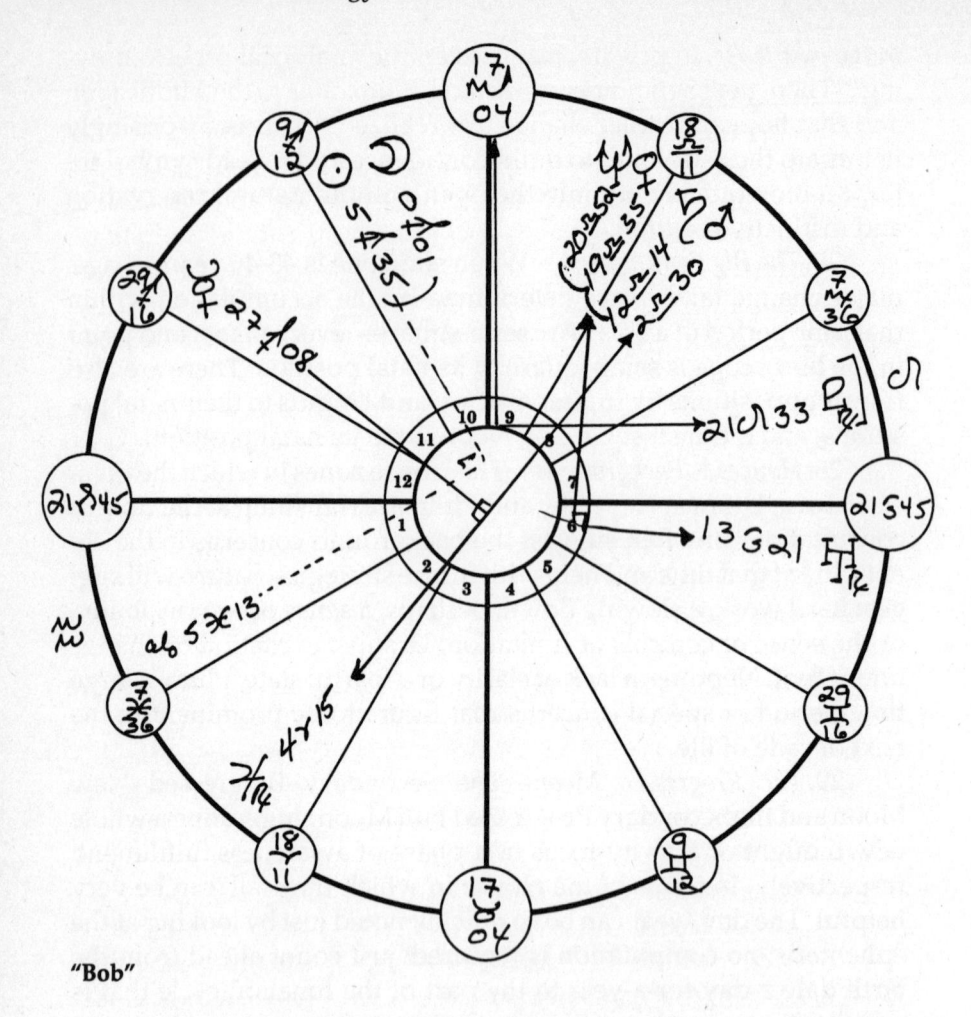

These 30 Aphorisms are predictive in their orientation, although they deal in the main with remembrance of things past. They represent a procedure with which to catch hold of development time, to sense periods of formative developmental tension, to begin to feel the essence of the individual's process of living. The flow out of the past into the future does become smooth and fluent. And, as we shall see in Chapter 7, it is done not by pronouncement by the astrologer but through inquiry.

Bob

The horoscope on page 144 is the most recent horoscope consultation I have had; specifically, yesterday afternoon. I did not search my files for a special demonstration of the aphorisms or of any special measurements. This is a normal, routine horoscope analysis for an individual who, by definition, is special in every way. Astrology always unlocks a personal drama within every human being for sharing, for appreciation in terms of development, and for projection into the future.

"Bob" expresses high energy and impulsiveness in his speech and in his opinions. *He* knows things and he wants others to *know that*. This made our telephone call a little awkward, but I understood it when I saw his horoscope with the Sun and Moon both in Sagittarius: the enormous need to have one's opinions respected as clarification of just who he is. This is very strong in this horoscope, and is inflated further by the trine with Jupiter in Aries (reward needs seen in terms of ego recognition).

As they would say in Tycho Brahe's time, "Saturn is lord of the horoscope," ruling the Ascendant. Our eyes go to Saturn and see the triple conjunction with Venus and Neptune. There is some kind of suppression possible here with emotions (Venus in its own Sign involved with Neptune and Saturn). Neptune is ruler of the self-worth IInd House, holding Jupiter retrograde. These two observations press for further study of self-worth development.* Bob is extremely talkative and, yet, not self-assured on the telephone; he is president of his own company—"I'm in the transportation business!"—an absolute confirmation of the strength of Sagittarius here and the prominent Mercury.

Pluto, ruler of the Midheaven, is square the Midheaven, part of the parental axis; the other arm of the axis, the fourth cusp, is ruled by Venus in the triple conjunction with Saturn and Neptune.—"Bob, there is a confusion here in reference to your parents. One of them, probably the father, is austere [Pluto], I think that would be the word, and your mother is more passive [Venus]...."

Bob interrupted me, "Yes, you're right. My father was in the military. He *was* austere. He was very controlling. My mother was spiritual, and she found it hard to show emotions."

---

* A personal note: after completing the preceding two chapters, I was taken aback to receive this client with a Saturn-Jupiter opposition in his horoscope!

146 / *Prediction in Astrology*

Here was a major clue to Bob's volubility as overcompensation perhaps for the suppression of emotions, suggested by the triple conjunction in Libra. (His mother was indeed very influential: the Sun is exactly square the Node.) I suggested this to him, and he smilingly agreed completely. He volunteered, "And my girlfriend is telling me all the time that it's OK to be vulnerable, to show emotions. I'm learning a lot from her about that."

Bob had been a nail-biter (Mercury square Mars; nervous energy). His sex drive is very strong (Mercury square Mars, Mercury ruling the Vth). He feels no upset, guilt, or frustration in that department of his life. He is "comfortable," good-looking, easy to be with (the Venus in Libra, of course; the settledness of its conjunction with Saturn and Saturn's rulership of the Ascendant), entertaining, smiling, positive, enthusiastic about life. In short, he has all the Sagittarian enjoyments one could hope for.

My eyes started to seek out timing developments. From the "Quick-Glance" Transit Tables reproduced in the back of this book, I was able to talk about developmental time smoothly, with little interruption, very conversationally.

1955

MONTH	MARS LONG	JUPITER LONG	SATURN LONG	URANUS LONG	NEPTUNE LONG	PLUTO LONG
Jan	20 ♓	27 ♋	18 ♏	26 ♋	28 ♎	27 ♌
Feb	12 ♈	23	20	25	28	26
Mar	02 ♉	20	21	24	29	25
Apr	23	20	20	24	27	25
May	13 ♊	23	18	24	27	24
June	04 ♋	28	16	25	26	24
July	23	04 ♌	15	27	25	26
Aug	13 ♌	10	15	29	26	26
Sept	03 ♍	17	16	00 ♌	26	27
Oct	22	23	19	02	27	28
Nov	12 ♎	28	22	02	28	28
Dec	01 ♏	01 ♍	25	02	29	29

—"Bob, was there a big move in September 1955 when you were just about four years old (transiting Saturn conjunct the Midheaven)?"

—Yes. There had been a cross-country move.

—"Then again early in 1961?"—(transiting Saturn conjunct the Ascendant; and my eyes had picked up the rapport measurement

SA Mars=Saturn in ten degrees/age 10, November birth, even arc expectation, 1961).

1961

MONTH	MARS LONG	JUPITER LONG	SATURN LONG	URANUS LONG	NEPTUNE LONG	PLUTO LONG
Jan	08 ♋	14 ♑	20 ♑	25 ♌	11 ♏	08 ♍
Feb	00	21	23	24	11	07
Mar	03	27	26	23	11	07
Apr	13	03 ♒	29	22	11	06
May	27	06	00 ♒	22	10	06
June	14 ♌	07	29 ♑	22	09	06
July	01 ♍	05	28	23	09	06
Aug	20	01	26	25	09	07
Sept	10 ♎	28 ♑	24	27	09	08
Oct	29	27	23	29	10	09
Nov	21 ♏	00 ♒	24	00 ♍	11	10
Dec	12 ♐	04	26	01	12	10

—Yes. Again there had been a cross-country move through his father's profession.

"You were moving so much!"

"Well that's what happens in the military."

"Yes, but might you say that it also kept you from getting the experience of peer group membership and allegiances, friendships, you know, the giving and taking of emotions, learning to express feelings?"

It is clear also that Venus, ruler of the IXth, under the press of the triple conjunction, suggested that his education had been interrupted. This, combined with the austerity of the home environment and inherited emotional suppression, would have to be considered and brought to Bob's attention.

—"What about March or so 1971? You were 20 then (the college education-time-reality). Was that the break up of your college plans (transiting Saturn conjunct the fourth cusp)? *Were they interrupted?*"

Again, Bob agreed completely with this deduction. This was important in our appreciation of his development in relationships and the prospects of marriage (which I had distilled in my private preparation of his horoscope before meeting with him).

—Yes. They had been, and a profitable discussion ensued about the value of education, especially to a Sagittarian, how he returned for his degree, what that meant, etc.

148 / *Prediction in Astrology*

1971

MONTH	MARS LONG	JUPITER LONG	SATURN LONG	URANUS LONG	NEPTUNE LONG	PLUTO LONG
Jan	16 ♏	28 ♏	16 ♉	13 ♎	03 ♐	00 ♎
Feb	06 ♐	03 ♐	16	13	03	29 ♍
Mar	23	06	17	13	03	29
Apr	12 ♑	06	20	12	03	28
May	28	04	24	10	02	27
June	13 ♒	01	28	10	01	27
July	21	27 ♏	01 ♊	10	01	27
Aug	19	27	04	10	00	28
Sept	12	29	06	12	00	29
Oct	15	03 ♐	06	14	01	00 ♎
Nov	27	09	05	15	02	01
Dec	14 ♓	15	03	17	03	02

My eyes had flashed to the IXth House and projected the Neptune to the Midheaven at age 27 (27 degrees), closely followed by Venus, one degree (one year) behind. What had happened here? The year would have been 1978; transiting Uranus would have been crossing his Midheaven, and Solar Arc Sun would have been square his Mars (project 27 degrees from the Sun position at 5 Sagittarius; 32 "Sagittarius" or 2 Capricorn, square Mars in 2 Libra). "The suggestion here is that you were 'wiped out,' if I may overstate it to get us talking. You should have been at the top of your form (the Uranus transit), but somehow it was other than what it seemed (a perfect phrase for Neptune). What happened?"

1978

MONTH	MARS LONG	JUPITER LONG	SATURN LONG	URANUS LONG	NEPTUNE LONG	PLUTO LONG
Jan	09 ♌	00 ♋	00 ♍	15 ♏	17 ♐	17 ♎
Feb	28 ♋	27 ♊	28 ♌	16	18	17
Mar	22	26	26	16	18	16
Apr	27	29	24	16	18	15
May	08 ♌	03 ♋	24	15	18	15
June	23	09	25	13	17	14
July	09 ♍	16	27	12	16	14
Aug	28	23	01 ♍	12	16	14
Sept	18 ♎	29	05	13	16	15
Oct	08 ♏	04 ♌	08	14	16	16
Nov	29	08	11	16	17	17
Dec	21 ♐	09	13	18	18	18

Bob had indeed been at top form. He had no problems with income (Neptune ruling the IInd), but Neptunian things entered his life, not necessary to go into for our timing discussion here. A romantic engagement did follow on the heels of this change in life direction. It was a very powerful time, a scary time for Bob, what with transiting Saturn's return to its natal position and many more measurements, including transiting Pluto opposed Saturn.

When did that difficult period end?

I suggested, "Did all that go on until mid-'87? (transiting Saturn conjunct the Midheaven)."

—Yes, it did. That's when it all stopped. (Bob's Angles were super-sensitive to transit and arc contacts. That had been proved in this process of discussion.)

Then Bob went on to found his own business. He was visiting with me showing brightness and eagerness, success, and hopefulness: "What's going to happen with my business? I want to relocate to the West Coast."

Of course: at the time of consultation in December, 1990, transiting Pluto was conjunct his Midheaven. All his concerns were about building his profession—with Pluto entering the Xth. Transiting Saturn has just crossed his Ascendant: he was at a peak of development and wanted to crystallize and consolidate all his achievements to date. He wanted to become a big businessman. Transiting Uranus and Neptune were still in his XIIth House and related to the concerns in his recent past.

Bob was just 39 years old: Solar Arc rapport projection of forty-degrees minus one. Simple: profession, relocation; Midheaven distance to Mercury is one sign and ten degrees, i.e., 40 years. Seen ahead of time, working into the future, I had made an exact measurement of that rapport connection: SA Midheaven will conjoin Mercury in April, 1991, seven months before his 40th birthday (a very fast Arc in November). Pluto in transit will sesquiquadrate his Jupiter in the IInd and go on to make the final conjunction with Midheaven through the Summer.

Yes, Bob would probably sell his business. Yes, the odds were very high that he would relocate in the Spring. And his relocation chart brought his Sun and Moon to the Ascendant, trined by Jupiter, its ruler placed in the IVth, with Mars moved to the Midheaven!

The consultation had gone from past to future effortlessly. Twenty of the thirty Predictive Aphorisms had come into use. Bob was literally creating his future at that moment, and his astrology was corroborating his reality. His past had built this time, and his new emotional freedom had become the spirit of adventure, for his profession and for his potential marriage to his lady in his new city. His time had come.

Mary

This horoscope portion shown here speaks dramatically in terms of past considerations molding future anticipations through basic analysis, rapport measurements of Solar Arcs, and the projections of simple transits. Look at this woman's horoscope for a moment before reading on.

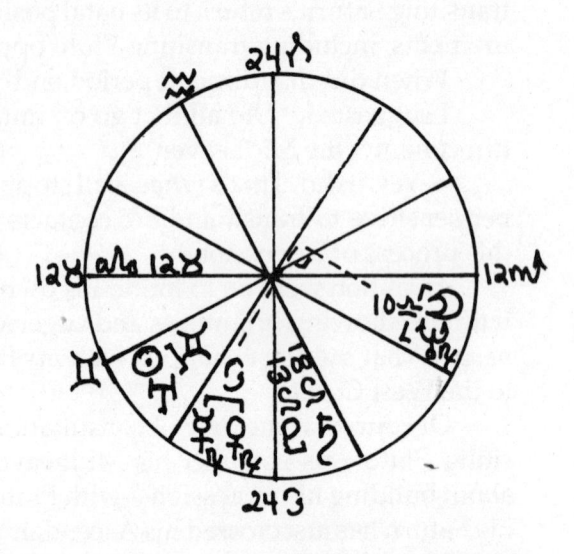

Let your eyes evaluate her self-worth consideration (Aphorisms 1, 2, 5, 7). How does this concern her XIth? Check the parental axis: what about that very powerful rapport measurement of five years between Pluto and Saturn in the IVth? Through Pluto, consider the VIIth House. Something in the early development time will affect relationships for all time. See the nodal conjunction with the Ascendant (Aphorism 4). What is the underlying anxiety that relates self-worth, homelife, maternal influence, the age five, and then something very formative and probably difficult at about age 32 (Neptune arced to the VIIth cusp)? Making connections among observations is the art of analysis.

The consultation took place in the Fall of 1989. What would the transit structure be throughout 1990, especially the transit of Saturn approaching her Midheaven?

There is a beautiful, gentle, earnest flow of energy from this attractive lady. "Mary" looks so nice, seems so poised, and she is president of her own sizeable company; yet there is a kind of shyness and timidity about her that the sharp eye can note. She is respected and liked by her employees (the need of the Moon in Libra, obviously; with the Neptune touch adding an alluring air). She is sharp and inventive and technologically analytical (Sun-Uranus conjunction in Gemini, etc.).

But the self-worth concerns are strong (Mercury, ruler of the IInd House is conjunct Venus—a conceptual idealism perhaps too hard to fulfill; reinforced by the retrogradation, there is another level of consciousness, especially involving Venus, ruler of Mary's Ascendant with the Node in conjunction—and square to the Moon-Neptune conjunction; additionally, the Sun-Uranus conjunction, disposited of by Mercury in the Venus conjunction, is in the IInd. There is an emphasis below the horizon for sure (only one planet is above in the full horoscope): "unfinished business."

The self-worth concerns will be important to discuss throughout the early development time because they undoubtedly affect her present relationship structures as well. Pluto, ruler of the VIIth is conjunct Saturn, one of the significators of the parental axis, ruling the Midheaven and placed in the IVth. The Moon, ruler of the IVth, the other parental significator, is conjunct Neptune. Self worth anxieties were taken on in the early years of development in the home through the relationship with the father—the enormous influence of the mother (Node conjunct Ascendant). A key time within all this would certainly have been at age 5+: rapport measurement SA Pluto conjunct Saturn, probably with transiting Uranus approaching the fourth cusp (Uranus transits approximately seven years per sign).

And finally, we can sense that an idealism about self-worth, about beauty, emerged to offset some difficult feelings. The young organism is eternally on guard to protect itself from self-doubt; it is a powerful, natural instinct, employing fantasy and many other devices to create security and a sense of sureness.

I suggested that Mary was anxious about her "loveability." Uranus with the Sun in the IInd rules her XIth, the fifth of the VIIth, the House of love-received, hoped for, needed, assumed, expected. (And the Sun rules the Vth, love given.)

In our consultation, I began talking about these concerns and her longing for an idealized home security (Mercury-Venus retrograde in Cancer; Moon ruling the IVth conjunct Neptune; Saturn-Pluto conjunct in the IVth). We discussed the extraordinary influence of her mother: "She was very domineering. She expected me to become a performer, a dancer. When I didn't, of course, I became a 'big disappointment.'"

When we talked about idealism (her mother's and her own), we learned a lot together. I introduced the concept of loveability, and we had a warm exchange about how true that was, that she had that anxiety, and how her professional position had, in a way, overcompensated for that need; but she was still longing for a special, good relationship (recently divorced), in spite of all her business success.

Then I asked her to focus with me on her fifth birthday year; specifically at five and a half by exact measurements. And her answer was so eloquently corroborative of all the astrology of her past and future: "It was Christmas time, and I remember seeing my father weeping. He was sobbing about not feeling loved. I really remember that." This was quite a moment between us, and it brought into focus all the dimensions inculcated within her own vulnerabilities in her early home life.

Her education had not been interrupted; she went far in education, despite the pressure on Saturn, ruler of the IXth. (This is one of the rare exceptions to Aphorism 8, explainable by the offsetting function of her Jupiter, which is extremely prominent in her horoscope and is withheld here, as are other details, to protect her privacy.)

Mary left home for college and "my mother flipped!" She had broken the bonds with her mother and had got out of the home environment. She earned her own college monies and paid her way. SA Midheaven opposed Pluto at 18-19 years of age. So clear, so obvious: a whole new life perspective.

The projections for Mary's year to come in 1990 were for a "boom" year of success for her firm, signaled by the transit of her powerful Saturn over the Midheaven three times during the year—with Solar Arc pictures, especially Jupiter and Sun, related to the midpoint of Pluto and the Midheaven, and much more. She couldn't miss. And it came to past: the finest year her firm has ever had; tremendous growth.

In 1991, she faces even more success—SA Pluto sesquiquadrate Sun/Midheaven.

But through it all, Mary waits to feel loved, personally special, within a warm relationship. She had been divorced with SA Neptune conjunct the VIIth cusp a few years ago and, during the boom year, we had both anticipated much from the transit of Uranus in opposition to her very important Venus. With no explanation, that did *not* come to pass.

A Bank President

A bank president just telephoned me. He has Solar Arc Neptune in contact with his Midheaven, exact this month, with transiting Pluto semi-square his Moon. In his horoscope, Neptune rules his Midheaven and is now the arcing planet making a tension aspect with the Midheaven. We had anticipated something nefarious in his business. The Pluto transiting semi-square his Moon reinforced this since his mother (the Moon in his IVth) owns the bank, and the Moon rules his Ascendant. It was reasonable to expect something *fishy* (a great Neptunian word in this instance) at the bank in December, 1990.

And so it came to pass: my client corroborated that several employees were found out embezzling funds. Guided by some other technical measurements, I suggested that this had been going on for about a month. The key employee involved had been hired 40 days earlier.

Another call: a businessman with natal Pluto in the IInd was facing up to the transit of Saturn in opposition to that Pluto, exact in three weeks. We had anticipated financial loss, rigorous attack somehow on his funds. But he was already on hard times, and we could not conceive of anything more or worse happening. And it was clear throughout some 28 years of life that every Saturn contact with the IInd House Pluto had accompanied financial difficulty. I had said to him some months ago, "Well, could there be something from the Internal Revenue Service (a clear Saturn symbolism as well as common sense)?"

My client called me to report that the IRS had started an investigation of a several year old report he had filed. The prediction any astrologer could have made had come to pass.

Ann

Predictions are not always as easy as those just cited here. For example, a woman longing for a romantic attachment has Solar Arc Venus square Jupiter forming in her horoscope—just the signal she and I were looking for! There were great expectations for sure, stimulating all kinds of conjecture of where they would meet, what he would look like, etc. The excitement was peaking during the consultation three months before the measurement would take place. Great expectations were getting out of hand.

The realities of the situation were that the woman was 48 years old and had never been married (one engagement called off at age 34 with SA Uranus, ruler of the VIIth, conjoining her Sun). She was a very successful businessperson, constantly busy, and very well-known. Venus, making this predictive Solar Arc contact as the arcing planet, was ruler of her Xth House with Taurus on the cusp. Jupiter, which was to receive the arc from Venus, was *in* the Xth! And, at the same time, transiting Jupiter was conjoining her Sun!

A very, very powerful time indeed. If she were not to meet a man for romance and strong relationship, she could certainly be successful in her business deals, which would be many in number at that time, according to her personal projections into her business future.

As we have seen, powerful direct Solar Arc contacts cast a Time Orb backward and forward in time. "Ann" was all set to meet her man, but time went by, business boomed, and no man showed until another part of the prediction fell into place: I had seen that, two months after the formation of her SA Venus square Jupiter supported by transiting Jupiter conjunct Sun, another Solar Arc would form with SA Uranus coming to her Mercury.

Previously, remembering her past engagement some five years earlier, we saw that SA Uranus, ruler of her VIIth, had figured strongly in conjunctions with her Sun (called off, with transiting Saturn thereafter opposing her Venus and then immediately opposing her Pluto). It was reasonable (and typical) that Uranus should again figure in the relationship prediction: here it was, coming to a conjunction with her natal Mercury, which was conjunct her Sun and Venus. Portents loomed large for relationship.

In other words, a full four-month *window of opportunity* presented itself through Solar Arcs and was supported by transits. The time period was from January, 1990 through May, 1990 (ending with the superb midpoint picture SA Pluto=Sun/Jupiter). Ann met the man in mid-March while, at the same time, setting up still another major business deal. He has recently proposed marriage.

Here we had two levels of bloom taking place simultaneously: business and relationship. What if there had been no business concerns or anything in the personal life that could also relate to the symbolisms? What if inactivity (underexposure), for example, did not allow the probability of any suitor? What would have happened to the measurements? What other level of manifestation could they fulfill ... or would they just not register in her life? How many measurements have indeed evaporated, disappeared, vanished in every astrologer's experience? For every person?

It is often a painful time, when expectations get so high, and the projection simply does not materialize. The astrologer must guard against this with great sensitivity and poise, with every strong set of measurements. There is no guarantee. And there is rarely any explanation. Alternate levels of symbolisms may manifest—and we have seen several examples of that in the book already—but there are times when there is nothing.

Such a set of circumstances is precisely the stimulus for my writing this book. I had known that one of the most powerful Solar Arc measurements possible was to form in my horoscope in July, 1990: SA Uranus conjunct the Ascendant, with many supportive transits, as introduced on page 97. Ordinarily, this measurement is backdrop to extraordinary individualistic development, so very often concomitant with geographic displacement, and, literally and figuratively, a whole new horizon.

Transits were backing this potential with "sledge hammers": transiting Saturn and Neptune had "lived" with my VIIth House Sun at 10 Capricorn for almost two years, and now transiting Uranus was to be there for a year. It is upon my Sun at this very moment in mid-December, 1990. We know that we can usually rely on the arcing planet's natal House rulership as an initial key to explain the particular Arc. Uranus rules my IXth. But I jumped the gun—with the explosiveness of this measurement. I saw myself as follows:

- Engaged to be married;
- Relocating to accommodate the marriage;
- Securing a high-level job position that would crown my career and reorganize several of my professional skills;
- Building new dreams.

But nothing happened to support these levels: my engagement to be married inexorably ground down to nothingness with the weight of VIIth House transits; all the apartment hunting was for naught; begrudgingly I extended my lease; the four major job thrusts I had mounted with enormous energy and pains, which would have taken me to different cities in each case, after protracted periods of scrutiny and evaluations, all collapsed; suddenly, I, the astrologer, was alone with my big powerful measurement(s) and nothing had happened except things to isolate me, stop me on one path, and perhaps move me to another.

I returned to the IXth House, the House the arcing Uranus rules. Yes, I faced lectures in Europe—but here was the signal, the *alternative* level for the manifestation to explain SA Uranus conjunct the Ascendant: *I had to write another book*. This House holding Venus had been activated with my last book, as we have seen. This new book would have to be the beginning of my new future time.

This personal example seems almost naively simplistic in the telling now, but it emerged out of great frustration, four months of deepest self-doubt, a loss of a dream, and that wrenching fortitude it takes to start a new vision. I, who for almost ten years was never again going to write a book, finally felt I had something more to share in our world of astrology. And that message came through loud and clear—as did the contract to write it—and I shall now build the next level of my individuation within those IXth House values.

My great expectations had introduced intense pressure into my life. With every "miss," embarrassment of the astrology followed. I could not believe it. But it is a lesson for us all to learn: the opportunities that emerge from the inexorable must be appreciated for what they are and not aggrandized to what they should be.

David

A second important problem in prediction involves neglecting the past as essential anchor for the future. We have seen over and over in Mundane Astrology (Chapter 5) how the charts of celestial phenomena of the past support the realities of the present and project to development in times to come.

A particular client of mine has been with me for almost eleven years. He is exquisitely intelligent, articulate, generous in his world to excess. However, he is a man whom few people can understand, I think. He is a giant of a man; he is black; he lives in the South; and he is in the world of the arts as a producer. On all fronts, he is not typical or expected or predictable. It all adds up to be intimidating to his worlds and confining to him.

I have lived through so many measurements with "David," so many powerful Solar Arc pictures and classic transits that did *not* correspond in any way to anything within his life development. As the past "failures" started to accumulate over the early years of our professional relationship, I began to temper and adjust suggestions about potentials when these cycles were due to repeat in future time. Gradually, we were diluting everything, and David's horoscope seemed to become just so much left-over skin after a plastic surgery.

David would bring me horoscope data for friends and associates, and quite rapidly in most cases, astrology would be able to zoom right in and illuminate these other lives. But astrology barely worked for David. We were both so frustrated.

Is his birthtime correct? Supposedly from his birth certificate; yet, we *have* tried adjustments, taken angular deficiencies into consideration, and more. Yet, every once in a while, a Solar Arc or transit situation *does* correspond with an anticipated reality, and the whole process of doubt is again readjusted with still more hope.

David kept a careful journal of happenings this past year, and wrote quite a long report to me. It was so awkward to read: major expectations such as transiting Saturn on his Sun with transiting Uranus crossing his Midheaven along with transiting Jupiter opposing his Sun; even with Solar Arc pictures such as SA MC= Sun/Mars and much more... *none of this* corresponded to much more than a blip here and there in his life, and the anguish was acute. He closed his report with these words, "I am certain that you will be just as bewildered as I about the failure of my 'reward period' to materialize. And despite all of these difficulties, I am not especially depressed. I became disgusted and oftentimes quite angry, but not depressed. As I said before, if you write another book, put me in it! Thank you for all your help and caring."

David is a Capricorn with Cardinal degrees everywhere across his horizon and upon his Meridian. The transits have been demanding, and somehow, throughout his past and now, he is in the wrong place on earth for his being to reach the Sun... as yet.

We learn from a story like this—and every astrologer has cases like this—*that no future measurement is going to transcend the grounding set up in the past*. David has some very difficult problematic concerns in his life; it is in those areas that the horoscope does seem "to work." If he were to take his case to another astrologer who did not check the past, see the failures and problems, that astrologer would have to relive the embarrassment David and I have been through and out of which we have emerged time and time again, not depressed, but indeed bewildered and still hopeful.

The third problem area of interpersonal astrological prediction faces the astrologer when reality structures do not accommodate potentials. For example, one's horoscope potentials are subsumed by a spouse's; or a woman's early development was spent in a geographic area and in a time when educational advantages were not offered to her, when highly stratified role expectations were placed upon her by the environment; when a young man is literally groomed from childhood to sail into his father's business with no say of his own. In these situations, individuation is somehow compromised, stunted, masked. Astrological measurements seem to push for expression and never register. There is always unhappiness.

As astrologers, we must know this, that *possibilities are built only upon personal potentials and what the environment will invite, admit, and reward*. Routine behavior is the rule—not the exception—in all society. Life gains security through predictability. Divergence from that norm is called abnormal, when personal, family, or social organization is threatened, with the environment rewarding change or squashing it. In short, we have the choice to reflect our environment for reward and constancy or to change it for greater individuation and self-aggrandizement.*

All this is only reasonable. The three-month sensation Rock groups, the flashes in the public pan, record one record, ride a crest of super-hype promotion into the ears of history, and disappear. The environment's needs—the market's needs—opened the door. The "package" was displayed. The effect is short-lived because it lacked other dimensions. A Quincy Jones, for example, has talents and potentials that belong "somehow" at the leadership level of the popular music industry. The song "We are the World" has "something" that somehow registers in the collective human mind—in market awareness, as special, fine, enduring, worthwhile. Some things have futures. Some things do not.

---

* See Tyl, *Holistic Astrology* for a thorough treatise on the individual's interaction with the environment in terms of horoscope symbology.

In prediction in astrology, there are these kinds of value judgments that definitely play a major role in consultations. Astrologers themselves must be able to understand the environmental prerequisites that each client faces *in terms of his or her potentials, plans, and dreams*. Dane Rudhyar said it well in *Astrology of Personality*: "No astrologer—and as well no psychoanalyst—can interpret a life and destiny at a level higher than that at which he himself functions."

Rolf

This next horoscope shown on page 160 portrays a young man of extreme drive (Sun-Uranus conjunction in Leo; Mars-Pluto conjunction in Leo; the do-your-own-thing Moon position in the Ascendant in Sagittarius), international acumen (the extraordinary emphasis on the IXth House, ruled by the Sun), keen sensibility (Mercury-Venus conjunction in Virgo), and precocious maturity (Saturn rising in Sagittarius square Mercury-Venus, trine Sun-Uranus). He and his wife, also foreign born, share some seven languages together, and enjoy very successful parallel careers in international banking. (His Saturn rules his IInd; Jupiter rules his Ascendant and is at the Midheaven; the Moon rules the VIIIth, other peoples' monies, and is in the Ascendant.)

The extreme emphasis seen in the expanded IXth House stellium corroborates that everything about Rolf will tend to be international, enterprising, engaging, and successful.

Rolf was born with an astrologer's list of predictions literally beside him: his parents had commissioned an astrologer to project the future for their son shortly after his birth.* So it was astrology-at-first-sight when Rolf became my next door neighbor 28 years later. He needed an update in a new land, in a new part of the world.

In terms of timing the horoscope past and future, it is really very simple: Saturn at the Ascendant will key developments throughout life. Without even yet checking the "Quick-Glance" Transit Table, we can see that, when Saturn makes its first square to the natal Moon position from 29 Pisces, it will be just about to cross his IVth cusp. This will be at about seven and a half years of age

---

* Rolf points to these predictions with amazement and pride: "He said I would be in business 'in new parts of the world,' obviously a reference to somewhere outside Europe. These predictions actually sparked my first interest in the potential of an international business career." (Read on. They were easy predictions to measure; demanding predictions to make for a new born!)

160 / Prediction in Astrology

"Rolf"

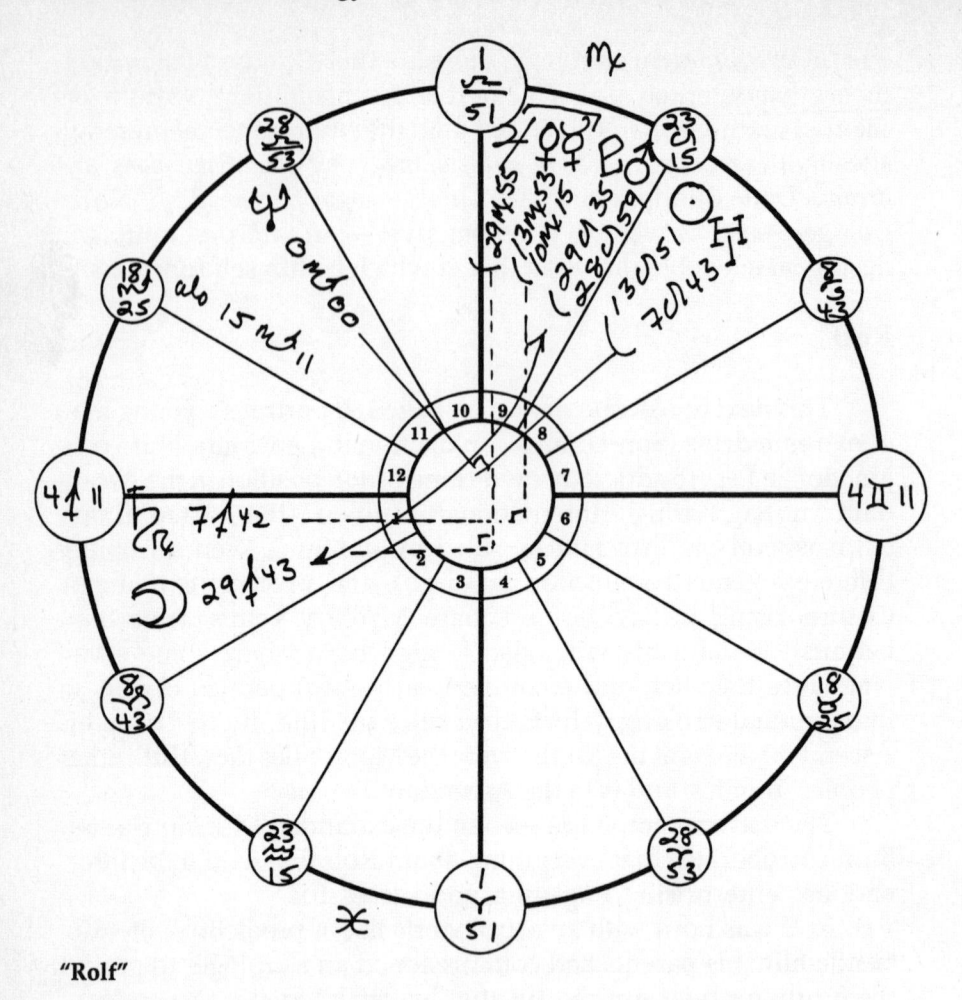

(quadrature of Saturn's 28-30 year orbit). Then, about 14 years later, transiting Spurn will oppose that IVth cusp position (one half of the cycle), age 21-22. Just before that, Saturn would be transiting the IXth House stellium.

And so it was: an extraordinary amount of life-change began for Rolf as Saturn moved through all those seven planets and as important Solar Arc measurements formed as well (August birth, very slow solar Arc accumulation; therefore more years of life to fulfill the number of degrees of measurement projection—recall page 62). For example, SA Mercury=Midheaven measures 21 degrees 36 minutes—and this will be enormously important since Mercury is in its own sign and, because of that, tends to dominate the horoscope; and, secondly, Rolf is a Mercury-in-Virgo archetype, fastidious, exacting, laser-memoried, and precise to beat the band. In the exact timing of this Solar Arc, his Mercury came to the Midheaven at age 22 years, seven months.

Working with the feel of transiting Saturn "lording it over the assembly of potentates in a foreign land," knowing that Saturn would be there, squaring its own natal position as well, at age 21-22; seeing also SA Uranus=Mars in 21 degrees, we could be positive that at about 22 years of age Rolf would experience a pivotal time in his development. This would be the time an astrologer prepares very close measurements prior to consultation.

Jupiter is prominent as the ruler of Rolf's Ascendant, and it is placed at the Midheaven. When he says that he is an international banker, your eyes go there and there only to begin with. Jupiter is basically $1^1/_2$ signs ahead of the Sun in this horoscope. This means that it will transit conjunct the Sun in about $10^1/_2$ years of age (within a regular 12-year cycle, very closely to one sign a year). The cycle then is set: $10^1/_2$ and then 22 (!), then 34 (1991, as we shall see). This is another powerful measurement that coincides with the general age orientation of 22.

Adding 22 degrees quickly to the Midheaven, we get 23-24 Libra. With a little practice and anticipation, one can then feel 45 degrees (semisquare) on top of that and come up with 68 "Libra," which is 8 Sagittarius, the position of Rolf's natal Saturn. This means that SA MC=Saturn would take place at the same time of development as all the other accumulating measurements.

Putting well-practiced pushes behind these generalized rapport measurements, one can then project the Sun 22 degrees further to 35 "Leo," which is 5 Virgo, and see that SA Sun is at the midpoint of Mercury/Pluto. Do this with Uranus and see that it has moved to the midpoint of Sun/Venus. Career development, possible marriage.

And one final predictive assumption from the radix: projecting the Moon to its first square with Saturn—68 degrees—divided by 12, and we can begin the Secondary Moon-Saturn cycle at roughly 5.6 years. Increased incrementally 6.5 to 7 years, we arrive at this series of ages for quadrature relationship with Saturn: the halfway points in the fifth, twelfth, nineteenth, twenty-sixth, thirty-third (etc.) years. Our important surmise about age 22 falls right in with developments after and before the Secondary Progressed Moon cycle contact with Saturn (and Mercury, since they are closely square).

Rolf visited the United States for the first time in August, 1979, when he was exactly 22 years old. All the measurements corroborate that very important time, especially transiting Jupiter exactly conjunct his Sun. Rolf decided to stay in the United States and take post-graduate study at a University in Washington D.C., where he did meet his bride-to-be, and began his swift rise to success in international business. This is where the Secondary Moon "kicked in," relating as well to Mercury, ruler of his VIIth.

It seems as if all these words about measurement may be hard to follow, not because of lack of clarity but because of the time it takes to read them. The deductions of time projections in a horoscope are so rapid after practice and confidence are accumulated that it is burdensome to slow things down to capture the nuance of the procedure. It is much like reading a book on sleight-of-hand magic with a deck of cards: the infinitesimally slight finger movements and even thought patterns have to be harnessed in detail for full comprehension; but the effect, when practiced and mastered with confidence, should be faster than the blink of an eye. Speed is not the goal; speed is a by-product of understanding and comfort.

Now that we know the core of Rolf's horoscope and his rise to success early in life, let us review it all quickly for confidence, and then add some considerations for predictions into the future:

- The stellium in the IXth promises international activity, academia, interest in philosophy, etc. Corroborated by his obvious language skills and his profession as an international banker.

- He is "old world" in grace and manners, but he is a very young man in a fast-moving country. (He still calls me "Sir" most of the time although we have been neighbors and friends for years!) This is the anchor of Saturn in Sagittarius at the Ascendant.

- Timing will probably be easy and reliable when we can project transiting Saturn up and into the stellium and start "clicking" off the Solar Arcs there as well.

- Age 22 would be of major importance by Solar Arc measurements and the transit of Jupiter over the Sun at the same time. Rolf came to the United States to further his education and build his career.

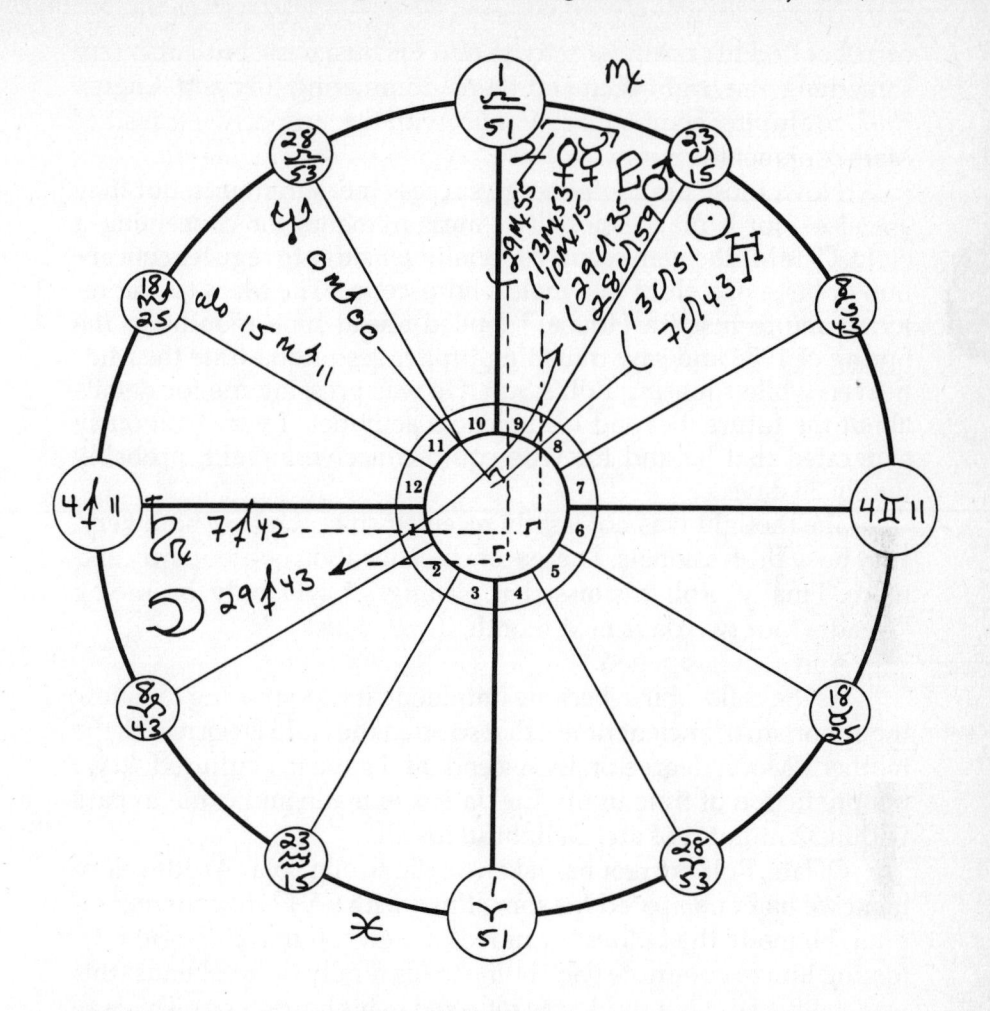

"Rolf"

What we have done over the last several pages, we have done with anticipation and feel, not with the dictates of a computer. Calculations then did help us zero in on precision, but it was always Rolf's reality that put meanings into the measurements that were made.

I have been through a lot of astrology with Rolf. He reminds me time and time again that on July 8, 1987, we sat for an update consultation. It was a very busy time for him and his wife: each was traveling in far-away countries for the whole Summer, so demanding were their jobs. I saw measurements in the horoscope that certainly corroborated his business activity and his busyness, but I also saw something else, right then and there, dominating July and August 1987: SA Jupiter semi-square Venus, with the supportive transit of Mars conjunct his Sun.

Now, those are high-energy success measurements, but they are also—for a man especially—measurements for conceiving a child. (The Midheaven seems especially sensitive to register conception or birth of a child in a male's horoscope.) The Mars transit referred me to his Vth House. I looked ahead nine months to the Spring of 1988 and saw transiting Jupiter sesquiquadrate the Midheaven while squaring Rolf's Sun. He was pressing me for details about the future, beyond his business activities. I very cautiously suggested that he and his wife could conceive a child, probably within 30 days.

The thought was not lightly received since they are both very, very busy professionals. There were worries about job jeopardy and more. Finally, Rolf dismissed it, saying, "I will only be seeing 'Neadra' for two days next month, if we're lucky!"

And so it happened.

As the child's birth became imminent, it was sporting to follow the aphorism of ancient times, that so often the child is born with the mother's Moon degree on its Ascendant. I gave it a cultured "try": the prediction of time upon due date was made and came to pass within 32 minutes of arc! Delightful for all.

Of late, Rolf's career has taken on the strong Solar Arc development we had anticipated for some time: with SA Pluto conjunct Jupiter, he made the boldest of moves, a new job in a different city, forcing him to commute back home to his family on weekends (this was a move I did not think was reflected in his horoscope). This was very, very difficult for the family. "How long will this last?" was the question I heard over and over again.

There was almost instant dissatisfaction with the new position Transiting Pluto constantly squaring Rolf's Sun at this time was pressing for even further change of perspective. The new job had placed him out of his field and into a whole new area of expertise. Rolf's horoscope showed only two potential breaks: SA Sun=Pluto/MC in July-August 1990, 18 months into the new job; and then the crowning SA Pluto conjunct his Midheaven five months later at age $33^{1}/_{2}$, with transiting Jupiter coming back again to conjoin his Sun. This would be the time of change, the biggest change of his life since he had come to the "new land" at age 22.

Rolf left the firm in July, 1990 and is now building his own international business arena, "big time," looking forward to the happiest of new years.

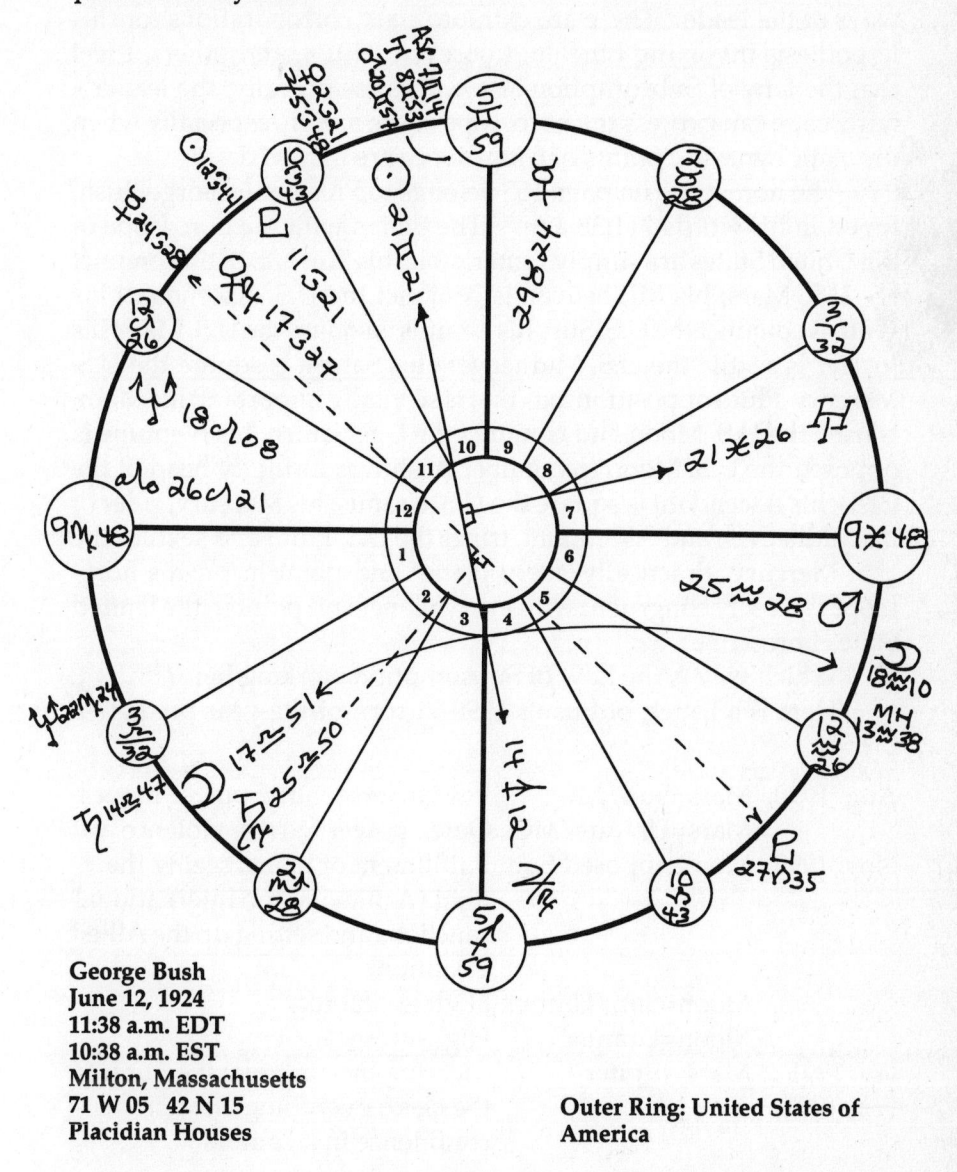

George Bush
June 12, 1924
11:38 a.m. EDT
10:38 a.m. EST
Milton, Massachusetts
71 W 05   42 N 15
Placidian Houses

Outer Ring: United States of America

In Mundane Astrology, there is an aphorism that the president or king of a country loses his identity to the country in terms of its horoscope. In other words, the country's horoscope takes the place of the leader's horoscope. This is called the "Law of Subsumption."[6] The national "field" is greater than the reference to an individual. If there are close synastric tie-ins, the national reference tells us the ways of the leader. There are extraordinary corroborations for this hypothesis involving Lincoln, Roosevelt, Hitler, and others. I feel that the Law of Subsumption also works reciprocally: the leader's horoscope can express the horoscope of the nation, especially when dramatic synastric points of congruence are involved.

The horoscope on page 165 belongs to President George Bush, timed in his words "11:38 a.m."[7] The tie-ins with the horoscope of the United States are simply remarkable: his Sun is exactly conjunct the U.S. Mars; his Midheaven is conjunct the U.S. Ascendant; his Pluto is conjunct the U.S. Sun; his Uranus is square the U.S. Mars; his Jupiter is sextile the U.S. Midheaven; his Saturn is square the U.S. Mercury-Pluto opposition axis that is so vitally important; his Moon is trine the U.S. Moon and conjunct the U.S. Saturn; his Neptune is opposed the U.S. Moon (remember Bush was formerly head of the CIA); his Ascendant is square the U.S. Uranus; his Mercury, ruler of his Midheaven and Ascendant, trines the U.S. Pluto and sextiles the U.S. Mercury. Practically every planet and point in Bush's horoscope is closely congruent with every planet and point in the United States horoscope!

Which way is the Law of Subsumption working here?

Here is a listing of Bush's 1990-91 turn-of-the-year predictive profile:

Aug. 1990:	Mars=Sun/MC	Power personality; power moves
	Mars=Uranus/MC	Quick power moves; violence
Nov. 1990:	Moon opposed Sun	Fulfillment of plans; seeing the light (Achieving the international sanctions and setting up the Allied Coalition)
Dec. 1990	Moon=Sun/Uranus	High excitability
	Moon=Uranus	High stress, anxiety
Jan. 1991	Mars=Jupiter	Clearing the air; breaking out into the clear; overdoing efforts; confidence in a gamble
Feb. 1991		

---

6. This insight is attributed to the British astrologer C.E.O. Carter, a leading personage in the field in the mid-20th century.
7. Eastern Daylight Time, told by Bush personally to a colleague of Lois Rodden of Los Angeles, CA, a specialist in the collection and refinement of birth times of the famous.

Getting Personal—Looking at the Past Ahead of Time / 167

Mar./Apr. 1991	Venus=Sun	Moratorium; peace or special alliance
May 1991	Jupiter=Neptune	Possible losses, scandal; terrorism
June 1991	Uranus=Mars	Extreme, sudden action; violence

These are the key Solar Arc pictures. The transits are clearly corroborating: the eclipse at 25 Capricorn, as we have seen, is so dramatic, taking place on January 15, 1991, the ultimate deadline date set by the United Nations, and it is exactly square Bush's Saturn, with transiting Mars conjunct his Mercury, ruler of Midheaven and Ascendant, and Uranus opposed his Pluto (tremendous exertion)... all at the same time.

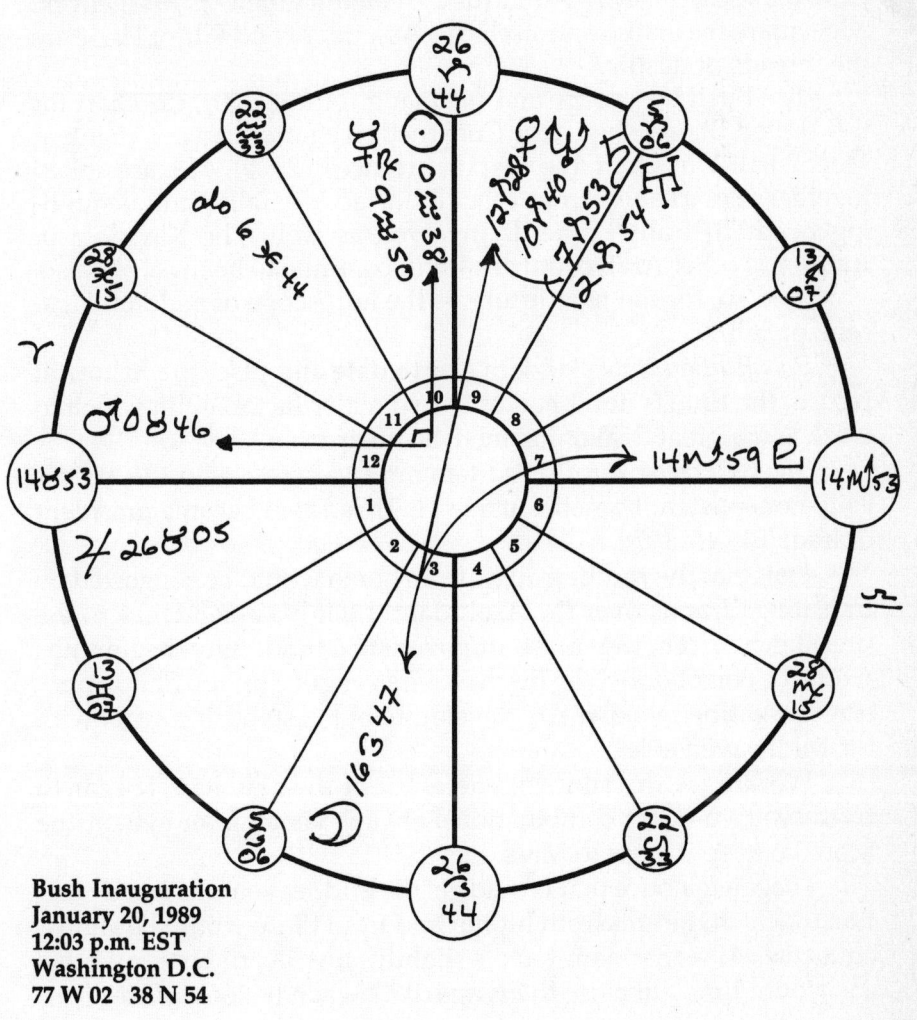

Bush Inauguration
January 20, 1989
12:03 p.m. EST
Washington D.C.
77 W 02   38 N 54

168 / Prediction in Astrology

And when we add the chart from the past, shown on page 167, for Bush's inauguration, we see even more portents of our president facing war, deploying aggression: the Sun is dramatically square Mars, and this Mars is *exactly the Mars position in the first degree of Taurus in the mid-way Jupiter opposed Saturn chart (see page 119).*

We can note with awe that the inauguration Pluto squares the U.S. Midheaven in Aquarius and that the inauguration Saturn is conjunct Jupiter-Saturn in the Great Conjunction chart of the Grand Mutation into the Earth Family of Signs in 1842 (page 129), and a demanding conjunction of transiting Mars and Saturn—which will color world history for some two years—takes place March 6, 1992 (5:51 p.m., GMT), at 13 Aquarius 29, conjunct the U.S. Midheaven, and square the inauguration chart's Ascendant and Pluto. These are the threads of destiny.

The Bush horoscope and the inauguration chart, the chart for the United States, the Great Conjunction charts (ingress, rising at Mecca, half-way chart, the next occurrence in 2000), ALL are linked together remarkably...not casually or accidentally, but astoundingly—fatalistically! Israel is involved as well. The Kingdom of Iraq—and other Arab countries—will continue to be involved also.

And so, for the near future, is the horoscope of Saddam Hussein, page 169.

Rectification Note: Saddam's birth date and place are historical record; the time is not. I had only two major factors with which to work and a great deal of instinctive anticipation.

The two facts were: 1) Saddam ran away from a hostile, practically non-existent homelife at age 11; 2) Saddam became president of Iraq, July 16, 1979.

I felt that the running away from home would be suggested by transiting Uranus over the Ascendant; I felt his ascendancy to the presidency from the most impoverished and ugly beginnings would be corroborated by his massive strength (Jupiter-Pluto opposition) rotating by Solar Arc development to establish contact with the Midheaven axis.

Working with a sunrise general lay-of-the-sky chart, I began to try these two-event combinations, always keeping an eye on the Moon to keep it close to Mars.

I began to notice that I could get the Midheaven axis into a position to which the arcs from Jupiter and from Pluto would be almost equal, i.e., 41°+; Saddam's arc is slightly slow, April birth, and this 41° would time out close to his age of 42 when he took office.

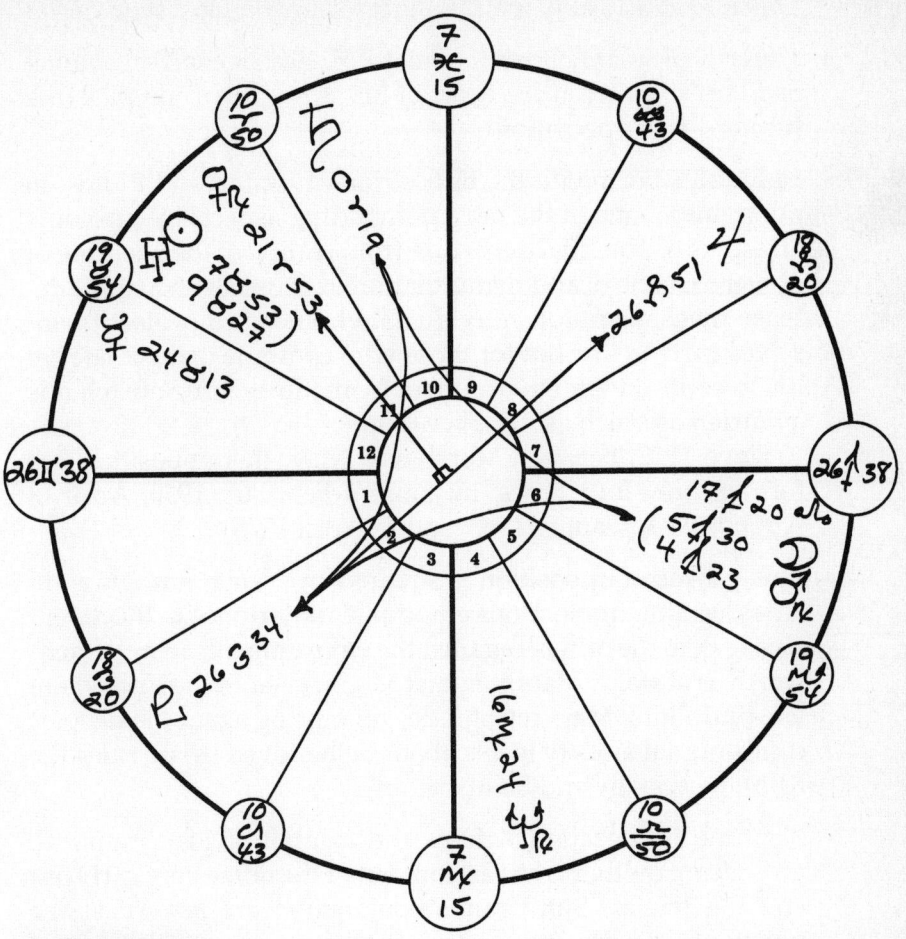

Saddam Hussein
Trial Rectification
April 28, 1937
8:18 a.m. BGT
Tikrit, Iraq
43 E 42   34 N 36

The process kept leading me to 8:18 a.m., and work with transits started to refine the rectification hypothesis: yes, transiting Uranus would be crossing the Ascendant during the Summer in 1948, just after Saddam's eleventh birthday, and SA Jupiter would conjoin the Midheaven in April, 1979, with SA Pluto upon the IVth cusp, opposing the Midheaven—one of the most powerful measurements in astrology—when he took over the country in July 1979.

The time of 8:18 a.m. is a fine start for further observation.

- The critical Solar Eclipse of January 15, 1991, is exactly conjunct Saddam's Jupiter at the heart of his strong-man complex (the Jupiter-Pluto opposition).

- Saddam is born with the opposition of Jupiter and Pluto—in my opinion, one of the most demanding aspects in astrology, an aspect of potential departure from reality, of the wielding of power, of control and manipulation. It is usually a helpful defense mechanism for individuals who need to protect themselves early in life; but for those who continue using it later in life to control their environment (sometimes ferociously), it is a burden as much as it is a weapon.

  Since 1937, between March and May, this opposition has formed only four times: in January-February 1950, April to August 1962; January 1963; and in April 1975.

- This powerful opposition is squared by Venus retrograde in Aries, adding tremendous emotional undertones to the defensiveness, to the outlash against the environment. So much self-worth is at stake: Mars conjunct Moon, ruler of the IInd where we find Pluto; Mars retrograde, suggesting again the deepest contrapuntal anxiety levels about being loved (Mars rules the XIth), personally and by his people.

- Neptune retrograde (perhaps the symbol of his tyrannical, non-caring mother who cast him out of the home very early on) and the intense Sun-Uranus conjunction are *peregrine!* The functions of overcompensation for the strangest of homelives (Neptune in the IVth, ruling the Xth) and the drive to be someone (Sun-Uranus) run away with the whole horoscope.

- Another defense mechanism working overtime is the fire Grand Trine among Saturn in Aries (ambition in ego terms), Pluto (over the signline in Cancer), and Mars-Moon in Sagittarius. This is an extraordinary configuration, tapping into the massive Jupiter-Pluto opposition. Mercury, ruler of the hypothetical Ascendant, has only one aspect: trine to Jupiter within the opposition with Pluto. In the XIIth, Mercury is unto itself, consumed with the wielding of defenses to structure an eventual show of the ego to satisfy emotional hurt and justify personal convictions.

There is a time-honored, significant tradition in astrology that imparts physical characteristics to the Ascendant. As the world has become more complicated, with peoples and races melted together, with populations drifted to extremes, and with so many personal potentials to change appearance, this tradition becomes conspicuously simplistic for modern usage and reliability. Yes, there are obvious "hits" that keep the tradition alive, but there are new problems to consider. To our perception, Saddam appears Scorpionicly swarthy, with many detailed points to fill out that classic image; but we must note that a tremendous portion of Iraqi males have this same look.

A second, certainly more dynamic reference from the Ascendant involves behavioral tendencies. But the astrologer must be sensitive to the level at which these potentials can manifest; i.e., *we too easily see what we look for*. Because Saddam has been portrayed as a murderous despot in his behavior, a bias is established to the sign Scorpio, to Scorpionic lore, which is certainly unfair to that sign on the Ascendant. In his case though, this inference may be valid, but we need to know much more about him and his behavior from within *his* milieu to do justice with our symbolisms.

The Gemini Ascendant could be valid as well, beyond the interesting timing focal points we have explored in our trial rectification: Saddam's skillful manipulation of the media; his penchant for long-winded rhetoric (by our standards); his suspected indecisiveness with war tactics; his apparent unemotional reaction to his world. But then again, we *are* seeing what we look for, and perhaps these values are equally unfair to the sign Gemini. In both conjectural instances, we are judging his Ascendant from our cultural, destined-to-win perspective.

Then there is a third consideration of the Ascendant which, along with the simplistic and the dynamic, completes a personal projection potential. This consideration involves the *ruler* of the Ascendant and its sign placement, aspect reinforcement, etc. In this case, Saddam's ruler would be Mercury in Taurus, *the tenacious polar complement of Scorpio*. This fuller view carries its validity as well. We must remember all three levels of Ascendant symbolism when we attempt to rectify a horoscope. We can never be sure with our deductions. Only time tells, and arcs and transits of time interplay with the Angles multi-dimensionally to give us our tightest grasp on the birth moment.

Fascinatingly, as we approach wartime in January-February, 1991, transiting Saturn conjoins Saddam's Jupiter and opposes his Pluto, exactly during the first 18 days of January. The entire Mid-East crisis is overwhelmingly involved with the same measurements, over and over and over again, all linked to the harbingers of the epoch, the lord called Jupiter and the lord called Saturn.

If this horoscope timing is close to correct, Saddam seized Kuwait with SA Moon conjunct his Pluto in June, 1990 and opposed his Jupiter in September, 1990. In other words, his SA Moon tapped into the reservoir of all Saddam's personal power, the core of his overcompensatory character development and his extremely sophisticated skills for environmental control, during the period May-September, 1990. The SA Moon-Pluto measurement is a measurement of enormous upheaval and potential violence, echoing his takeover of the government in 1979, in the past. In reciprocity to the Law of Subsumption, perhaps the country is being seen here through its president, and what is shown is an entirely new perspective for an ancient nation.

In mid-February for Saddam, as for the United States and Bush, there is an intensification during the second week: transiting Mars opposes Saddam's Moon, semi-squares his Venus, squares his Midheaven. There will be a major change of tactics on both sides between February 10 and 14, triggered by the Mars transit of the U.S. Ascendant and Uranus.

Then in March/April, there is nothing new in terms of aggression. For all constituents, there seems to be a lull in April—a suspension. For Bush and the United States there is frustration; for Iraq there is positivism (Sun=Jupiter), and for Saddam there is only the midpoint picture of May casting a Time Orb back into March/April: SA Jupiter=Saturn/MC, unreliable because of the involvement of the recitified Angle. But should this be tenable, the suggestion is for doing things right, the way they are expected to be done. He will be made to toe the line by March/April. A Time Orb may cast this earlier.

This lull in March/April will coincide with Ramadan, perhaps to avoid exacerbating the issues further with the drama of religious martyrdom. But in July/August, 1991, regardless of the exact time of his birth, Saddam experiences SA Mars opposed Pluto—upheaval and brutality, possibly absorbing injury one way or another. At this time, we can say no more.

These measurements out of past cycles focus the present and forge the future. We see within this crisis the specter of nihilism, this time curiously in the name of God.

Chapter Seven

Working with Clients—Talking about Predictions

Almost 1900 years ago Ptolemy applied an astrological grid over all his known world in terms of national temperament, in terms of behavior patterns learned through trade and discourse, historians' reports, and rumor; he was working with one sense of the Law of Subsumption (page 166). Even now, we talk about "national character," about how Israel *is* its well-timed chart, how Germans behave in such ways, Turks another, etc. Does astrology inspire culture? Does culture define astrology?

And so with us. We Americans individually reflect the national "field," the overview of the nation that permeates our growth and projections, naturally, with necessity, and certainly with extraordinary judgmental pressure. We can become only what our environment will allow; we can grow only to the extent our environment will support. We are part of our nation; Americans away from home are quite obvious.

Our public image, our international poise, is of invincibility: our Cancer Sun portrays us as nurse to the world; our Aquarian Moon justifies all our activities (including historically annotated intrusion) as humanitarian to all. Indeed, we Americans *have* saved the modern world, and we continue to do so at every opportunity; that is what we think; that is what we are told.

There is nothing unnatural about any of this. And that is our discussion point. What is important however is that every client we astrologers serve feels this same sense of rightness, the rectitude of the American prerogative. Our clients *expect* fulfillment and success. Somehow, someway, in one language idiom or another, at one level of achievement or another, we naively expect to be successful, to be happy, to be proud, to be respected.

Not everyone in the world has these personal assumptions of nobility and grandeur. We cannot conceive that this is true, but it is. Other nations with other temperaments think in other perspectives about personal fulfillment and so-called success, about the meaning of life, and they are rarely so expressive about it as we Americans are. They fit into the scheme of things. What is the ethos of the Norwegians, Belgians, Japanese, Nicaraguans?

Americans fear realism.*

It is very difficult for an American to anticipate hearing a "bad bottom line." The person may be disadvantaged, oppressed, or victimized, but hope is always there. This is not necessarily the human condition, but it *is* the American way.

We can combine this extremely important, nationally intrinsic personality trait with a Zen teaching: that any earnest question has its answer within it. The client wants to be the hero. More often than not, the client will provide most of the answers, if the astrologer will listen, especially about the significance of things past and the potentials of things to come.

First, the astrologer must be *organized* to listen, to hear the assessment of the present and projection of the future from clients proud and secure, from clients at the fringes of self-doubt, from clients holding on to the American dream, to the projection of eventual success. These statements can be framed within many different levels: from finding romance to becoming president of a grand corporation; from improving the self-worth concept to choosing a profession. Organized measurements and a general plan of discussion must be prepared ahead of client consultation time. Following the prediction aphorisms (page 138) will be helpful to get the essential organization started.

All of these concerns came vividly to my mind recently when I called a friend for advice. My friend is highly intelligent and extremely experienced in life, and we share an intellectual rapport. Although my concerns when I called him were indeed clearly reflected in my horoscope, my call to him had nothing to do with astrology.

When we began our conversation, I led the dialogue and found

---

* The U.S. Neptune is sextile its retrograde Mercury, square to the U.S. Mars and sesquiquadrate to the Midheaven.

myself saying, "I need your advice on something, *but hold your tongue!* I want you to hear me out! Don't give me your reactions until I'm finished, OK?"

Listen to that! What I was saying here is that *I wanted to be heard* in the midst of my consternation. I wanted to regain the feeling of being a champion, of being on top of a complicated situation. Was it that, somehow, the answer to my dilemma was *going to be my statement of my problem?* I wanted time for that to get out; then I would have reinforced my integrity, my wholeness within the situation, and I would then be able to hear (take, endure) what my wise friend would have to say. I wouldn't be fragmented.

I was conscious of all this all the while during our talk. In fact, I realized I was listening to myself more than I would probably listen to him, probably because I feared he would tell me what I did not want to hear or what I thought would set me back... which, in turn, tells me I already knew the correct solution to my bind! Was it that I could only hear myself through my friend?

As it turned out, he gave me very sound advice—I agreed with it, which he backed up with examples from his own past experience. He characteristically and instinctively spoke in terms of cycles, of how these kinds of problems seem to repeat themselves when certain conditions are right. His "bottom line" was certainly the best bottom line of the several choices I had before me.

But I chose a different bottom line, the one through which I would sacrifice something to gain a sense of nobility, of rightness. I could always go back to the other alternative, but, for the moment, I needed to feel very good about myself rather than exploit my personal position.

I was fascinated with this process. I realized how often this happens to one degree or another every day, "Hey George, what do you think of this idea?... Jane, what do you *really* think of our sex life?"* In fact, I called my friend back two days later, thanked him again for helping, and told him what I had decided to do and why. I was patting myself on the back! I could hear him smiling on the telephone. I think he understood what was going on—doing anything to feel good about oneself—because this *is* the human condition, especially in our society.

---

* The interjection "really" in our language structure suggests that we doubt the veracity of a statement told to us or we feel our own statement is being doubted...or the expression of it is incomplete. "Really" is a way to get to the bottom line or behind the scenes: what *really* happened?

We so desperately need to feel good about ourselves. So many things in our world of development affect our progress. As suggested in the predictive aphorisms (page 138), seeking out the concomitants of self-worth and the timing of its development cycle is to study the whole of personality: parental influence, relationship dynamics, the giving and receiving of love, the comfort with sexual matters, the support of education, the maintenance of health, and inspiration through that personal example to our offspring.

Before we deal with the specifics of managing communication of prediction within the astrological consultation, I want to recall the seeds of thoughts presented in Chapter 2, "Great Expectations": just by the fact that we are astrologers, that we deal with this "thing" called astrology, we set up enormous expectations and the assumption of accuracy: why should I pay for something that isn't accurate?—We even inspire revelation! "You're my last hope. You've got to help me get out of this!"

When someone comes to an astrologer, he or she usually holds one of three views: "I believe in astrology, and this is going to be great!" Here the expectations are very high. The client expects a performance by the astrologer.

The second view is, "You were right on the button for my friend, who just hasn't stopped talking about you!" Here expectations have been raised by the friend. The client expects a similar excitement, resolution, promise of reward, etc. But the cases would undoubtedly be totally different; the new client could discover old problems that have been locked away for a long time, could learn the probable extension of a dull life routine for several years into the future, or could break down and accost very special anxieties, none of which was even thought of in relation to the friend's experience.

The third view is caution or outright testing. The client has been "sent" to the astrologer for one reason or another, or the client is "checking it out" for quite private reasons. What is usually happening here is the client is intrigued that astrology "may work," and is embarrassed about trying to find out or is afraid of what might happen, afraid that astrology *may* work. Here expectations will be reasonable most of the time in this point of view. Yet, as soon as accuracy pushes a few pressure buttons, the client will either become totally engrossed and helpful or will recoil in surprise and anxiety.

We astrologers also have great expectations. Enthusiasm for what we *can* do spills over all too easily to an over-sell of that which we *hope* we can do. We are not taught uniformly or completely enough about the extraordinary dynamics of counseling, of using astrological measurements and the "stuff" of life to make creative connections. We astrologers are left to our own devices—figuratively and literally—to make ourselves feel proud, prized, significant, and special. As we deal with doubt and unknowing to one degree or another—of our systems, our style, and our selves—we beef up our craft and image all the more. Expectations get larger still.

When we quote or make reference to the past to give evidence for the future, we pick out the great predictions of history or the nifty prediction that turned out for a client "just last year," and we neglect the predictions that failed. In that sense, by selective quoting of precedent, we reinforce an understandably flawed system.

Astrology definitely has its strengths and its vagaries: the former are related more to science and the latter are related more to art: on the one hand, life is measured and, on the other, measurements live. There is no magical coalescing solution possible here; it is *recognition of the situation* we face that can give us balance and poise within this swirl of concerns.

Expectations of one-sided performance by the astrologer must be changed to eagerness for dialogue between client and astrologer; the astrologer must give the parameters of sharing—of understanding and appreciating development—to the client's anticipation of success, instead of the prospect of revelation and the marshaling of fate. In this way, great expectations give way to the experience and expression of togetherness. The astrologer—along with astrology—achieves excellence, and the client indeed becomes a hero, which is his or her own birthright.

How much accuracy?* Whenever prediction is mentioned in astrological textbooks or lectures, it is almost always linked to the concept of "events." Indeed, in this book as well, much of the technique of measurement has been demonstrated through events, especially in the Mundane arena, since it is there that our symbology plays out its potential correspondences mono-directionally: we speak our mind, give our assessment, and there are no ramifi-

---

* This is always a major theme throughout astrological history, serving as a blend of self-protection and a cry for research. For example, in 1607, just after Brahe's death and just as Kepler was coming forth with his laws of planetary motion, Ilario Altobelli was giving a cardinal of the Church a list of predictions about the fate of Venice. He lamented enough for the history books about the inaccuracy of Mars positions, this "unobservable erratic since the world began."—Thorndike VII, page 16.

cations except that which the future will bring. History records the evaluation of our assessments, say, of a Great Conjunction of Jupiter and Saturn.

But this event orientation, so environmentally dependent, does not capture the essence of personal astrology. Indeed, our lives *are* compiled through a continuous flow of events, big and small, and events are our life history. But our *reactions*, our management of what these events mean, are existential, not environmental, and those reactions become our life character.

This is why the past tells us so much: we find out how someone reacted. Through time, we see accumulated reactions. The person becomes known through those reactions. And those reactions become predictable in the future. In this sense, we gain the feeling of free will: we are reacting as who we are. Life is happening somehow through us rather than to us. That is how the American especially needs to think.

Our textbooks speak of orbs applying with broader tolerances to "major events" and smaller tolerances to other events. Where is the line drawn to demarcate a "major event?" Or are we ever so gradually accumulating in our literature an apology for what we yet do not know in astrology, for not being able to be as accurate as others and we ourselves expect, as frequently as we would like? Are we saying, "the big stuff we can handle, but the small stuff eludes us still"? We miss a lot of "big stuff," too.

A more graceful way to present this difficult, soul-searching point is to say that the value of major and not-major events is established by the client, not the astrologer. For example, the death of a parent is not always a "major" event in the life of the son or daughter who could be 50 years old at the time, estranged from the parent for a very long time, be living some 5,000 miles away. Perhaps society expects such an event to be major, but to your client it is not. Should it be seen in the horoscope? Was it that my own mother did die six months *late*?

A still more graceful way to present this point is to say that events which will be given significance by the client—and perhaps reinforced or polished with the astrologer in earnest dialogue about the meaning of an event—*are carried into the client's life by cycles* and that, through the measurement of these cycles, we are able to use astrology to define the events that do have special developmental significance... more often than not.

That sense of cycles, tied to those steps and concerns that we know are extremely, formatively important in life in our society, is the thrust behind the prediction aphorisms presented in Chapter 6. Just as we know in our culture that our children leave the home to go to school at 6, enter the changes of adolescence at 13-14, take on an automobile at 16, go off to college at 18, gain the right to vote at legally prescribed ages, marry in the early twenties, seem to change job direction or level conspicuously at 28-30, etc., so do we know the astrological cycles that support those changes, and others, others that are individualistic to the extreme.

For example, if the client has a Leo Midheaven and, somewhere in the horoscope, the Sun is square with Uranus, we know instantly that the rulers (significators) of the parental axis are in high developmental tension. The astrologer will have to investigate this tension in the early home and beyond, guided by strong transits and Solar Arcs to those significators especially across the angular IVth and Xth cusps.

The thrust for the astrologer cannot end then with just establishing an event or two; it must continue to assess the client's reaction, and the pattern of reactions, thereafter during development. Perhaps the independence drive suggested by this Sun-Uranus aspect is presently activated, say at age 42, with transiting Uranus squaring the Sun and opposing its own natal position. Perhaps the natal Sun is in the VIIth House. Such a pattern of behavioral tensions develops throughout life, linking past and future in terms of the experience of the aspect, which becomes the key to prediction. What lessons have been learned through time? Is something threatening independence within the marriage? Is marriage itself the threat? Why all-of-a-sudden?

A client of mine for some years just came to see me for an update. In the main, we talked about his recent past, tied to our earlier meetings and discussions over the years, and began to make some projections about two things: his relationship with his daughter, and his potential for very strong adjustments of his job position relating to the near and distant future.

The discussion about his relationship with his daughter was based more on *her* horoscope than on his, and this discussion was very rewarding.

The job situation study was built upon dominant Solar Arc midpoint pictures in the next two months: Pluto=Sun/Saturn,

MC=Mars/Pluto, Jupiter=Mars/Pluto and then, nine months into the future, MC square Pluto.

Pluto, the arcing planet in the first picture, rules his XIth (his reward from his job—second of his Xth), and is prominent in his horoscope in conjunction with Mars, dispositor of his Aries Moon. Saturn is conjunct his Virgo Sun.

What we see here in these few measurements is an enormous rush of almost rebellious energy potential along with a heavy down-to-earth sobriety. The midpoint pictures and supportive transits are obvious job-energy indicators. And, indeed, his job situation adjusted itself on schedule strongly for his new future; he is now able to plan strategically for the "major" development next Summer.

But—the instructive point here is that something else happened in this man's life that we had talked about in the consultation only fleetingly. For a hobby, he is an avid motorcyclist and strong campaigner for motorcycle safety. (Aries Moon with Mars conjunct Pluto natally; Sagittarian Ascendant; yet his personal presentation is deeply subdued: Saturn conjunct the Sun in Virgo.)

After our consultation, I received a long, wonderful letter from him about an extraordinary breakthrough in his relationship with his young daughter, and then three telephone calls about his positive job adjustments and other matters. But what was really important was the recognition he had received as a District Safety Representative for a prominent motorcycle firm. He told me this three times, and this is as far afield from his financial management job as one could imagine.

Where was *this* event in his horoscope? It is a minor event, relatively, but it brought about a major feeling within him, a major reaction. Returning to the horoscope, I saw, indeed, transiting Jupiter was semi-squaring the Sun...but that was tied in with the exact time of his job improvement. This transit corresponded to a generally fortunate time. But this assessment feels weak, incomplete, meaningless. The dilemma is that we have great expectations for something astrological to say "Recognition Award Certificate received for Motorcycle Safety Representation," and astrology simply can not do that.

It was enough in our discussion to see that he was in good shape with regard to his job, that his energies were strong, that a general timing of adjustment fit his projections of possibilities, that nothing was threatening. That he received the award of recognition is a *delight*...not an event that was missed because it was not "major."

There are scores of events that happen every day which are not "major" but we feel should somehow be harnessed descriptively by our predictive astrology. Astrologers can not do that yet. Astrology may not be able to do it ever. Can we not be content with cycles and the translation of time into opportunity? Can we not trust our communication and listening skills as much as we explore our measurement skills? Can we relate the horoscope not to what we know about astrology but to the life our client is living? Can we adjust expectations to let astrology shine the way it can most of the time? If we do, astrology will become more meaningful, and *astrologers will become more accurate.*

I can vividly remember sitting with a client whose Virgo Sun was in her VIth House, opposed by Saturn in the XIIth. When we were at the point of the discussion when I was inquiring about the transit of Saturn over her Sun at approximately age 13-14, I sensed she had little faith in what we were trying to do. And almost in a fit of pique, masked with humor, I said, "Well, June, I could just say right out what these symbols could mean: for example, at this time, you had a black cat that died, and you buried it ceremoniously in your backyard!"

I was right in every detail! How had that happened? All I did was stretch the symbolism of Virgo, VIth House and pets, Saturn and black, concerns of death; and then adolescent involvements with sorrow and ceremony (Virgo reactions), burying the cat, etc. I had said this to get her attention.—Her father was even a minister and officiated at the burial!

That does not happen yet in astrology, *but it does happen sometimes in astrologers*. Every seasoned professional has had jolts-of-knowing like that, and the scores of professional astrologers from four countries with whom I have spoken about this agree: the occurrence of such awareness of specifics appears accidental; it flows from some other level, because it cannot be explained methodologically or repeated reliably. Some expert astrologers reiterated that such specificity is not the role of astrology; but, being fair, I must comment that this may be the rationale protecting our incompleteness.

And then again, when a dear friend and client of mine went,

with her husband and their three children up into the sky in their private plane, heading for their vacation home in New England...a trip they had made many times...and I with them once...how could I know that they would all die in a horrible crash? Before the fact and after the fact, there was no evidence astrologically in her horoscope whatsoever that such an event would happen. The fact that her husband was the pilot and not she? The fact that another plane was involved? Those are only *more measurements*, not clarification of principle. When someone dies, the horoscope should show it, right? It is major!

Or do we not know what to look for?

Yes, we can see debilitation in someone ill and, from empirical reasoning, as a doctor does, make the judgment that death could come at a time of added stress. Yes, we can see *circumstances* of death in the horoscope but, again, we are on the periphery of fate. Maybe that is where we are supposed to be. Maybe that should give us comfort with VIIIth House matters and take the pressure off our feelings that we should know all.

Going further: in my opinion, there is extremely little evidence *before the fact* for the assassination of John F. Kennedy.[1] There is evidence of important potential changes in his life (such as a divorce), which has been corroborated by recent books about Kennedy, his marriage tensions, and problems with Congress. But evidence for death? No.

This discussion is an exercise to relax our great expectations about predictions, to champion the flow of cycles over the capture of specifics, and to set the stage in that spirit for the counseling aphorisms that follow. These Aphorisms can help us explore our strengths in counseling about prediction, give us greater efficiency with our skills, greater accuracy with our techniques, and greater grace in our contact with clients.

Counseling Aphorisms

1. *Clarification for the Client*—Clarifying expectations immediately upon first contact with the prospective client improves astrological accuracy enormously. Astrologer and client get onto the same wave length; the consultation is anticipated for the right

---

1. Tyl, *The Houses.*

reasons and the parameters for its conduct and objectives are shared by astrologer and client alike:

> "I look forward to our visit together, Mr. Grissom. It usually lasts about an hour and ten minutes—more if needed, of course—and we have a thorough discussion together about your life development and the time ahead."

A statement along these lines does wonders to calm the client, to defuse expectations that may be off the track, and to start the process of introspection within the client. The key words are "we have a thorough discussion together about your life development." The emphasis is on give-and-take conversation and away from any one-sided performance that may be expected from the astrologer.

Often prospective clients will ask if they can tape-record the consultation. This is a tip-off that the client is indeed expecting a performance by the astrologer, a "proclamation" of astrology, rather than a sharing of understanding. Throughout my entire career, my answer to this request has always been: "That won't be necessary, Mrs. Hobbins. Believe me. Our time together will be a time of sharing, a time of dialogue. You may even be doing most of the talking! And we will probably be talking about deep, very personal, even intimate concerns. The tape machine puts us both on stage, and that's not the best thing for us. My job is to be clear in what we come up with together. You'll be able to remember it, I promise. You may want to take notes. At the end, if we really think it's needed, I will speak a summary into your recorder. All right?"

That statement is loaded with persuasion, rationale, and, yes, situational control. We are discussing not just the taping request but the entire perception of the astrological consultation. From the very beginning, the astrologer must be the choreographer. The astrologer must make realistic promises and avoid the cliches of great expectations. The key words are: together, we, us, the best thing, a time of sharing.

There is no astrologer who cannot do his or her best with a client when the conditions of meeting with the client are as the astrologer wants them.

2. *Preparation*—Preparation is vitally important: knowing the lay of the land before the client arrives. The client should see that you have done your homework—from your eyes, from your folder, from your notes. For prediction, cycles in the past should be lined up

for questions to the client in order to learn about important, formative events and character-building reactions; cycles into the future should be noted, but rarely beyond a year-and-a-half ahead. Projections any further into the future put enormous responsibility on the astrologer and change what is practical and helpful into what is conjectural and unrelated; they also put enormous expectations and preoccupations upon the client.

The shorter the time projection, the more accurate the prediction: projection into the future is then closer to the realities of the present. Common sense can more easily reinforce speculation. (This is not an apology for or a weakness in the astrologer; rather, it is an adjustment of perspective about astrology that permits it to be what it is, not what it has been fashioned to be.)

Specifically, it is mandatory to make a list of rapport measurement Solar Arcs through the early part of life combined with strong transits. (Please recall the Prediction Aphorisms, page 138.) These measurements will be the best guide for client discussion for most of the consultation time.

Carefully measured Solar Arc and transit measurements made into the future should be carefully organized on a computer printout or a transit graph for the year ahead, to be seen and evaluated easily, at a glance. The astrologer should be free then to listen, to make creative connections among symbols throughout time as conversation develops and to be part of the life as times to come into focus.

3. *Pressure Points*—Thorough preparation helps get to the answer of an important question: "Where's the action? Where is the pressure building that brings the client to the astrologer?"

If there is dramatic Solar Arc and/or transit activity with particular Angles or key planets, the answers are clear. Perhaps the build-up of developmental tension is yet ahead, and the client feels it approaching. This is the kind of sensitivity that can best support strategy; the client is involved with the process and is close to the controls of the situation.

There will always be some pressure point obvious; the astrologer will be seeing what prompted the client to make the appointment for the consultation.

The client may be concerned about something that has nothing to do with an event or with change. Perhaps it is depression or boredom or jealousy or job dissatisfaction—an attitude, which indeed may be tied to an event or a series of events; perhaps the evaluation of those experiences has become awkward or uncomfortable.

When a client states why he or she has come for astrological consultation, the reason is usually not the "bottom line" real reason. The astrologer has to be able to infer the real reason by going several steps further, beyond the client's statement, working through the measurement clues in the horoscope.

I submit that there are basically only three sets of developmental problems for individuals in our society: status/identity concerns (represented by the Angular Grand Cross of Houses), self-worth/ materialism concerns (by the Succeedent Grand Cross), and information/perspective concerns (by the Cadent Grand Cross). These are all keyed by the significators of the Houses involved, and the client will manifest the particular focus of the problem with some specific reference that is echoed by some set of astrological measurements.

"Where's the action?" It is rarely where the first description from the client may suggest. It is deeper and perhaps elsewhere. It is at the beginning of conversation, not the end. Marriage dissatisfaction may really be a projection of job frustration or a by-product of in-law tensions; job upset can mask frustration in sex and relationships or an embarrassment about a lack of education.

4. *Abbreviation*—With a new client, a practical suggestion is to allocate only 20% of consultation time to prediction. Keeping the time for prediction to, say, ten or fifteen minutes out of an hour condenses the period the astrologer must prepare for, permitting more care and depth, permitting the client's past development to be assessed more completely, and connections to be made analytically between astrological measurements and event reactions throughout the client's life. This builds rapport between client and astrologer and prepares both for realistic discussion about the future.

Additionally, the astrologer feels less pressure in the predictive department. What is suggested in discussion then, together with the client, takes on greater viability than if a time period twice as long had to be filled with "pronouncements" of one sort or another.

With these insights about abbreviation, about leanness, we are talking about closing our window of responsibility to where the draft is maximally controllable. In this way, we astrologers improve accuracy and become more meaningful to our clients, more than if we open our windows wide and let a full wind blow through the delicate frameworks of personal time.

It is improper for the astrologer to say too much, hoping through quantity to chance upon something relevant.

5. *Jargon*—Using jargon in client consultation is a defense mechanism for the astrologer; it gets in the way of success. If astrologers will delete the technical jargon from their consultations, they will find that a remarkable amount of time will be freed up to discuss *something significant* with the client. Jargon is too easily used in place of what is important. Again, here is the "performance" mentality at work, the sense of parading fate in front of someone, rather than settling down to a productive exchange of understandings. Jargon itself has never helped anyone.

6. *Objectification*—Throughout the horoscope consultation, in order to be maximally helpful to clients, astrologers must be objective. Our observations should in no way be subjective: they must be explicitly anchored to measurements in the horoscope.

For example, the astrologer Zoltan Mason of New York City is the only astrologer I have ever commissioned to do my horoscope. Our consultation took place, long, long ago when I knew absolutely nothing about astrology. I impulsively had barged into his bookstore and asked all the typical naive questions, and I received some reply like "Don't be afraid of what you don't know." Anyhow, Mr. Mason did my horoscope, and I've never forgotten a moment of it.

At the conclusion of our time together, Mr. Mason said, in his very heavy Hungarian accent, which certainly added to the mystique of what he said, "But there is yet another thing, Noel. You could be a great astrologer, a great teacher and writer in astrology." I interrupted strongly and with laughter. At that time, I was an emerging opera singer on my way to European career opportunities: "Oh, Mr. Mason, you just want me to buy a lot of your books! I'm an opera singer."

Using all the objectivity his half-century of experience had taught him, Mr. Mason replied, "Well, Noel, I don't see it in you, but I see it in your horoscope."

That's objectivity! What one says need not be "you"-oriented. A psychologist will say, "What did *you* mean by that?" or "What do you really feel about that?" And, indeed, the astrologer should learn to talk that way too, to an extent, to get at feelings and interpretations. But, we have to appreciate as well the strength of objectification of the horoscope drawing. Implicit in all we say is that "it is not I who is talking or evaluating; it is here in the horoscope." This is certainly comforting to the client. It may be one of the rare times in life when the client is not implicated or accused personally for something difficult! It is extremely liberating for us astrologers to have faith in the analysis presented to us by the horoscope and to present it that way.

Approaching prediction objectively, the astrologer establishes that something *outside* the client is saying something: "What I see here suggests that...." The more corroboration that is received about past events within this awareness of symbolic objectification (the parallelism between events and astrological measurements), the greater the efficiency of communication about the future and probably the greater the accuracy.

7. *Asking Questions*—The best projector of the future is the client; he or she instinctively and pragmatically understands or at least appreciates the realities of the present and the potential of the future. The client has the impetus of dreams and hopes. Realistically or not, the client is best equipped to make the first step into future time.

This is best facilitated by the astrologer asking a simple question: "Now that we've got an understanding of these lines of development over the years, what do you project for yourself over the next six months?"

Certainly, should strong Solar Arc measurements and/or transits focus themselves eight months from the time of consultation, the astrologer should extend the time period of self-projection. The number of months is not what is important. What is important is that the client is invited to place himself or herself into the future in terms of what has been brought forward from the past to the present during the consultation.

8. *Routinization*—The astrologer should be alert to the stifling affects of routinization in the life of the client. Has routine prevailed to maintain the status quo, to ward off the insecurity that is bound up with change, to take the place of adventure? Is there something between the client and his or her spouse or parents or job that keeps things as they are? Are opportunities (especially Jupiter transits, strong Saturn/Angle contacts, etc.) being ignored or passing the client by?

The astrologer must know that many people seem to "unrelate" the potential of their horoscope by their adherence to behaviors prescribed by the environment; there are the do-nothings, the passively content. It may be environmentally impossible for the client to respond to powerful measurements that suggest opportunity, change, new dreams, etc. The energies are then imploded. Tensions and stress take other forms for release. The astrology changes level. Illness can develop.

A predictive press relating to IXth House matters may not be long distance travel or legal concerns for a client who is locked into a routine. It may rather be taking adult education courses at the local college or simply the joy of a grandchild (the IXth is the fifth of the Vth).

9. *The Hot-Spot*—Is there one particularly sensitive area in the horoscope that time after time in analysis of the past responds reliably, measurably, anticipatably? Is there an axis that responds to relationship difficulty? To job change? To anxiety about sickness? Such areas or axes will often carry many levels of symbolism: not only high potential outcome in the future but, as well, overcompensatory manifestation with regard to other dimensions of life expression.

For example, a woman has Uranus in exact conjunction with Venus retrograde in Taurus in the XIth House. This very intense conjunction is opposed by the Moon in Scorpio within 42 minutes of arc from the Vth. Venus rules the Vth and the Moon rules the Ascendant.

This is a highly charged axis of love-given and love-received, V-XI. It is frustrated somehow or diverted (the Venus retrogradation).

The lady has a scant relationship history. She has been alone most of her life and has been dedicated to the extreme to being a successful, lone mother rather than a woman fulfilled in relationship.

Whenever this axis has been touched by a powerful transit or involved one way or another in Solar Arc symbolization, there has not been any romance, no dimension normally tied to the Vth-IXth axis and Venus. Instead, there has been gynecological anxiety (Moon in Scorpio, ruler of her Ascendant) about ill health, disease, test complications. The Moon is caught up in the frustration axis that is keyed by the retrograde Venus. Pluto, ruler of the VIth and dispositor of the Moon, is prominently aspected in the horoscope as well. This is a "hot axis," an antenna that gains high reliability throughout a lifetime at many different levels of behavioral reaction.

There are many horoscopes that have such hot-spots. Some horoscopes have many of them. The hot-spot is the place upon which predictions can be built to be most helpful to the client.

10. *Improving Answers*—A "Yes" or "No" answer does not fit into astrological consultation. Such polarization suggests the fallacy of dichotomous reasoning: there is no situation that is entirely wrong or entirely right. There are degrees of rightness and degrees of wrongness. Astrologers need to be very sensitive about their answers to questions that ask for such polarized response.

11. *Vagueness*—Astrologers should consider how unhelpful "I think so" is as an answer to a client's question. The client is paying for professional judgment. "I think so" is not worth it.

"I think so" can be expressed differently, in order to become helpful: "Throughout all my study...in our literature...in my experience this set of measurements usually corresponds with..." This alternative approach allies the astrologer with a store of knowledge and experience beyond the individual focus; the caution of "usually" sets acceptable parameters for graceful sharing with the client.

12. *Managing the Negative*—When the apparently negative is present or imminent, it is usually already known by the client. It must be brought out tactfully and objectively: "In a worst case scenario, what do you think you would do if...?" In this way, the astrologer is collecting responses ahead of time; the astrologer can then match these responses to responses in the past within specific cycles of development. How many times have I heard, "Yes, I knew you would see this too! I'm just going to have to get through it the way I always have."

13. *The "What If" Strategy*—"What if" statements are extremely helpful in consultation about the future. "What if" captures the creativity of change.

For example, "George, you just said that you've felt there was going to be a major shake-up at your job; that you've been feeling this for three or four months. Well, I can see that build up of tension in your horoscope (the transits and Solar Arc measurements of the recent past gaining corroboration from the client). From all my experience, though, and the research astrologers have done about job security, it appears you're going to make out just fine in this next step of your development. But first, *what if* something *does* go wrong and doesn't fit the pattern we expect? What if we saw that as a new opportunity for you to go into one of those new directions we were just talking about, something even bigger and better?"

This type of discussion is typical, for astrological consultation and for life strategy. "What if" is not threatening, and, in the paragraph above, the astrologer was able to relax the client with a positive prognosis first before introducing the alternative. But then the alternative had a twist into still another positive direction. Reward measurements need the client's courage and enthusiasm to come to pass. Rewards rarely arrive as surprises.

"What if" questions can also be startling: "What if you started to behave differently with your husband on this matter and not just keep the routine going? It's not getting anywhere as it is; what if you just made a few small changes? What would happen?"

The client is being asked a straight forward question that forces new thinking and evaluation, especially after perhaps 45 minutes of deep, honest sharing with the astrologer about life development to the present.

"What if" is better in syntax than "What do you have to lose," or "Why don't you...." The latter statements are not really on target. They are actually about something else: one is about losing something, which is certainly threatening; the other one is a question about *not* doing something.

"What if" statements are also friendly; they permit intimacy. For example, "Now Janet, since we see that this is a time now for you to start learning about oil painting, something you've been thinking about for so long; now that you have time and are going to start those Adult Education Courses...and really develop a hobby (measurements that would involve the IXth House or its significator; Jupiter, Venus, Neptune, perhaps with Mercury; perhaps activation of a natal quintile aspect (72°) that has been dormant in the horoscope for a lifetime; the client's wish projections), you're going to start to feel so much better about yourself. It's a new era!

"So, let me ask you, what if—in this new spirit of things—what if you relaxed that difficulty you've been having with your husband about sex. Remember, we determined the difficulty was really that you don't feel desirable anymore, what with the weight you've gained and those other things. *That's* the problem. You've started the diet; it's working, and now the painting course. Your husband is supportive. That's wonderful! What if you also started a new program with him as well—sexually. Surprise him; learn some new things together. What if you tried that; interesting? Exciting? Think how each of you would feel!"

Here is a way the astrologer has through conversation of reviewing discussion of the past, weaving into the dialogue different levels of symbolisms, reinforcing development and change, and addressing problem areas with common sense conjecture about behavioral adjustment. At all times, the astrologer—with conversational grace—can *protect* the client and avoid confrontational thinking.

In thinking about the potential of "What if" statements, it is helpful to review the impact one can have (for example) on a child who is in a crying snit: "Johnnie, what would happen if you *stopped* crying?" There really is no answer; yet there are many answers. The point is that *there is a pause* within the routine, a way to get out of it. There is the capacity then to consider change.

14. *Points of View*—When there is disagreement between astrologer and client, perhaps about the evaluation of a relationship or a set of reactions within the Saturn retrograde phenomenon or Nodal axis involvement, the chances are that the client is still expressing attitudes that have been routinized to an extreme over many years.

This is especially valid as a defense mechanism when the significators of the Cadent Houses (especially the IIIrd and IXth), are under high developmental tension: *the point of view*, whatever it is, is sacred; it helps the organism grow in prestige and it constantly protects the status quo. A very strong focus of Pluto in the IXth, for example, can show tremendous opinionation, the sense of "knowing all the answers" especially under pressure; a powerful gift, a rigorous responsibility.

When points of view become moments of contention between astrologer and client, it is helpful to ask the client to re-evaluate. For example: "What you say makes a lot of sense. I can certainly see how you needed to feel that way about your father. But what we're saying here in trying to understand all this is nothing *against* him. We want to have some identification with *his* problems at the time (which you didn't know anything about, of course) which caused behaviors that may not have helped you in the ways you needed. Let's be fair: do you think you might have gotten lost in his traffic pattern? Maybe he just couldn't say 'Dottie, I love you.' He didn't know how. He had too many other things hurting in his life. What do you think?"

Basically, the astrologer can helpfully ask the client to rethink any situation when the purpose is not to change it but to clarify it. Accumulated clarification throughout the astrological consultation is what builds the base for clearer vision into the future.

15. *Putting Symbols in Their Place*—The planets *do* nothing; neither natally, in transit, nor in progressions of any kind. They are symbols of existence and change all within the cycles of time. *People* make things happen in ways that become routinized throughout life experience.

This is why jargon is useless for client consumption. This is why measurement precision tends to waver in personal astrology or we see justifications that are completely arbitrary, such as "An aspect applying within one degree for a major event is more powerful at that time than when exact or departing." But the measurement orb is a span of consciousness. It is an astrological way of showing our "togetherness" within ourselves.

Series of books have been written about this kind of detailed accuracy, all in the pursuit of control. The old-time astrologers had the same desire, infinitely less to work with, extraordinarily less accurate measurements, and the same human frailties. And today with all our computer strengths, we still face the same problems in interpretation, complicated by Nature which often DOES put the exact measurements together with the reality manifestation. So the quest is ever there, ever elusive. But caution can become sensitive and creative, and it is then that the human condition is more accurately captured by our astrology, more often, more meaningfully.

16. *Stories Can Help*—Parables and projected drama are the "stuff" of all discourse on prediction. Recall the Sermon on the Mount, the mysterious quatraines of Nostradamus, the prediction scenario of any news documentary: we are told stories of how things worked in the past, and we are given projections into the future.

The sense of cycle is dominant: "He has risen *again* from the dead." The preponderant worldview of reincarnation dogma, the repetition of history through the affairs of nations. Things happen to others as they happen to us; things happen over and over and over again, predictably. Yet things can change; new cycle levels can be birthed.

The astrologer can make a forceful presentation by telling a persuasive story to help objectify a client's decision-making process during a time of change. Projecting a scenario into the future to help with behavioral modification can introduce a new perspective. Behavioral modification is simply adjusting reactions to improve the process of development.

For example, this horoscope portion (cast for a high northern latitude, thus the double interception), presents almost in a flash "where the action is" in terms of analysis first and then in prediction: the Moon rules the VIIth and is conjunct Mars in the XIIth; Mars rules the self-worth IInd holding the Jupiter-Saturn conjunction with Saturn ruling the Ascendant, Jupiter ruling the Midheaven; and this conjunction, in turn, is squared Pluto in the VIIth. There are definite self-worth anxieties linked to the parents in the early homelife, and these anxieties have spilled over into strong relationship tensions.

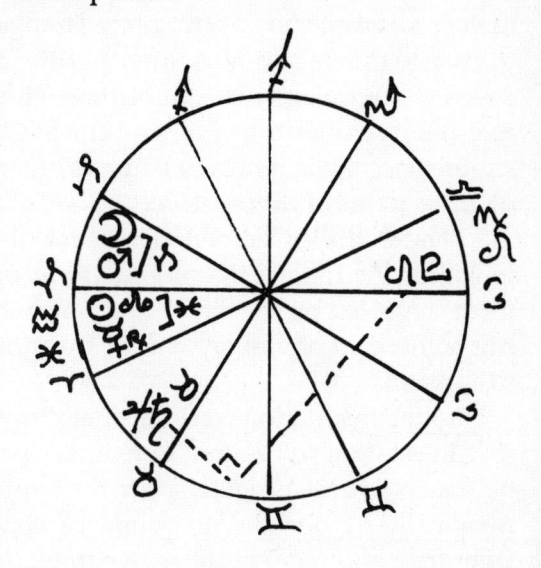

Mercury, ruler of the IVth and Vth, is retrograde at the Ascendant: giving love and self-expressing sexually will probably be difficult because of the self-worth anxieties; the Sun-Node conjunction introduces a strong maternal influence factor; and all of this points attention to the parental axis through rulerships by Jupiter and Mercury.

This is a swift vignette that is absolutely undeniable as the orientation of analysis. And indeed, every single point was corroborated within three or four minutes of the consultation as I mapped out the results of my preparation and where we were going to go in discussion.

For prediction orientation, major transits in mid and late 1990 (the ahead-of-time period for this horoscope projection) focused on Capricorn, on the Ascendant: Solar Arc measurements were clear (but need not be indicated here).

To bring out the relationship anxiety syndrome after it was corroborated—since it had dominated this woman's life and, with important change in the offing, was not bound to continue—I simply told her a few success stories of people with whom I had consulted in the past *who had similar concerns*. I told her how well they had done to change things and how, after putting away parental anxiety factors and routinized self-doubt through understanding that objective and dynamic, they had found ways to feel worthwhile and desirable once again, ways of being proud to be a mother and getting over the pains of divorce, etc.

These stories helped. They usually do. The astrologer best looks for the details that stimulate recognition and identification most (revealed on the client's face or in body language). These are the points that obviously will be most important for more helpful discussion.

Our consultation was at a small convention where I was speaking. In relation to the freedoms that were in the offing for her—a new way of presenting herself to the world professionally and interpersonally—I decided to reinforce some behavior modification right then and there at the convention.

With humanity and authority, I asked her if she would "cooperate with a very nice suggestion I was going to make." (Notice the phrasing; there is no way to say "No.") She agreed right away. And then we agreed together that, anytime we saw each other at the convention, no matter where it was, no matter if it were five minutes after the time before, anywhere at all throughout the hotel, we would greet each other fondly and *touch* somehow, shake hands, offer a hug, whatever. The point was to be free with sincere appreciation for another human being and to confirm the beginning of bonding activity, to establish that it would not be threatening. This was an antidote for the situation presented in the horoscope.

Parables about the past, stories about other clients, helped her feel less alone and gave her confidence. The little experiment of our time together at the convention as a bridge to her confirming new thoughts about herself helped with behavior modification and reinforcement of new attitudes...and her relationship to all others at the convention. It was a lovely experience to see this woman shine and begin to bloom over a three-day period. I will never forget it; nor will she.

Another projected drama, a scenario for behavioral modification that always stays with me, involved a male with very strong concerns about never having pleased his father (who had died some years before). My client was in a different profession than his father would have enjoyed and supported. There were many problems, much "unfinished business." My client was getting very tense about things in his high-exposure, public media work; the anxieties were strong and temperamentally roiling.

Astrological projections for him involved a Jupiter transit of his Sun. In checking other transit contacts between Jupiter and his Sun in the past (quadratures as well as conjunction), I ascertained that the odds would be very high for this next conjunction in his reward cycle to represent a fine time in his life, a breakthrough time for success.

What would help all of that, of course, would be an alleviation of the father anxieties: all those tensions that were bubbling back to the surface during a period of job insecurity.

I asked him if he would "do an experiment with me" (This is a strong counseling technique which binds client and astrologer together in the process of change): if he would set aside 15 minutes a day, at the same time every day, to think through his father relationship and lead up to a time when he would visit his father's grave—within four months (the time the Jupiter transit was due to begin along with reinforcing Solar Arcs). At the grave, he would then be prepared to say his final "farewell!"

This touched him deeply. He promised to do the experiment. Two months later, he came to see me unannounced: he had made the visitation; he was crying with release; it was over. And, "coincidentally," he had just received major reinforcement in his career. (Jupiter was alive and well!) This man was a television personality, and all of the dramatic touches fell into place with extra special meaning. Astrology calls for a therapeutic boost. That's what astrolo*gers* are for.

17. *Fair Warning*—When pre-consultation preparation reveals extremely strong transit activity and/or vivid Solar Arc measurements, especially direct planet-to-planet arcs, "where the action is"

will be clear to the astrologer. It is very important then *to give the client* preparation time in advance, at the very beginning of the consultation: "We've got much to talk about for sure! We're looking ahead for some very important, strategic changes, as you surely sense or know. (Watch for reaction, for acknowledgment, and continue accordingly.) "And we'll get to that, but first I want us to share your life development together. In that way, astrology can be most helpful about the times ahead."

This cues the client that at the end of the consultation you will together recognize the exigency of times ahead. That's *why* the consultation is taking place! Observing pressure points in a general way ahead of time tips the client to the astrologer's preparation and foreknowledge. It also gives the client a sense of comfort that things are well in hand professionally, and that he or she then can build responses about the past with maximum candor and, so very often, *with an instinctive sensibility to the times that are to come*—coloring the past with awareness of the future.

Major transits of Uranus, to the Angles especially, most specifically conjunction with the Ascendant or IVth cusp, suggest a very high percentage of the time that a geographic relocation will be involved. The consultation should then have that probability in mind; the particular Angle should be tested for measurement accuracy and responsiveness throughout life development.

Transits of Pluto will usually correspond to dominatingly important changes of life perspective, but with slower and, as well, longer lasting development.

Transits of Neptune that are in high relief within the future horoscope usually will present times of uncertainty, the diffusion of self-awareness, the introduction of idealism, a kind of withdrawal or covering up, or upset of reality. These measurements are very difficult to manage, but, again, the entire consultation should be devoted to checking and rechecking sensitivities from the past, brought forward into the future, involving Neptune, the area of transit, reactions in the past, all with an eye to what is developed within the present and projected into the future by the client.

In short, the major future measurement conditions rely on the bulk of the consultation about the past in order for the prediction to gather support, meaningfulness, and a proper position within the client's Reality Principle.

18. *Knowing about Life*—While most astrologers only qualify as

lay practitioners in terms of formal psychological therapeutic programs, we must remember that we are gifted sensitives as well, schooled in people-awareness and objectivity. Astrologers must become well informed about other fields of the human condition, such as stress management, dispelling depression, resources to help working through alcoholism, proper diet management, sexual concerns (especially female orgasmic dysfunction), and certain protocols with regard to legal support in connection with divorce, contract negotiations, lease management and suits, especially the time elements involved with these complicated processes.

When astrologers enrich themselves with this extra knowledge, their skills mature commensurately. The suggestion of antidotes is certainly part of our being in touch with the future.

19. *Intuition*—In dealing constantly with the time dimension, past and future, astrologers develop a greater sensibility about the future than most people do. Intuition becomes a very special point of sensitivity within the astrologer's skill, and it too must be recognized and managed with discipline.

Philosophically, recalling our discussion on page 55, the phenomenon of precognition can be balanced by the phenomenon of memory: both are mental processes that defy rational measurement and both can be faulty, incomplete, erroneous, and simply wrong. Intuition does not exist in astrology; it exists in the astrologer. When its energy is felt, it can not be allowed to transcend the discipline of *pro forma* astrology: it must consciously enrich the astrologer's understanding of the symbologies and the circumstances of projected potentials. Intuition must lead to substantiation by measurements and evaluation by common sense.

That is the extent of the magician in each of us. It is real, but it must be controlled.

20. *Explaining Causes*—Clients are extremely uncomfortable—as all human beings are—when they see themselves as *causes* of difficulty. I caused you unhappiness; I caused the automobile accident; I caused myself to get fired; I caused the unhappiness in our marriage; I caused the failure of my child.

As we have seen, causes are dreadfully unnerving because they somehow speak of inalterability, of fatalistic inexorability. In Chapter 2, we discussed the admonition of St. Augustine that we should claim the stars as "signs, not causes" of effects. Being a cause comes too close to God.

Margaret Thatcher

Date	Aspect		
JAN 15, 1990	♂	☌	♃/♄
JAN 16, 1990	☉	∠	♃/MC
FEB 03, 1990	AS	⚼	♂/☊
FEB 11, 1990	♇	∠	♆/♇
FEB 26, 1990	♇	∠	☿/AS
MAR 02, 1990	♀	⚼	☉/♆
	♂	□	♄/♇
	☉	⚼	♇/MC
MAR 29, 1990	♃	⚼	♃/♆
APR 09, 1990	♆	∠	♃/♄
MAY 11, 1990	☿	∠	♄
MAY 14, 1990	♃	⚼	♆/♇
MAY 24, 1990	♆	∠	♄/♇
MAY 27, 1990	☿	□	☿/MC
MAY 28, 1990	♃	⚼	☿/AS
JUN 11, 1990	♀	⚼	♄/☊
JUN 12, 1990	♄	⚼	MC
JUN 21, 1990	♄	☌	♅/AS
JUL 06, 1990	☽	☌	☿/♄
JUL 08, 1990	MC	∠	☿/♆
JUL 30, 1990	MC	∠	☽/☉
SEP 05, 1990	MC	☌	♃/MC
SEP 21, 1990	♄	∠	☿/♃
OCT 09, 1990	♀	∠	♅
OCT 10, 1990	☽	∠	☽/♂
OCT 11, 1990	♂	☌	♃/AS
OCT 21, 1990	MC	□	♇/MC
OCT 30, 1990	☊	□	☉/♅
NOV 06, 1990	♄	⚼	☿/♇
NOV 26, 1990	♂	□	♇/AS
JAN 02, 1991	♆	∠	♃/AS
JAN 09, 1991	♅	⚼	☿/♆
JAN 13, 1991	☊	☌	☽/♄
JAN 30, 1991	☽	☌	♃/♆
JAN 31, 1991	♄	□	☉
FEB 04, 1991	☿	∠	♄/AS
FEB 17, 1991	♆	∠	♇/AS
FEB 23, 1991	☿	⚼	☽/☊
MAR 07, 1991	♀	⚼	☊/AS
MAR 17, 1991	☽	□	♆/♇
APR 01, 1991	☽	☌	☿/AS
MAY 16, 1991	♇	∠	♀/♂
MAY 30, 1991	♂	⚼	☊
JUL 01, 1991	♅	□	☽
JUL 22, 1991	♀	∠	♀/♃
JUL 26, 1991	♄	⚼	♂/☊
AUG 16, 1991	♃	⚼	♀/♂
AUG 18, 1991	☉	∠	☉/♀
AUG 21, 1991	♆	□	☊
SEP 06, 1991	♀	⚼	♀/♇
SEP 18, 1991	AS	□	☉/☿

It is only natural for the client to feel causally related in many situations that may be astrologically projected into the future: "What does this prediction mean? Why must it be? Am I going to do something that will make this happen? What can I do about it?"

The Solar Arc chart shown on this page calls our attention to the period June, 1990 through January, 1991 (the exact dates are irrelevant; they are necessry for the computer to do its work).

Saturn=Sun in January, 1991 suggests a concern for major professional change: the lord of ambition is in tension with one's place in the Sun. Something is altered, controlled, held back, or negated—as the astrologers some 350 years ago would have said most accurately.

If we inspect for a Time Orb backward (in application), we see echoes of this tension in November, 1990 with Mars=Pluto/ASC, and even earlier in June, 1990, with Saturn=Midheaven.

There is simply no doubt about it: this is extremely important Solar Arc activity. We must check transit activity involved at these same important times.

When we study the horoscope itself, with its 14 Scorpio Ascendant, it is instantly obvious that Pluto, ruler of the Ascendant, was transiting the Ascendant—in fact, was stationary on the Ascendant for a month (in July, 1990) at the beginning of the Solar Arc Time Orb period shown above.

This is an amplification of Margaret Thatcher's horoscope again, the measurements upon her resignation as Prime Minister of England. During the last two weeks of her campaign for reelection and her resignation, transiting Saturn, within the embrace of the strong Solar Arcs, was exactly square her natal Mercury, ruler of her Virgo Midheaven.

"What does this prediction mean: that I do not look good for election in November? It is mid-Summer now. Must it be? Am I going to do something that will make this happen? Can astrology tell what I can do about it?"

There is only one answer, the answer for any client, even if we had seen Mrs. Thatcher four months before her end of term or, indeed, quite some time before that. And that answer is, "The prediction is what time is bringing to you; now a new time is presenting itself. It will probably come to pass, and the preparation for it now will add grace and efficiency to the times yet to come."

Yes, the words sound pretty. And they must. But *that* is the answer. There is no other, and somehow...remarkably...somehow clients begin to understand difficult dialogues like this when they are presented with sensitivity, grace, and enduring hope.

"Let's go forward, Mrs. Thatcher. Let's get ready for the Spring and Summer (SA Uranus=Moon): just think of the book you're probably going to write about international affairs!" (Uranus, the arcing planet, rules the IIIrd; the Moon rules the IXth and is in the IXth close to the Midheaven.)

These Counseling Aphorisms were built up from the simple to the complex. In the process, the observations have gone farther away from measurement and more toward communication. In the end, in astrological counseling, subjective judgment and creative communication do displace any objective rules, no matter how old, tried and tested, or accurate they are professed to be.

This process is not dictated by astrology; rather, the process *responds* to human beings, to the complexity of individuals, to each one in his or her own portion of living space and life time.

While there is certainly a difference in the application of astrology between the Mundane level of symbology and the personal sphere of experience, the recognition of each of us as a product of the nation and a focal point of time is the essence of all we do.

In astrological consultation, neither client nor astrologer is alone. And for that time together, in relation to times that were and times that are to come, both are heroes.

Chapter Eight

Working with the Indeterminate

"I don't see it in you, but I see it in your horoscope!" Please recall that statement from the one and only reading of my horoscope reported on page 188. What a way to reinforce a prediction! That phrase has never left my astrological consciousness for a quarter of a century!

But what if we turn that thought around? We come much closer to the concerns and position all astrologers face all too often: "I see it in you, but I do not see it in your horoscope." All too often, the indeterminate confronts us: some "thing," some happening, some concern explodes or emerges in the client's life and simply defies astrology as we know it at this time.

Some examples, beginning with the very simple: I see that you are a man and not a woman. For starters, astrology can not define gender, certainly a vital prerequisite for any interpretation!

I cannot infer your social level from your horoscope—your placement within the economical, religious, ethnic, and racial demarcation that are part of social order and disorder. I cannot tell a prostitute from a president, a Catholic from Boston from a Baptist from Alabama. The astrologer *needs* this kind of information to frame expectations realistically within analysis.

Study the horoscope shown on the next page for a moment. You will see it presents a great deal of "softness": the Sun in Cancer conjunct Neptune in the VIIth, the essence of "softness," although this dimension is given some robust drive by the square from Mars in the Xth, along with the Moon, which, in the Xth, usually suggests

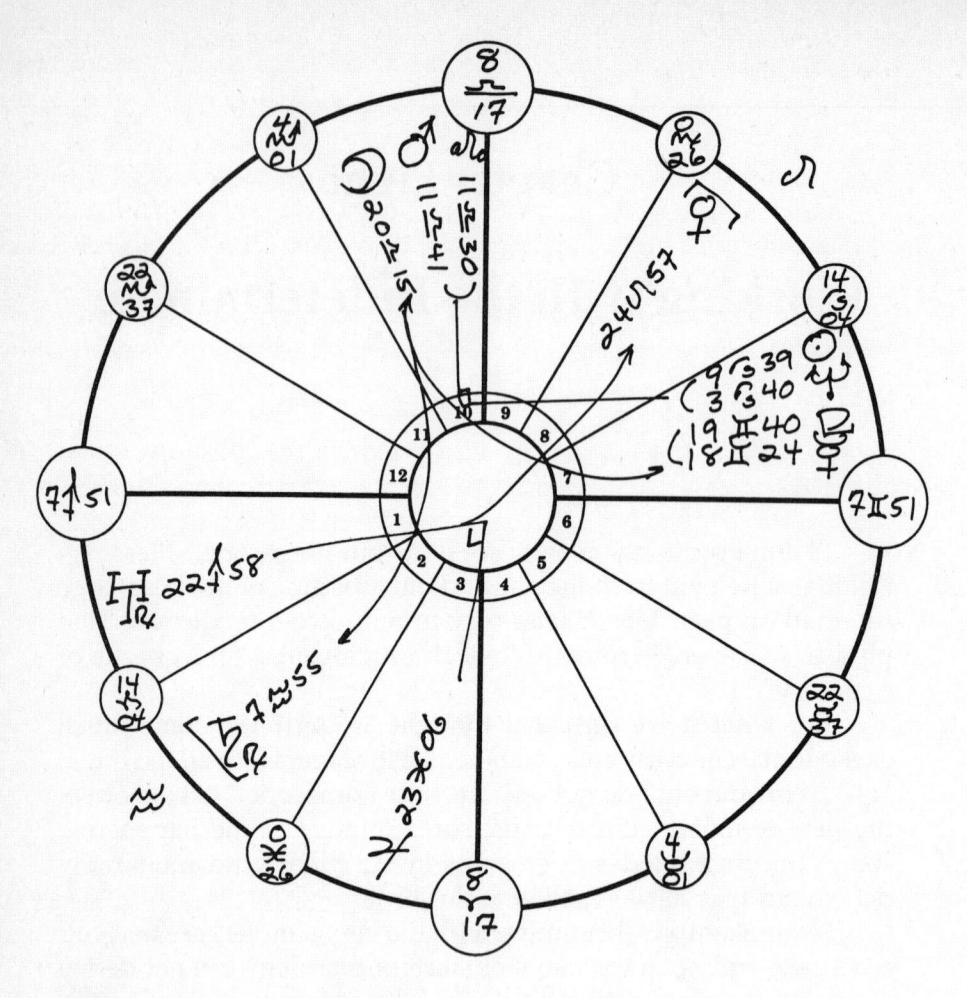

Male
July 2, 1903
5:50 p.m. GMT
00 E 31   52 N 50
Placidian Houses

a "take charge" personality, and in Libra, the need to be well received socially. But the Mars is itself softened in its conjunction with the Node, suggesting a tremendous maternal influence in how this man would learn to apply himself in life.

In turn, the Moon in Libra is sextiled by Uranus rising retrograde in the Ascendant. So far we have a suggestion over all of personal magnetism and public appeal.

And then note the Saturn retrograde in the IInd, suggesting the phenomenon we associate with a difficult or absent father relationship and potential feelings of inferiority, especially in the IInd, the House this Saturn rules. This complex, combined with the Mars-Node dimension, shows extraordinary family influence upon this male; and all of that is part of public presentation "adjustment" (quincunx) from Saturn to the Sun-Neptune conjunction, and, probably, an unruffling self-presentation through it all, again suggested by the Saturn trine to Mars in the Xth. In addition, there may be an overcompensatory belligerence in private (the Mars square to the Sun).

Without getting lost in a maze of aspect routings, one *can* feel the reserve in basic character development, but also a game posture of poise and potential success. Finally, three more echoes: Jupiter, ruler of the Ascendant, is in Pisces; and Venus, ruler of the Midheaven, is sextile to the Moon. We have here a natal midpoint picture (a Yod) of Jupiter=Moon/Venus, usually a picture supporting a most loving nature.

Would you anticipate that this is the horoscope of a king? King Olav of Norway.

"Sir, I see it in you in your reality, but I could not see it in your horoscope."[1]

King Olav died on January 17, 1991, and his son has become King Harald V.

Harald's horoscope offers some very interesting dimensions, again not usually associated with our expectations of kingly profiles (page 206): the Cancer Ascendant has its ruler in the XIIth; Neptune, ruler of the Midheaven, is opposed Saturn in the Xth, in the parental axis. We can start to sense the similarities between this son and his father. The "softness" was robust in Olav but is probably shy in Harald. (Harald's wife is the very forthright Queen Sonja.)

Another point we are making here with regard to the indeterminate is that these two men are individual human beings. They are kings in spite of themselves, but being kings is essential to who they are. In an effort to make the measurements of astrology mean *everything* securely, astrologers easily overlook the indeterminate human element that cannot be codified.

---

1. Olav's father was a powerful man, formerly Prince Carl of Denmark, becoming King Haakon VII of Norway in 1905. Olav's mother was Queen Maud, a princess of Great Britain, daughter of the Prince of Wales who later became Edward VII. Olav was born at Sandringham Castle just north of London.

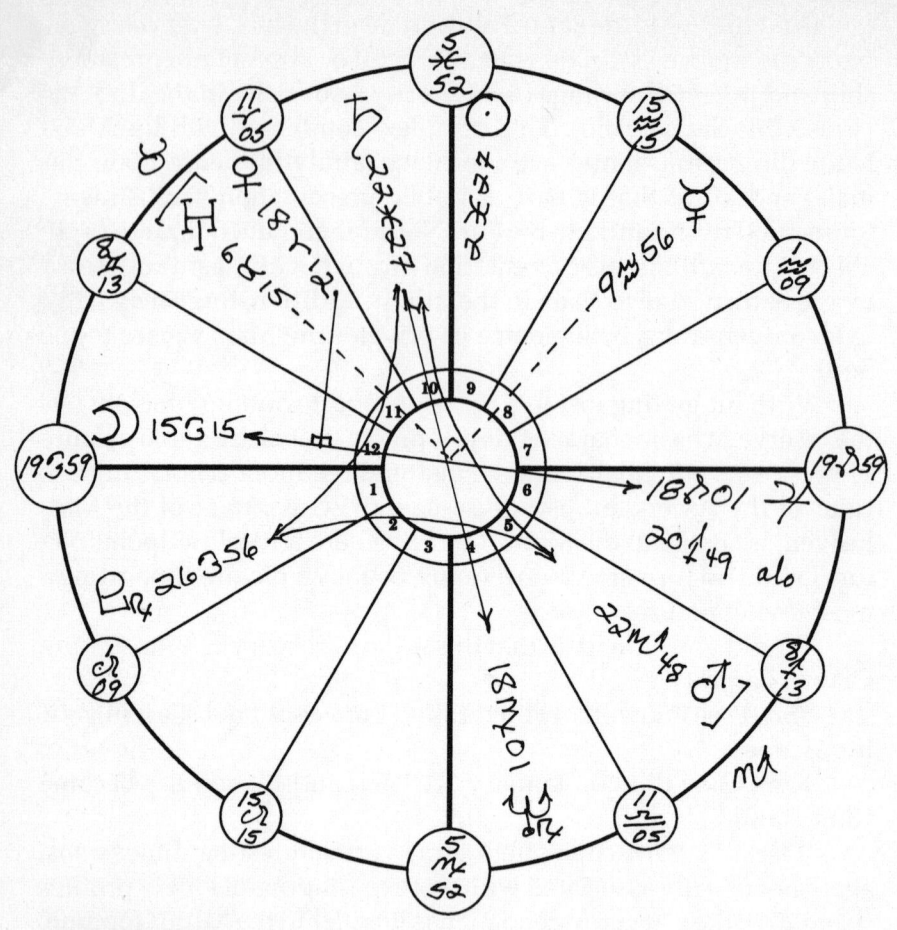

King Harald V of Norway
February 21, 1937
00:45 p.m. CET
Skaugum, Norway
10 E 26   59 N 51
Placidian Houses

Nothing can bring this to our attention more than the observations that, as Nectanebus managed the birth of Alexander, at that same moment, *other sons* were being born in Pella, Macedonia and elsewhere in the region but there was only one Alexander. Was that because he was the son of a king (Nectanebus, the former pharaoh), or of a god (Ammon, Jupiter, Zeus) or born into a king's family (Philip of Macedonia); or would Alexander have become Alexander if he had been born in another part of town? Contrary to Nectanebus's ministrations, Alexander's horoscope *did not make him Alexander*. Something we do not understand took the suggestions of the heavens and illuminated them to blaze into history.

In that early morning in Bethlehem, undoubtedly, another child was being born. And as the world population has grown, literally millions of persons share very similar horoscopes or, at least, especially auspicious measurements. We do not know what makes the individual difference. Will the world hear especially from someone born February 4, 1962 with the seven-planet cluster in Aquarius? Isn't it about time?

There are many stories in the literature about birth coincidences and startling similarities in the lives lived by the people involved; about birth coincidences and extremely divergent life manifestations, though remarkably linked in ways that defy credulity—king and stable boy born at the same time, depart into different lives, but within the same castle community; both great horsemen, both sharing major turns of life at their respective different levels, both dying similarly on the same day.

An astrologer needs a lot of information in order to understand what I call the Reality Principle of a human being's horoscope. The data we need is the beginning of the all-important corroboration process of astrological deductions, essential to understanding individual development, appreciating individual reactions, and projecting substantively and gracefully into the individual's future. To establish the Reality Principle for every client as clearly and surely as possible is why astrologers should ask questions more than they should make pronouncements. This brings the horoscope to life. To Francis Bacon is attributed the instructive insight: "A prudent question is one-half of wisdom."

A star football player in the national championship game plays the game of his life, has the success that will assure so much of his future, proudly visits his mother the next morning and finds her dead on the living room floor. True. No amount of glib after-the-fact articulation can possibly suggest that these practically contemporaneous moments could have been seen astrologically before the fact. Yet, we expect that our astrology in its present stage of development should have this capability. This is our ever-present need to fulfill the greatest of expectations.

A woman suffers a deeply emotional blow: her prominent ex-husband (from whom she was divorced after a long rich marriage) with his new wife, and four children aged three to twelve years are killed in an auto accident. The ex-wife was the only one left to settle the man's estate. What does the astrologer say, do, think? Three Solar Arc measurements in her horoscope relate closely to the time of the accident. Two of them do suggest family upset and potential violence (Neptune=Moon/Mars; Pluto sesquiquadrate Mars, respectively), but there is absolutely no possibility that this singular tragedy could have been specifically conceived of through astrology ahead of time. Whatever upset was suggested would have been related to the levels of life experience closer to the woman within *her* Reality Principle, namely, what would be possible, what would be probable in terms of her present life situation. No one could think of such a tragedy. And that is a major point here: the symbols and our measurements are just that, nothing, until the mind of the astrologer gives them significance and value. In this case, whose mind would dare make the connection that did become reality?

The indeterminateness of the human dimension and of astrological measurements is reflected as well within the multiplicity of astrology's prediction systems. There are many, too numerous to list here. They record our continuous search and research for some way to grasp the unfoldment of life reality more exactly.

It was a major decision in the conceptualization of this book to concentrate on Solar Arc progressions and transits. Along with much of the astrological world, I believe that these two systems, the former symbolic and the latter real-time, work extremely well together to appreciate development in the past and to project development into the future. This was a most assertive stand to take in the face of the emphasis in the United States particularly upon the system of Secondary Progressions. But my stand rests on much experience and my need to see astrologers keep on learning.

Rudhyar suggested that *all* systems work because they are symbolic; we astrologers give our meanings to the measurements within the systems. We work with a clear and sound rationale, and the systems develop meaning.

Robert Hand says, "Every technique works the first time, especially in retrospect"—so serendipitous is the astrological process.

There is the extraordinary allure of the Solar Return chart drawn for the natal Sun's return exactly to the degree, minute, and second of its birth position, on or about one's actual birthday every year. But there is the baffling problem still about whether to draw this chart for the birthplace, or for where the person is domiciled, or for where the person actually happens to be at the moment of the return, or accounting for the phenomenon of the precession of the equinoxes.

There is the extraordinary allure of eclipses in personal horoscopes. For example, the Solar Eclipse of January 15, 1991, was crucial within the complex of measurements linked to the war with Iraq. But every person in the world born any year on January 15 took on this Solar Eclipse as a transit and as the year's Solar Return. What can that mean?

Here again, we are not even partly sure: we simply can not yet apply our knowledge reliably, as reliably as we can with transits, Solar Arcs, and, to a degree, Secondary Progressions.

My thrust here is not to evaluate systems; there is intrinsically much measurement agreement among them all. Rather, I want to assert strongly and helpfully that all our systems are *incomplete*. This incompleteness reflects the indeterminateness of the human condition.

However, we often see in Mundane Astrology an extraordinary exactness through measurements. The indeterminateness is not there. This is astrology at a different level, akin to the magical objectivity of horary astrology. We have seen how celestial phenomena do not have psyches or individuation concerns; and we have seen how these celestial phenomena are clear-sighted witness to the creation of history.

In personal astrology, the incompleteness of our systems reflecting human indeterminateness manifests in inconsistencies in measurement success. Saying this another way, the inconsistencies that every astrologer must face—the divergence of the personal Reality Principle from great astrological expectations—are caused by the intrinsic human condition, that which makes us who we are. What makes us king, hero, stable boy, leader, soldier, doctor, lawyer, Indian chief, successful, sick, happy, depressed etc.? We find parallels in our astrology, definite correspondences, almost always after the fact, but what makes us happen? As reality data is increased, astrology takes human shape.

Within the scope of astrological prediction, the vagaries return: there is little reinforcement of projections possible except through the valuable record of the past extrapolated and arced into the unfoldment of continuing cycles.

Then there is the vast concern of karma, the reincarnationist doctrine espoused by an enormous portion of the people on earth. There is miraculous evidence suggesting other lives working out the process of soul refinement, but in practical application in astrology, *we are still incomplete* with this undeniably relevant study.

Being incomplete in many dimensions in our fulfilling and frustrating study of astrology does not mean that astrology is wrong. Instead, ascertaining and acknowledging incompleteness tells us what we do and do not know. That becomes our wisdom. That is our humanness. And by working to remove the expectation of infallibility, we earn for astrology more dignity and respect.

As we saw in the Nectanebus legend and, I believe, in the Evangeline Adams fire prediction—and, indeed, in practically every tale of astrology old and new—there is something beyond astrology, something beyond the measurements in each of us. Cycles of time flow through us as mediums; cycles we can define and cycles we have yet no idea of; and often we give stunning meaning to these concentric phases of time experience.

Sometimes, we do not know why or how we deduce what we do; or how it is possible to make eloquent observations from incorrect data. We rush to explore the potentials of different sets of measurements; we put into these measurements more and more and more meaning to satisfy ourselves and the circumstances of the client's Reality Principle. This is how astrologers work with the indeterminate; this is the indeterminate dimension of a sensitive astrologer; and this is how astrology grows as a discipline.

A word must be said about death, the ultimate indeterminate. Obviously, death is part of everyone's Reality Principle. In fact, the whole of life, from one point of view, is the process of dying, which makes the birth horoscope also the death horoscope. Perhaps this is why astrologers, especially of olden times, thought they could find this ultimate measurement in the radical figure.

But then again, astrologers of old were pressed into searching for success of political struggles and wars through the demise of the rival king. Death in those days was a common, strategic concern, and probably a less subjectively painful fear. The symbolic representations of hundreds of Fixed Stars were established to help with

Working with the Indeterminate / 211

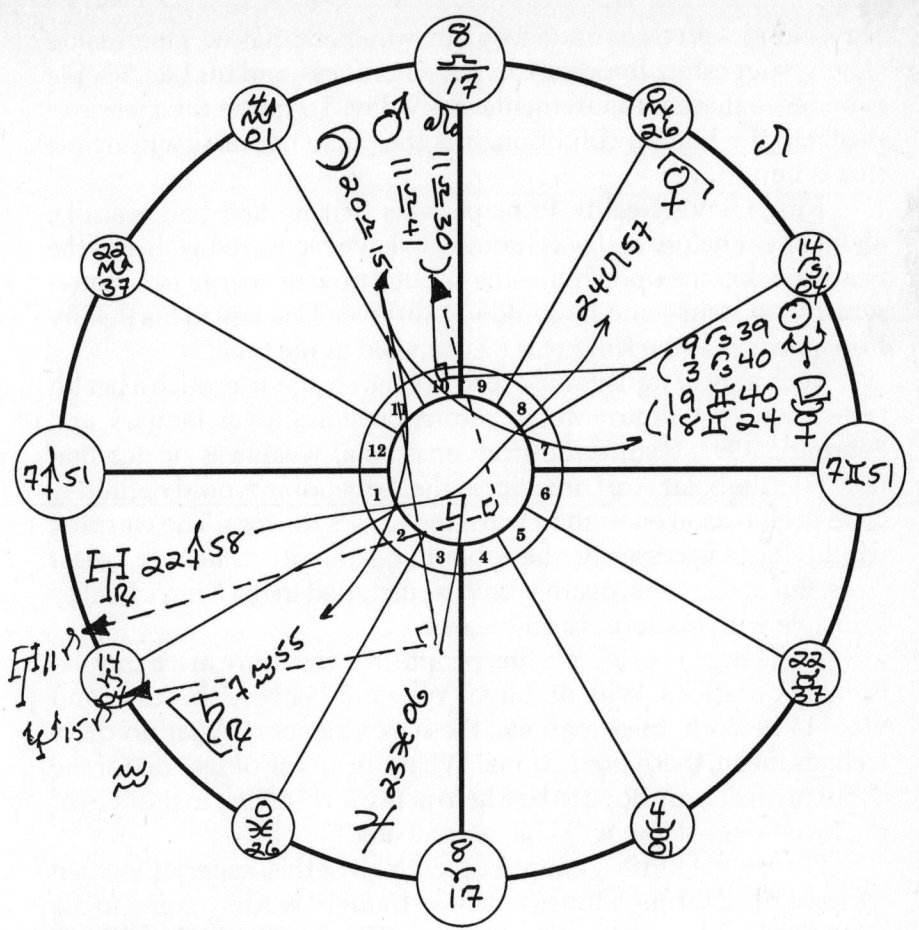

King Olav of Norway
Transits for death: January 17, 1991

explaining and predicting misfortune and calamities. Times then were undeniably fatalistic.

When we look at Norwegian King Olav's horoscope and note the transits for his death of a heart attack on January 17, 1991, we note with alarm the exact transit position of Uranus square the King's Mars in the Midheaven (again, the accent upon the 10th-11th degrees of the cardinal signs, as we have seen throughout our examples in this book); and the transiting Neptune square beginning to form with the Moon, ruler of the VIIIth.

Astrology can be trapped by such measurements *after the fact*. Before the fact, we would simply have felt high energy, sudden energy, along with a contradictory measurement that was increasing slowly, suggesting hypersensitvity, moodiness, and the like. People experience these measurements every day. To frame the measurements to the human condition, it is the personal Reality Principle that is important.

King Olav's Reality Principle was that he had had a stroke about a year before and was thought to have recovered well. But the heart attack came upon him—the sudden flow of energy to a hypersensitive system—and he could not survive. Also key to his Reality Principle is that the King was 87 years old at the time!

Such a set of transits absorbed at such an age after such a health crisis—with SA Pluto=Moon/Saturn presiding over January and February, 1991: ("suffering from emotional weakness or debilitation"; see the Solar Arc Directory in the Appendix), would definitely have been reason enough to warn the King's doctors. The warning would not necessarily be about death; *it would be about crisis*. But at this time, death would be included in the King's Reality Principle with obvious, caring reason.

In the urge to celebrate life, people in our culture ask many existential questions. Why do I live? Why did I choose this time and place to be born, these parents, these experiences? What do these feelings mean, these predictions? What can an astrologer do for me about my fears, my hope to be a hero at my level of life, in the eyes of my loved ones? How will I be remembered?

We can get terribly caught up with all of this, especially when we have lived through times when we thought we *were* going to die or we were told somehow that we were. We can ask, why is meaning so elusive if purpose is truly the stimulus of creation?

Through VIIIth House references in the main, common-sense understanding of life's progress, and respect of an individual's Reality Principle, we become aware not of death itself or of one's own death, but, rather, of *the circumstances about death*, not personalized except in having *to deal* with such circumstances—concerns of inheritance, for example, or someone's death circumstances that affect us. Anything else does not matter since we would not be alive to be concerned.

Just a short study of John F. Kennedy's horoscope (May 29, 1917; 3:15 p.m., LMT; 71W08, 42N20) and Harry S. Truman's horoscope (May 8, 1884; 3:43 p.m., LMT; 94W15, 37N29—Source: Doane), both of which have particular VIIIth House emphases within their Reality Principles, should tell us simply that VIIIth House dimensions do not necessarily keep anyone from fulfillment during life.

We have seen how the old astrologers relied so much upon conjunctions, planetary clusters, Fixed Stars, eclipses, and the drama of language to make their predictions. We have seen all of these observations plus Solar Arcs and transits work most accurately in Mundane Astrology. We have seen how measurements become less reliable, how symbolisms change in nuance, and how communication of astrology changes from pronouncement to dialogue *when astrology gets personal*. The indeterminate enters.

Our incompleteness glaringly calls for research of the Fixed Stars and of eclipses in personal astrology, and, as well, into the intriguing premise of Solar Return calculations. In our study in this book, we can see and sense the progress in astrology over the last 300 years. What will the next 25 computer-assisted years bring to our craft?

In conclusion, for prediction in astrology, there are four primary considerations we should respect, which we have covered in many different ways in this book:

First, there is the enormous importance of the Reality Principle to help us determine the possibilities and probabilities in any individual's horoscope. The Principle is founded within the person first, before it is tracked in the horoscope. The horoscope is brought into the life, not vice versa. The most important question about the future becomes a projection of the client into time ahead: "What do you project for yourself in the next six months?" The door is then opened appropriately for the maximum significance and reliability in prediction.

Second, there is the enormous importance of *past reactions* to fill out the Reality Principle as a basis for projection of those reactions on the waves of cycles into the future. The greatest security we have in astrological prediction is this reliability of cycles. These cycles can be quickly determined by reference to the "Quick-Glance" Transit Table (exclusively produced in the Appendix), used with rapport measurements and Solar Arcs to track development.

Rudhyar said it so well in *The Astrology of Personality*: "Very few persons, indeed, realize which events of their past have really been significant; neither do people usually grasp the true significance of these events. The greatest value of astrology is probably to be found in the aid it gives man in discovering the significance of what has already happened."

Third, in the measurement of powerful solar Arcs, there is the vitally important concept of Time Orb for maximum efficiency. The more slowly the planets move intrinsically, the longer the Time Orb seems to be of significance. For example, Saturn=Pluto will arc forward and back in time from its measured position (or rapport projection) for more months (perhaps four in each direction) than either the Solar Arc picture Mercury=Mars or most indirect midpoint pictures. Yet, midpoint pictures involving Angles and the outer planets seem to have proportionately longer Time Orbs.

The Time Orb sets up a time of significant development potential that is measured approximately as five minutes of arc per month of time (60 minutes divided by 12 months). As we have discussed in Chapter 3, this is a very tight astrological orb to work with, yet the resulting life time-opening allows for an appropriate transit to trigger symbolic correspondences.

And fourth, we astrologers must know keenly the danger of great expectations, recognize incompleteness, communicate with the greatest of care, and finally, know completely that the process of analysis is what prediction is all about. It is *the process* that makes time happen and gives it meaning.

Appendix I

"Quick-Glance" Transit Tables 1940-2040

Planet Positions
Mars through Pluto
for the First Day of Every Month

1940

MONTH	MARS LONG	JUPITER LONG	SATURN LONG	URANUS LONG	NEPTUNE LONG	PLUTO LONG
Jan	28 ♓	01 ♈	24 ♈	18 ♉	26 ♍	02 ♌
Feb	19 ♈	06	26	18	25	02
Mar	09 ♉	12	28	18	25	02
Apr	29	19	01 ♉	20	24	01
May	19 ♊	26	05	21	23	01
June	09 ♋	03 ♉	09	23	23	01
July	28	09	12	25	23	02
Aug	18 ♌	14	14	26	24	03
Sept	08 ♍	16	15	26	25	03
Oct	27	15	14	26	26	04
Nov	17 ♎	11	12	25	27	04
Dec	07 ♏	07	09	24	27	04

1941

MONTH	MARS LONG	JUPITER LONG	SATURN LONG	URANUS LONG	NEPTUNE LONG	PLUTO LONG
Jan	27 ♏	06 ♉	08 ♉	23 ♉	28 ♍	04 ♌
Feb	18 ♐	07	08	22	27	03
Mar	08 ♑	11	10	23	27	02
Apr	29	17	13	24	26	02
May	20 ♒	25	17	25	25	02
June	11 ♓	01 ♊	21	27	25	02
July	29	08	24	29	25	03
Aug	15 ♈	14	27	00 ♊	26	04
Sept	23	19	28	00	27	05
Oct	20	21	28	00	28	05
Nov	12	21	26	29 ♉	29	06
Dec	14	17	24	28	00 ♎	06

1942

MONTH	MARS LONG	JUPITER LONG	SATURN LONG	URANUS LONG	NEPTUNE LONG	PLUTO LONG
Jan	25 ♈	13 ♊	22 ♉	27 ♉	00 ♎	05 ♌
Feb	10 ♉	11	22	26	00	04
Mar	26	12	23	27	29 ♍	04
Apr	15 ♊	16	26	28	28	04
May	03 ♋	21	29	29	27	04
June	22	28	03 ♊	01 ♊	27	04
July	10 ♌	05 ♋	07	03	27	05
Aug	00 ♍	12	10	04	28	05
Sept	19	18	13	05	29	06
Oct	09 ♎	22	12	04	00 ♎	07
Nov	29	25	11	04	01	07
Dec	20 ♏	25	09	02	02	07

217

1943

MONTH	MARS LONG	JUPITER LONG	SATURN LONG	URANUS LONG	NEPTUNE LONG	PLUTO LONG
Jan	11 ♐	22 ♋	07 ♊	01 ♊	02 ♎	07 ♌
Feb	04 ♑	18	06	01	02	06
Mar	24	15	06	01	01	05
Apr	18 ♒	16	08	02	00	05
May	10 ♓	19	11	03	00	05
June	03 ♈	24	15	05	29 ♍	05
July	25	00 ♌	20	07	29	06
Aug	16 ♉	07	23	08	00 ♎	07
Sept	04 ♊	14	25	09	01	08
Oct	17	19	27	09	03	08
Nov	22	24	26	08	03	09
Dec	15	27	24	07	04	09

1944

MONTH	MARS LONG	JUPITER LONG	SATURN LONG	URANUS LONG	NEPTUNE LONG	PLUTO LONG
Jan	05 ♊	27 ♌	24 ♊	06 ♊	04 ♎	08 ♌
Feb	08	24	20	05	04	08
Mar	17	20	20	05	03	07
Apr	02 ♋	17	21	06	03	06
May	18	18	24	07	02	06
June	05 ♌	20	28	09	01	07
July	23	25	01 ♋	11	02	07
Aug	12 ♍	01 ♍	05	12	02	08
Sept	02 ♎	08	08	13	03	09
Oct	22	14	10	13	04	10
Nov	13 ♏	20	11	12	05	10
Dec	04 ♐	25	09	11	06	10

1945

MONTH	MARS LONG	JUPITER LONG	SATURN LONG	URANUS LONG	NEPTUNE LONG	PLUTO LONG
Jan	26 ♐	27 ♍	07 ♋	10 ♊	06 ♎	10 ♌
Feb	20 ♑	27	05	09	06	09
Mar	11 ♒	24	04	09	06	08
Apr	05 ♓	20	04	10	05	08
May	29	18	07	11	04	08
June	22 ♈	18	10	13	04	08
July	14 ♉	21	14	15	04	09
Aug	06 ♊	25	18	16	04	10
Sept	26	01 ♎	21	17	05	11
Oct	13 ♑	08	24	17	06	11
Nov	27	14	25	17	07	12
Dec	03 ♌	20	24	16	08	12

1946

MONTH	MARS LONG	JUPITER LONG	SATURN LONG	URANUS LONG	NEPTUNE LONG	PLUTO LONG
Jan	28 ♋	25 ♎	22 ♋	14 ♊	09 ♎	11 ♌
Feb	17	27	20	14	08	11
Mar	14	27	18	13	08	11
Apr	21	24	18	14	07	10
May	04 ♌	20	19	15	06	09
June	19	18	22	17	06	10
July	06 ♍	18	26	19	06	10
Aug	25	21	00 ♌	20	06	11
Sept	14 ♎	25	04	21	07	12
Oct	04 ♏	01 ♏	07	22	08	13
Nov	26	08	09	21	09	13
Dec	18 ♐	14	09	20	10	13

1947

MONTH	MARS LONG	JUPITER LONG	SATURN LONG	URANUS LONG	NEPTUNE LONG	PLUTO LONG
Jan	11 ♑	20 ♏	07 ♌	19 ♊	11 ♎	13 ♌
Feb	05 ♒	25	05	19	11	12
Mar	27	27	03	18	10	12
Apr	21 ♓	27	02	18	09	11
May	15 ♈	24	03	19	09	12
June	08 ♉	21	05	21	08	11
July	00 ♊	18	08	23	08	12
Aug	21	18	12	25	08	13
Sept	12 ♋	21	16	26	09	14
Oct	00 ♌	25	19	26	10	14
Nov	17	02 ♐	22	26	12	15
Dec	00 ♍	08	23	25	12	15

1948

MONTH	MARS LONG	JUPITER LONG	SATURN LONG	URANUS LONG	NEPTUNE LONG	PLUTO LONG
Jan	07 ♍	15 ♐	22 ♌	24 ♊	13 ♎	15 ♌
Feb	04	21	20	22	13	14
Mar	23 ♌	26	18	22	12	13
Apr	18	29	16	23	12	13
May	24	29	16	24	11	13
June	06 ♍	26	17	25	10	13
July	21	22	20	27	10	13
Aug	09 ♎	19	24	29	11	14
Sept	28	19	28	00 ♋	11	15
Oct	19 ♏	22	01 ♍	01	13	16
Nov	11 ♐	27	04	00	14	16
Dec	03 ♑	03 ♑	06	29 ♊	15	17

219

1949

MONTH	MARS LONG	JUPITER LONG	SATURN LONG	URANUS LONG	NEPTUNE LONG	PLUTO LONG
Jan	27 ♑	10 ♑	07 ♍	28 ♊	15 ♎	16 ♌
Feb	21 ♒	17	04	27	15	15
Mar	14 ♓	23	02	27	15	15
Apr	08 ♈	29	00	27	14	14
May	01 ♉	02 ♒	29 ♌	28	13	14
June	24	02	00 ♍	29	13	14
July	15 ♊	00	02	01 ♋	12	15
Aug	06 ♋	26 ♋	06	03	13	16
Sept	26	23	09	04	14	17
Oct	15 ♌	23	13	05	15	18
Nov	03 ♍	25	16	05	16	18
Dec	19	00 ♒	19	04	17	18

1950

MONTH	MARS LONG	JUPITER LONG	SATURN LONG	URANUS LONG	NEPTUNE LONG	PLUTO LONG
Jan	02 ♎	07 ♒	19 ♍	03 ♋	17 ♎	18 ♌
Feb	10	14	18	02	17	17
Mar	09	20	17	01	17	16
Apr	29 ♍	27	14	01	16	16
May	22	03 ♓	13	02	15	16
June	26	06	13	04	15	16
July	08 ♎	07	14	05	15	17
Aug	24	06	17	07	15	18
Sept	13 ♏	02	21	09	16	18
Oct	04 ♐	28 ♒	25	09	17	19
Nov	26	28	28	09	18	20
Dec	19 ♑	00 ♓	01 ♎	09	19	20

1951

MONTH	MARS LONG	JUPITER LONG	SATURN LONG	URANUS LONG	NEPTUNE LONG	PLUTO LONG
Jan	13 ♒	05 ♓	02 ♎	07 ♋	19 ♎	19 ♌
Feb	07 ♓	11	02	06	20	19
Mar	29	18	00	05	19	18
Apr	23 ♈	25	28 ♍	06	18	18
May	15	02 ♈	26	06	18	17
June	07 ♊	08	26	08 ♊	17	18
July	28	12	26	10	17	18
Aug	19 ♋	14	29	11	17	19
Sept	09 ♌	13	02 ♎	13	18	20
Oct	28	09	06	14	19	21
Nov	16 ♍	06	09	14	20	21
Dec	04 ♎	04	12	13	21	22

1952

MONTH	MARS LONG	JUPITER LONG	SATURN LONG	URANUS LONG	NEPTUNE LONG	PLUTO LONG
Jan	21 ♎	06 ♈	14 ♎	12 ♋	22 ♎	21 ♌
Feb	05 ♏	10	15	11	22	21
Mar	15	16	14	10	21	20
Apr	18	23	12	10	21	19
May	11	01 ♉	09	11	20	19
June	02	08	08	12	19	19
July	04	14	09	14	19	20
Aug	15	18	10	16	19	21
Sept	03 ♐	21	13	17	20	22
Oct	22	20	17	18	21	23
Nov	14 ♑	17	20	19	22	23
Dec	08 ♒	13	24	18	23	23

1953

MONTH	MARS LONG	JUPITER LONG	SATURN LONG	URANUS LONG	NEPTUNE LONG	PLUTO LONG
Jan	01 ♓	11 ♉	26 ♎	17 ♋	24 ♎	23 ♌
Feb	25	12	27	15	24	22
Mar	16 ♈	16	27	15	24	22
Apr	09 ♉	21	25	14	23	21
May	00 ♊	29	23	15	22	21
June	21	05 ♊	21	16	21	22
July	11 ♋	12	21	18	21	22
Aug	01 ♌	18	22	20	21	22
Sept	21	23	24	22	22	23
Oct	10 ♍	26	27	23	23	24
Nov	00 ♎	26	01 ♏	23	24	25
Dec	18	23	05	23	25	25

1954

MONTH	MARS LONG	JUPITER LONG	SATURN LONG	URANUS LONG	NEPTUNE LONG	PLUTO LONG
Jan	07 ♏	19 ♊	07 ♏	22 ♋	26 ♎	25 ♌
Feb	25	17	09	20	26	24
Mar	10 ♐	17	09	19	26	23
Apr	25	20	08	19	25	23
May	06 ♑	25	06	20	24	23
June	08	02 ♋	04	21	24	23
July	01	08	03	22	23	23
Aug	26 ♐	15	03	24	23	24
Sept	03 ♑	22	05	26	24	25
Oct	17	27	08	27	25	26
Nov	07 ♒	00 ♌	12	28	26	27
Dec	28	00	15	27	27	27

1955

MONTH	MARS LONG	JUPITER LONG	SATURN LONG	URANUS LONG	NEPTUNE LONG	PLUTO LONG
Jan	20 ♓	27 ♋	18 ♏	26 ♋	28 ♎	27 ♌
Feb	12 ♈	23	20	25	28	26
Mar	02 ♉	20	21	24	29	25
Apr	23	20	20	24	27	25
May	13 ♊	23	18	24	27	24
June	04 ♋	28	16	25	26	24
July	23	04 ♌	15	27	25	26
Aug	13 ♌	10	15	29	26	26
Sept	03 ♍	17	16	00 ♌	26	27
Oct	22	23	19	02	27	28
Nov	12 ♎	28	22	02	28	28
Dec	01 ♏	01 ♍	25	02	29	29

1956

MONTH	MARS LONG	JUPITER LONG	SATURN LONG	URANUS LONG	NEPTUNE LONG	PLUTO LONG
Jan	21 ♏	01 ♍	29 ♏	01 ♌	00 ♏	28 ♌
Feb	12 ♐	28 ♌	01 ♐	00	00	28
Mar	01 ♑	25	03	29 ♋	00	27
Apr	22	22	02	28	00	26
May	10 ♒	22	01	29	29 ♎	26
June	29	24	29 ♏	00 ♌	28	26
July	14 ♓	29	27	01	28	27
Aug	23	05 ♍	26	03	28	28
Sept	21	11	28	05	28	29
Oct	14	18	29	06	29	00 ♍
Nov	16	24	02 ♐	07	00 ♏	00
Dec	27	29	06	07	02	00

1957

MONTH	MARS LONG	JUPITER LONG	SATURN LONG	URANUS LONG	NEPTUNE LONG	PLUTO LONG
Jan	14 ♈	01 ♎	09 ♐	06 ♌	02 ♏	00 ♍
Feb	02 ♉	01	12	05	03	00
Mar	19	29 ♍	14	04	02	29 ♌
Apr	09 ♊	25	14	03	02	28
May	28	22	13	03	01	28
June	17 ♋	22	11	04	00	28
July	06 ♌	24	09	06	00	29
Aug	25	29	08	07	00	29
Sept	15 ♍	05 ♎	08	09	01	00 ♍
Oct	04 ♎	11	10	11	01	01
Nov	25	18	12	12	03	02
Dec	15 ♏	24	16	12	04	02

1958

MONTH	MARS LONG	JUPITER LONG	SATURN LONG	URANUS LONG	NEPTUNE LONG	PLUTO LONG
Jan	06 ♐	29 ♎	19 ♐	11 ♌	04 ♏	02 ♍
Feb	28	01 ♏	23	10	05	02
Mar	18 ♑	01	25	08	05	01
Apr	11 ♒	29 ♎	26	08	04	00
May	03 ♓	25	25	08	03	00
June	25	22	23	08	02	00
July	17 ♈	22	21	10	02	00
Aug	07 ♉	24	20	12	02	01
Sept	23	29	19	14	03	02
Oct	02 ♊	05 ♏	20	15	04	03
Nov	29 ♉	11	23	16	05	04
Dec	19	18	26	16	06	04

1959

MONTH	MARS LONG	JUPITER LONG	SATURN LONG	URANUS LONG	NEPTUNE LONG	PLUTO LONG
Jan	17 ♉	24 ♏	29 ♐	16 ♌	07 ♏	04 ♍
Feb	26	29	03 ♑	14	07	03
Mar	09 ♊	01 ♐	05	13	07	03
Apr	25	02	07	12	06	02
May	12 ♋	29 ♏	07	12	05	02
June	00 ♌	25	06	13	05	02
July	18	23	03	14	04	02
Aug	07 ♍	22	01	16	04	03
Sept	27	25	00	18	05	04
Oct	16 ♎	29	01	20	06	05
Nov	07 ♏	05 ♐	03	21	07	06
Dec	28	12	06	21	08	06

1960

MONTH	MARS LONG	JUPITER LONG	SATURN LONG	URANUS LONG	NEPTUNE LONG	PLUTO LONG
Jan	20 ♐	19 ♐	09 ♑	21 ♌	09 ♏	06 ♍
Feb	13 ♑	25	13	19	09	05
Mar	05 ♒	00 ♑	16	18	09	05
Apr	29	03	18	17	08	04
May	22 ♓	03	18	17	08	04
June	16 ♈	01	18	18	07	04
July	08 ♉	27 ♐	16	19	06	04
Aug	29	24	13	21	06	05
Sept	19 ♊	24	12	23	07	06
Oct	05 ♋	26	12	24	08	07
Nov	16	01 ♑	14	25	09	08
Dec	18	07	16	26	10	08

1961

MONTH	MARS LONG	JUPITER LONG	SATURN LONG	URANUS LONG	NEPTUNE LONG	PLUTO LONG
Jan	08 ♋	14 ♑	20 ♑	25 ♌	11 ♏	08 ♍
Feb	00	21	23	24	11	07
Mar	03	27	26	23	11	07
Apr	13	03 ♒	29	22	11	06
May	27	06	00 ♒	22	10	06
June	14 ♌	07	29 ♑	22	09	06
July	01 ♍	05	28	23	09	06
Aug	20	01	26	25	09	07
Sept	10 ♎	28 ♑	24	27	09	08
Oct	29	27	23	29	10	09
Nov	21 ♏	00 ♒	24	00 ♍	11	10
Dec	12 ♐	04	26	01	12	10

1962

MONTH	MARS LONG	JUPITER LONG	SATURN LONG	URANUS LONG	NEPTUNE LONG	PLUTO LONG
Jan	05 ♑	10 ♒	00 ♒	00 ♍	13 ♏	10 ♍
Feb	29	18	03	29 ♌	13	10
Mar	21 ♒	24	07	28	13	09
Apr	15 ♓	01 ♓	09	27	13	08
May	09 ♈	07	11	26	12	08
June	02 ♉	11	11	27	11	08
July	24	13	10	28	11	08
Aug	16 ♊	11	08	29	11	09
Sept	06 ♋	08	06	01 ♍	11	10
Oct	24	04	05	03	12	11
Nov	10 ♌	03	05	05	13	12
Dec	21	05	07	05	14	12

1963

MONTH	MARS LONG	JUPITER LONG	SATURN LONG	URANUS LONG	NEPTUNE LONG	PLUTO LONG
Jan	25 ♌	09 ♓	10 ♒	05 ♍	15 ♏	12 ♍
Feb	16	15	14	04	16	12
Mar	07	22	17	03	16	11
Apr	07	29	20	02	15	10
May	15	06 ♈	22	01	14	10
June	29	12	23	01	14	10
July	15 ♍	17	23	02	13	10
Aug	03 ♎	19	21	04	13	11
Sept	22	19	18	06	13	12
Oct	13 ♏	15	17	08	14	13
Nov	05 ♐	11	17	09	15	14
Dec	27	10	18	10	16	14

1964

MONTH	MARS LONG	JUPITER LONG	SATURN LONG	URANUS LONG	NEPTUNE LONG	PLUTO LONG
Jan	20 ♑	11 ♈	20 ♒	10 ♍	17 ♏	14 ♍
Feb	15 ♒	15	24	09	18	14
Mar	08 ♓	20	27	08	18	14
Apr	02 ♈	27	01 ♓	07	17	12
May	25	04 ♉	03	06	17	12
June	18 ♉	12	05	06	16	12
July	10 ♊	18	05	07	15	12
Aug	01 ♋	23	03	08	15	13
Sept	21	26	01	10	15	14
Oct	10 ♌	26	29 ♒	12	16	15
Nov	27	23	28	14	17	16
Dec	12 ♍	19	29	15	18	16

1965

MONTH	MARS LONG	JUPITER LONG	SATURN LONG	URANUS LONG	NEPTUNE LONG	PLUTO LONG
Jan	24 ♍	16 ♉	01 ♓	15 ♍	19 ♏	16 ♍
Feb	28	17	05	14	20	16
Mar	23	20	08	13	20	15
Apr	11	25	12	12	20	14
May	09	02 ♊	15	11	19	14
June	18	09	17	11	18	14
July	01 ♎	16	17	12	17	14
Aug	18	22	16	13	17	15
Sept	07 ♏	28	14	15	18	16
Oct	28	01 ♋	12	17	18	17
Nov	20 ♐	01	11	18	19	18
Dec	13 ♑	29 ♊	11	19	20	18

1966

MONTH	MARS LONG	JUPITER LONG	SATURN LONG	URANUS LONG	NEPTUNE LONG	PLUTO LONG
Jan	07 ♒	24 ♊	12 ♓	20 ♍	21 ♏	18 ♍
Feb	01 ♊	22	15	19	22	18
Mar	23	22	19	18	22	17
Apr	17 ♈	24	22	17	22	17
May	10 ♉	29	26	16	21	16
June	02 ♊	05 ♋	28	16	20	16
July	23	12	00	16	20	16
Aug	14 ♋	20	29 ♓	17	19	17
Sept	04 ♌	25	28	19	20	18
Oct	23	01 ♌	25	21	20	19
Nov	11 ♍	04	23	23	21	20
Dec	28	04	23	24	23	21

225

1967

MONTH	MARS LONG	JUPITER LONG	SATURN LONG	URANUS LONG	NEPTUNE LONG	PLUTO LONG
Jan	14 ♎	02 ♌	24 ♓	24 ♍	24 ♏	21 ♍
Feb	27	28 ♋	27	24	24	20
Mar	03 ♏	25	00	23	24	20
Apr	00	25	03 ♈	22	24	19
May	19 ♎	27	07	21	23	18
June	15	01 ♌	10	20	23	18
July	22	07	12	21	22	18
Aug	06 ♏	14	12	22	22	19
Sept	24	21	11	24	22	20
Oct	14 ♐	27	09	26	22	21
Nov	07 ♑	02 ♍	07	27	23	22
Dec	29	05	06	29	25	23

1968

MONTH	MARS LONG	JUPITER LONG	SATURN LONG	URANUS LONG	NEPTUNE LONG	PLUTO LONG
Jan	23 ♒	06 ♍	06 ♈	29 ♍	26 ♏	23 ♍
Feb	18 ♓	03	08	29	26	23
Mar	10 ♈	00	11	28	27	22
Apr	03 ♉	27 ♌	15	27	26	21
May	25	26	19	26	26	20
June	16 ♊	28	22	25	25	20
July	07 ♋	02 ♍	24	25	24	20
Aug	27	08	26	27	24	21
Sept	17 ♌	15	25	28	24	22
Oct	06 ♍	21	23	00 ♎	25	23
Nov	25	27	21	02	26	24
Dec	13 ♎	02 ♎	19	03	27	25

1969

MONTH	MARS LONG	JUPITER LONG	SATURN LONG	URANUS LONG	NEPTUNE LONG	PLUTO LONG
Jan	01 ♏	05 ♎	19 ♈	04 ♎	28 ♏	25 ♍
Feb	18	06	20	04	28	25
Mar	02 ♐	04	23	03	29	24
Apr	13	00	26	02	28	23
May	17	27 ♍	00 ♉	00	28	23
June	10	26	04	00	27	22
July	02	28	07	00	26	23
Aug	05	02 ♎	09	01	26	23
Sept	18	08	09	03	26	24
Oct	06 ♑	14	08	05	27	25
Nov	27	21	05	06	28	26
Dec	19 ♒	27	03	08	29	27

1970

MONTH	MARS LONG	JUPITER LONG	SATURN LONG	URANUS LONG	NEPTUNE LONG	PLUTO LONG
Jan	12 ♓	02 ♏	02 ♉	09 ♎	00 ♐	27 ♍
Feb	05 ♈	05	03	09	01	27
Mar	26	06	05	08	01	26
Apr	18 ♉	04	08	07	01	26
May	08 ♊	00	12	05	00	26
June	29	27 ♎	16	05	29 ♏	25
July	19 ♋	26	19	05	29	25
Aug	09 ♌	28	22	06	28	26
Sept	29	02 ♏	23	07	28	27
Oct	18 ♍	08	22	09	29	28
Nov	07 ♎	15	20	11	00 ♐	29
Dec	26	21	18	13	01	29

1971

MONTH	MARS LONG	JUPITER LONG	SATURN LONG	URANUS LONG	NEPTUNE LONG	PLUTO LONG
Jan	16 ♏	28 ♏	16 ♉	13 ♎	03 ♐	00 ♎
Feb	06 ♐	03 ♐	16	13	03	29 ♍
Mar	23	06	17	13	03	29
Apr	12 ♑	06	20	12	03	28
May	28	04	24	10	02	27
June	13 ♒	01	28	10	01	27
July	21	27 ♏	01 ♊	10	01	27
Aug	19	27	04	10	00	28
Sept	12	29	06	12	00	29
Oct	15	03 ♐	06	14	01	00 ♎
Nov	27	09	05	15	02	01
Dec	14 ♓	15	03	17	03	02

1972

MONTH	MARS LONG	JUPITER LONG	SATURN LONG	URANUS LONG	NEPTUNE LONG	PLUTO LONG
Jan	03 ♈	22 ♐	00 ♊	18 ♎	04 ♐	02 ♎
Feb	24	29	00	18	05	02
Mar	13 ♉	04 ♑	00	18	05	01
Apr	03 ♊	07	03	17	05	00
May	23	08	06	15	05	00
June	12 ♋	06	10	14	04	29 ♍
July	01 ♌	03	14	14	03	29
Aug	21	29 ♐	17	15	03	00 ♎
Sept	11 ♍	29	20	16	03	01
Oct	00 ♎	01 ♑	21	18	03	02
Nov	20	05	20	20	04	03
Dec	10 ♏	11	18	22	05	04

1973

MONTH	MARS LONG	JUPITER LONG	SATURN LONG	URANUS LONG	NEPTUNE LONG	PLUTO LONG
Jan	01 ♐	18 ♑	15 ♊	23 ♎	06 ♐	04 ♎
Feb	22	25	14	23	07	04
Mar	12 ♑	01 ♒	14	23	07	04
Apr	04 ♒	07	16	21	07	03
May	25	11	18	20	07	02
June	17 ♓	12	22	19	06	02
July	07 ♈	11	26	19	05	02
Aug	24	07	00 ♋	19	05	02
Sept	07 ♉	03	03	21	05	03
Oct	08	02	05	22	05	04
Nov	29 ♈	04	05	24	06	06
Dec	25	08	03	26	07	06

1974

MONTH	MARS LONG	JUPITER LONG	SATURN LONG	URANUS LONG	NEPTUNE LONG	PLUTO LONG
Jan	03 ♉	14 ♒	01 ♋	27 ♎	08 ♐	07 ♎
Feb	16	22	28 ♊	28	09	07
Mar	01 ♊	28	28	27	10	06
Apr	19	05 ♓	29	26	10	05
May	06 ♋	11	01 ♋	25	10	05
June	25	16	05	24	08	04
July	13 ♌	18	08	24	07	04
Aug	03 ♍	17	12	24	07	05
Sept	22	14	16	25	07	06
Oct	12 ♎	10	18	27	07	07
Nov	02 ♏	09	19	29	08	08
Dec	23	09	18	01 ♏	09	09

1975

MONTH	MARS LONG	JUPITER LONG	SATURN LONG	URANUS LONG	NEPTUNE LONG	PLUTO LONG
Jan	15 ♐	13 ♓	16 ♋	02 ♏	10 ♐	09 ♎
Feb	07 ♑	19	13	02	11	09
Mar	28	26	12	02	12	09
Apr	22 ♒	03 ♈	12	01	12	08
May	15 ♓	10	14	00	11	07
June	08 ♈	17	17	29 ♎	10	07
July	00 ♉	22	21	28	10	07
Aug	21	24	25	29	09	07
Sept	10 ♊	24	28	00 ♏	09	08
Oct	25	21	01 ♌	01	09	09
Nov	02 ♋	17	03	03	10	10
Dec	28 ♊	15	03	05	11	11

228

1976

MONTH	MARS LONG	JUPITER LONG	SATURN LONG	URANUS LONG	NEPTUNE LONG	PLUTO LONG
Jan	17 ♊	16 ♈	01 ♌	06 ♏	13 ♐	12 ♎
Feb	15	19	29 ♋	07	13	12
Mar	23	24	27	07	14	11
Apr	06 ♋	01 ♉	26	06	14	10
May	22	08	27	05	13	10
June	09 ♌	16	00 ♌	04	13	09
July	26	22	03	03	12	09
Aug	15 ♍	27	07	03	11	09
Sept	05 ♎	01 ♊	11	04	11	10
Oct	25	02	14	06	12	11
Nov	16 ♏	28 ♉	16	08	12	13
Dec	07 ♐	24	17	09	14	14

1977

MONTH	MARS LONG	JUPITER LONG	SATURN LONG	URANUS LONG	NEPTUNE LONG	PLUTO LONG
Jan	00 ♑	22 ♉	16 ♌	11 ♏	15 ♐	14 ♎
Feb	23	22	14	12	16	14
Mar	15 ♈	24	11	12	16	14
Apr	09 ♓	29	10	11	16	13
May	03 ♈	06 ♊	10	10	16	12
June	26	13	12	09	15	12
July	18 ♉	20	15	08	14	11
Aug	10 ♊	26	19	08	14	12
Sept	00 ♋	02 ♋	23	09	13	13
Oct	17	05	26	10	14	14
Nov	02 ♌	06	29	12	15	15
Dec	11	04	00 ♍	14	16	16

1978

MONTH	MARS LONG	JUPITER LONG	SATURN LONG	URANUS LONG	NEPTUNE LONG	PLUTO LONG
Jan	09 ♌	00 ♋	00 ♍	15 ♏	17 ♐	17 ♎
Feb	28 ♋	27 ♊	28 ♌	16	18	17
Mar	22	26	26	16	18	16
Apr	27	29	24	16	18	15
May	08 ♌	03 ♋	24	15	18	15
June	23	09	25	13	17	14
July	09 ♍	16	27	12	16	14
Aug	28	23	01 ♍	12	16	14
Sept	18 ♎	29	05	13	16	15
Oct	08 ♏	04 ♌	08	14	16	16
Nov	29	08	11	16	17	17
Dec	21 ♐	09	13	18	18	18

229

1979

MONTH	MARS LONG	JUPITER LONG	SATURN LONG	URANUS LONG	NEPTUNE LONG	PLUTO LONG
Jan	15 ♑	08 ♌	14 ♍	20 ♏	19 ♐	19 ♎
Feb	09 ♒	03	13	21	20	19
Mar	01 ♓	01	11	22	20	19
Apr	25	29 ♋	08	20	20	18
May	18 ♈	01 ♌	07	19	20	17
June	12 ♉	05	08	18	19	17
July	03 ♊	11	09	17	19	16
Aug	25	17	12	17	18	17
Sept	15 ♋	24	16	17	18	18
Oct	04 ♌	00 ♍	20	19	19	19
Nov	21	06	23	20	19	20
Dec	05 ♍	09	26	22	20	21

1980

MONTH	MARS LONG	JUPITER LONG	SATURN LONG	URANUS LONG	NEPTUNE LONG	PLUTO LONG
Jan	14 ♍	10 ♍	27 ♍	24 ♏	21 ♐	22 ♎
Feb	14	08	26	25	22	22
Mar	04	05	25	26	23	21
Apr	26 ♌	01	22	25	23	21
May	29	00	21	24	22	20
June	10 ♍	02	20	23	22	19
July	25	06	21	22	21	19
Aug	12 ♎	12	24	21	20	19
Sept	02 ♏	18	27	22	20	20
Oct	22	25	01 ♎	23	20	21
Nov	14 ♐	01 ♎	05	25	21	22
Dec	07 ♑	06	08	27	22	23

1981

MONTH	MARS LONG	JUPITER LONG	SATURN LONG	URANUS LONG	NEPTUNE LONG	PLUTO LONG
Jan	01 ♒	10 ♎	10 ♎	28 ♏	23 ♐	24 ♎
Feb	25	10	10	00 ♐	24	24
Mar	17 ♓	09	08	00	25	24
Apr	12 ♈	05	06	00	25	23
May	04 ♉	02	05	29 ♏	25	22
June	27	00	03	28	24	22
July	18 ♊	02	04	27	23	22
Aug	09 ♋	06	06	26	22	22
Sept	29	12	09	26	22	23
Oct	18 ♌	18	12	27	22	24
Nov	06 ♍	25	16	29	23	25
Dec	23	01 ♏	19	01 ♐	24	26

230

1982

MONTH	MARS LONG	JUPITER LONG	SATURN LONG	URANUS LONG	NEPTUNE LONG	PLUTO LONG
Jan	07 ♎	06 ♏	21 ♎	03 ♐	25 ♐	27 ♎
Feb	17	09	22	04	26	27
Mar	19	10	22	05	27	27
Apr	10	08	20	04	27	26
May	01	05	17	04	27	25
June	03	01	16	02	26	24
July	13	11	16	01	25	24
Aug	29	02	17	01	25	24
Sept	17 ♏	06	20	01	24	25
Oct	08 ♐	12	23	02	24	26
Nov	00 ♑	18	27	03	25	27
Dec	23	25	00 ♏	05	26	28

1983

MONTH	MARS LONG	JUPITER LONG	SATURN LONG	URANUS LONG	NEPTUNE LONG	PLUTO LONG
Jan	17 ♒	01 ♐	03 ♏	07 ♐	27 ♐	29 ♎
Feb	11 ♓	07	04	08	28	00 ♏
Mar	03 ♈	10	04	09	29	29 ♎
Apr	27	11	03	09	29	29
May	19 ♉	09	00	08	30	28
June	11 ♊	06	28 ♎	07	28	27
July	01 ♋	02	28	06	28	27
Aug	22	01	28	05	27	27
Sept	12 ♌	03	01 ♏	05	26	28
Oct	01 ♍	07	04	06	27	29
Nov	20	12	07	08	27	00 ♏
Dec	07 ♎	19	11	09	28	01

1984

MONTH	MARS LONG	JUPITER LONG	SATURN LONG	URANUS LONG	NEPTUNE LONG	PLUTO LONG
Jan	25 ♎	26 ♐	14 ♏	11 ♐	29 ♐	02 ♏
Feb	10 ♏	03 ♑	16	13	00 ♑	02
Mar	22	08	16	13	01	02
Apr	28	12	15	13	01	01
May	24	13	13	13	01	00
June	14	11	11	12	01	00
July	13	08	10	10	00	29 ♎
Aug	22	04	10	10	29 ♐	29
Sept	08 ♐	03	12	10	29	00 ♏
Oct	27	05	14	10	29	01
Nov	19 ♑	09	18	12	29	02
Dec	11 ♒	15	21	14	00 ♑	03

231

1985

MONTH	MARS LONG	JUPITER LONG	SATURN LONG	URANUS LONG	NEPTUNE LONG	PLUTO LONG
Jan	05 ♓	21 ♑	25 ♏	15 ♐	01 ♑	04 ♏
Feb	29	29	27	17	03	05
Mar	20 ♈	05 ♒	28	18	03	05
Apr	12 ♉	11	28	18	04	04
May	03 ♊	15	26	17	03	03
June	24	17	24	16	03	02
July	14 ♋	16	22	15	02	02
Aug	04 ♌	12	21	14	01	02
Sept	24	09	23	15	01	03
Oct	13 ♍	07	25	15	01	04
Nov	03 ♎	08	28	16	02	05
Dec	21	12	02 ♐	18	02	07

1986

MONTH	MARS LONG	JUPITER LONG	SATURN LONG	URANUS LONG	NEPTUNE LONG	PLUTO LONG
Jan	11 ♏	18 ♒	05 ♐	19 ♐	04 ♑	07 ♏
Feb	29	25	08	21	05	07
Mar	15 ♐	03 ♓	09	22	05	07
Apr	02 ♑	09	10	22	06	07
May	15	15	08	22	06	06
June	23	20	06	21	05	05
July	20	23	04	20	04	05
Aug	12	22	03	19	04	05
Sept	14	19	04	18	03	05
Oct	26	15	05	19	03	06
Nov	14 ♒	13	08	20	04	07
Dec	03 ♓	14	12	22	05	09

1987

MONTH	MARS LONG	JUPITER LONG	SATURN LONG	URANUS LONG	NEPTUNE LONG	PLUTO LONG
Jan	25 ♓	18 ♓	15 ♐	24 ♐	06 ♑	09 ♏
Feb	16 ♈	23	18	25	07	10
Mar	06 ♉	00	20	26	08	10
Apr	27	07 ♈	21	27	08	09
May	17 ♊	14	20	26	08	09
June	07 ♋	21	18	25	07	08
July	26	26	16	24	07	07
Aug	16 ♌	29	15	23	06	07
Sept	06 ♍	29	15	23	05	08
Oct	25	27	16	23	05	09
Nov	15 ♎	23	19	24	06	10
Dec	04 ♏	20	22	26	07	11

1988

MONTH	MARS LONG	JUPITER LONG	SATURN LONG	URANUS LONG	NEPTUNE LONG	PLUTO LONG
Jan	25 ♏	20 ♈	25 ♐	28 ♐	08 ♑	13 ♏
Feb	16 ♐	23	29	29	09	13
Mar	05 ♑	28	01 ♑	01 ♑	10	13
Apr	26	05 ♉	02	01	10	13
May	16 ♒	12	02	01	10	11
June	06 ♓	20	01	00	10	10
July	24	26	28 ♐	29 ♐	09	10
Aug	07 ♈	02 ♊	27	28	08	10
Sept	11	05	26	27	08	10
Oct	04	06	27	27	07	11
Nov	0058	04	29	28	08	12
Dec	04 ♈	00	02 ♑	00 ♑	09	14

1989

MONTH	MARS LONG	JUPITER LONG	SATURN LONG	URANUS LONG	NEPTUNE LONG	PLUTO LONG
Jan	20 ♈	27 ♉	06 ♑	02 ♑	10 ♑	15 ♏
Feb	07 ♉	26	09	03	11	15
Mar	24	29	12	05	12	15
Apr	13 ♊	03 ♊	14	05	12	15
May	01 ♋	10	14	05	12	14
June	20	17	13	04	12	13
July	09 ♌	23	11	03	11	12
Aug	28	00 ♋	09	02	10	12
Sept	18 ♍	06	07	01	10	13
Oct	07 ♎	10	08	02	10	14
Nov	28	11	09	02	10	15
Dec	18 ♏	09	12	04	11	16

1990

MONTH	MARS LONG	JUPITER LONG	SATURN LONG	URANUS LONG	NEPTUNE LONG	PLUTO LONG
Jan	10 ♐	05 ♋	16 ♑	06 ♑	12 ♑	17 ♏
Feb	02 ♑	02	19	08	13	18
Mar	22	01	22	09	15	18
Apr	15 ♒	03	24	10	15	17
May	08 ♓	07	25	09	15	17
June	01 ♈	13	25	09	14	16
July	22	19	23	08	13	15
Aug	13 ♉	26	21	06	13	15
Sept	00 ♊	03 ♌	19	06	12	15
Oct	12	08	19	06	12	16
Nov	14	12	20	07	12	17
Dec	04	14	22	08	13	19

233

1991

MONTH	MARS LONG	JUPITER LONG	SATURN LONG	URANUS LONG	NEPTUNE LONG	PLUTO LONG
Jan	28 ♉	12 ♌	26 ♋	10 ♑	14 ♑	20 ♏
Feb	03 ♊	08	29	12	15	20
Mar	14	05	02 ♒	13	16	20
Apr	29	04	05	14	17	20
May	15 ♋	05	07	14	17	19
June	01 ♌	10	07	13	16	18
July	21	14	05	12	16	18
Aug	10 ♍	21	03	11	15	18
Sept	00 ♎	28	01	10	14	18
Oct	19	04 ♍	00	10	15	19
Nov	10 ♏	09	01	11	14	20
Dec	01 ♐	13	03	12	15	21

1992

MONTH	MARS LONG	JUPITER LONG	SATURN LONG	URANUS LONG	NEPTUNE LONG	PLUTO LONG
Jan	24 ♐	15 ♍	06 ♒	14 ♑	16 ♑	22 ♏
Feb	17 ♑	13	09	15	17	23
Mar	09 ♒	10	13	17	18	23
Apr	03 ♓	06	16	18	19	23
May	26	05	18	18	19	22
June	20 ♈	06	18	17	19	21
July	12 ♉	10	18	16	18	20
Aug	04 ♊	15	16	15	17	20
Sept	23	21	13	14	16	20
Oct	10 ♋	28	12	14	16	21
Nov	23	04 ♎	12	15	17	22
Dec	28	10	14	16	17	24

1993

MONTH	MARS LONG	JUPITER LONG	SATURN LONG	URANUS LONG	NEPTUNE LONG	PLUTO LONG
Jan	20 ♋	13 ♎	16 ♒	18 ♑	18 ♑	25 ♏
Feb	10	15	20	19	20	25
Mar	10	13	23	21	20	26
Apr	18	10	27	22	21	25
May	01 ♌	06	29	22	21	25
June	17	05	00 ♓	22	21	24
July	04 ♍	06	00	21	20	23
Aug	23	10	28 ♒	19	19	23
Sept	13 ♎	15	26	19	19	23
Oct	03 ♏	21	24	18	18	24
Nov	24	29	24	19	19	25
Dec	16 ♐	04 ♏	25	20	19	26

1994

MONTH	MARS LONG	JUPITER LONG	SATURN LONG	URANUS LONG	NEPTUNE LONG	PLUTO LONG
Jan	09 ♑	10 ♏	27 ♒	20 ♑	21 ♑	27 ♏
Feb	03 ♒	13	00 ♓	23	22	28
Mar	25	15	04	25	23	28
Apr	19 ♓	13	07	26	23	28
May	13 ♈	10	10	26	23	27
June	06 ♉	06	13	26	23	26
July	28	05	12	26	22	26
Aug	19 ♊	06	11	24	22	25
Sept	10 ♋	10	09	23	21	25
Oct	28	15	07	22	21	26
Nov	14 ♌	22	06	23	21	27
Dec	27	28	06	24	22	28

1995

MONTH	MARS LONG	JUPITER LONG	SATURN LONG	URANUS LONG	NEPTUNE LONG	PLUTO LONG
Jan	03 ♍	05 ♐	08 ♓	25 ♑	23 ♑	00 ♐
Feb	27 ♌	10	11	27	24	00
Mar	17	14	14	29	25	01
Apr	13	15	18	00 ♒	25	00
May	20	14	21	00	26	00
June	03 ♍	11	24	00	25	29 ♏
July	18	07	25	29 ♑	25	28
Aug	06 ♎	06	24	28	24	28
Sept	26	07	22	27	23	28
Oct	16 ♏	10	20	27	23	29
Nov	08 ♐	16	18	27	23	00 ♐
Dec	00 ♑	22	18	28	24	01

1996

MONTH	MARS LONG	JUPITER LONG	SATURN LONG	URANUS LONG	NEPTUNE LONG	PLUTO LONG
Jan	24 ♑	29 ♐	19 ♓	29 ♑	25 ♑	02 ♐
Feb	19 ♒	06 ♑	22	01 ♒	26	03
Mar	11 ♓	12	25	03	27	03
Apr	06 ♈	16	29	05	28	03
May	29	18	03 ♈	05	28	02
June	22 ♉	17	06	04	27	01
July	14 ♊	13	07	04	27	01
Aug	04 ♋	10	07	02	26	00
Sept	24	08	06	01	25	00
Oct	13 ♌	09	04	01	25	01
Nov	01 ♍	13	02	01	25	02
Dec	16	18	01	02	26	03

235

1997

MONTH	MARS LONG	JUPITER LONG	SATURN LONG	URANUS LONG	NEPTUNE LONG	PLUTO LONG
Jan	29 ♍	25 ♑	01 ♈	03 ♒	27 ♑	04 ♐
Feb	06 ♎	02 ♒	04	05	29	05
Mar	03	09	07	07	29	06
Apr	21 ♍	15	10	08	00 ♒	05
May	17	20	14	09	00	05
June	23	22	17	09	00	04
July	05 ♎	21	20	08	29 ♑	03
Aug	22	18	20	07	28	03
Sept	11 ♏	14	20	05	28	03
Oct	01 ♐	12	18	05	27	03
Nov	24	13	15	05	27	04
Dec	17 ♑	17	14	06	28	06

1998

MONTH	MARS LONG	JUPITER LONG	SATURN LONG	URANUS LONG	NEPTUNE LONG	PLUTO LONG
Jan	11 ♒	27 ♒	14 ♈	07 ♒	29 ♑	07 ♐
Feb	05 ♓	29	15	09	00 ♒	08
Mar	27	06 ♓	18	10	01	08
Apr	21 ♈	13	22	12	02	08
May	13 ♉	20	26	13	02	07
June	06 ♊	25	29	13	02	07
July	26	28	02 ♉	13	01	06
Aug	17 ♋	28	03	11	01	05
Sept	07 ♌	25	03	10	00	05
Oct	27	21	02	09	29 ♑	06
Nov	15 ♍	18	00	09	00 ♒	07
Dec	03 ♎	19	28 ♒	10	00	08

1999

MONTH	MARS LONG	JUPITER LONG	SATURN LONG	URANUS LONG	NEPTUNE LONG	PLUTO LONG
Jan	18 ♎	22 ♓	27 ♈	11 ♒	01 ♒	09 ♐
Feb	02 ♏	27	28	13	02	10
Mar	10	04 ♈	01 ♉	14	03	10
Apr	11	11	03	16	04	10
May	02	18	07	17	04	10
June	25 ♎	25	11	17	04	09
July	29	00 ♉	14	16	04	08
Aug	11 ♏	04	16	15	03	08
Sept	29	05	17	14	02	08
Oct	19 ♐	03	16	13	02	08
Nov	11 ♑	29 ♈	14	13	02	09
Dec	04 ♒	26	12	13	02	10

2000

MONTH	MARS LONG	JUPITER LONG	SATURN LONG	URANUS LONG	NEPTUNE LONG	PLUTO LONG
Jan	28 ≈	25 ♈	10 ♉	15 ≈	03 ≈	11 ♐
Feb	22 ♓	28	11	16	04	12
Mar	14 ♈	03 ♉	12	18	05	13
Apr	07 ♉	09	15	20	06	13
May	28	16	19	21	07	12
June	20 ♊	23	23	21	06	12
July	10 ♋	00 ♊	27	20	06	11
Aug	00 ♌	06	29	19	05	10
Sept	20	10	01 ♊	18	04	10
Oct	09 ♍	11	01	17	04	11
Nov	28	10	29 ♉	17	04	11
Dec	16 ♎	06	27	17	04	13

2001

MONTH	MARS LONG	JUPITER LONG	SATURN LONG	URANUS LONG	NEPTUNE LONG	PLUTO LONG
Jan	05 ♏	02 ♊	25 ♉	19 ≈	05 ≈	14 ♐
Feb	23	01	24	20	06	15
Mar	07 ♐	03	25	22	07	15
Apr	21	08	28	23	08	15
May	28	13	01 ♊	25	09	15
June	26	20	05	25	09	14
July	18	17	09	24	08	13
Aug	16	04 ♋	12	23	07	13
Sept	26	10	14	22	07	13
Oct	13 ♑	15	15	21	06	13
Nov	03 ≈	16	14	21	06	14
Dec	24	14	12	21	07	15

2002

MONTH	MARS LONG	JUPITER LONG	SATURN LONG	URANUS LONG	NEPTUNE LONG	PLUTO LONG
Jan	17 ♓	11 ♋	09 ♊	22 ≈	07 ≈	16 ♐
Feb	09 ♈	07	08	24	09	17
Mar	00 ♉	06	08	26	10	18
Apr	21	07	10	27	10	18
May	12 ♊	11	14	28	11	17
June	02 ♋	17	17	29	11	16
July	22	23	21	29	10	16
Aug	12 ♌	00 ♌	25	28	10	15
Sept	02 ♍	06	28	26	09	15
Oct	21	12	29	25	08	15
Nov	10 ♎	16	29	25	08	16
Dec	00 ♏	18 ♑	27	25	09	17

2003

MONTH	MARS LONG	JUPITER LONG	SATURN LONG	URANUS LONG	NEPTUNE LONG	PLUTO LONG
Jan	20 ♏	17 ♌	24 ♊	26 ♒	10 ♒	18 ♐
Feb	10 ♐	13	23	28	11	19
Mar	28	10	22	29	12	20
Apr	17 ♑	08	23	01 ♓	13	20
May	05 ♒	09	26	02	13	20
June	22	13	00 ♋	03	13	19
July	05 ♓	18	03	03	13	18
Aug	10	24	07	02	12	17
Sept	04	01 ♍	11	01	11	17
Oct	00	07	13	29 ♒	11	18
Nov	07	13	13	29	10	18
Dec	21	17	12	29	11	19

2004

MONTH	MARS LONG	JUPITER LONG	SATURN LONG	URANUS LONG	NEPTUNE LONG	PLUTO LONG
Jan	09 ♈	19 ♍	10 ♋	00 ♓	12 ♒	20 ♐
Feb	28	18	07	02	13	21
Mar	17 ♉	14	06	03	14	22
Apr	07 ♊	11	07	05	15	22
May	26	09	09	06	15	22
June	16 ♋	10	12	07	15	21
July	04 ♌	13	16	07	15	20
Aug	24	19	20	06	14	20
Sept	14 ♍	25	23	05	13	20
Oct	03 ♎	01 ♎	26	04	13	20
Nov	23	08	27	03	13	21
Dec	13 ♏	13	27	03	13	22

2005

MONTH	MARS LONG	JUPITER LONG	SATURN LONG	URANUS LONG	NEPTUNE LONG	PLUTO LONG
Jan	04 ♐	17 ♎	25 ♋	04 ♓	14 ♒	23 ♐
Feb	26	19	22	05	15	24
Mar	16 ♑	18	21	07	16	24
Apr	08 ♒	14	20	09	17	25
May	00 ♓	11	22	10	18	24
June	22	09	25	11	18	24
July	13 ♈	10	28	11	17	23
Aug	02 ♉	13	03 ♌	10	16	22
Sept	17	19	06	09	16	22
Oct	23	25	09	08	15	22
Nov	17	01 ♏	11	07	15	23
Dec	09	08	11	07	15	24

2006

MONTH	MARS LONG	JUPITER LONG	SATURN LONG	URANUS LONG	NEPTUNE LONG	PLUTO LONG
Jan	11 ♉	13 ♏	10 ♌	08 ♓	16 ♒	25 ♐
Feb	22	17	08	09	17	26
Mar	06 ♊	19	05	11	18	27
Apr	23	18	04	12	19	27
May	10 ♋	14	05	14	20	26
June	28	11	07	15	20	26
July	17 ♌	09	10	15	19	25
Aug	06 ♍	10	14	14	19	24
Sept	25	13	18	13	18	24
Oct	15 ♎	18	21	12	17	24
Nov	06 ♏	25	24	11	17	25
Dec	26	02 ♐	25	11	17	26

2007

MONTH	MARS LONG	JUPITER LONG	SATURN LONG	URANUS LONG	NEPTUNE LONG	PLUTO LONG
Jan	18 ♐	08 ♐	24 ♌	12 ♓	18 ♒	27 ♐
Feb	11 ♑	15	22	13	19	28
Mar	02 ♒	18	20	14	20	29
Apr	26	20	18	16	21	29
May	19 ♓	19	18	18	22	29
June	12 ♈	16	20	18	22	28
July	04 ♉	12	22	19	22	27
Aug	26	10	26	18	21	27
Sept	15 ♊	11	00 ♍	17	20	26
Oct	01 ♋	14	03	16	20	26
Nov	11	20	06	15	19	27
Dec	11	26	08	15	20	28

2008

MONTH	MARS LONG	JUPITER LONG	SATURN LONG	URANUS LONG	NEPTUNE LONG	PLUTO LONG
Jan	00 ♋	03 ♑	08 ♍	15 ♓	20 ♒	29 ♐
Feb	24 ♊	10	07	17	21	00 ♑
Mar	29	16	05	18	22	01
Apr	11 ♋	20	03	20	23	01
May	25	22	02	21	24	01
June	12 ♌	22	02	22	24	00
July	00 ♍	19	05	23	24	00
Aug	18	15	08	22	23	29 ♐
Sept	08 ♎	13	12	21	22	29
Oct	28	13	15	20	22	29
Nov	19 ♏	17	19	19	21	29
Dec	11 ♐	22	21	19	22	00 ♑

2009

MONTH	MARS LONG	JUPITER LONG	SATURN LONG	URANUS LONG	NEPTUNE LONG	PLUTO LONG
Jan	04 ♑	29 ♑	22 ♍	19 ♓	22 ♒	01 ♑
Feb	27	06 ♒	21	20	24	02
Mar	19 ♒	13	19	22	25	03
Apr	13 ♓	19	17	24	26	03
May	07 ♈	24	15	25	26	03
June	00 ♉	27	15	26	26	03
July	22	27	17	27	26	02
Aug	14 ♊	24	19	26	26	01
Sept	04 ♋	20	23	25	25	01
Oct	22	17	27	24	24	01
Nov	07 ♌	18	00 ♎	23	24	01
Dec	17	21	03	23	24	02

2010

MONTH	MARS LONG	JUPITER LONG	SATURN LONG	URANUS LONG	NEPTUNE LONG	PLUTO LONG
Jan	19 ♌	26 ♒	05 ♎	23 ♓	25 ♒	03 ♑
Feb	09	03 ♓	04	24	26	04
Mar	01	10	03	26	27	05
Apr	03	17	01	27	28	05
May	13	24	29 ♍	29	28	05
June	27	29	28	00 ♈	29	05
July	13 ♍	03 ♈	29	01	28	04
Aug	01 ♎	03	01 ♎	00	28	03
Sept	21	01	04	29 ♓	27	03
Oct	11 ♏	27 ♓	08	28	26	03
Nov	03 ♐	24	11	27	26	03
Dec	25	24	15	27	26	04

2011

MONTH	MARS LONG	JUPITER LONG	SATURN LONG	URANUS LONG	NEPTUNE LONG	PLUTO LONG
Jan	18 ♑	27 ♓	17 ♎	27 ♓	27 ♒	05 ♑
Feb	13 ♒	02 ♈	17	28	28	06
Mar	05 ♓	08	16	29	29	07
Apr	29	15	14	01 ♈	00 ♓	07
May	22 ♈	22	12	03	01	07
June	15 ♉	29	11	04	01	07
July	07 ♊	05 ♉	11	05	01	06
Aug	28	09	12	04	00	05
Sept	19 ♋	10	15	04	29 ♒	05
Oct	07 ♌	09	19	02	29	05
Nov	25	05	22	01	28	05
Dec	09 ♍	01	26	01	28	06

2012

MONTH	MARS LONG	JUPITER LONG	SATURN LONG	URANUS LONG	NEPTUNE LONG	PLUTO LONG
Jan	20 ♍	00 ♉	28 ♎	01 ♈	29 ♒	07 ♑
Feb	23	03	29	02	00 ♓	08
Mar	15	07	29	03	02	09
Apr	05	13	27	05	02	10
May	05	20	25	07	03	09
June	15	28	23	08	03	09
July	29	04 ♊	23	08	03	08
Aug	16 ♎	10	24	08	02	07
Sept	05 ♏	15	26	08	02	07
Oct	26	16	29	06	01	08
Nov	18 ♐	15	03 ♏	05	00	07
Dec	11 ♑	12	07	05	00	08

2013

MONTH	MARS LONG	JUPITER LONG	SATURN LONG	URANUS LONG	NEPTUNE LONG	PLUTO LONG
Jan	05 ♒	08 ♊	10 ♏	05 ♈	01 ♓	09 ♑
Feb	29	06	11	06	02	10
Mar	21 ♓	08	11	07	03	11
Apr	15 ♈	12	10	09	04	12
May	08 ♉	17	08	10	05	11
June	00 ♊	24	06	12	05	11
July	21	01 ♋	05	12	05	10
Aug	12 ♋	08	05	12	05	10
Sept	03 ♌	15	07	12	04	09
Oct	21	18	10	11	03	09
Nov	10 ♍	20	14	09	03	09
Dec	26	20	17	09	03	10

2014

MONTH	MARS LONG	JUPITER LONG	SATURN LONG	URANUS LONG	NEPTUNE LONG	PLUTO LONG
Jan	12 ♎	16 ♋	20 ♏	09 ♈	03 ♓	11 ♑
Feb	23	12	23	09	04	12
Mar	28	10	23	11	05	13
Apr	22	11	23	12	06	14
May	11	15	21	14	07	14
June	10	20	18	15	08	13
July	18	27	17	16	07	12
Aug	03 ♏	03 ♌	17	16	07	12
Sept	22	10	18	16	06	11
Oct	12 ♐	16	21	15	05	11
Nov	04 ♑	20	24	14	05	11
Dec	27	23	27	13	05	12

2015

MONTH	MARS LONG	JUPITER LONG	SATURN LONG	URANUS LONG	NEPTUNE LONG	PLUTO LONG
Jan	21 ≈	22 ♌	01 ♐	13 ♈	05 ♓	13 ♑
Feb	15 ♓	18	04	13	06	14
Mar	07 ♈	15	05	14	07	15
Apr	00 ♉	13	05	16	08	15
May	22	13	03	18	09	15
June	14 ♊	17	01	19	10	15
July	04 ♋	22	29 ♏	20	10	14
Aug	25	28	28	20	09	14
Sept	15 ♌	04 ♍	29	20	08	13
Oct	04 ♍	11	01 ♐	19	08	13
Nov	23	17	04	18	07	13
Dec	11 ♎	21	08	17	07	14

2016

MONTH	MARS LONG	JUPITER LONG	SATURN LONG	URANUS LONG	NEPTUNE LONG	PLUTO LONG
Jan	29 ♎	23 ♍	11 ♐	17 ♈	08 ♓	15 ♑
Feb	15 ♏	22	14	17	08	16
Mar	28	19	16	18	10	17
Apr	07 ♐	15	16	20	11	17
May	08	13	15	22	12	17
June	28 ♏	14	13	23	12	17
July	23	17	11	24	12	16
Aug	29	22	10	25	11	16
Sept	14 ♐	28	10	24	11	15
Oct	02 ♑	05 ♎	12	23	10	15
Nov	25	11	14	22	09	15
Dec	16 ≈	17	18	21	09	16

2017

MONTH	MARS LONG	JUPITER LONG	SATURN LONG	URANUS LONG	NEPTUNE LONG	PLUTO LONG
Jan	10 ♓	21 ♎	21 ♐	21 ♈	10 ♓	17 ♑
Feb	03 ♈	23	25	21	11	18
Mar	23	22	27	22	12	19
Apr	16 ♉	19	28	24	13	19
May	07 ♊	15	27	25	14	19
June	28	13	26	28	14	20
July	17 ♋	14	23	28	14	18
Aug	07 ♌	18	22	29	14	18
Sept	27	23	21	28	13	17
Oct	16 ♍	28	22	27	12	17
Nov	06 ♎	05 ♏	25	26	12	17
Dec	25	11	28	25	11	18

242

2018

MONTH	MARS LONG	JUPITER LONG	SATURN LONG	URANUS LONG	NEPTUNE LONG	PLUTO LONG
Jan	14 ♏	17 ♏	01 ♑	25 ♈	12 ♓	19 ♑
Feb	03 ♐	21	05	25	13	20
Mar	20	23	07	26	14	21
Apr	08 ♑	22	09	27	15	21
May	23	19	09	29	16	21
June	05 ♒	16	08	01 ♉	16	21
July	09	13	06	02	16	20
Aug	03	14	04	03	16	20
Sept	29 ♑	17	03	02	15	19
Oct	06 ♒	22	03	01	14	19
Nov	21	28	05	00	14	19
Dec	09 ♓	06 ♐	08	29 ♈	14	20

2019

MONTH	MARS LONG	JUPITER LONG	SATURN LONG	URANUS LONG	NEPTUNE LONG	PLUTO LONG
Jan	0056	12 ♐	11 ♑	29 ♈	14 ♓	21 ♑
Feb	21 ♈	18	15	29	15	22
Mar	10 ♉	22	18	00 ♉	16	22
Apr	00 ♊	24	20	01	17	23
May	20	24	21	03	18	23
June	10 ♋	21	20	05	19	23
July	29	17	18	06	19	22
Aug	19 ♌	15	16	07	18	21
Sept	09 ♍	15	14	06	18	21
Oct	28	18	14	06	17	21
Nov	18 ♎	23	15	04	16	21
Dec	08 ♏	00 ♑	18	03	16	21

2020

MONTH	MARS LONG	JUPITER LONG	SATURN LONG	URANUS LONG	NEPTUNE LONG	PLUTO LONG
Jan	28 ♏	07 ♑	21 ♑	03 ♉	16 ♓	22 ♑
Feb	19 ♐	14	25	03	17	23
Mar	09 ♑	20	28	04	18	24
Apr	01 ♒	24	01 ♒	05	19	25
May	22	27	02	07	20	25
June	13 ♓	27	02	09	21	25
July	02 ♈	24	00	10	21	24
Aug	18	20	28 ♑	11	21	23
Sept	28	18	26	11	20	23
Oct	25	18	25	10	19	22
Nov	16	21	26	09	18	23
Dec	17	26	28	08	18	23

243

2021

MONTH	MARS LONG	JUPITER LONG	SATURN LONG	URANUS LONG	NEPTUNE LONG	PLUTO LONG
Jan	27 ♈	03 ♒	02 ♒	07 ♉	18 ♓	24 ♑
Feb	13 ♉	10	05	07	19	25
Mar	28	17	08	08	20	26
Apr	16 ♊	23	11	09	21	27
May	05 ♋	28	13	11	22	27
June	24	02 ♓	13	12	23	27
July	12 ♌	02	12	14	23	26
Aug	01 ♍	00	10	15	23	25
Sept	21	26 ♒	08	15	22	25
Oct	10 ♎	23	07	14	21	24
Nov	01 ♏	23	07	13	21	24
Dec	21	25	09	12	20	25

2022

MONTH	MARS LONG	JUPITER LONG	SATURN LONG	URANUS LONG	NEPTUNE LONG	PLUTO LONG
Jan	13 ♐	01 ♓	12 ♒	11 ♉	21 ♓	26 ♑
Feb	05 ♑	07	15	11	21	27
Mar	26	14	19	12	22	28
Apr	19 ♒	21	22	13	24	28
May	13 ♓	28	24	15	25	29
June	05 ♈	04 ♈	25	16	25	28
July	27	07	25	18	25	28
Aug	18 ♉	09	23	19	25	27
Sept	07 ♊	07	21	19	24	26
Oct	20	03	20	18	24	26
Nov	26	00	19	17	23	26
Dec	19	29 ♓	20	16	23	27

2023

MONTH	MARS LONG	JUPITER LONG	SATURN LONG	URANUS LONG	NEPTUNE LONG	PLUTO LONG
Jan	09 ♊	01 ♈	22 ♒	15 ♉	23 ♓	28 ♑
Feb	10	06	26	15	24	29
Mar	19	12	29	16	25	29
Apr	03 ♋	19	03 ♓	17	26	00 ♒
May	20	26	05	18	27	00
June	07 ♌	03 ♉	07	20	27	00
July	24	09	07	22	28	00
Aug	13 ♍	14	06	23	27	29 ♑
Sept	03 ♎	16	03	23	27	28
Oct	23	14	01	23	26	28
Nov	14 ♏	11	01	22	25	29
Dec	05 ♐	07	01	20	25	28

2024

MONTH	MARS LONG	JUPITER LONG	SATURN LONG	URANUS LONG	NEPTUNE LONG	PLUTO LONG
Jan	27 ♐	06 ♉	03 ♓	19 ♉	25 ♓	29 ♑
Feb	21 ♑	07	06	19	26	00 ♒
Mar	13 ♒	11	10	20	27	01
Apr	07 ♓	17	14	21	28	02
May	00 ♈	24	17	22	29	02
June	24	01 ♊	19	24	0040	02
July	16 ♉	08	19	26	00	01
Aug	08 ♊	14	19	27	00	01
Sept	28	19	17	27	29 ♓	00
Oct	15 ♋	21	14	27	28	00
Nov	29	20	13	26	28	00
Dec	06 ♌	17	13	25	27	00

2025

MONTH	MARS LONG	JUPITER LONG	SATURN LONG	URANUS LONG	NEPTUNE LONG	PLUTO LONG
Jan	02 ♌	13 ♊	15 ♓	24 ♉	27 ♓	01 ♒
Feb	20 ♋	11	17	23	28	02
Mar	17	12	21	24	29	03
Apr	24	16	24	25	00 ♈	04
May	06 ♌	21	28	26	01	04
June	21	29	00 ♈	28	02	04
July	08 ♍	05 ♋	02	00 ♊	02	03
Aug	26	12	02	01	02	02
Sept	16 ♎	18	00	01	01	02
Oct	06 ♏	22	28 ♓	01	01	01
Nov	27	25	26	00	0048	01
Dec	19 ♐	25	25	29 ♉	29 ♓	02

2026

MONTH	MARS LONG	JUPITER LONG	SATURN LONG	URANUS LONG	NEPTUNE LONG	PLUTO LONG
Jan	13 ♑	21 ♋	26 ♓	28 ♉	0031	03 ♒
Feb	07 ♒	17	29	27	00 ♈	04
Mar	29	15	02 ♈	28	01	05
Apr	23 ♓	16	06	29	02	05
May	16 ♈	19	09	00 ♊	03	05
June	10 ♉	24	12	02	04	05
July	02 ♊	00 ♌	14	04	04	05
Aug	23	07	15	05	04	04
Sept	13 ♋	14	14	06	04	04
Oct	02 ♌	20	12	06	03	03
Nov	19	24	09	05	02	03
Dec	02 ♍	27	08	03	02	04

2027

MONTH	MARS LONG	JUPITER LONG	SATURN LONG	URANUS LONG	NEPTUNE LONG	PLUTO LONG
Jan	10 ♍	26 ♌	08 ♈	02 ♊	02 ♈	04 ♒
Feb	07	23	10	02	02	05
Mar	27 ♌	20	13	02	03	06
Apr	21	17	17	03	04	07
May	26	17	21	04	05	07
June	07 ♍	20	24	06	06	07
July	22	25	27	08	07	07
Aug	10 ♎	01 ♍	28	09	07	06
Sept	29	08	27	10	06	05
Oct	19 ♏	14	26	10	05	05
Nov	12 ♐	20	23	09	04	05
Dec	04 ♑	25	22	08	04	05

2028

MONTH	MARS LONG	JUPITER LONG	SATURN LONG	URANUS LONG	NEPTUNE LONG	PLUTO LONG
Jan	28 ♑	27 ♍	21 ♈	07 ♊	04 ♈	06 ♒
Feb	22 ♒	27	22	07	04	07
Mar	15 ♓	24	25	06	05	08
Apr	09 ♈	20	28	07	07	08
May	02 ♉	18	02 ♉	08	08	09
June	25	18	06	10	08	09
July	16 ♊	21	09	12	09	08
Aug	07 ♋	26	11	13	09	08
Sept	28	02 ♎	11	14	08	07
Oct	16 ♌	08	10	14	07	06
Nov	05 ♍	15	08	13	07	06
Dec	21	20	06	12	06	07

2029

MONTH	MARS LONG	JUPITER LONG	SATURN LONG	URANUS LONG	NEPTUNE LONG	PLUTO LONG
Jan	04 ♎	25 ♎	04 ♉	11 ♊	06 ♈	08 ♒
Feb	13	27	05	10	07	09
Mar	13	27	07	10	08	09
Apr	02	24	10	11	09	10
May	25 ♍	20	14	12	10	10
June	29	18	18	14	11	10
July	10 ♎	18	21	16	11	10
Aug	26	21	24	17	11	09
Sept	15 ♏	26	26	18	11	09
Oct	05 ♐	01 ♏	24	19	10	08
Nov	28	08	23	18	09	08
Dec	21 ♑	15	20	17	08	08

2030

MONTH	MARS LONG	JUPITER LONG	SATURN LONG	URANUS LONG	NEPTUNE LONG	PLUTO LONG
Jan	15 ≈	21 ♏	18 ♉	16 ♊	08 ♈	09 ≈
Feb	09 ♓	25	18	15	09	10
Mar	01 ♈	27	20	15	10	11
Apr	25	27	22	15	11	12
May	17 ♉	24	27	16	12	12
June	09 ♊	20	00 ♊	18	13	12
July	00 ♋	18	04	20	13	12
Aug	20	18	07	22	13	11
Sept	10 ♌	21	09	23	13	10
Oct	29	26	09	23	12	10
Nov	18 ♍	02 ♐	07	22	11	10
Dec	06 ♎	09	05	21	11	10

2031

MONTH	MARS LONG	JUPITER LONG	SATURN LONG	URANUS LONG	NEPTUNE LONG	PLUTO LONG
Jan	22 ♎	15 ♐	03 ♊	20 ♊	11 ♈	11 ≈
Feb	07 ♏	22	03	19	11	12
Mar	17	26	03	19	12	12
Apr	22	29	05	19	13	13
May	15	29	08	21	14	14
June	05	26	12	22	15	14
July	06	22	16	24	16	13
Aug	17	19	19	26	16	13
Sept	04 ♐	20	22	27	15	12
Oct	23	22	23	27	14	11
Nov	15 ♑	27	22	27	14	11
Dec	08 ≈	03 ♑	20	26	13	12

2032

MONTH	MARS LONG	JUPITER LONG	SATURN LONG	URANUS LONG	NEPTUNE LONG	PLUTO LONG
Jan	02 ♓	10 ♑	18 ♊	25 ♊	13 ♈	12 ≈
Feb	26	17	16	24	13	13
Mar	17 ♈	23	16	23	14	14
Apr	10 ♉	29	18	24	15	15
May	01 ♊	02 ≈	21	25	16	15
June	23	02	24	26	17	15
July	13 ♋	00	28	28	18	15
Aug	03 ♌	26 ♑	02 ♋	00 ♋	18	14
Sept	23	23	05	01	17	13
Oct	12 ♍	23	07	02	17	13
Nov	01 ♎	25	07	01	16	13
Dec	20	00 ≈	06	00	15	13

2033

MONTH	MARS LONG	JUPITER LONG	SATURN LONG	URANUS LONG	NEPTUNE LONG	PLUTO LONG
Jan	09 ♏	07 ♒	03 ♋	29 ♊	15 ♈	14 ♒
Feb	27	14	01	28	15	15
Mar	12 ♐	21	00	28	16	16
Apr	28	27	01	28	17	16
May	09 ♑	03 ♓	03	29	18	17
June	12	06	07	01 ♋	19	17
July	06	07	11	02	21	16
Aug	00	05	15	04	20	16
Sept	06	01	18	05	20	15
Oct	20	28 ♒	20	06	19	15
Nov	09 ♒	28	21	06	18	14
Dec	00 ♓	00 ♓	21	05	18	15

2034

MONTH	MARS LONG	JUPITER LONG	SATURN LONG	URANUS LONG	NEPTUNE LONG	PLUTO LONG
Jan	22 ♓	05 ♓	18 ♋	04 ♋	17 ♈	15 ♒
Feb	14 ♈	11	16	03	18	16
Mar	04 ♉	18	15	02	18	17
Apr	25	25	15	02	19	18
May	15 ♊	02 ♈	16	03	21	18
June	05 ♋	08	19	05	22	18
July	25	12	23	06	22	18
Aug	15 ♌	14	27	08	22	17
Sept	04 ♍	13	01 ♌	10	22	17
Oct	24	09	03	10	21	16
Nov	13 ♎	05	05	10	20	16
Dec	03 ♏	04	05	10	20	16

2035

MONTH	MARS LONG	JUPITER LONG	SATURN LONG	URANUS LONG	NEPTUNE LONG	PLUTO LONG
Jan	23 ♏	06 ♈	04 ♌	08 ♋	20 ♈	17 ♒
Feb	13 ♐	10	01	07	20	18
Mar	02 ♑	16	29 ♋	07	21	19
Apr	22	23	28	07	22	19
May	12 ♒	00 ♉	29	07	23	20
June	01 ♓	07	02 ♌	09	24	20
July	16	14	05	11	24	19
Aug	27	18	09	12	25	19
Sept	27	21	13	14	24	18
Oct	19	20	16	15	24	18
Nov	20	17	18	15	23	17
Dec	00	13	19	14	22	18

2036

MONTH	MARS LONG	JUPITER LONG	SATURN LONG	URANUS LONG	NEPTUNE LONG	PLUTO LONG
Jan	15 ♈	11 ♉	18 ♌	13 ♋	22 ♈	18 ♒
Feb	03 ♉	12	16	12	22	19
Mar	21	16	14	11	23	21
Apr	11 ♊	21	12	11	24	21
May	29	29	13	12	25	21
June	19 ♋	05 ♊	14	13	26	21
July	08 ♌	12	17	15	27	21
Aug	27	18	21	17	27	20
Sept	17 ♍	23	25	18	27	20
Oct	06 ♎	26	28	19	26	19
Nov	26	26	01 ♍	20	25	19
Dec	16 ♏	23	03	19	24	19

2037

MONTH	MARS LONG	JUPITER LONG	SATURN LONG	URANUS LONG	NEPTUNE LONG	PLUTO LONG
Jan	08 ♐	19 ♊	03 ♍	18 ♋	24 ♈	20 ♒
Feb	00 ♑	16	01	17	24	21
Mar	20	17	29 ♌	16	25	21
Apr	13 ♒	20	27	16	26	22
May	05 ♓	25	26	16	27	23
June	27	02 ♋	27	17	28	23
July	19 ♈	08	29	19	29	22
Aug	09 ♉	15	03 ♍	21	29	22
Sept	26	22	07	23	29	21
Oct	05 ♊	27	10	24	28	21
Nov	04	29	14	24	27	20
Dec	23 ♉	29	16	24	27	21

2038

MONTH	MARS LONG	JUPITER LONG	SATURN LONG	URANUS LONG	NEPTUNE LONG	PLUTO LONG
Jan	21 ♉	27 ♋	16 ♍	23 ♋	26 ♈	21 ♒
Feb	28	23	15	21	27	22
Mar	11 ♊	20	13	20	27	23
Apr	27	20	11	20	28	24
May	13 ♋	23	09	21	29	24
June	02 ♌	28	10	22	00 ♉	24
July	20	04 ♌	12	23	01	24
Aug	09 ♍	10	14	25	01	23
Sept	28	17	18	27	01	23
Oct	18 ♎	23	22	28	01	22
Nov	09 ♏	28	25	29	00	22
Dec	00 ♐	01 ♍	28	28	29 ♈	22

249

2039

MONTH	MARS LONG	JUPITER LONG	SATURN LONG	URANUS LONG	NEPTUNE LONG	PLUTO LONG
Jan	22 ♐	01 ♍	29 ♍	27 ♋	29 ♈	23 ♒
Feb	15 ♑	28 ♌	29	26	29	23
Mar	06 ♒	25	27	25	29	24
Apr	00 ♓	22	25	25	00 ♉	25
May	23	22	23	25	01	26
June	17 ♈	24	23	26	02	26
July	09 ♉	29	24	28	03	25
Aug	00 ♊	05 ♍	26	00 ♌	04	25
Sept	20	11	29	01	03	24
Oct	06 ♋	18	03 ♎	03	03	24
Nov	18	24	07	03	02	23
Dec	21	29	10	03	01	24

2040

MONTH	MARS LONG	JUPITER LONG	SATURN LONG	URANUS LONG	NEPTUNE LONG	PLUTO LONG
Jan	12 ♋	01 ♎	12 ♎	02 ♌	01 ♉	24 ♒
Feb	03	01	12	01	01	25
Mar	05	29 ♍	11	00	02	26
Apr	15	25	08	29 ♋	02	26
May	29	22	06	00 ♌	04	27
June	16 ♌	22	05	01	05	27
July	03 ♍	25	06	02	05	27
Aug	22	29	08	04	06	26
Sept	11 ♎	05 ♎	11	06	06	26
Oct	01 ♏	11	14	07	05	25
Nov	22	18	18	08	04	25
Dec	14 ♐	24	21	08	04	25

Appendix II

Solar Arc Analysis Directory

These modern word-images of analysis for all possible Solar Arcs, direct and indirect, were inspired by the superb work done by Reinhold Ebertin throughout his long career, and published in *The Combination of Stellar Influences* in 1940 and 1972.

Preface

Symbolism. The theory of Solar Arcs is founded totally on symbolism, which is constantly updated and refined through deduction and experience. The symbolic projection of one planet to new aspect contacts with natal planets and sensitive points depends entirely upon word-images for significance. These word-images, presented in this Appendix, must be creatively related to the individual realities depicted in the horoscope and manifested in life.

Significance. No Solar Arc—and, as well, no astrological measurement of any kind—can be expected to be significant in every occurrence. The degree and frequency of actual manifestation appear to be tied to two considerations: the aptness and timeliness of the Arc to the individual's reality; and the tie-in with strategic transit activity.

Irrelevance. In Midpoint Pictures, when the same planet appears on both sides of the "equation," i.e., Mars=Mars/Neptune (Solar Arc Mars makes a fourth harmonic aspect with the midpoint between natal Mars and natal Neptune), the particular equation appears to be irrelevant. For efficiency in management of the many pictures sometimes presented in the horoscope, such an equation should be overlooked.

Synthesis. When several Solar Arcs are presented in the same "month" time-period, Direct Arcs (planet to planet) should predominate over Midpoint Pictures in the ordering of analysis. When word-images of Arcs contrast strongly in the same time period, analysis must be carefully guided by reality, practicality, the areas of pertinence, and the potentials in the individual's horoscope life.

For example, the following Solar Arc measurements and accompanying transits present several "pictures." The astrologer is challenged to find a way to organize the measurements meaningfully within the client's personal reality.

	June		**July**
SA MC=☿/♅	Success with all-around resourcefullness.	SA ☽=♆/AS	Great sensitivity; open to hurt; fear of being deceived.
SA ♄=♀/MC	Controlling the love urge; loss of relationship	SA ♅=♂/♇	A chip on the shoulder; fight before talk.
		SA MC=♃/♇	Attaining a power position.
		SA ♂=♇	Extreme force; control; brutality.
Tr. ♄ ☍ ♇	Potential loss; Saturn rules her VIIth house.	Tr. ♅ □ ☿	Nervous tension; heated conversation.

The woman's personal reality preceding June and July was clear: she reported the pain of a relationship in the process of stormy upset, which had begun nine months earlier with the transit of Uranus over her seventh cusp (along with other similar measurements). Looking ahead, it was clear that the Solar Arc Mars=Pluto in July would dominate the period, backing up the powerful transit Saturn-opposed-Pluto exact in June. The prognosis was for loss of the relationship under stormy conditions, through perhaps some vengeful act on her part.

The Saturn Arc in June certainly echoed the Mars/Pluto signal and was also manifested by the fact that my client had forced a four-month moratorium upon interaction with the man, speaking with him only by telephone.

The MC Arc in June did not seem to fit the reality, unless the resourcefulness suggested was to support vengeful actions. There seemed to be no peace overtures forthcoming from her; she appeared in total control of things. As it turned out, as a kind of diversion within the tense time period, my client began helping a friend with some office work in her own business, innovating very resourcefully to get some trying tasks done expeditiously. This Arc then, involving the MC, was allocatable to a contemporaneous but different area of life activity. Very often, it is the case that some measurements apply to the job area while others in the same time period apply to the personal life. Two or three levels of concern can be operating at the same time, of course.

In July, the woman obviously would be open to continued hurt and would probably react in vengeful fashion. There was sure to be a confrontation. Yet her man's horoscope showed a strong SA MC=Sun/Venus in July, promising a sense of fulfillment in the love union! But at the same time, he had Mars transiting square his Midheaven and Uranus transiting sesquiquadrate his Moon. Here again, there were conflicting measurements: a comfortable fulfillment measurement in the Solar Arc and jarring, tense measurements in the transits.

My client soon reported that the man had pressed for a meeting. The prediction was clearly that he expected the best, she feared the worst, and he would feel temperamentally attacked (transiting Mars square his Midheaven). This would probably be the showdown.

As it turned out, there were two meetings: one between my client and the man and a second shortly thereafter with an arbitrator. The first meeting went beautifully: although she was still distrusting and doubting, she felt great love once again; she reported that he was thrilled and thought everything was going to be alright again. She doubted it.

At the second meeting—on the day of the man's Mars transit square his Midheaven—my client paraded all the accusations once again into the open. All the tensions were revived. In the man's opinion, everything had been calmed; he saw her "surprise" as unyielding, forceful, and extreme. He aborted the meeting, walked out, and the relationship ended.

Technically, the multiplicity of measurements and, indeed, the contradiction among them can be daunting. Efficiency is learned by allocating measurements to different areas of life experience—job or personal life—following the lead of the dominant measurements (the Direct Arcs), if they exist, and strong transits; the Midpoint Pictures that hold together within the same image-sense and accompanying transits). *Measurements that are not immediately applicable to a reality situation should be overlooked.* It is a rare horoscope or person who responds even to the majority of measurements of any kind in astrology.

Again, this is not an indictment of astrology as fallible. Rather, it is recognition that astrology is ever incomplete in its relation to the lives of individuals who are infinitely complex. Always, symbolic significances in astrology depend upon the art of the analyst to gain application and importance to the individual. Almost always, though, it is the artfully chosen few measurements that tell the tale.

Using the Directory

All possible Arcs are indexed at the upper right corner of each page. The presentation is in customary planetary order from Sun/Moon out to Pluto and then to the Lunar Node, Ascendant (AS), and Midheaven (MC in most computer notation; Medium Coeli).

All equation relationships reflect the fourth harmonic: the conjunction, the opposition, the square, semi-square, or sesquiquadrate.

To find the Arc relationship or Midpoint Picture of Mars and Jupiter, for example, locate the "♂/♃" page and study the word-images of Mars=Jupiter or the appropriate Midpoint Picture. To find the Arc of Jupiter=Mars, locate the page led by the equation planet (first planet) nearer the Sun—Mars, specifically the same "♂/♃" page. To repeat: the Directory pages are keyed to planetary pairs proceeding out from the Sun in customary order.

An additional use of the Directory is in analytical reference to natal aspect contacts and, especially, to natal Midpoint Pictures. Please be reminded that, in application to natal analysis, these word images do not take into consideration the dimensions of retrogradation, house positions, or rulerships.

Sun and Moon ☉/☽

☉ = ☽		Male and Female; illuminated achievements, needs, and sensitivities; highlighted relationships, seeing the light.
☽ = ☉		Sensitivity to need-fulfillment; seeing the light; female influence.

☿ =		Thoughts about male-female principles, including marriage; relationships in general; plans for fulfillment.
♀ =		Friendship; love awareness; harmony.
♂ =		Energy helping or upsetting relationship; sexual awareness in partnership; drive for fulfillment.
♃ =		Happy relationship; enthusiasm for life; success.
♄ =		Difficult concerns in relationship; addressing problems; possible inhibition or separation; weakened system.
♅ =		Intensification of independence within relationship; sudden developments; possible breakup.
♆ =		Misunderstandings in relationship; deception; discontent.
♇ =		Potential new perspective in relationship; critical time of development; separation to start anew.
☊ =		Making contact; new associations.
AS =		Openness to others; feeling secure.
MC =		Ego fulfillment in relationship; marriage.

Sun and Mercury ☉/☿

☉	= ☿	Illumination of intelligence; thoughts; common sense.
☿	= ☉	Thinking about ego potentials; new ideas

☽	=	Awareness of needs; emotional thoughts.
♀	=	Idealization of thoughts about relationships and love; thoughts about sexual matters; writing about love.
♂	=	Excitement; nervous drive; energies to tackle a project; possible quarrelsomeness.
♃	=	Optimism; broadening one's horizon; successful travel, speech-making, publishing; uplifting thoughts about religion.
♄	=	Seriousness in mental outlook; possible depression; sadness about potential separation; a new maturity.
♅	=	High excitability in the nervous system and thinking process; sudden eruptions of temperament; quick trips; new circumstances.
♆	=	Fantasy; imagination; spiritual wondering; possible deception by others; something undermining the perceived reality.
♇	=	The dramatic push to new perspectives; big plans.
☊	=	New social contacts; sales presentations; meetings.
AS	=	Exchanging ideas; sharing with others; pleasant mental state.
MC	=	Ego awareness; helping one's plans work and standing up to the test; successful communications.

Sun and Venus ☉/♀

☉	= ♀	Romance; love relationship; illumination of one's sense of beauty; aesthetics; marriage; birth.
♀	= ☉	Idealization of outlook; feeling love; the artistic "touch."
☽	=	Strong feelings of love in relationship; feeling good about life.
☿	=	Thinking about love, usually in an idealized way; dialogues about feelings; a beautiful trip.
♂	=	Desire for love; sexual feelings; the application of creativity.
♃	=	Happiness; success; idealized relationship; a grand vacation.
♄	=	Strain within love relationship; hard work to make feelings right again, to make ends meet; fears of separation.
♅	=	Intensified sexuality; "love-crazy"; sudden romantic meetings.
♆	=	Dreaminess about love potential; overindulgences of all kinds for ego gratification or defense; self-deception.
♇	=	Extreme intensification of emotions; a waste of feelings and possible squandering of relationship values; the feeling of fate within relationship perspectives.
☊	=	Meetings under lovely circumstances; artistic people and events; making new friends.
AS	=	Being at one's best; attractiveness to others.
MC	=	The love-union; marriage; feeling of fulfillment.

Sun and Mars ☉/♂

☉ = ♂   Energy applied directly, naturally, vigorously.

♂ = ☉   Temperament; feeling attacked; possible accident; intensified sex drive.

☽ =   Awareness of relationship dynamics in balance with individual needs; the feminine influence; thoughts for marriage.

☿ =   Alertness; ready for action; fast-talk; busy travel.

♀ =   The feelings of love; sex; conception; birthing.

♃ =   Optimism; expansive energy application; success.

♄ =   Difficulties in energy application; obstacles against work advancement; inhibitions; worries and indecision.

♅ =   High excitability; intense reflex actions; impulse; sudden events and forceful adjustment of new circumstances; militarism; over-exertion causing break-down of efficiency.

♆ =   Possible loss of vitality; difficulty concentrating; feeling "off the track."

♇ =   Force; ruthless application of energy; defensiveness to an extreme; warring relationships; severe health strain possible.

☊ =   Meeting new associates in work situation; teamwork; dating.

AS =   Feeling robust; being seen as hearty and confident.

MC =   Success; loving one's work; efficiency; ready to fight for one's principles.

Sun and Jupiter ☉/♃

☉	= ♃	Recognition; success; feeling great.
♃	= ☉	Being rewarded; success; a great vacation.

☽ = The feeling of needs fulfilled; good health; fine relationship.

☿ = Efficient and successful thinking; good news; writing, publishing, contracting, traveling; healthy mental outlook.

♀ = Happy relationship; expansive romance; recognition; honors.

♂ = Successful application of will-power; zeal; enthusiasm that "catches on."

♄ = A "collision" between what one wants and what is demanded; a quandary of law and order; a curtailment; negativism; loss.

♅ = Sudden success; great expectations; expansive outlook; the sense of good luck.

♆ = Increased sensitivity; the sense of things spiritual; loss of concentrated orientation.

♇ = Successful efforts; great good luck; fulfillment in a big way; an estate; an inheritance.

☊ = Meeting happy/wealthy/successful people; new plans with others that feel "bound to succeed."

AS = Great enthusiasm; infectious happiness; successful teamwork.

MC = Good luck, success, and fulfillment; ego recognition; time of great good fortune.

Sun and Saturn ☉/♄

☉ = ♄ Illumination of ambition; testing if one is on the right track; awareness of responsibility; importance of the father.

♄ = ☉ The sense of difficulty, overwork, depletion, confinement, discipline; the fear of loss; "aloneness"; possibly grief.

☽ = A sense of loneliness; separation from females; personal needs under wraps; feeling inferior; hurt.

☿ = Serious thinking; grave decisions; possible depression; striving for a new way of seeing things.

♀ = Feelings of an inhibited love-life; suppressed feelings in relationship; feeling victimized.

♂ = Running "hot and cold"; energies feel confined; the sense of futility.

♃ = A break-up of a relationship or value system for eventual recovery and gain; the cloud with a silver lining.

♅ = The clash between new ways of doing things and long-establishedways; crises within relationship; the fight for individuality.

♆ = Sadness; loss of hope; delusions within relationship leading to the feeling of aloneness.

♇ = The threat of loss in relationship or health; a pressure to change one's entire value system.

☊ = Difficult meetings with others.

AS = Being misunderstood; possible threat to health.

MC = Lacking the feeling of success; feeling devalued; working hard to win; the "lone wolf."

Sun and Uranus ☉/♅

☉ = ♅		Independent, even revolutionary spirit; being oneself and getting away with it.
♅ = ☉		Intensified feeling of ego aggrandizement; excited state in relationship; possible break up.

☽ = Emotional excitability; the intense woman; demand for need fulfillment.

☿ = Quickness of mind; the spark of understanding; the harsh word; seeing things too analytically for comfort.

♀ = Sudden love feelings; instant attraction; sexiness.

♂ = Rash action; possible injury; combativeness; temperament; sudden breakdown of relationship; "hitting a brick wall."

♃ = Rewards for innovation; ego recognition; surprise and success.

♄ = A struggle for individual freedom; the fight against the routine, old, or traditional way of doing things; separation.

♆ = Possible loss of the sense of individuality; self-deluding schemes for ego recognition; threat to relationship and personal health.

♇ = The demand for new perspectives; a new individual reality; reforms; a strong drive for power; twists of fate.

☊ = Meeting unusual or intense people; quick new associations.

AS = Appearing at one's best; high excitability; sudden events.

MC = Major events in support of big plans; hopeful triumph for the ego.

Sun and Neptune ☉/♆

☉ = ♆   Illumination of sensitivity, imagination, aesthetics; possible befuddlement, remoteness, impracticality.

♆ = ☉   The sense of ego loss; hypersensitivity; potential spiritual rationalization, inspiration; deception; illegality.

☽ =   Moodiness; high impressionability; very special inner experiences not easily understood; gynecological concerns.

☿ =   Mental sensitivity; self-deception; worrisome; fear from a lack of resourcefulness.

♀ =   Reveling in love impractically; emotional disappointments.

♂ =   Magnetism; sexual discovery; nefarious scheming to exalt the ego.

♃ =   Success through inspiration or imagination; possible overindulgence.

♄ =   Emotional struggle or pain; concerns about the blood; bereavement about separation.

♅ =   Sudden impressionability or even psychic awareness; nervous reactions for unclear reasons; relationship disputes.

♇ =   Extreme sensitivity; use of the spiritual, psychic, or illusory as a force for persuasion; fateful deception.

☊ =   Deception in relationships; support of the needy.

AS =   A sensitive show to others, true or fabricated; difficulties being accepted.

MC =   Loss of ego strength or aesthetics taking over ego presentation; depression; emotional stress in the profession; artistic strength.

Sun and Pluto   ☉/♇

☉ = ♇   Illumination of power needs; the need to control; new perspectives confirmed in life.

♇ = ☉   Powerful force creates major change in the life; identity change; sudden prominence; exhibitionism.

☽ =   Attempts to project power and persuasion; feelings possibly trampled in relationship.

☿ =   Extraordinary mental projection; "lording it over" someone; great salesmanship.

♀ =   Emotional upset; creative force; strength in the arts.

♂ =   Enormous drive; strenuous self-application; carving new perspectives in one's life; strong sexual interest.

♃ =   Expansion of power base; success; international opportunities.

♄ =   Potential loss in relationship through power struggle; ruthlessness; separation.

♅ =   New individual perspectives; sudden change; rebellion; reform.

♆ =   Self-sacrifice in relationship or to a cause; high impressionability; vocation problems.

☊ =   Very special new attachments; meeting the powerful.

AS =   Enormous power projection; being forced to fight.

MC =   Striving for power and control; vocational upset and change to adopt new perspectives; power games with important consequences.

Sun and Lunar Node ☉/☊

☉ = ☊   Experiences shared with others become important; the public.

☊ = ☉   New contacts come into the life.

☽ =   Feelings shared with others; the relationship dynamics of wife and husband are highlighted.

☿ =   Communications with others; business contacts; news; commentary.

♀ =   Lovely associations; the arts; beginning of a romantic relationship.

♂ =   Vigorous drives with others to gain personal importance.

♃ =   Public recognition; associations with the wealthy or international; positive legal involvements; good fortune.

♄ =   Reserve in relationships; maturation; patience with others.

♅ =   Attraction to unusual individuals; upsets through intensity; the drive for popularity.

♆ =   Feeling that relationships are threatening or bothersome; feeling let down by others.

♇ =   Being persuasive; ordering and controlling others; exerting influence; public prominence.

AS =   Making personal contacts.

MC =   Becoming prominent through associations.

Sun and Ascendant ☉/AS

☉	= AS	Recognition; being seen for who one is.
AS	= ☉	Testing the identity; personality clarification through the reactions of others.

☽	=	Feelings and needs in relationships become very important, especially for females or with females.
☿	=	Thinking about who one really is in relation to others; existential awareness and sensitivity.
♀	=	Affections; love of others; peace.
♂	=	Making things happen; strong self-projections; disputes and possibly anger; the sense of self-promotion.
♃	=	Philanthropic or social welfare outlook; successful relationship.
♄	=	Inhibition or discretion; reserve or depression; separation.
♅	=	Intensification of self-image; pushy behavior; upsets.
♆	=	High sensitivity about others' opinions; being duped; being disregarded.
♇	=	The power play through personal persuasion; fated events.
☊	=	Personal acquaintances; business contacts.
MC	=	Personal recognition, especially through the profession; the influence of the parents.

Sun and Midheaven ☉/MC

☉	=MC	Ego recognition; potential glory; usually successful; fulfillment.
MC	= ☉	Professional fulfillment; getting what one deserves.
☽	=	Finding one's position in life, usually through the profession.
☿	=	Thinking about one's position in life.
♀	=	Feelings about love, the arts, aesthetics; sociability.
♂	=	Strong power maneuvering in the profession; promotion and success.
♃	=	Optimism; publicity; fulfillment.
♄	=	Maturation through sobering experiences; refinement of ambition; learning from apparent mistakes.
♅	=	Sudden changes; shifts of position.
♆	=	Something threatens ego definition; confusion; insecurity.
♇	=	Very strong drive for fulfillment of objectives; changes in life perspective; upset in relationships.
☊	=	Forming relationships.
AS	=	Personal relations.

Moon and Mercury ☽/☿

☽	= ☿	Thinking with the feelings; emotional perception.
☿	= ☽	Mental stimulation about personal needs and how to fulfill them; improved communication; the advice of a woman.

☉	=	Realism; practical planning.
♀	=	Lovely thoughts; the sense of beauty; art appreciation.
♂	=	Critical, perhaps nervous thought processes; clarification of objectives.
♃	=	Rational thought; good judgment; sound planning; interests in travel, communication sciences, educational institutions.
♄	=	Solving problems to grow in wisdom; thoughts about patience; possible depression if the tide has turned.
♅	=	Sudden, innovative thoughts and plans; irritability about progress; getting on with things hastily.
♆	=	An active imagination; reverie; hypersentience; falsehood.
♇	=	New perspectives; persuasion or being persuaded; the force of thought.
☊	=	Sharing thoughts with others; making contacts.
AS	=	Letting people know how one thinks; sharing opinions.
MC	=	Making decisions, usually about one's profession or social position.

Moon and Venus ☽/♀

☽	= ♀	Love and sensitivity.
♀	= ☽	Grace; good social reception; cooperation.

☉	=	The love in a marriage; art appreciation.
☿	=	Thinking about love.
♂	=	Potential overindulgence; living passionately.
♃	=	Good luck; lots of good feelings; feeling loved.
♄	=	Sternness within feelings; tightness entering romance.
♅	=	Sudden romantic feelings and attachments; intensification of sexuality.
♆	=	Dreaminess; fantasies about love, the erotic; possible misdirection of love; being duped.
♇	=	Powerful awakening of the emotions, more sexual than temperamental; procreation; complications and a waste of emotions.
☊	=	Lovely association; rewarding social contacts; maternal feelings.
AS	=	Affectionate behavior toward others; being well-received.
MC	=	Success; feeling valuable.

Moon and Mars ☽/♂

☽ = ♂		Emotional excitement; emotional conviction.
♂ = ☽		Strong drive to fullfill needs, to "let it fly"; disruption; hyperactivity.

☉ =		The working bond within a marriage; prosperity through relationship.
☿ =		Nervousness; being irritable; worrisome preoccupations.
♀ =		Sexual desires; creativity; promoting things artistic.
♃ =		Principles; justified actions.
♄ =		Caught in the middle of the road; frustration.
♅ =		Intensified temperament; eruption; anger; arguments leading to emotional wear and tear.
♆ =		Emotional magic; possible duplicity; weaving a spell for personal gain.
♇ =		Powerful opinionation; demanding nature.
☊ =		Energetic activity with others; good teamwork.
AS =		Personal enterprise; leadership.
MC =		Marriage thoughts; self-promotion; getting things off the ground.

Moon and Jupiter ☽/♃

☽ = ♃		Feeling happy; being successful; contentment; religiousness or the judiciary becoming important.
♃ = ☽		Opportunity; reward; publicity; success.

☉	=	Optimism; a fine relationship.
☿	=	Making expansive plans; learning; traveling.
♀	=	Lovingness; artistry; relating rewardingly through the emotions.
♂	=	Enthusiasm; get-up-and-go; making success happen.
♄	=	Interference possible through outside restrictions; separation from an important female or becoming distant from important emotions.
♅	=	Confidence; expectation of reward.
♆	=	Losing focus of objectives; success feels like it is leaving one's grasp.
♇	=	Major plans for major triumph; the big picture and the power to make it appear.
☊	=	Sociability; successful contacts.
AS	=	Expansive nature; being happy and well-accepted.
MC	=	Popularity; confidence; possible religious significances; good fortune, especially through a female.

Moon and Saturn ☽/♄

☽ = ♄		Awareness of ambition, strategy, direction.
♄ = ☽		Self-control; loneliness.

☉ = Sobering times; feelings of enforced controls; possible separation in relationship.

☿ = Prudence; maturity; the wise thought; sadness and perhaps depression, especially among women.

♀ = Emotional changes; restrictions in expression; the grace "to start over again."

♂ = The sense of real problems; difficulty getting off the ground except by very careful, strategically planned exertion of energy.

♃ = The sense of law and order prevails; the sense of duty; feeling confident about structure; appreciating why certain controls are necessary.

♅ = Reaching for emotional freedom; exploding out of frustration.

♆ = Feelings of inferiority; melancholy.

♇ = The threat of loss; feeling isolated; needs repressed.

☊ = Making contacts is difficult; loneliness.

AS = A reserved self-presentation.

MC = Making things happen carefully; structuring ambition.

271

Moon and Uranus ☽/♅

☽	= ♅	Emotional individuation, emotional tensions.
♅	= ☽	Intensification of self; impulsivity to fulfill needs.

☉	=	The sense of free-will; sudden attachments; anxiety about accomplishment.
☿	=	Excited mental activity; expecting a surprise; innovative ideas; short trips.
♀	=	Excitability of emotions; sudden sexual activities; artistic creativity.
♂	=	Lack of self-control; self-aggrandizement.
♃	=	Large plans to put the self forward; sudden success.
♄	=	Striving for independence in order to solve things; the struggle between the traditional and the avant-garde; changes in emotional expression.
♆	=	Nervousness about a sense of futility; things are unclear and insecure for no apparent reason.
♇	=	Bombast; the fanatical push for fulfillment of needs; sensationalism.
☊	=	Restlessness in contact with others.
AS	=	Excitability; consideration of geographic relocation.
MC	=	Much excitement about ambition, potential gains; sudden changes of plans.

Moon and Neptune ☽/♆

☽	= ♆	The awakening of aesthetics, special sensitivities, or the spirit.
♆	= ☽	Subconscious awareness emerges, refinement or bewilderment.

☉	=	A delicate relationship; the man trying to support the woman; illuminated aesthetics; the importance of the spirit.
☿	=	Fantasy; imagination; remembrance of things past; saying one thing and meaning another; vagueness.
♀	=	Highly romanticized feelings of love; art appreciation; being deceived through the emotions.
♂	=	Personal magic; hypersensitivity; weakened system.
♃	=	Grand imaginings and plans; artistic interests and success.
♄	=	A sense of suffering under the yoke; hard work to restructure ambition; shaking off indolence.
♅	=	Temperamental impulse; emotional unpredictability.
♇	=	Emotional shock, upheaval, change.
☊	=	The projection of passivity or confusion.
AS	=	The feeling of having lost ego definition.
MC	=	Artistic talent possible; artsy temperament; imagination can pay off significantly; emotional concerns from the early homelife come to consciousness.

Moon and Pluto ☽/♇

☽ = ♇   Zeal; intensity of self-application.

♇ = ☽   Extreme emotional intensity; upheavals; exaggerated new plans.

☉ =   Tight team effort in relationship; special far-reaching plans; emotional excitement.

☿ =   Strategizing, planning, conceptualization; the power of persuasion.

♀ =   Intensification of feelings; romance; anything amorous and need-fulfilling.

♂ =   Often an intense emotional crisis; great tension; too much energy not knowing where to go; frustration and anger.

♃ =   Big plans; luck and success; rich emotionalism.

♄ =   Inclination to feelings of loss; depression; constraint; the pressure to regroup forces and plan anew.

♅ =   Possible nervous crisis; intensity that can get out of hand; tremendous projection of self is possible; identification with the world; sudden upsets.

♆ =   The supernatural is added to the emotional life; the feeling of fate; the fear of the unknown; feeling weakened somehow.

☊ =   Emotionalism disrupts teamwork and getting along with others.

AS =   Tremendous self-projection in reaction to the environment; temperamental upset.

MC =   Ego consciousness prevails; one-sided emotional intensity.

Moon and Lunar Node ☽/☊

☽	= ☊	Association with others, usually emotionally based.
☊	= ☽	Contacts with others brings assistance and comfort.

☉	=	Harmony in relationships.
☿	=	Thinking about interpersonal reactions; getting along with others; building cooperation.
♀	=	Affectionate attachments with others; contacts with artistic people or cultural events.
♂	=	Energetic associations and teamwork.
♃	=	Confidence; good luck through interaction with others.
♄	=	Working hard with others; sometimes having then to "go it alone."
♅	=	Meeting exceptional people or experiencing unusual events with or through others; sudden new attachments.
♆	=	The potential undermining of relationships or contacts with others; sentimentality.
♇	=	Powerful forces affect interpersonal relationships; the sense of fated attraction.
AS	=	The importance of interpersonal relationships is brought forward.
MC	=	Ego-involvement intensified in emotional relationship.

Moon and Ascendant ☽/AS

☽ = AS		Focus on personal needs and relationships to fulfill them.
AS = ☽		Focus on personal needs and relationships to fulfill them.

☉ = Evaluation of interpersonal relationships for one's own benefit; interaction of marriage partners from one's personal perspective.

☿ = Thinking about how to put one's best foot forward; creating confidence.

♀ = Adaptability to preserve the love in a relationship; social events that put one forward.

♂ = Energetic self-projection; temperamental change at the slightest sense of frustration.

♃ = Expansive confidence; gregariousness; largesse; publicity.

♄ = The process of maturation; heavy moods of deliberation; severity; depression; feelings of constraint.

♅ = Excited self-projection; sudden relationships.

♆ = Self-delusion is possible; feeling "wiped out"; loneliness; deception by a female.

♇ = Over-dramatization or obsessive importance of relationship; dramatic personal projection to others.

☊ = Desire for contacts; importance of women as associates.

MC = Learning about one's position in the world; revival of concerns from the early homelife.

Moon and Midheaven   ☽/MC

☽	=MC	One's strongest needs are out in the open.
MC =	☽	Ego-consciousness alerts all one's senses.

☉	=	Positive attitude toward life; the spirit of enterprise.
☿	=	Thinking about one's position in life.
♀	=	Graceful social positioning; success with the emotions; significant relationships are possible.
♂	=	Strong work orientation; promotion; strength on the job; the introduction of a man to a woman.
♃	=	High enthusiasms; probably professional success; an awakening of religion or the study of philosophy becomes important.
♄	=	Sobering experiences affect the emotional life; greater efficiency; depressing longing.
♅	=	High degree of emotional excitement; nervousness in reaction to changes; the sense of vocational instability or the threat of pending upset; anxiety.
♆	=	Sensing a loss of ego-identification; feeling devalued; perhaps the awakening of aesthetics or things spiritual.
♇	=	Tremendous thrust forward, usually accompanied by intense emotion; the biggest picture; rejuvenation.
☊	=	Professional contacts.
AS	=	Awareness of one's emotional orientation; self-evaluation.

Mercury and Venus ☿/♀

☿ = ♀		Idealization; thoughts of love.
♀ = ☿		Romanticizing; thoughts of love.

☉ = Awareness of things beautiful; the arts; sunny disposition.

☽ = The emotions gain creative expression.

♂ = Alerting the passions; making strong, emotional statements; creativity.

♃ = Expansive idealization; perhaps religiousness; aesthetics; publishing; artistic achievement.

♄ = Serious attitude toward life; maturation; trimming down ideals to be more practical; adjusting to realism.

♅ = Intensification of innovation; the spontaneous idea of feelings becoming dominant; extraordinary communication.

♆ = Fantasy; seeing through a special dimension; spiritual thoughts; deluding oneself about reality.

♇ = Highly focused aesthetics, argumentative position, or expectations; the sense of mission; the successful "hard sell."

☊ = Sociability; relationship to the arts.

AS = Pleasantness; being well-mannered; appreciated by others.

MC = Possibly a profession in the arts; the profit from things creative; acknowledging things beautiful or ideal.

Mercury and Mars ☿/♂

☿	= ♂	Nervous drive.
♂	= ☿	Energized thinking; making plans.

☉ = Putting one's foot down; making a point strongly; standing up for one's position; enjoying a good argument; quick decisions.

☽ = Emotions are added to the issue at hand; arguments get an extra level of meaning; one needs to be heard.

♀ = Arguments about love; excited plans about romance; creative inspiration; insight.

♃ = Constructive thinking; sound judgment; knowing how to "sell" an idea with enthusiasm.

♄ = Concentration; focused thought; efficiency and practicality; knowing how to close the sale; knowing how to wound.

♅ = Tremendous excitability; thinking and planning on the run; potentially rash judgment; losing self-control.

♆ = Vagaries; deception; not telling all; avoiding key points; intrigue; fantasy channeled into creativity.

♇ = Criticism with a passion; knowing just what's wrong with the world; involved in big arguments.

☊ = Discussions with others; easily argumentative.

AS = Being seen as a talker; known to be impulsive.

MC = Bravura; the champion salesperson; ready to win the fight.

Mercury and Jupiter ☿/♃

☿ = ♃   Good common sense; writing, publishing; traveling.

♃ = ☿   Intellect; thoughts about the spirit; legal issues; travel.

☉ =   Success with the intellect; creative ideas are born; solutions are illuminated.

☽ =   Emotions inspire impressive ideas and welcomed solutions.

♀ =   Idealized thinking; appreciation of one's world; thoughts and plans for romance; a lovely vacation.

♂ =   Energetic opinionation is well-accepted; making one's point effectively.

♄ =   Sober decisions; rational thought; withdrawing from disputes to avoid a fight; the lonely stand.

♅ =   Excited presentation of ideas; curiosity about new things; sudden inspiration; effective advertising.

♆ =   Inspiration; beguiling fantasy; magnetism; losing the focus of an issue; lack of realism.

♇ =   The powerful salesperson; the big proposal; dramatic persuasion.

☊ =   Sociability; the exchange of thoughts with others; meetings.

AS =   Acceptance of one's well-organized thinking; successful teamwork.

MC =   Optimistic hope; looking for the best side of things to come about; successful planning.

Mercury and Saturn ☿/♄

☿ = ♄		Hard work; analysis.
♄ = ☿		Wisdom through duress; maturation through depression; the sense of heavy responsibility.

- ☉ = Making a go of it; getting down to work; discipline paying off; knowing what's got to be done.
- ☽ = Emotional quandary; emotional indecision because of fear of losing; frustration; taxing learning process.
- ♀ = Frustration in romance; fickleness; needing reassurance.
- ♂ = Risking everything to make one's point; turning drive into tyranny; arguments; no compromise.
- ♃ = Logic; reasoning; success through concentration and industry.
- ♅ = Great tension between the old way of thinking about things and a new way; anxiety about change of the status quo; quick decisions.
- ♆ = Depression; a sad spirit looking for a ray of hope.
- ♇ = Contemplating loss; fearing wipe-out; feeling resourceless.
- ☊ = Making contact with hard-working people who can be helpful.
- AS = Tendency to be aloof; backing off from responsibilities.
- MC = The heavy thinker; mind over matter; winning through planning.

Mercury and Uranus ☿/♅

☿	= ♅	Impulsive action; provocative ideas; inspiration.
♅	= ☿	Intensification of the nervous system; acuteness of thought; sharpness; speed, sudden travel plans.

☉ = Ready-to-go; temperament is well-received; "up to speed"; able to create the surprising move.

☽ = Emotional excitability; quick mood changes; valid instincts about the situation.

♀ = A sense of artistry; the tendency to love spontaneously.

♂ = Nervous drive finds the mark and usually can pay off; the instincts of a fighter hitting home; courage.

♃ = Impressive presentation of ideas; successful solutions spring to mind.

♄ = Nervous antipathy toward any state of tension or frustration; tendency to intolerance; trying always for quick extrication.

♆ = The higher levels of the mind; inspiration; psychic feelings brought into focus; magical persuasiveness; deductive analysis.

♇ = Tremendous power for work, action, leadership; getting the biggest job done in a commanding way.

☊ = Creative interchange with others; quick conferences.

AS = Accident-prone through fast action or recklessness.

MC = The inventor; success with all-around resourcefulness.

Mercury and Neptune ☿/♆

☿ = ♆		Thinking about what to feel; alert imagination; special awarenesses.
♆ = ☿		Feeling what to think; fantasy; special awarenesses.
☉ =		Creativity; successful imaginative conceptualization; possibly allowing oneself to be deceived.
☽ =		Emotional sensitivity; possible paranormal awarenesses; personal impressions dominate the thinking process.
♀ =		Sensual thoughts; rapture; expecting a great deal of personal attention; demanding in love; impractical expectations; artistic expression.
♂ =		Putting imagination to work; inspired planning pays off.
♃ =		Expansive fantasy; the large picture becomes personalized; dramatic hopefulness; inspiration in the arts.
♄ =		A gloomy reaction to real or imagined circumstances; looking at the down side of things, which may not be valid.
♅ =		Sudden new ideas; inspiration; going "far out"; individual participation in the arts.
♇ =		Instincts supporting the power drive.
☊ =		Creative contact with others.
AS =		Potential overreaction to others; being exploited.
MC =		Spiritual awareness; living among the clouds with or without practical orientation.

Mercury and Pluto ☿/♇

☿ = ♇		The ability to persuade; communicating new perspectives.
♇ = ☿		The ability to persuade; demanding new perspectives.
☉ =		The need for recognition; championing an idea or attitude that prevails; communication skill.
☽ =		Emotional communication power.
♀ =		Artistic communication power; advertising; promotions of any kind; "up front" sexual expression.
♂ =		The ability to grasp a situation quickly, right or wrong, and take action confidently and persuasively; attacking the issue without reservation.
♃ =		Teaching lessons; gaining a good reputation; publicity; persuasion brings success.
♄ =		Insistence of a point of view; unrelenting demands; driven by fear of failure; needing control.
♅ =		The bright idea saves the day; extreme self-confidence; ready to chart new territory.
♆ =		Overdoing issues drains energy and wears out one's welcome.
☊ =		Being recognized by others for persuasion and communication skills.
AS =		Exercizing influence.
MC =		Resourcefulness; great perception of any situation; leadership.

Mercury and Lunar Node ☿/☊

| ☿ = ☊ | Exchanging ideas with others. |
| ☊ = ☿ | Meeting others to exchange ideas. |

☉ =	Putting together a philosophy of life.
☽ =	Sharing emotional thoughts with others.
♀ =	Socialization; sharing affection with others; kindness.
♂ =	Making things happen in group sharing.
♃ =	Teaching; communication; philosophizing; partnership.
♄ =	Reticence about sharing one's point of view with others; perhaps too much self-control or modesty.
♅ =	Stimulating ideas shared; sudden business contacts; self-aggrandizement that disturbs relationships.
♆ =	Confusion about how to fit into the group.
♇ =	The thrust of intelligence; lording it over others.
AS =	Making contacts is easy and pays off.
MC =	Placed in the forefront in social and business circles.

Mercury and Ascendant ☿/AS

☿ = AS		Social attitude becomes important
AS = ☿		What one thinks is "on the line"; open to evaluation.

☉ =		Putting together a philosophy of life.
☽ =		Projection of emotions to others.
♀ =		Projection of feelings about love, intimacy, and the arts.
♂ =		Negotiating with others; deciding on the best course of action in collaboration with advisors.
♃ =		Teaching; successful meetings; sharing ideas easily.
♄ =		Adopting a strategic reserve in expression; withdrawing from a social circle; protecting one's position.
♅ =		Impetuous opinionation can irk others; being critical.
♆ =		Not knowing quite what to think about something or someone; openness to deception.
♇ =		Becoming prominent and influential; putting one's personal stamp on something.
☊ =		Easy interchange with others.
MC =		Baring one's soul; taking one's stand; communicating without fear.

Mercury and Midheaven   ☿/MC

☿ =MC		Following one's way of thinking to the hilt; changes as a result.
MC = ☿		Having one's point of view clarified or recognized.

☉ = Feeling confident about one's life philosophy; further change.

☽ = Feelings get expressed through a sense of rightness and usually are effective.

♀ = Thinking about love and relationships and feeling "right."

♂ = Making a decision about where one stands, usually with regard to the profession or one's social position.

♃ = Large thoughts are easy to come by and are easily communicated for success; almost a "can't lose" position; teaching, publishing; traveling for gain; philosophizing.

♄ = One's point of view comes under scrutiny by authority figures.

♅ = Formulating new objectives; making a sensation; throwing caution to the winds because of great confidence; nerve.

♆ = Self-absorbed thinking may lose the track on the public course.

♇ = A major turning point is possible; the power picture is clear; persuasion dominates.

☊ = Open interaction with others; telling the truth.

AS = Self-absorption; losing contact with others; change brewing.

Venus and Mars   ♀/♂

♀	= ♂	Feelings for love; romance; sexual relationship; creativity in the arts.
♂	= ♀	Passion; impulsive sexual drive; excitement.
☉	=	Potential marriage; physical attraction; opportunity in the arts; conception.
☽	=	Emotional impulses; maternal feelings; fulfillment through the arts.
☿	=	Physicality, love, and togetherness influencing the mental outlook; writing about love.
♃	=	Success in the arts and/or in plans to make relationships, attract love, marry, have children.
♄	=	The sense of being controlled in love matters, of losing freedom; inhibitions; possible relationship with someone of conspicuous age difference; renunciation.
♅	=	Intense passion; high nervous involvement with things sexual; sexual experimentation; dangerous liaison.
♆	=	Reveling in desire; spiritual bonds; rationalization of passionate attractions; self-sacrifice to another; being taken advantage of.
♇	=	Powerful sexual drive; the conquest.
☊	=	Attractiveness among others.
AS	=	Showing love easily, with few conditions.
MC	=	Intense relationship; desire for marriage or the actual event; giving birth.

Venus and Jupiter ♀/♃

♀ = ♃		Happiness in love; success; humanism; birthing.
♃ = ♀		Success in love; artistic success; philanthropy; birthing.

☉ = Being popular, successful, particularly well-appreciated; advancement in life; good will.

☽ = Charm; good nature; pleasant circumstances.

☿ = Happy thoughts; good humor; writing beautifully; communicating with grace.

♂ = Preoccupation with opportunity; trying to make things happen successfully; stirred up feelings; a good time.

♄ = Realism is introduced to expansive hopes; possible coming down to earth with a thud; caution; loss of faith.

♅ = Sudden turn of events to joy and success; exhilaration.

♆ = A loss of focus in love relationship; a change of direction for no clear reason; being taken advantage of, deceived.

♇ = Publicity; popularity; the world view; unbounded enthusiasm.

☊ = Unselfishness; sharing.

AS = A bright disposition; good cheer.

MC = Wonderment at the feelings of love and/or success.

Venus and Saturn ♀/♄

♀ = ♄		Grace given to ambition; the arts introduced to the life; the hurt of love-lost.
♄ = ♀		Suppression of love feelings; relationship with someone of conspicuous age difference; learning trust in romance; trying to understand peacefulness and calm.

☉ = Possible trouble in relationship; a difference in objectives; lack of satisfaction; conservatism.

☽ = Emotional hurt, probably from loneliness or feeling unimportant.

☿ = Thinking about ways to feel fulfilled, to improve relationship, to feel wanted; preoccupation; searching for the ideal.

♂ = Driving a wedge into relationship harmony; wanting more than is there; fearing competition; disputes; possible separation.

♃ = Learning respect for the status quo; keeping to oneself.

♅ = Tension in relationship; jealousies; split-off affairs; boredom with the past; arguments; possible separation.

♆ = Pretense in relationships; thinking the grass is greener elsewhere; dreaminess deceives; possible separation.

♇ = Unusually strong tensions toward separation; wasting emotions.

☊ = Contacts with similar souls on the downside of life; needing sympathy.

AS = Hiding one's light; withdrawing; fear of not being accepted.

MC = Feeling unimportant; never successful enough.

Venus and Uranus ♀/♅

♀	= ♅	Grace added to individuality; being appreciated, desired.
♅	= ♀	Intensification of love desires and emotional excitement.
☉	=	Love adventures; ready-to-go; proud of excitability.
☽	=	Sudden excitement in fulfillment of one's needs in love, in sex, in the arts; new ideas for a new future.
☿	=	Sudden ideas about seeking out love adventure, sex; ready ideas to solve problems innovatively, aesthetically.
♂	=	Strong excitability in love; creative activity.
♃	=	Expansive artistic ideas; appreciation of the arts; an adventurous vacation.
♄	=	Strategic controls are applied to the passionate nature; coming down to earth.
♆	=	Seduction; off-the-norm in sexual experience and fantasy; relationship problems that are not easily defined and threaten togetherness.
♇	=	Fated attraction; enormous thrust of love needs and activity; potential notoriety; possible exhibitionism.
☊	=	Intense feelings seek out the same in others.
AS	=	A projection of sexiness; artistic temperament.
MC	=	Getting involved with someone quickly; an affair breaking open to public view; success in artistic endeavors.

Venus and Neptune ♀/♓

♀ = ♓		Love in a swoon; erotic imaginings; artistic ideas.
♓ = ♀		Potential delusion in love; feeling unrequited; creative outlets.

☉ = Falling in love with love; secretiveness.

☽ = A dreamy emotional projection; impracticality.

☿ = Sympathy for others; artistic creativity; idealization.

♂ = Sexual drive has difficulty being fulfilled; there is magnetic attractiveness but trouble settling down; easy self-delusion.

♃ = Romantic reverie; luxury consciousness; keeping up a good front.

♄ = Fear of losing the dream; a new look at realism is needed.

♅ = Intensified fantasy setting up impractical expectations; going too far; susceptibility to exploitation through ego aggrandizement.

♇ = Extremely emotional; sexual needs pack a primal punch.

☊ = Relationships become unclear in their value structure.

AS = Possibly a libertine image; reveling in love ideals.

MC = Losing oneself in illusion; profiting through artistic endeavors, creativity.

Venus and Pluto ♀/♐

♀ = ♐		Grace is brought to power; improved acceptance for the indomitable.
♐ = ♀		Intensification of love desires; affairs; compulsiveness; wasting emotions.

☉ =		Creative thrusts in love, in the arts, and in general lifestyle are illuminated conspicuously but non-threateningly.
☽ =		Enormous feeling of emotions from the depths of being.
☿ =		Thinking about sexual relationships; artistic creativity.
♂ =		The sex drive dominates expression; temperamental emotionalism.
♃ =		Creativity; publicity; sex adventures on vacation; problems in the courts, possibly involving revenge.
♄ =		The fear of losing love; the, sense of tragedy.
♅ =		Immediate love impulse; experiences off-the-beaten-track.
♆ =		A love narcosis; possible instability in relationships.
☊ =		Meeting people seems to present a gamble instead of security.
AS =		Fascinating personality attracts others.
MC =		Artistic success; love affairs brought out into the open; fated union.

Venus and Lunar Node ♀/☊

♀ = ☊		Nice meeting with someone; romantic contact,
☊ = ♀		Contact with someone or an event in the arts; cultural; get-togethers; romance; emotional meetings.

⊙ = Politeness; sociability; geniality; others coming to one's assistance.

☽ = Showing one's feelings.

☿ = Communication about romance or artistic matters to others.

♂ = Making sexy contact with someone; making an important romantic date.

♃ = Enjoying someone's company enormously; entertainment.

♄ = Being brought up short in a situation that was potentially emotionally rewarding; shyness; withdrawal.

♅ = Intense, sudden attraction to someone; quick liaison; making friends with someone out of the ordinary.

♆ = Idealizing someone; making promises that are hard to keep; indulgent with love.

♇ = Romantic contact that may be extremely strong and lasting.

AS = Affectionate nature; cordiality; popularity.

MC = Being known for one's art or appreciation of things cultural; significant romantic fulfillment.

Venus and Ascendant ♀/AS

♀ = AS		Niceness; being appreciated.
AS = ♀		Niceness; being appreciated.

☉ =		A sense of all that is lovely; showing oneself at one's best in terms of appearance.
☽ =		The show of emotions; affections shown to others.
☿ =		Sociability; entertaining nature; telling stories.
♂ =		Using one's charm or sexiness to make something happen.
♃ =		Enthusiasm galore; a show of luxury.
♄ =		Tightening up the budget; pulling back the affections; being known as frugal, tight.
♅ =		Intense flair; attractiveness to others; one's sense of individual style.
♆ =		Fooling oneself about personal popularity or attractiveness; sadness about romantic loss.
♇ =		Extreme show of self-awareness, probably in terms of style, flair, beauty, or arts appreciation; clothing; gender pride.
☊ =		Being sweet, interested in others.
MC =		A sense of beauty; a recognized "romantic."

Venus and Midheaven ♀/MC

♀	=MC	Falling in love; reinforcing a deep relationship; peace, kind support of others.
MC	= ♀	Falling in love; reinforcing a deep relationship; forwarding a career, in the arts or other métier; getting a raise.

☉	=	Being very strongly aware of oneself; confident sense of attractiveness; success.
☽	=	Feelings about romance; relating to others deeply; being valued for one's work; recognition for a job well done.
☿	=	Artistic ideas; beautiful communications for profit; working as a writer or some other kind of artist.
♂	=	Impulsive expression of creativity; showing *joie de vivre*.
♃	=	Philanthropy; giving love; enthusiasm; happiness; success.
♄	=	Ambition focused in the arts; controlling the love urge; loss of relationship; being frugal; facing a cut-back of some kind professionally.
♅	=	Excitability in love; new ideas on the job, perhaps "zany"; openness about relationships.
♆	=	Imagination; artistic achievement; losing touch with the most satisfactory ways of relating and loving.
♇	=	Tremendous focus on an artistic career; cultural exposure; publicity; emotional expression; love relationship.
☊	=	Seen as an affectionate person.
AS	=	Being at harmony.

Mars and Jupiter ♂/♃

♂ = ♃   A fortunate course of action; clearing the air; successful creative activity.

♃ = ♂   Tremendous energy; enterprise; making things happen in a big way; "making waves" effectively.

☉ =   Success; organizational talent; leadership.

☽ =   Opinionation; emotional, "gut" feelings guide action; pride.

☿ =   Planning capability; publishing; showing the fruits of one's labors and creativity.

♀ =   Success; romantic expression; creative activity.

♄ =   Struggling with impulse; having to toe the line; pulling in one's sails.

♅ =   Explosive expression; breaking loose; domination.

♆ =   Imagining success; letting reality get away; being near a mistaken course of action.

♇ =   Extreme creative self-application; enterprise; demanding success from the environment; the really big picture.

☊ =   Cooperation with others; getting their support.

AS =   Being respected as a doer; getting things done.

MC =   The excitement of being "on top"; opportunity for success.

Mars and Saturn ♂/♄

♂ = ♄		The clash of hot and cold, action and control; stalemate.
♄ = ♂		Putting a damper on things; ups and downs; indecision; failing.

☉ = Possible threat to the body or health; breaking down under stress and strain; the sense of loss; eking it out.

☽ = Moodiness; possible depression; feelings about losing something.

☿ = Thoughts don't know where to go; any alternative seems inappropriate; indecision; separating from issues.

♀ = Emotions are cooled; frustration; feeling loveless or unloved, unsupported; passionately trying to make something work.

♃ = Tremendous concentration; fast production of fine work; wisdom; weighing all matters and making a pronouncement.

♅ = Intense drive; breaking loose; gaining independence through struggle; sudden accident.

♆ = Confusion; feeling threatened; self-torment about identity.

♇ = The need to take control; forcing an issue; strong anger.

☊ = Unsatisfactory liaisons.

AS = Struggling for every step of advance; possible health threat.

MC = Overcoming obstacles stoically; silent pride.

Mars and Uranus ♂/♅

♂ = ♅		Intense self-awareness; tremendous urge to action; test of nerves.
♅ = ♂		Sudden application of great energy; dominant will.
☉ =		Making something happen; sudden new circumstances; strong sense of self-confidence; feeling invulnerable.
☽ =		Intensification of the emotions; the strong need for love; a desire for recognition.
☿ =		Nervousness; planning independent action; strategy.
♀ =		Passionate excitability; increased romantic activity.
♃ =		Planning one's future, one's new position in life; looking to rewards; planning the course of action.
♄ =		A clash between controls and the freest spirit; potential battles and separations; controls can not be tolerated.
♆ =		Inspiration for vigorous selfhood; a dream leading the action; something coming out of "nowhere"; a loss of the usual orientation.
♇ =		Force; a "Higher Power"; intervention of the big shock.
☊ =		Hyperexcitability with others.
AS =		Accident-prone temperament and personality.
MC =		"Putting a gun to someone's head"; getting one's way; the sense of "either/or"; taking drastic measures.

Mars and Neptune ♂/♆

♂ = ♆ Inspiration; imagination made applicable; personal magnetism.

♆ = ♂ Change of course of action due to dissatisfaction; going to where the grass seems greener; losing focus.

☉ = New plans are illuminated; situational changes.

☽ = Emotional sensitivity; indecision; feeling off course.

☿ = Imagination may lose anchor; difficulty coping.

♀ = Erotic musings; differently directed sensuality.

♃ = Enjoying the cloud's silver lining; a break in the knick of time.

♄ = Being taken advantage of; reticence; the sense of futility; persevering in spite of fear.

♅ = Energetically following one's personal dream; reaching for "pie in the sky."

♇ = Apparently irresponsible attitude; selfish pursuit of one's objectives; devil-may-care attitude.

☊ = Sense of suspicion in associations.

AS = Giving off a magnetic or off-the-norm emanation; being different.

MC = Apparent loss of ego-consciousness; one's own world prevails; losing contact defensively; rebuilding the inner spirit.

Mars and Pluto ♂/♇

♂ = ♇   Extreme force; persuasion; control; brutality; excessive effort.

♇ = ♂   Extreme force; persuasion; control; brutality; excessive effort.

☉ =   Hard work; passionate attack to achieve an objective; accident potential; intervention of some undeniable force or authority; upset of plans that is unredeemable.

☽ =   Daring; taking a chance; playing the powerful hunch; self-belief; publicity.

☿ =   Seeing is achieving; tenacious pursuit of plans; publicity; effective salesmanship.

♀ =   Passionate disposition; sexual adventure or even danger; an affair.

♃ =   Unusual success; the big plan comes into focus; the energy and resources are available to make things happen; publicity.

♄ =   Hard, hard work; extraordinary discipline is needed and usually prevails.

♅ =   Tremendous energy; dangerous sense of attack; a chip on one's shoulder; fight first, talk later.

♆ =   Cunning strategies; subterfuge; plotting rebellion.

☊ =   Working with others to change the world.

AS =   Showing the hero image; the fighter who dares the impossible; aggression.

MC =   Confidence; ambition; dealing with might on either side of any issue; major job maneuver.

Mars and Lunar Node ♂/☊

♂ = ☊		Getting along with others; combined efforts pay off.
☊ = ♂		Meeting others to get the work done.

☉	=	Good cooperation dynamics; good blending of energies with others.
☽	=	Emotional attitude toward others shows and leads activity.
☿	=	Plans to collaborate, cooperate, share; promotion through partnerships; community-minded; salesmanship; publicity.
♀	=	Getting together affectionately, passionately.
♃	=	Successful teamwork; lots of enthusiasm; taking a trip with someone; planning togetherness for the long term.
♄	=	Something or someone always stepping on one's shadow; difficulty making the sale; withdrawing because of poor reception; one's ardor is squashed; looking for more amenable associations.
♅	=	Organizing others; getting people stirred up; sharing excitement; sudden events that affect lots of people.
♆	=	Self-absorption within a group; charismatic or off-putting.
♇	=	Others must "get on the train" or get left behind!
AS	=	Easy camaraderie.
MC	=	Excellent teamwork; partnership values important.

Mars and Ascendant ♂/AS

♂ = AS		The fighting spirit.
AS = ♂		Robustness.

☉ = Getting involved with arguments or operating in an inhospitable milieu; having to adjust things forcefully.

☽ = Emotional temperament easily shown to others.

☿ = A sharp tongue; verbal disputes; angry letters; telling someone off; intolerance.

♀ = Passion; love and sex are first concerns in relationships; the arts become important for personal expression.

♃ = Enthusiasm and leadership; harmonious public outreach.

♄ = Anxiety comes from feeling controlled somehow; frustration and rebellion; others don't cooperate as they should.

♅ = Testiness; argumentation; temper; picking a fight; inclination to intimidate others; ego-aggrandizement.

♆ = Magnetism, charisma; out of the mainstream; others may not understand; withdrawal as an option.

♇ = Premature action; intensity; "bitchiness"; easily provoked to anger.

☊ = Excellent teamwork.

MC = Work fulfillment with others.

Mars and Midheaven ♂/MC

♂ =MC		Ego awareness; action; fire; change of status.
MC = ♂		Recognition; responsibility grows; change of status.

☉	=	The drive to be important; self-promotion.
☽	=	Emotional excitability; impulsiveness; publicity; an emotional appeal; changing status through emotional "feel."
☿	=	Acting with vigor according to plan; important news or strategically helpful information.
♀	=	Social desires; sexual desires; romance on the job; self-promotion.
♃	=	Great success; promotion in professional status; energy and opportunity.
♄	=	The demand is to bring energies, plans, and enthusiasms into line; elimination of the overdone or exaggerated.
♅	=	The big push; the quick advance; winning right away; rashness; argumentative; inflamed.
♆	=	Creativity may be off the mark; discipline is needed to use one's talents in the best way; diffusion needs focus.
♇	=	Zeal, energy, promotion, publicity, power; the big picture.
☊	=	Leadership qualities; success potential.
AS	=	Confidence; projection of sureness and pizazz.

Jupiter and Saturn ♃/♄

♃ = ♄		Law and order; ambition given the go-ahead signal; patience pays off; feeling righter than right; dogmatic.
♄ = ♃		Control tempers zeal; opportunities are carefully evaluated; success takes on long-term security; one has "made it happen"; strategy.

☉ =		Taking destiny into one's own hands; major changes according to plan; or, if nothing has been prepared, becoming gripped by the status quo and having to make the best of things.
☽ =		Emotional conviction; hypersensitive about one's ego-position.
☿ =		Studying one's philosophy of life; a long trip; speaking with great maturity; studying hard; asking the right questions.
♀ =		Maturation of romantic needs and projections; feeling a little older than one's age; a touch of reserve.
♂ =		Ambition emerges out of discontent; feeling unrewarded and making a change; not wanting to toe the line.
♅ =		Terribly upset with the status of things; forceful change of direction, which can upset many dimensions of life.
♆ =		Bewilderment; not knowing which "master" to follow; loneliness.
♇ =		Tremendous perseverance; dramatic thrust of self; control of the situation; fearless; major change of situation.
☊ =		Working well with others; being just with others.
AS =		Keeping properly in one's place; the tactician.
MC =		The philosopher; thinking with grandeur.

Jupiter and Uranus ♃/♅

♃	= ♅	The big break; success or going one's independent way to greener pastures.
♅	= ♃	The big break; boundless optimism.
☉	=	Great success; the illumination of one's best position in any situation, in life in general; individuality in full bloom.
☽	=	Opportunity for major change; looking ahead to success.
☿	=	Planning on success; confidence; a series of fortunate breaks.
♀	=	Happy feelings about love, artistic things; fascination with being a man or a woman; narcissism.
♂	=	Drive and determination toward success; a love of individual freedom; specualtion; changing fortunes.
♄	=	The introduction of patience and practicality to boundless self-projection; temperance over excess.
♆	=	Inspiration; gain from the unexpected; strange conditions seem to heighten individual awareness; a silver lining.
♇	=	Tremendous drive to success; publicity; gains.
☊	=	Individuality attracts enthusiasm and new friends.
AS	=	Optimism and personal self-confidence; knowing the best will happen; success; fortunate twists in the way things transpire.
MC	=	Comfortably becoming known for who one is.

Jupiter and Neptune ♃/♆

♃ = ♆   Idealism; grand spirit; feeling quietly special; looking ahead to nice times; self-indulgences; rumor and scandal.

♆ = ♃   Emphasis on things spiritual, philosophical, religious, extra-sensory; benevolence; self-indulgences; tricky legalisms.

☉ =   Potentially misguided states; feeling the spirit; trying to capture the essence of things; following a dream.

☽ =   Dreaminess; an emotional swoon; going with the wind.

☿ =   Active imagination; learning to communicate fancifully; visualization; changing character; inspiration.

♀ =   Eroticism; optimism in love.

♂ =   Strong idealism; the need for practical focus.

♄ =   Breakdown of idealization; pessimism; possible self-delusion.

♅ =   Charisma; intuitively innovative; lifting the shades.

♇ =   Unreasonable plans; self-projection out of hand; major adjustment of life circumstances.

☊ =   Dealing with others naively or simplistically.

AS =   Appearing to live in a world lighted by personal imagination and an emotionally rationalized agenda.

MC =   A visionary; the potential for all kinds of self-indulgence.

Jupiter and Pluto ♃/♇

♃	= ♇	Establishing new perspectives; feeling personal power and resourcefulness; building the big picture; keeping in control of things.
♇	= ♃	Tremendous optimism; a thrust for power; leadership.
☉	=	Successful use of strong personality power; doing well with all resources; keeping things in one's own grip.
☽	=	Emotional conviction guides a new start; establishing one's new position with a gut feeling.
☿	=	Persuasion; influence; promotion of a cause.
♀	=	Creativity; flair.
♂	=	Leadership; publicity; organizing talent; applying controls to suit one's particular purposes.
♄	=	Adjusting the big picture to meet more with convention; strategy becomes necessary.
♅	=	Intense application of resources to establish a new perspective; overturning the tables; getting back onto the track or finding a better one.
♆	=	Inclination to be deceptive; adjusting the data; omitting key facts; working a situation into one's own format.
☊	=	Working together with others for success.
AS	=	Being known as an organizer and special achiever.
MC	=	Hard-working attainment of power position.

Jupiter and Lunar Node   ♃/☊

♃ = ☊		Good relationships, profitable associations; "connections."
☊ = ♃		Meeting others; making profitable liaisons; "connections."

☉ =	Feeling good about one's self in relation to others; building confidence to support action.
☽ =	An emotional and enthusiastic projection to others pays off.
☿ =	Thinking about others' welfare; sharing success; appreciating the complementation of partnership.
♀ =	Pleasantness with others; a graceful image; caring.
♂ =	Successful teamwork.
♄ =	Working with others by the rules; getting things perfectly clear; holding back in strategic reserve; slowing things down for safety; maybe "missing the boat" through caution.
♅ =	Entertaining image; inventive; enthusiastic; new associations.
♆ =	Lack of clarity about the objectives of being or working together; sharing the spirit with others but not much else, especially in the way of grounding.
♇ =	Strong personal projection of sociability; "collecting" well-known people.
AS =	Pleasantness with others.
MC =	Recognition for one's humanity and agreeableness.

Jupiter and Ascendant ♃/AS

♃ = AS		Enthusiasm; harmony.
AS = ♃		Enthusiasm; harmony.

☉ = Pleasantness with others; enthusiasm brought to the fore.

☽ = Largesse, kindness; a happy time.

☿ = Delight in social contact.

♀ = Affectionate relationship with others.

♂ = Easy, enthusiastic cooperation with others.

♄ = Appreciating the rules; maturity; comfortable with convention.

♅ = Optimism; enthusiasm; fortunate adjustment to one's status saves the day.

♆ = Living with hope and speculation; dreaming; projecting the niceness of things; not admitting the adverse.

♇ = Strong image; influential; leadership.

☊ = Needing to be with other people for their support and appreciation of who one is.

MC = Being in the right place at the right time; successul positioning.

Jupiter and Midheaven ♃/MC

♃ =MC		Success, recognition, good fortune; sense of purpose.
MC = ♃		Success; professional gains; internationalism; legalism.

☉ = Illumination of one's purpose in life; new opportunities; recognition and success.

☽ = Fulfillment of personal needs to a high degree; recognition; a deserved sense of importance.

☿ = Publishing; lots of ideas; voluble communication; plans that prove successful.

♀ = Success; reward; artistic appreciation and achievement; happiness; love relationship; engagement; marriage; birth.

♂ = Creating opportunities; making success happen; being inspired.

♄ = Cautious pursuit of opportunity; respect for the rules; long-lasting endeavors pay off with long-lasting rewards.

♅ = Great good luck with new enterprise; good fortune appears suddenly.

♆ = Projecting the best of all worlds; needing anchor to avoid disappointments; befuddlement; lack of realism.

♇ = Great gains; potential for extraordinary achievement and recognition; publicity.

☊ = Enthusiastic contacts with others.

AS = Pleasant contact with others who support one's personal success.

Saturn and Uranus ♄/♅

♄ = ♅		Tension between the avant garde and the conventional; the new and the old; feeling controls; need to fight for gains.
♅ = ♄		Pep-up for ambition; exciting the status quo into new development; a jolt to consider freedom; separation.

☉ = Tendency to rebel; egocentric drive against controls; separations in order to find one's way.

☽ = Emotional courage emerges under duress; changes for freedom.

☿ = Demands on nervous energy; decisions to be made about doing things a new way; necessary stages of re-thinking.

♀ = Tensions in romantic life; hot and cold; off again, on again; feeling personally limited.

♂ = Tremendous upheaval possible in rebellion, through calamity, overexertion, or anxiety about how things will get on; challenges leading to a fight.

♃ = Resolution of tensions comes rewardingly from without.

♆ = Break down under emotional pressure; new vision fighting to be understood; sadness; feeling lost.

♇ = Tremendous fear of loss; upheaval to protect assets; rebellion.

☊ = Too much combative energy to fit teamwork requirements easily.

AS = The loner's position is established; indecision.

MC = Break away from the old; recognition of one's thrust for individuality or loss of self to the grip of controls.

Saturn and Neptune ♄/♆

♄ = ♆		Suffering as a martyr to a cause; losing focus; wanting to give up under stress; denial.
♆ = ♄		Losing focus of ambition; depression; sense of being wronged.

☉ =		Painstaking attention to hard work to fulfill plans; feeling alone in the effort.
☽ =		Emotional drain; feeling inhibited.
☿ =		Pessimism; depression; slowness of mind; strangely nervous.
♀ =		Deluded love feelings; inhibitions; diminished emotional expression, sexual activity; unrequited love; longing for attention; lack of popularity; appreciated more by senior people.
♂ =		Diminution of energy; preoccupations that can't be explained; lack of zest.
♃ =		Very upset with the ways of the world; losing the will to fight.
♅ =		Irritability; frustration.
♇ =		Strong depression; feeling downtrodden; tremendous awareness of potential for loss; fear.
☊ =		Not getting along easily with others; withdrawal.
AS =		Being a loner; feeling confined; sense of being "out group."
MC =		Peculiar loss of ambition; moodiness; giving up or capitulating to demands of the environment totally.

Saturn and Pluto ♄/♇

♄ = ♇		The threat of loss in any area of life; potential self-destruction; hard, hard work.
♇ = ♄		The threat of loss in any area of life; potential self-destruction; hard, hard work.

☉ = Threat of loss; hard work; enforced change; separation; potential ill-health.

☽ = Emotional coldness; renunciation; giving up giving.

☿ = Depression; morbid thoughts; deep study; stark realism.

♀ = Troubled by the loss of love.

♂ = Fighting battles to keep life going; enormous undercurrent of frustration; a gun with a cork in its barrel.

♃ = Trouble with authority; adoption of the austere; staying out of trouble; trying to save what's left.

♅ = Brutal efforts to start a new order; an attack, regardless of potential losses.

♆ = Being doubted; not being seen for who one is; instable life situation because of the inexplicable, because of fear.

☊ = Suffering shared with others.

AS = Saddness; mourning.

MC = Hard, hard work to rise again from difficulty; major separation as a last resort.

Saturn and Lunar Node ♄/☊

♄	= ☊	Serious attitude in relation to others; aloneness.
☊	= ♄	Meetings of a serious nature; a lonely position.

☉	=	Setting oneself apart from others for defense or for prestige; appearing self-contained.
☽	=	Appealing to senior persons; showing precocious maturity; qualifying for responsibility.
☿	=	Thoughts that appeal to others because they are sound, conservative, and respectful; strategy; news of sadness.
♀	=	Difficulty expressing emotions to others; inhibitions; depression in relationship.
♂	=	Difficult surrounding situations; looking for personal freedom; confused motivation.
♃	=	The generation gap; rebellion; freeing oneself from stress.
♅	=	Upsetting the established way of doing things; going against group expectations; separatist activities.
♆	=	Confusion in one's environment; confusing others about one's personal stand; deception; fraud; lies.
♇	=	Sacrifice; loss through others; giving up the struggle.
AS	=	Pulling back; appearing alone; going away.
MC	=	Standing alone in life; mourning for others; little joy from accomplishments.

Saturn and Ascendant ♄/AS

☉ = AS Controlled or inhibited personality.

AS = ♄ One's position of maturity, wisdom, control, and patience is shown openly.

☉ = Taking responsibility squarely into one's life plan; strategizing personal freedom; making something happen through hard work; overtaxing body-health system.

☽ = Depression due to the environment; difficulty being accepted.

☿ = Others influencing how one thinks; wanting to be alone, to get away from it all.

♀ = Inhibition of expression to others; sour disposition.

♂ = Getting mad at the status quo; trying to put things right; struggling with inhibitions and control.

♃ = Being seen as "above it all"; *c'est la vie!* or one works very hard to reestablish a new order that is reliable and predictable.

♅ = Upsets and disputes over change; demanding personal freedom.

♆ = Depressing and introverted life situations; arguments about strange dimensions or obscure things; overmaking a point.

♇ = Violent upset; deep anguish; being put down by others.

☊ = Unpleasant circumstances with others.

MC = Feeling like the victim; trying to justify one's position.

Saturn and Midheaven ♄/MC

♄ =MC Major change in the family or in the profession; possible death concerns within the extended family circle; the father figure; an extremely important time of life development.

MC = ♄ Focus upon ambition; professional change; significant family development; a major move.

☉ = Need to fight hard and having the capacity to do so.

☽ = Renunciation of one thing and the adoption of another to fulfill needs better; an attack on private emotions.

☿ = Melancholy; separation thoughts; bad news; professional decisions that are hard to make.

♀ = Improvement in job situation; dryness in relationships.

♂ = A battle in the job situation; tendency to give in, pull back, lose ground; controls adopted.

♃ = Doing things right, the way they are expected to be done; keeping things as they are; or changing things to how they should be done for maximum security.

♅ = The great effort; intensity; a new way of doing things; sudden crisis on the job or in the family; surprise.

♆ = A lack of clarity; one's position is vague; feeling fears.

♇ = Great demands; fear of loss; the grand struggle.

☊ = Potential on the job or in the family; major stroke of fate may affect all development.

AS = Working with others in compassion and serious understanding.

Uranus and Neptune ♅/♆

♅ = ♆ Exploring individuation through imagination; through speculation; through creativity; possible use of underhanded means (artfully rationalized) to do the job.

♆ = ♅ Loss of ego-focus is possible if socio-professional position is unstable; spiritual world is awakened; amorphous states; irritability.

☉ = Great creativity; ultra-sensitive; impressionable; vaunted self-regard.

☽ = Emotional conviction, realistic or fanciful; the sense of being on the right track to do one's best.

☿ = Aware of the metaphysical; the mind plays tricks; high curiosity; perhaps needing a reorientation to common sense.

♀ = High sensitivity; fantasy life; reveling in love.

♂ = Applied creativity could be very strong; impatience; a nervous feeling of foreboding.

♃ = Good luck coming out of nowhere; rejuvenation of the spirit.

♄ = A clash among ambitions and projections; need for recognition; changes of direction; staying put causes depression and loss of self-confidence.

♇ = The big picture commands a certain course of action, which must be followed; very little option to do otherwise.

☊ = Meeting with people who care about one's future.

AS = Wearing anxieties on one's sleeve; needing sympathy.

MC = Supernatural concerns come into play; guidance is sought from other realms or never-before-tapped sources.

Uranus and Pluto ♅/♇

♅	= ♇	Overturning the status quo; creating a whole new perspective for ego-recognition.
♇	= ♅	Tremendous intensification of ego-awareness; attainment of great goals through great effort; upsets and tension enroute.

☉	=	The urge for independence and freedom; great tension; revolution.
☽	=	Change through force; indomitable, emotional conviction.
☿	=	Intense thought activity; new ideas, new plans, all for a new personal perspective; forcing individuality into focus.
♀	=	Creativity; a conquest for love.
♂	=	Enormous energy; fanaticism is possible; coercion.
♃	=	Enormous success potential.
♄	=	Egotism; tendency toward autocratic leadership; "my way is the best way"; pressure from others; toppled from position.
♆	=	Deep study of specialized subject; sympathetic understanding of others; peculiar nervous state when excited.
☊	=	Untiring colleague; teamwork paying off, but one's own ego is put first in line.
AS	=	Force active in one's environment.
MC	=	Grand awareness of what's going on; the opportunity to rise to leadership.

Uranus and Lunar Node ♅/☊

♅	= ☊	Meetings with unusual people pay off; sudden relationships.
☊	= ♅	Shared experiences are particularly rewarding.

☉	=	High tension; a group taking action.
☽	=	Excitability; a team taking a stand.
☿	=	Excited thoughts shared with others; impetuousness.
♀	=	Sudden attachments, romantic or just like-minded: the camaraderie is what is important.
♂	=	Tremendous energy and tension; having an axe to grind and gaining support.
♃	=	The big opportunity comes to those demanding it.
♄	=	Difficulties encountered together with others; the acceptance of controls by "group vote."
♆	=	Meeting with people off the beaten path.
♇	=	The strong need to be influential, persuasive; rocking the boat, and people approving the motion.
AS	=	Sudden new acquaintances.
MC	=	Teamwork paying off; professional recognition.

Uranus and Ascendant ♅/AS

♅ = AS		Major new start; high probability of geographic relocation.
AS = ♅		Showcase opportunity for individuality; "show off" time.

☉	=	Show of restlessness; anxiety about putting one's best foot forward; hoping for success.
☽	=	Emotionalism spills into view; needs sympathy, support and approval.
☿	=	Nervous planning; fault-finding; sharp witted; caustic.
♀	=	Being sexy; showing oneself in exciting fashion; emphasizing individual "new looks" of any kind.
♂	=	Making things happen raucously; devil-may-care attitude.
♃	=	Working feverishly to earn recognition.
♄	=	The clash of controls and the avant garde; indecision; airing dilemmas.
♆	=	Strange experiences may be revealed; emotions are shared; a feeling of martyrdom can be exploited.
♇	=	Force; commanding success.
☊	=	Getting like-minded people on board.
MC =		Major change potential in job status, with the parents, or through the spouse's job position or family.

Uranus and Midheaven ♅/MC

♅ =MC An extraordinary time of life; probable reorganization of family life in the early home; dramatic adjustment of job status as an adult; change of profession possible; sudden change of direction in practically every department of life; individuality reigns; geographic relocation.

MC = ♅ Brings the power of selfhood forward; assertion is recognized; strong developmental tensions for job and social position.

☉ = Strong illumination of individuality; getting what one deserves; unrest; eagerness for achievement; nervous drive.

☽ = Prominent shift of direction for emotional fulfillment; excitement about making a new bid for life advancement.

☿ = Nervous excitability in expectation of change; new ideas.

♀ = Possible promiscuity; feelings are exposed; creativity; eagerness to please.

♂ = Temperamental drive for ego recognition; argumentative and challenging; rash action; upping the tempo.

♃ = Optimistic outlook for success; recognition; publicity.

♄ = Possible rebuff in one's bid for recognition; having to temper idiosyncratic behavior; pull-back for gain.

♆ = Creativity; expecting recognition; withdrawal if frustrated.

♇ = Extraordinary power-drive to win success and command attention; over-exertion threatens the nervous system.

☊ = Climbing over others to fulfill one's own needs for recognition.

AS = Sudden adjustments to much of the life; change that has far-reaching significance; "this is it" for years to come.

Neptune and Pluto ♆ / ♇

♆ = ♇ The supernatural; other realms seem to be involved with life occurrences; unusual problems; peculiar experiences; possible concerns about death matters; creative enterprise.

♇ = ♆ Enormous intensification of sensory sensitivity; possible loss of the frame of reality; subterfuge; possible introduction of drugs or alcohol dysfunctionally.

☉ = Creative enterprise; possible drain on the system through over-indulgences; rationalization reigns over realism.

☽ = Extreme creativity possible; high sensitivity; big mood sweeps and fluctuations; anxiety about being appreciated.

☿ = Preoccupation with out-of-the-world thoughts and experiences; communications are other than they appear; deception as a strategy; nervous irritability; loss of centering.

♀ = Creativity; respect for mysticism; intense love fantasy; sensuality; over-indulgence with anything pleasant.

♂ = Great personal magnetism to set things right or rejection of actions because of misunderstanding.

♃ = In love with love, with life; feeling at one with the way things should be; a "Thank God" position; possibly religiousness.

♄ = Grief, weakness, torment.

♅ = Disruption to gain recognition; adventurous ego-thrust; courage; making waves to get to shore; possibly aberrant behavior.

☊ = Sharing other-worldliness and curiosity with others; group study projects.

AS = The mystical air flavors personal image.

MC = Profit through the occult or the spiritual; recognition of idiosyncrasies.

Neptune and Lunar Node ♆/☊

♆ = ☊		Possible breakdown of relationships; sense of being out of the group, or bound together through spiritual sharing.
☊ = ♆		Meeting with others interested in paranormal dimensions.

☉ =		Seeking to establish contacts with others through artistic or spiritual exchange; or else feeling misunderstood.
☽ =		High sensitivity; feeling ostracized; being misunderstood.
☿ =		Imagination shared with others; expecting too much from others; being let down by occurrences; undependability.
♀ =		Vagueness about emotional values; suspicions; promiscuity.
♂ =		Charisma; resourceful adaptation to others.
♃ =		Spritual bonds with others; religiousness tightens relationships.
♄ =		Emotional hurt through deception, unfaithfulness, duplicity.
♅ =		Self-willed motives disrupt group ideas.
♇ =		Difficulty blending personal perspective with others' views.
AS =		Appearing strange to others; being duped.
MC =		Taking a position off the mainstream of life.

Neptune and Ascendant ♆/AS

♆ = AS		High sensitivity, impressionability; spiritual projection; loss of ego.
AS = ♆		Gaining acceptance for one's specialness.

☉ =		Projection of aesthetics, creativity; the arts as a profession; sensitivities are used for gain, or there is discomfort and frustration.
☽ =		Great sensitivity; open to hurt; easily deceived.
☿ =		Great imagination; special perceptions; aware of special levels of interaction with others; open to deception.
♀ =		Sensual image; longing to understand love and share it.
♂ =		Charisma possible; fighting for one's vision; disputes about ethereal premises.
♃ =		Good fortune is assumed; one's peaceful nature.
♄ =		Loss of get-up-and-go energy; pull-back; feeling out of the group; slow progress through the martyring of earlier ideas.
♅ =		Hoping for luck; someday one's ship comes in.
♇ =		Feelings of an oppressive environment; difficulty tuning in.
☊ =		Hurt through others; deception, rumor.
MC =		Recognition for aesthetics or alone in one's specially sensitive realm.

Neptune and Midheaven ♆/MC

♆ =MC Very important time of life: there can be the sense of ego disappearance; the identity somehow gets lost in situations through disregard or through drugs or alcohol in emotional defensiveness; possible success through the arts, imagination, aesthetics; peculiar states in the early homelife; job vagaries for the adult.

MC = ♆ Accentuation of creativity on the job; disruption in the homelife; being pushed around; feeling lost; "losing it."

☉ = Illumination of aesthetics and creativity on the job or in the social life; possible discontent with life-position and the creativity to begin change; reaching for the vision.

☽ = High sensitivity; artistic expression dominates; being lost in one's own world.

☿ = Imagination; losing orientation to the mainstream; rumor; creative communication.

♀ = Idealized love out in the open; holding high the image of what love should be.

♂ = Charisma for professional gain through the arts; personal artistic flair; sensual image; playing a role.

♃ = Dreaming, hoping, feeling sure somehow that all will be well.

♄ = The feeling of being wiped out; needing to correct past mistakes with honest, open, clear statements and plans.

♅ = Intense impatience; self-righteousness; creativity.

♇ = The supernatural as a professional focus; strange happenings on the job or in the home.

☊ = Difficult relationships; peculiarities.

AS = The tendency to live in one's own foggy realm; defenses against insecurity.

Pluto and Lunar Node ♇/☊

♇	= ☊	Identification with a large group; making very important contacts; a life-significant relationship.
☊	= ♇	New associations of significance and importance.

☉	=	The urge to impose one's will on others.
☽	=	Reaching for the big picture; making the big scene emotionally; ambition is magnified; or there is too much fear for any action.
☿	=	Thinking big; hearing the grass grow; intellectual dominance.
♀	=	Important love contact; possible tragic melodrama.
♂	=	Exhibition of personal power; tyranny.
♃	=	Forcing oneself into a power position; self-promotion; attaining success through others.
♄	=	Potential loss through others; the end of relationships.
♅	=	Intense need for recognition; publicity; crush the opposition.
♆	=	The power of the half-truth; deception as a tool; win at any cost.
AS	=	The need for influence.
MC	=	Associations with others are the *sine qua non* of success.

Pluto and Ascendant ♇/AS

♇	= AS	Extremely important time of life: dramatic changes of perspective are possible; identity transformation; geographic relocation; taking command of things; a life-milestone.
AS	= ♇	The use of personal power and persuasion.

☉	=	Seeing a whole new avenue for development and success; "full steam ahead."
☽	=	Strong reaction to stimuli; emotional eruption.
☿	=	Domination of others mentally; the thrust of intellect.
♀	=	Emotionalism used to excite others; love relationship; propaganda.
♂	=	Ruthless energy deployment; courage; upset and change; accident-prone.
♃	=	Drive to major success; receiving a bounty.
♄	=	High potential for great difficulty and loss; oppressive dealings with others.
♅	=	Unusual events fan the fires further; success at all costs.
♆	=	Something paranormal influences situations; fight against rumor; vision to fulfill; embarrassment to transcend.
☊	=	Identification of the ego with a larger group.
MC	=	Power and authority and success; ego-ascendancy.

Pluto and Midheaven ♇ /MC

♇ =MC Extremely important time of life: dramatic changes of perspective are practically assured; identity transformation is possible; job adjustment is major; professional developments are life-significant; parental adjustments in the early home are personally significant; separations; a life-milestone.

MC = ♇ Recognition and the ultimate power position are probable; past mistakes can be opened to view and threaten ruin.

☉ = The potential for major life-change is illuminated; wanting to spread one's wings and fly; getting on with excitement.

☽ = Emotional power; leadership through such power; highly influential.

☿ = Thinking big; recognition of intelligence; planning.

♀ = Attractiveness; emotional charisma; appearing sexy.

♂ = Striving for power; drive to dominate; explosively argumentative.

♃ = Unusual scope of reward; assumption of success; righteousness.

♄ = The conspicuous threat of loss; potential scandal; major business reversal; hard, hard work; circumstances of death; bereavement.

♅ = Impatience; nervousness; sudden changes; publicity; rewards.

♆ = Potential scandal; other-worldliness; peculiarities; disappointments; away from the middle of the road; power run amok.

☊ = Leadership of a group of people.

AS = Importance and fame; being out in front of everyone.

Lunar Node and Ascendant ☊/AS

| ☊ = AS | Personal relationships. |
| AS = ☊ | Personal relationships. |

☉ = Helpful social contacts; gregariousness; an entertaining personality.

☽ = Emotional bonds with others; sympathy; caring for others.

☿ = Entertainment; gossip; exchanging ideas; getting input from others; news; traveling to meetings.

♀ = Pleasantness; affectionate associations.

♂ = Working for the common good; the "doer."

♃ = Sociability; humanitarianism; congeniality.

♄ = Prevailing with realism and wisdom; conservatism.

♅ = All for the avant-garde; unusual associations; upbeat ways of doing things with other people.

♆ = Making relationships with others through sensitivities and even interests in the paranormal; impressionability.

♇ = Power-plays with others for personal advancement.

MC = Sense of community.

Lunar Node and Midheaven ☊/MC

☊ =MC	Being recognized.
MC = ☊	Being recognized.

☉ =	The importance of contacts and friends for success; easy social ascendancy.
☽ =	The challenge and fulfillment of sharing emotions with others.
☿ =	The exchange of ideas for personal gain.
♀ =	Sociability; congeniality; talking about feelings to someone.
♂ =	Getting things done together; partnership work.
♃ =	Social life and entertainment; church groups; togetherness.
♄ =	Being comfortable in the loner's position; being the serious person in the group; respect; conservatism.
♅ =	The sudden experience; possible rashness; being seen as "zany"; solving problems innovatively with others.
♆ =	The tendency to impracticality in dealing with others.
♇ =	Leadership; success.
AS =	Harmony.

Ascendant and Midheaven   AS/MC

AS =MC   Identity awareness.

MC = AS   Identity awareness.

☉ =   The quest to be one's own person; to do well by one's self-image; to clarify the persona.

☽ =   Showing others how one feels about things.

☿ =   Thinking about one's place in the world.

♀ =   The sense of beauty; harmony; comfort.

♂ =   Individual talents put into action.

♃ =   Glad to be alive; optimism; pleased with things; justification.

♄ =   Austerity is important as part of maturity and reliability; conservatism is comfortable.

♅ =   Excitability; emotional; quickly responsive; adventurous.

♆ =   Idealization; spirituality; quiet.

♇ =   Power performances become well known.

☊ =   Pleasantness; contacts come easily.

Bibliography

Adams, Evangeline. *Astrology—Your Place Among the Stars*. New York: Dodd, Mead, and Company, 1930.

───────. *Astrology—Your Place in the Sun*. New York: Dodd, Mead & Company, 1927.

Aristotle. *Rhetoric to Alexander*, trans. H. Rackham. Cambridge, MA: Harvard University Press. 1965.

Braudy, Leo. *The Frenzy of Renown*. New York: Oxford University Press, 1986.

Campion, Nicholas. *The Book of World Horoscopes*. Wellingborough, England: The Aquarian Press, Thorsons Publishing Group, 1988.

Christianson, Gale E. *In the Presence of the Creator: Isaac Newton & His Times*. London: Collier Macmillan, Publishers, 1984.

Cirlot, J. E. *A Dictionary of Symbols*. New York: Philosophical Library, 1962.

DeLuce, Robert. *Complete Method of Prediction*. DeLuce Publishing Company, 1935, 1962.

Dewey, Edward R. *Cycles*. New York: Hawthorn Books, Inc., 1971.

Dobyns, Zipporah. *Progressions, Directions, and Rectification*. Los Angeles, CA: T.I.A. Publications, 1975.

Ebertin, Reinhold. *The Combination of Stellar Influences*. Aalen, Germany: Ebertin-Verlag, 1972.

Encyclopedia of Philosophy. London: Collier Macmillan, 1967.

Glass, Justine. *They Foresaw the Future*. G. P. Putnam's Sons, 1969.

Gleadow, Rupert. *The Origin of the Zodiac*. London: Ebenezer Baylis and Son, Ltd., 1968.

Graubard, Mark. *Astrology and Alchemy—Two Fossil Sciences*. New York: Philosophical Library, 1953.

Grun, Bernard. *The Timetables of History*. New York: Simon and Schuster, 1975.

Hand, Robert. *Planets in Transit*. Gloucester, MA: Para Research, 1976.

Howe, Ellic. *Urania's Children*. London: William Kimber, 1967.

Jacobs, Don "Moby Dick." *Astrology's Pew in Church*. San Francisco, CA: Joshua Foundation, 1982.

Jansky, Robert Carl. *Interpreting Eclipses*. San Diego, CA: Astro Computing Services, 1979.

Johndro, L. Edward. *The Stars*. New York: Samuel Weiser Inc., 1970.

Leo, Alan. *The Progressed Horoscope*. Edinburgh: International Publishing Company, 1964.

Lilly, William. *Christian Astrology* in three volumes, Houston, Texas: JustUs & Associates, 1986.

McCaffery, Ellen. *Graphic Astrology*. New York: Macoy Publishing Company, 1952.

Munkasey, Michael P. *Midpoints—Unleashing the Power of the Planets*. San Diego, CA: ACS Publications, 1991.

Nierenberg, Gerard I. *How to Give & Receive Advice*. Editorial Correspondents, Inc., 1975.

Pagan, Isabelle M. *From Pioneer to Poet*. London: Theosophical Publishing House, Ltd., 1969.

Ptolemy. *Tetrabiblos*. North Hollywood, CA: Symbols & Signs, 1976.

Roberts, Henry C. *The Complete Prophecies of Nostradamus.* New York: American Book-Stratford Press, Inc., 1971.

Rudhyar, Dane. *The Astrology of Personality.* Netherlands: Servire/ Wassenaar, 1963.

Thorndike, Lynn. *History of Magic & Experimental Science,* in eight volumes. New York, Columbia University Press, 1964.

Tyl, Noel. *Holistic Astrology.* McLean VA: TAI Books/Llewellyn Publications, 1980.

———. *The Principles and Practice of Astrology,* in twelve volumes: III, *The Planets, Their Signs and Aspects;* VII, *Integrated Transits;* IX, *Special Horoscope Dimensions,* St. Paul, MN: Llewellyn Publications, 1974, 1976.

———. "The Second House," and "The Eighth House," *Houses: The Power Places of the Horoscope,* ed. Joan McEvers. St. Paul, MN: Llewellyn Publications, 1989.

Van Norstrand, Frederic. *Precepts in Mundane Astrology.* New York: Macoy Publishing Company, 1962.

Index

A
Abraham, 103-104, 133
Accidents, 54, 73, 80, 199, 208
Accuracy, 20, 49-50, 178, 179, 184, 187, 189, 194, 195
Adams, Evangeline, 6, 50
Addey, John, 74
Air Family, 102-103, 106, 110
Alexander the Great, 1-11
Archetypes, 3, 6, 161
Arcing Planets, 87, 91, 121, 123, 125, 131, 140, 182, 201
Augustine, Saint, 52

B
Bacon, Francis, 207
Birthday Month, 66, 69
Black Death, 14-15
Brahe, Tycho, 19-25
Bush, George, 108, 165-167, 172

C
Cardinal Signs, 98, 115, 212
Celestial Phenomena, 101, 114, 156, 209
Christian IV, 20-21
Christmas Star, 11, 102
Communication, 13, 68, 91, 106, 137, 178, 183, 189, 201, 213
Conjunctions, 11-12, 14-15, 17-18

Counseling Aphorisms, 183
Cycles, 14, 53-55, 76-80, 101-103, 110, 118, 120, 128, 131, 133, 137, 142-143, 157, 160-161, 172-173, 177-178, 180-181, 183-185, 191, 194-195, 197, 210, 213

D
Death, 209, 211
Dee, John, 59
Dobyns, Zipporah, 51-53

E
Earth Family, 102, 128-129, 136, 168
Ebertin, Rheinhold, 71, 74, 76, 78, 100, 110
Eclipses, 4, 12, 14-18, 25, 53, 73, 90, 102, 108, 110-114, 117-118, 120, 122-124, 127, 209, 213
Effects, 12, 52, 199
Environment, 7, 53, 94, 98, 141, 147, 158-159, 170, 172, 175, 180, 190
Exactness, 68, 70, 79, 81, 125, 209

F
Fire of London, 26, 28

G
Galileo, 61
Grand Mutation, 102-103, 110, 113, 128-129, 133, 168

H
Hagar, 103-104
Hand, Robert, 208
Harald, King, 205-206
Harmonic, 73-75, 91, 141
Hussein, Saddam, 124, 168, 169

I
Isaac, 104, 133
Ishmael, 103-104, 133
Iraq, Kingdom of, 108-109, 126
Israel, 132

J
Jacobs, Don, 11-13, 58
Jargon, 188, 194
Jesus, 11-14
Jones, Marc Edmund, 96
Jung, Carl Gustav, 3

K
Kepler, Johannes, 11, 20, 49-50, 61, 179

L
Law of Subsumption, 166, 175
Leo, Alan, 4, 6, 58, 60
Lilly, William, 26-30
Lunar Nodal Axis, 99-100, 138

M
Maginus, Antonius, 59-60, 63
Mason, Zoltan, 188
Memory, 55, 200
Midpoints, 18, 31-32, 46, 74-75, 205, 214

Mundane Astrology, 84, 101-102, 114, 115, 117, 121, 133, 156, 165, 209, 213

N
Nabod (or Naibod), 60-62
Nations, Astrology of, 101
Nectanebus, 1-11
Nihilism, 136
Nostradamus, 30, 194

O
Olav, King, 203, 210
Olympias, 2-5

P
Pagan, Isabelle, 6-7, 9
Parental, Axis, 138, 141, 145, 150-151, 181, 195, 205
Precision, 66, 68, 96, 163, 194
Prediction Aphorisms, 137
Presidents, 102, 115
Primary Directions, 20, 24, 29, 49, 57-59, 64
Proust, Marcel, 135
Ptolemy, 6, 12, 26, 28, 57-60, 63, 114, 175

R
Rapport, 63-70, 77-79, 88-89, 92, 95-96, 99, 139, 142, 146, 149-151, 161, 176, 186-187, 213-214
Reality Principle, 206-209, 211-212
Rectification, 8, 11-13, 31, 33-35, 37-41, 43, 47, 61-62, 65, 96, 125, 169, 171
Regulus, 5-9, 107
Responsibility, 25, 51, 103, 143, 186-187, 193
Right Ascension, 5, 57, 58, 60
Rudhyar, Dane, 63, 66, 80, 84, 136, 159, 208, 213

S

Sarah, 104
Saturn Retrograde, 138, 193, 205
Secondary Progressed Moon, 76-78, 85, 154-156, 162
Self-worth, 95, 138-139, 141, 145, 150-151, 170, 176, 178, 187, 195
Sepharial, 60
Simmonite, W. J., 62-63
Sirius, 21-22
Stars, Fixed, 5-6, 12, 15, 17, 20, 22, 25-26, 30, 102, 107, 210, 213
Steiger, Brad, 55

T

Tension, developmental, 14, 65-66, 73, 75-76, 86, 91, 98, 144, 181, 186, 193

Thatcher, Margaret, 50-51, 201
Time Orb, 15, 65, 69, 70-71, 85, 88, 90, 98, 124-126, 154, 172, 200, 214
Tyl, Noel, 67, 110, 137, 157, 183

U

United States of America, 72

W

Witte, Alfred, 74

Z

Zadkiel, 26-27, 60
Zen, 176

On the following pages you will find listed, with their current prices, some of the books now available on related subjects. Your book dealer stocks most of these and will stock new titles in the Llewellyn series as they become available. We urge your patronage.

TO GET A FREE CATALOG

You are invited to write for our bi-monthly news magazine/catalog, *Llewellyn's New Worlds of Mind and Spirit*. A sample copy is free, and it will continue coming to you at no cost as long as you are an active mail customer. Or you may subscribe for just $10 in the United States and Canada ($20 overseas, first class mail). Many bookstores also have *New Worlds* available to their customers. Ask for it.

In *New Worlds* you will find news and features about new books, tapes and services; announcements of meetings and seminars; helpful articles; author interviews and much more. Write to:

Llewellyn's New Worlds of Mind and Spirit
P.O. Box 64383-L814, St. Paul, MN 55164-0383, U.S.A.

TO ORDER BOOKS AND TAPES

If your book store does not carry the titles described on the following pages, you may order them directly from Llewellyn by sending the full price in U.S. funds, plus postage and handling (see below).

Credit card orders: VISA, MasterCard, American Express are accepted. Call us toll-free within the United States and Canada at 1-800-THE-MOON.

Special Group Discount: Because there is a great deal of interest in group discussion and study of the subject matter of this book, we offer a 20% quantity discount to group leaders or agents. Our Special Quantity Price for a minimum order of five copies of *Prediction in Astrology* is $71.80 cash-with-order. Include postage and handling charges noted below.

Postage and Handling: Include $4 postage and handling for orders $15 and under; $5 for orders *over* $15. There are no postage and handling charges for orders over $100. Postage and handling rates are subject to change. We ship UPS whenever possible within the continental United States; delivery is guaranteed. Please provide your street address as UPS does not deliver to P.O. boxes. Orders shipped to Alaska, Hawaii, Canada, Mexico and Puerto Rico will be sent via first class mail. Allow 4-6 weeks for delivery. **International orders:** Airmail – add retail price of each book and $5 for each non-book item (audiotapes, etc.); Surface mail – add $1 per item.

Minnesota residents add 7% sales tax.

Mail orders to:
Llewellyn Worldwide, P.O. Box 64383-L814, St. Paul, MN 55164-0383, U.S.A.

For customer service, call (612) 291-1970.

Prices subject to change without notice.

HOLISTIC ASTROLOGY: THE ANALYSIS OF INNER AND OUTER ENVIRONMENTS
by Noel Tyl

When an individual's life does not reflect what is expressed in his or her chart, it doesn't mean the chart is wrong! Holistic astrology demands that the horoscope be related to the life as it is lived by the individual, that we take into consideration environmental as well as planetary influences.

This landmark study of astrology and parental influences, generational differences, defense mechanisms, and the patterns of environmental pressures provides incisive techniques for becoming better astrologers/analysts. Here are clues to the meaning of anxiety, a new look at communication and points of view, and a new understanding of Pluto and Neptune. Learn practical and effective counseling techniques, the dynamics of loving, and the significance of the sexual profile. Ten case studies demonstrate the practical application of this method. Original, creative, human—and hopeful.

0-9356200-00-1, 363 pgs., hardcover $15.95

THE MISSING MOON
by Noel Tyl

This delightful collection of ten short stories illustrate principles of astrological counsel and practice with deliciously absurd wit. Read about the mysterious man whose horoscope has no Moon, and learn what the famous poem "Casey at the Bat" really means!

Follow Tyl's hero-astrologer through a series of trials and misadventures on his journey around the horoscope. This book will help you understand astrology to a far deeper level than ever before, and what's more, you'll enjoy it while you're learning.

0-87542-797-9, 172 pgs., softcover $2.97

THE PRINCIPLES AND PRACTICE OF ASTROLOGY
by Noel Tyl

Seven volumes of the most complete course of instruction in astrology ever published. These important source books will open horizons and expand your knowledge and understanding of astrology as never before.

- 0-87542-803—ASPECTS & HOUSES IN ANALYSIS
- 0-87542-805—THE EXPANDED PRESENT
- 0-87542-807—ANALYSIS & PREDICTION
- 0-87542-808—SPECIAL HOROSCOPE DIMENSIONS
- 0-87542-809—ASTROLOGICAL COUNSEL
- 0-87542-810—ASTROLOGY-MUNDANE, ASTRAL, OCCULT
- 0-87542-811—TIMES TO COME

Order by number, softcover $3.95 each

ASTROLOGY'S SPECIAL MEASUREMENTS
How to Expand the Meaning of the Horoscope
Edited by Noel Tyl

Every new student of astrology looks with bewilderment at that first horoscope and asks, "What's it mean when there's nothing in my 7th house? Won't I ever get married?" The student feels the strong need to *measure*. He needs something to define the space in the house and give meaning to the picture. Measurements are the lenses that help us see nearer, farther, and with greater contrast and clarity. In the process of analysis, measurement becomes diagnosis.

In this volume, ten experts discuss the finer points of measurement and meaning, analysis, and diagnosis. How many measurements do you need? Not all measurements work in every horoscope or for every astrologer—and too many can present so much data that you lose confidence. Furthermore, no matter how precise the measurements, they still rely on the astrologer to adapt them to the human condition. *Astrology's Special Measurements* will help you put those special measurements to work easily and without fear.

ISBN: 1-56718-864-8, 6 x 9, 352 pgs., charts, tables, softbound $12.00

THE NEW A TO Z HOROSCOPE MAKER AND DELINEATOR
by Llewellyn George

A textbook ... encyclopedia ... self-study course ... and extensive astrological dictionary all in one! More American astrologers have learned their craft from the NEW A TO Z than any other astrology book. First published in 1910, it is in every sense a complete course in astrology, giving beginners ALL the basic techniques and concepts they need to get off on the right foot. Plus it offers the more advanced astrologer an excellent dictionary and reference work for calculating and analyzing transits, progression, rectifications, and creating locality charts. This new edition has been revised to met the needs of the modern audience.

0-87542-264-0, 592 pgs., 6 x 9, softcover $12.95

HORARY ASTROLOGY
The History and Practice of Astro-Divination
by Anthony Louis

Here is a how-to guide for the intermediate astrologer on the art of astrological divination. It's the best method for getting answers to questions of pressing personal concern based on the planets' positions at the time of inquiry. Delves deeply into the heritage and the modern applicability of the horary art. Author Anthony Louis is a practicing psychiatrist, and brings that knowledge to this scholarly textbook.

Written beautifully and reverently in the tradition of William Lilly, the book translates Lilly's meaning into modern terms. Other features include numerous case studies; tables; diagrams; and more than 100 pages of appendices, including an exhaustive planetary rulership list, planetary key words and a lengthy astrological/horary glossary. Dignities and debilities, aspects and orbs, derivative houses, Arabic parts, fixed stars, critical degrees and more are explored in relation to the science of horary astrology. Worksheets supplement the text.

0-87542-394-9, 592 pgs., 6 x 9, illus., softcover $19.95

Prices subject to change without notice.

THE LLEWELLYN ANNUALS

Llewellyn's MOON SIGN BOOK: Approximately 400 pages of valuable information on gardening, fishing, weather, stock market forecasts, personal horoscopes, good planting dates, and general instructions for finding the best date to do just about anything! Article by prominent forecasters and writers in the fields of gardening, astrology, politics, economics and cycles. This special almanac, different from any other, has been published annually since 1906. It's fun, informative and has been a great help to millions in their daily planning. **State year $4.95**

Llewellyn's SUN SIGN BOOK: Your personal horoscope for the entire year! All 12 signs are included in one handy book. Also included are forecasts, special feature articles, and an action guide for each sign. Monthly horoscopes are written by Gloria Star, author of *Optimum Child*, for your personal Sun Sign and there are articles on a variety of subjects written by well-known astrologers from around the country. Much more than just a horoscope guide! Entertaining and fun the year around. **State year $4.95**

Llewellyn's DAILY PLANETARY GUIDE and ASTROLOGER'S DATEBOOK: Includes all of the major daily aspects plus their exact times in Eastern and Pacific time zones, lunar phases, signs and voids plus their times, planetary motion, a monthly ephemeris, sunrise and sunset tables, special articles on the planets, signs, aspects, a business guide, planetary hours, rulerships, and much more. Large 5 1/4 x 8 format for more writing space, spiral bound to lay flat, address and phone listings, time zone conversion chart and blank horoscope chart. **State year $6.95**

Llewellyn's ASTROLOGICAL CALENDAR: Large wall calendar of 52 pages. Beautiful full color cover and color inside. Includes special feature articles by famous astrologers, introductory information on astrology. Lunar Gardening Guide, celestial phenomena, a blank horoscope chart for your own chart data, and monthly date pages which include aspects, lunar information, planetary motion, ephemeris, personal forecasts, lucky dates, planting and fishing dates, and more. 10 x 13 size. Set in Central time, with conversion table for other time zones worldwide.
State year $8.95

SYNTHESIS & COUNSELING IN ASTROLOGY
The Professional Manual
by Noel Tyl

One of the keys to a vital, comprehensive astrology is the art of synthesis, the capacity to take the parts of our knowledge and combine them into a coherent whole. Many times, the parts may be contradictory (the relationship between Mars and Saturn, for example), but the art of synthesis manages the unification of opposites. Now Noel Tyl presents ways astrological measurements—through creative synthesis—can be used to effectively counsel individuals. Discussion of these complex topics is grounded in concrete examples and in-depth analyses of the 122 horoscopes of celebrities, politicians, and private clients.

Tyl's objective in providing this vitally important material was to present everything he has learned and practiced over his distinguished career to provide a useful source to astrologers. He has succeeded in creating a landmark text destined to become a classic reference for professional astrologers.

1-56718-734-X, 720 pgs., 7 x 10, 115 charts, softcover $29.95

Solar Arcs on Software!

As a service to readers of Noel Tyl's recently published *Prediction in Astrology*, Matrix Software now offers Tyl's Solar Arcs & Midpoint Pictures Directory in computer disk format. Using your birth data, this software gives you all Solar Arc aspects for any period of your life. Printed with every aspect, you have Tyl's images to give meaning to prediction using the master-technique of Solar Arcs.

For IBM PC and its clones. Requires printer. Call toll-free for more details. A free catalog of all Matrix Software programs will be sent first class upon your request. You can use this and other programs to print ready-to-sell reports for clients and friends.

Matrix Software
COMPUTER ASSISTED ASTROLOGY

315 Marion Ave • Big Rapids, MI 49307 • (616) 796-2483   **800-PLANETS** ext. 17